Rwanda Revisited

Journal of International Peacekeeping Leadership

Volumes published in the ***Journal of International Peacekeeping Leadership*** are listed at *brill.com/joup*

Rwanda Revisited

Genocide, Civil War, and the Transformation of International Law

Edited by

Phillip Drew
Bruce Oswald
Rob McLaughlin
Jeremy Farrall

TUTA SUB AEGIDE PALLAS · 1683 ·

BRILL

BRILL | NIJHOFF

This book was previously published as Special Issue of the *Journal of International Peacekeeping*, Volume 22 (2018), Issue 1-4 (published April 2020); with updated introduction.

Cover illustration: 'Rwanda Revisited', drawing by Emilia Drew, 2021. With kind permission by the artist.

Library of Congress Cataloging-in-Publication Data

Names: Drew, Phillip, editor. | Oswald, Bruce, editor. | McLaughlin, Rob, editor. | Farrall, Jeremy Matam, editor.
Title: Rwanda revisited : genocide, civil war, and the transformation of international law / edited by Phillip Drew, Bruce Oswald, Robert McLaughlin, Jeremy Farrall.
Description: Leiden ; Boston : Brill Nijhoff, [2022] | Series: Journal of international peacekeeping leadership | Summary: "In Rwanda Revisited: Genocide, Civil War, and the Transformation of International Law, the contributing authors seek to recount, explore, and explain the tragedy that was the Rwanda genocide and the nature of the international community's entanglement with it. Written by people selected for their personalized knowledge of Rwanda, be it as peacekeepers, aid workers, or members of the ICTR, and/or scholarship that has been clearly influenced by the genocide, this book provides a level of insight, detail and first-hand knowledge about the genocide and its aftermath that is clearly unique. Included amongst the writers are a number of scholars whose research and writings on Rwanda, the United Nations, and genocide are internationally recognized. Contributors are: Major (ret'd) Brent Beardsley, Professor Jean Bou, Professor Jane Boulden, Dr. Emily Crawford, Lieutenant-General the Honourable Romeo Dallaire, Professor Phillip Drew, Professor M.A. Drumbl , Professor Jeremy Farrall, Lieutenant-General J.J. Frewen, Dr. Stacey Henderson, Professor Adam Jones, Ambassador Colin Keating, Professor Rob McLaughlin, Linda Melvern, Dr. Melanie O'Brien, Professor Bruce 'Ossie' Oswald, Dr. Tamsin, Phillipa Paige, Professor David J. Simon, and Professor Andrew Wallis. This book was previously published as Special Issue of the Journal of International Peacekeeping , Volume 22 (2018), Issue 1-4 (published April 2020); with updated introduction"— Provided by publisher.
Identifiers: LCCN 2021037635 (print) | LCCN 2021037636 (ebook) | ISBN 9789004422223 (hardback) | ISBN 9789004430129 (ebook)
Subjects: LCSH: Rwanda—History—Civil War, 1994—Law and legislation. | Humanitarian intervention—History—20th century. | Responsibility to protect (International law)—History—20th century.
Classification: LCC KZ6795.R83 R883 2022 (print) | LCC KZ6795.R83 (ebook) | DDC 345.67571/0251—dc23
LC record available at https://lccn.loc.gov/2021037635
LC ebook record available at https://lccn.loc.gov/2021037636

Typeface for the Latin, Greek, and Cyrillic scripts: "Brill". See and download: brill.com/brill-typeface.

ISBN 978-90-04-42222-3 (hardback)
ISBN 978-90-04-43012-9 (e-book)

This book is printed on acid-free paper and produced in a sustainable manner.

Contents

PART 2
The "G" Word

PART 3
Prosecuting Genocide

PART 4
Rwanda's Legacy

List of Abbreviations

AWM	Australian War Memorial (record series)
BBGNU	(Rwandan) Broad-Based Government of National Unity
CDR	Coalition pour la Défense de la République
DFAT	(Australian) Department of Foreign Affairs and Trade
MFAT	(New Zealand) Ministry of Foreign Affairs and Trade
MRND	National Republican Movement for Democracy and Development
NAA	National Archives of Australia (record series)
NMOG I/II	(OAU) Neutral Military Observers Group
OAU	Organisation of African Unity
Parmehutu	Hutu Emancipation Movement Party
RPA	Rwandan Patriotic Army
RPF	Rwanda Patriotic Front
RTLM	Radio Télévision Libre des Mille Collines
SA	Sturmabteilung (also known as the 'Brown Shirts')
UNOMUR	UN Observer Mission Uganda–Rwanda
UNAMIR	United Nations Assistance Mission in Rwanda
UNHCR	United Nations High Commission for Refugees

Notes on Contributors

Major (retired) Brent Beardsley
is a retired Canadian Infantry Officer. He was General Dallaire's Military Assistant from August 1993 until May 1994, at which time he was medically evacuated from Rwanda. He is a co-author of the best-selling book *Shake Hands With the Devil* (Da Capo Press, 2004). Since his retirement from the Canadian Military in 2009 he has been working with Romeo Dallaire on the Dallaire Child Soldiers Initiative.

Jean Bou
is a historian at the Strategic and Defence Studies Centre at the Australian National University. He wrote the chapters dealing with the Australian deployment to the United Nations Assistance Mission in Rwanda (UNAMIR) for volume 4 of the *Official History of Australian Peacekeeping, Humanitarian and Post-Cold War Operations: The Limits of Peacekeeping* (Cambridge University Press, 2018).

Jane Boulden
is a Professor at the Royal Military College of Canada. From 2004-2014 she held a Canada Research Chair in International Relations and Security Studies at RMC. From 2000 until 2004 she was a MacArthur Research Fellow at the Centre for International Studies, University of Oxford. Her books include, *Responding to Conflict in Africa, the United Nations and Regional Organizations*, ed. (Palgrave Macmillan, 2013); *The United Nations and Nuclear Orders*, co-edited with Ramesh Thakur, and Thomas G. Weiss (United Nations University Press, 2009); *Terrorism and the UN: Before and After September 11th*, co-edited with Thomas G. Weiss (Indiana University Press, 2004).

Dr Emily Crawford
is an Associate Professor in the University of Sydney Law School and an associate of the Sydney Centre for International Law (SCIL). Previously at the Law Faculty at the University of New South Wales (UNSW), Emily completed her Arts and Law degrees before working as a researcher at the Australian Broadcasting Corporation, before returning to UNSW to undertake her Ph.D. Her doctoral thesis on the disparate treatment of participants in armed conflicts was published by Oxford University Press in 2010.

Dr. Crawford has taught International Law and International Humanitarian Law, and has delivered lectures both locally and overseas on international humanitarian law issues, including the training of military personnel on behalf of the Red Cross in Australia. A member of the International Law Association's Committee on Non-State Actors, as well as the Australian (NSW) Red Cross International Humanitarian Law (IHL) Committee, Emily's most recent research project examined major developments in the conduct of armed conflicts in the 21st century, such as cyber warfare, targeted killings, and the increasing presence of civilians directly participating in armed conflicts. The research project was published in 2015 by Oxford University Press as *Identifying the Enemy: Civilian Participation in Armed Conflict.*

Lieutenant-General Roméo Dallaire
was the Force Commander of the United Nations Assistance Mission for Rwanda prior to and during the 1994 genocide. A career military officer, he served in the Canadian Armed Forces from 1964 until he was medically released in 2000.

A devoted Humanitarian, Romeo Dallaire is an outspoken advocate for human rights, especially in regards to child soldiers and military veterans. He is the founder and president of the Lieutenant-General Roméo Dallaire Foundation which is aimed at inspiring young people from underprivileged backgrounds to develop their leadership potential, and the Roméo Dallaire Child Soldiers Initiative, a project aimed at eradicating the recruitment and use of children in violence.

His courage and leadership during the Rwanda mission earned him the Meritorious Service Cross, the United States Legion of Merit, the Aegis Award on Genocide Prevention, and the affection and admiration of people around the globe. His defiant dedication to humanity during that mission has been well-documented in films and books, including his own award-winning account: *Shake Hands with the Devil: the Failure of Humanity in Rwanda.*

General Dallaire was appointed as an Officer of the Order of Canada in 2002 and to the Canadian Senate in 2005. In May 2014, he resigned from the Senate so that he could devote more time to international humanitarian causes and advocating for military veterans who have been affected by Post Traumatic Stress Disorder.

Dr. Phillip Drew
is the Assistant Dean – Juris Doctor and Graduate Studies at the Faculty of Law, Queen's University (Kingston). He is also an Associate Professor at the Australian National University College of Law where he teaches courses international law, including The Law of Peacekeeping Operations. He was the Canadian Contingent Intelligence Officer in Rwanda from July 1994 until February 1995. He is a co-author of the San Remo Handbook on Rules of Engagement, and was special advisor to the NATO Working Group on Rules of Engagement (ROE) training from 2011–2013.

M.A. Drumbl
is the Class of 1975 Alumni Professor at Washington and Lee University, School of Law, where he also serves as Director of the University's Transnational Law Institute. He has held visiting appointments and has taught intensive courses at law schools world-wide, including Oxford University (University College), Université de Paris II (Panthéon-Assas), Vrije Universiteit Amsterdam (VU), University of Ottawa, Masaryk University, Trinity College-Dublin, University of Western Ontario, University of Melbourne, Monash University, Vanderbilt University, University of Sydney, and the University of Illinois. Professor Drumbl's research and teaching interests include public international law, global environmental governance, international criminal law, post-conflict justice, and transnational legal process. His work has been relied upon by the Supreme Court of Canada, the United Kingdom High Court, United States Federal Court, and the Supreme Court of New York.

Dr. Jeremy Farrall
is Associate Dean (Research) at the Australian National University (ANU) College of Law and Professor of Law in the ANU Law School. Professor Farrall has worked for the United Nations in a range of capacities, serving as a Political Affairs Officer for the UN Security Council at UN Headquarters in New York (2001–2004) and for the UN Mission in Liberia (2004–2006). He was also a UN Facilitator for the UN Secretary-General's Good Offices team that mediated peace talks in Cyprus (2004, 2008).

Lieutenant-General J.J. Frewen
is the Principal Deputy Director of the Australian Signals Directorate. In August 1994, he deployed to Rwanda as the Operations Officer with the Australian Contingent to the United Nations Assistance Mission for Rwanda (UNAMIR).

Lieutenant-General Frewen has held a range of senior staff appointments, most notably Military Assistant to the Chief of Army, Chief of Staff Headquarters Forces Command, and Head Military Strategic Commitments in Australian Defence Headquarters. His operational service includes Rwanda, the Solomon Islands, and Afghanistan. Throughout 2017 he was the national commander of Australian Defence Forces in the Middle East, including Iraq and Afghanistan.

Dr Stacey Henderson
is a Lecturer at the University of Adelaide Law School. She is an early career researcher who successfully completed her Ph.D. focusing on non-forceful responses to atrocity crimes under Responsibility to Protect (R2P), for which

she was awarded a Dean's Commendation for Doctoral Thesis Excellence, in early 2018. Her research focuses on the protective capacity of law, including international law generally, responsibility of States, and governance of outer space and space technology particularly in the context of off-Earth human settlement.

Adam Jones, Ph.D.
is Professor of Political Science at the University of British Columbia Okanagan in Kelowna, Canada. He is the author of *Genocide: A Comprehensive Introduction* (Routledge, 3rd edition, 2017), and author or editor of over a dozen other books, mostly on genocide and crimes against humanity. He has worked as an expert consultant with the United Nations Office on Genocide Prevention and the Responsibility to Protect.

Colin Keating
was New Zealand's Ambassador to the UN in New York between 1993 and 1996, serving on the Security Council in 1993 and 1994, and as Council President during the 1994 genocide in Rwanda. In 2005, he became the founding Executive Director of Security Council Report, an independent non-profit organisation based in New York which produces reports and analysis about the work of the Council. He has contributed chapters on the Rwanda crisis in various publications. These include chapters focusing on the internal political dynamics of the Security Council and on the Security Council's actions in the face of genocide.

Professor Rob McLaughlin
is the former Director of the Australian Centre for the Study of Armed Conflict and Society at UNSW Canberra. Before becoming an academic, Professor McLaughlin served in the Royal Australian Navy for several decades as both a Seaman officer and a Legal officer. As a lawyer, he served as Fleet Legal Officer, the Strategic Legal Adviser, Director of the Naval Legal Service, and Director of Operations and International Law in the Department of Defence. He holds degrees in history, law, and international relations, and earned his Ph.D. at Cambridge.

Linda Melvern
is a British investigative journalist. For several years she worked for *The Sunday Times* (UK), including on the investigative Insight Team. Since leaving the newspaper she has written six books of non-fiction and is widely published in the British press and academic journals. For the past twenty years she has concentrated on the circumstances of the 1994 genocide in Rwanda. A consultant

to the Military One prosecution team at the International Criminal Tribunal for Rwanda, part of her archive of documents was used to show the planning and progress of the 1994 genocide. She is the author of the best-selling books, *A People Betrayed: The Role of the West in Rwanda's Genocide* (Zed Books, 2000), and *Conspiracy to Murder. The Rwandan Genocide* (Verso, 2004). Her latest book is entitled *Intent to Deceive,* which examines the phenomenon of genocide denial in Rwanda (Verso, 2020).

Dr Melanie O'Brien
is Senior Lecturer in International Law at the University of Western Australia, an award-winning teacher of International Humanitarian Law, Public International Law, and Legal Research. Her research examines the connection between human rights and the genocide process; and sexual exploitation by peacekeepers. She has conducted fieldwork and research in 20 countries on 6 continents.

Dr. O'Brien is on the Editorial Boards of *The International Journal of Human Rights* and *Human Rights Review*, and the WA International Humanitarian Law Committee of the Australian Red Cross. She is 2nd Vice-President of the International Association of Genocide Scholars (IAGS) and co-convened the 2017 IAGS conference at University of Queensland, serving on the Editorial Board of *Genocide Studies and Prevention* 2013–2017. Dr. O'Brien was the distinguished keynote speaker at the 2019 Australian National Armenian Genocide Commemoration.

She is an admitted legal practitioner who has previously worked at several Australian universities; the National Human Rights Institution of Samoa; and the Legal Advisory Section of the Office of the Prosecutor at the International Criminal Court. She is the author of *Criminalising Peacekeepers: Modernising National Approaches to Sexual Exploitation and Abuse* (2017, Palgrave) and tweets @DrMelOB.

Bruce "Ossie" Oswald
is a Professor and Director of the Asia Pacific Centre for Military Law in the Melbourne Law School at the University of Melbourne. His interests in law and practice are in the areas of international humanitarian law, peace operations, state building, accountability and responsibility, and the application of human rights law to military operations. More specifically, his interests are in examining the law and practice surrounding the protection of civilians, the taking and handling of detainees during military operations, and militias undertaking law and order functions.

Professor Oswald has served in the Australian Regular Army as a legal officer. He has seen operational service in Rwanda, the Former Yugoslavia, East Timor, Iraq and Afghanistan.

For his service as the Legal Officer for the Australian Contingent serving in Rwanda, Professor Oswald was awarded the Conspicuous Service Cross (CSC).

Tamsin Phillipa Paige
is a Lecturer with Deakin Law School and consults for the UN Office on Drugs and Crime in relation to Maritime Crime. Prior to this, she was a Postdoctoral Fellow with the research centre: Conflict and Society, in the School of Humanities and Social Sciences at UNSW Canberra at ADFA. Her work is interdisciplinary in nature, using qualitative sociological methods to analyse international law. She was awarded an Endeavour Scholarship by the Australian Government for her Ph.D. research (conducted at the University of Adelaide and Columbia Law School) on the Security Council and 'threat to the peace'. Prior to her Security Council work she conducted research into the application and impact of international law in counter-piracy operations in Somalia. In a former life, she was a French trained, fine dining pâtissier.

David J. Simon
is a Senior Lecturer in Political Science at Yale University and the Director of Yale's Genocide Studies Program. He studies international regimes to confront mass atrocities as part of a broader interest in atrocity prevention. He also works on the post-genocide efforts to rebuild nations, states, and societies. He graduated from Princeton University and holds a Ph.D. in Political Science from the University of California, Los Angeles.

Andrew Wallis
is a freelance journalist, academic, and author, and a leading expert in the African Great Lakes Region, especially Rwanda. He holds a Ph.D. in Political Science from the University of Cambridge and is a qualified (NCTJ) journalist, with works featured in a wide range of media, including *The Times, The Guardian, USA Today, Thisworld.org, CS Monitor, opendemocracy.net, The New Times,* ABC-CLIO, *The New Jurist,* Institute for Public Policy Research and Rwandan, Ugandan and South African radio and television. His current book *Stepp'd in Blood: Akazu and the Architects of the Rwandan Genocide Against the Tutsi* (Zero Books, 2019) is the result of seven years of detailed investigative research, uncovering the lives and motivations of the leading perpetrators of the 1994 horror.

Foreword

Lieutenant-General the Honourable Romeo Dallaire

It has been more than a quarter of a century since I was appointed as the Commander of the United Nations Assistance Mission in Rwanda (UNAMIR). When I took on the task, I knew very little about the tiny country, located in the heart of Africa, just below the equator. At that point in history, the internet was nowhere nearly as developed as it is today, so my primary source of information on current events for the region came from the scant coverage that the country received in the media. To say the least, Rwanda was not a place that attracted much attention from the western world before 1994, and we had no indication that within five months of the mission's commencement we would find ourselves in the middle of genocide that was unprecedented in violence and intensity. Nor could we have foreseen that our small peacekeeping force would become part of what is now recognized as a major juncture in post-cold war history, law, and politics.

It is clear that when the United Nations was contemplating the creation of UNAMIR in the summer of 1993, it was optimistic that the mission would be short, conducted with little risk of casualties, and most importantly, inexpensive. In spite of numerous warnings that pointed to a resurgence of ethnic violence as early as August 1993, the Security Council pushed forward with its plan to deploy a lightly armed peacekeeping mission that was approximately fifty percent smaller than had been recommended. As reports of massacres and the threat of wider violence increased during the first few months of the mission, the United Nations ignored the numerous warnings, and when faced with irrefutable evidence of impending violence, forbade UNAMIR from taking decisive action to intervene. Rather than reinforcing UNAMIR as Rwanda spiraled into genocide, the Security Council reduced the size of the mission and deliberately chose to avoid using the word "genocide" to describe the ethnic massacres that were consuming an average of 8,000 lives per day. It was not until the genocide and civil war were concluded by the Rwandan Patriotic Army's victory in the middle of July 1994, that my beleaguered force began to be reinforced, and the true extent of the genocide became known. In the subsequent months and years, evidence of horrible atrocities entered the public record, as the International Criminal Tribunal for Rwanda brought the most notorious leaders of the genocide to justice. Although it was too little and too late for the hundreds of thousands who perished, the establishment of the ICTY signaled a turning point in international law, providing notice to those who engage in

 | DOI:10.1163/9789004430129_001

genocide and crimes against humanity that there would be no guaranteed impunity, and no safe refuge for perpetrators of such egregious violence.

It is my distinct pleasure to have been invited to write the foreword for this collection of articles. This work is the first of its kind, providing an examination of the Rwanda tragedy from a wide variety of contributors, including a former ambassador to the Security Council, persons who were on the ground as part of UNAMIR, prosecutors in the ICTR, and dedicated international law scholars and journalists who have spent decades studying Rwanda and the role United Nations played in dealing with the genocide; before, during and after. The articles provide unique insight into how and why the events of 1994 unfolded, and how those events have influenced post-cold war politics and the over-all development of international law.

The legacy of Rwanda is not just one of the failure of the international community to react. It is also a story of how the world can respond in a positive manner when it realizes that colossal errors made at all levels have contributed to catastrophe. To that end, the Rwandan tragedy has inspired reform and innovation in how the international community seeks to prevent and respond to mass atrocities, as well as how to support societies recovering from violent conflict. In many respects the development of doctrines such as the Responsibility to Protect; Transitional Justice; the Protection of Civilians; and the advancement of the Women, Peace and Security agenda, can trace their origins to the Rwandan calamity.

As I have stated so often, we cannot afford to tolerate egregious abuses of human rights or human security; nor can we turn a blind eye to racism and other forms of intolerance. As the second decade of the twenty-first century draws to a close, it is apparent that isolationism is on the rise and that the Security Council has been paralyzed by the self-serving political and strategic interests of its permanent members. The current situations in Syria, Myanmar and Yemen are glaring examples of the human price that is exacted in this environment.

This publication should serve as a reminder of what can happen when national self-interests trump the requirements of humanity. The genocide in Rwanda was preventable, and it could have been stopped in its tracks had the international community responded appropriately. The world has the capacity to intervene to prevent or stop humanitarian disasters; all we need is the leadership and will to do what is right. Peux ce que veux. Allons-y.

Introduction

Phillip Drew, Jeremy Farrall, Rob McLaughlin, and Bruce Oswald

In April 1994, the long-simmering animosity between Rwanda's two primary groups, the Hutu and Tutsi, erupted into civil war and Genocide. Boldened by decades of propaganda, impunity and racially motivated violence, the ethnic Hutu government and its supporters engaged in a campaign of extermination that, over a 100-day period, would leave some 800,000 people (primarily Tutsis and moderate Hutus) dead; an event that was largely ignored by the rest of the world at the time.

While the international community's reaction to Rwanda's genocide was, by any standard, deplorable, the case of Rwanda proved to be a seminal turning point in post-cold-war international relations and international law. The legacy of Rwanda has inspired reform and innovation in how national governments and the international community can seek to prevent and respond to mass atrocities, as well as how they help societies to recover and rebuild after conflict. To this end, when we created this project, we did so not with the intent of explaining what happened in Rwanda, but examining why and how the events of 1994 occurred, and how they can serve to better direct the international community's responses to atrocities and government-sponsored violence in the future.

The contributors to the chapters in this work have been selected for their personalized knowledge of Rwanda, and/or scholarship that has been clearly influenced by the genocide. Included amongst the writers are a number of scholars whose research and writings on Rwanda, the United Nations, and genocide are internationally recognized. Additionally, we have sought out contributions from people who have first-hand experience from Rwanda, be it as peacekeepers, aid workers, or members of the ICTR. As a result, readers might note that some of the authors remain affected by their experiences in Rwanda, and that even after the passage of a quarter of a century, their reflections have awakened raw and painful memories. These aspects have not been edited out of the contributors' articles; it is the opinion of the editors that these recollections and the authors' handling of them add to the value of the over-all work. To that end, we would also like to acknowledge those who were invited to take part in this special issue, but either declined outright or were ultimately unable to contribute due to the fact that their experiences in Rwanda continue to haunt them. The fact that they cannot tell their stories is one of the lasting legacies of Rwanda.

 | DOI:10.1163/9789004430129_002

The Approach We Took to Building This Book

The chapters of this book seek to recount, explore, and – where we can – explain the tragedy that was the Rwanda genocide and the nature of the international community's entanglement with it. We have, consequently, focussed the chapters around three themes:

1. The context – what went before, and how did (or didn't?) this set the conditions that allowed, or even facilitated, the genocide.
2. The crisis – how did the genocide evolve, and what parts did the wide range of, by turns, appalled, fretful, powerless, mislead - but nevertheless implicated – international community actors and witnesses play in the events.
3. The consequences – what happened after; what shadow has the Rwanda genocide cast since 1994 in relation to UN operations, UN doctrine, and (yet again) the 'never again' hopes of the international community.

Additionally, the chapters in this book are generally of three types: personal accounts; comment; and analysis. Many of the contributions mix all three moda, and we have encouraged this rather than sought to limit or compartmentalise the contributions; indeed, we think this a real strength of the editorial approach we have adopted, and the contributions provided. It is, after all, not possible to be dispassionate about genocide in the way that it is possible to be dispassionate about the legal limits of coastal state authority in the eez, the practicalities of detention on the battlefield, or the most recent GDP figures.

Outline of the Book

Part One: Rwanda, UNAMIR and the International Community

Chapter 1 - Rwanda's Forgotten Years: Reconsidering the Role and Crimes of Akazu 1973–1993

Author: Andrew Wallis

Andrew Wallis, a journalist and scholar deeply familiar with Rwanda, leads off the book by examining how one element of the permissive context for the genocide was established well in advance of the crisis itself. Wallis focusses upon the role and crimes of the coterie around President Habyarimana and his wife, Agathe. The power and longevity (two decades) of this network of self-interested, kleptocratic, violent, and to some degree internationally tolerated groups – the Akazu, Network Zero, and eventually the Interahamwe – ensured that an environment of ethnic tension, impunity, liberal resort to violence, and ultimately active undermining of the Arusha Accords, was well and truly in place by 1993. Indeed, as Wallis observes, the fact that 'the success of the peace process… would inevitably involve some form of compromise and power sharing was treated as treason' by many of those in power, threatened as they were by what that process could portend. Reading Wallis' short history of this fundamental contextual tinder almost leaves one with a despairing sense of consequential inevitability.

Chapter 2 - Rwanda: the Political Failure of the UN Security Council

Author: Colin Keating

Colin Keating was the New Zealand Permanent Representative in the UNSC when the crisis unfolded, and he played a central role in trying to ensure the UNSC lived up to its international peace and security mandate in relation to Rwanda. His article is a searing and honest account from someone who witnessed the descent into genocide from the vantage point of unny. It is a challenging read, tracing (as it does) the sense of frustration, and even helplessness, at the UNSC as a general sense of post-Cold War international optimism was suddenly confronted by a series of almost simultaneous peacekeeping crises – Somalia, Bosnia-Hercegovina, and Rwanda. Uncertainty as to information; the absence of mechanisms for due diligence and incorporation of alternative intelligence; a retreat on the part of some States from the required level of political will; unwillingness to fund, adequately empower, and resource missions; and the ever present influence of domestic politics - all acted to frustrate and even mislead the UNSC. Obstruction, distraction, obfuscation, fear, and ignorance all played a role in the Secretariat's response as well. As Keating explains, although some States saw quite clearly what was unfolding and called it out for what it was, the unsc as an institution was to some extent taken by surprise – a shocking, condemnatory, but systemically and politically almost inevitable indictment on the UNSC, Secretariat, and some closely engaged States. And even though the UNSC ultimately – albeit to some extent with only minimal effect – shifted gears once the genocide was an undeniable fact, Keating assesses that subsequent introspection was perhaps fleeting, for he still finds it 'difficult to escape the conclusion that much of what should have been learned by the Security Council from the Rwanda tragedy is either absent or eroding'.

Chapter 3 -Wilfully Blind: the Security Council's Response to Genocide in Rwanda

Author: Tamsin Phillipa Paige

In her contribution to this book, Tamsin Paige, an innovative scholar of UNSC history and practice, analyses the 'inadvertent complicity' of the UNSC in the genocide. By analysing the discourse employed in assessing the nature of the threat to the peace represented by the situation in Rwanda, Paige lays bare the nuanced differences in argument and approach employed by each of the

P5. Her assessment indicates several fundamental points. The first is the expressed preference amongst the P5 for a negotiated solution – in many ways, an almost blind unwillingness to change course, even after the genocide commenced, from the initial commitment to negotiations and (failed) peace accord implementation. The second is that the P5 as a collective were committed to public institutional reliance upon reports from the Secretariat for UNSC situational awareness and recommendations. That is, despite their own independent access to information, and the fact that some of the E10 – such as NZ – worked hard to bring these alternative sources of information to the table, the P5 were collectively reluctant to allow these independent assessments and reports to enter the chamber in any meaningful way. This was a consequence of both P5 management of their own situational interests but also of deeper predilections and beliefs about the role of the UNSC in such situations. Her conclusion is that 'When all of this is considered the only reasonable conclusion that we can reach is that the Security Council, at the behest of the French, was complicit through their inaction in the Rwanda genocide.'

Chapter 4 - Underpowered and Mostly Unwanted: A Short History of UNAMIR

Author: Jean Bou

In his concise and pithy contribution, Jean Bou - one of Australia's official historians of peacekeeping – describes the rise, fall, and partial resurrection of the UN mission – UNAMIR. From its origins as the Uganda based UNOMUR, through the creation and almost extinction of UNAMIR, to the part resurrection of UNAMIR (ii), Bou outlines how the mandate, resourcing, and contextual stars were never in alignment for UNAMIR, fatally compromising from the very outset any chance the mission had of preventing, or in any event stopping, the genocide: 'Unable to affect a peace that neither side wanted and lacking the strength, mandate and political backing to stop the genocide, UNAMIR was limited to the significant but ad hoc roles of protecting the few people it could, exhorting the belligerents to talk and, perhaps most importantly, reporting on the atrocities around them'. UNAMIR, he concludes, was variously 'disdained' or 'tolerated' by all sides – rpf, Hutu militia, Rwandan Army – and this speaks powerfully to its effectively pre-ordained weaknesses. Even subsequent to the mid-1994 revamp, the same essential 'paradox' continued to vex and hamstring UNAMIR – that is, quite apart from resource incapacities, 'the mandate and reality were not in sympathy'. Subsequent atrocities such as Kibeho, the evolving political context, and increasing local contempt for the brave but utterly inadequate UNAMIR, meant that its ultimate withdrawal in March 1996 was for many States, and for the UN, an ongoing embarrassment, but a relief nonetheless.

Chapter 5 - Rwanda Revisited: UNAMIR II - Australian Reflections on the Mission and the Mandate

Author: Lieutenant-General J.J. Frewen

John Frewen – at the time an Australian Army Captain, now a Lieutenant-General – provides us with a gripping personal perspective of the day to day tactical and operational frustrations of UNAMIR II. But, perhaps more importantly, he also delivers a very open account of the human costs and consequences of, but also the initiative and resourcefulness of an under-strength and weakly mandated UN Force which was mismatched to its context. Both UNAMIR and UNAMIR II, he writes 'failed the grand ideals of humanitarian intervention assigned them', which meant that the UN was ultimately relegated to the role of 'bystander to the ensuing carnage'. A confused mandate, and associated confusion as to use of force authorisations, inadequate resourcing, misjudgements as to the intentions of the main actors (and, indeed, the degree of respect they would afford the UN), failure of collective will, and misconceptions as to role, all played a part in UNAMIR and UNAMIR II trying – often heroically – to act as 'representatives of peace, where no true peace had yet settled'.

Chapter 6 - UNAMIR: a Deployed Legal Officer's Retrospective

Author: Bruce 'Ossie' Oswald

In a similar vein, Bruce 'Ozzie' Oswald – also an Australian Army participant in UNAMIR II and now a greatly respected analyst of UN mandates and operations – also provides an insider's perspective on the mission. Oz was the Australian contingent Legal Officer and is almost uniquely qualified to comment upon the legal ills and opportunities that attended UNAMIR. It is also fair to say that the academic Oz is in very many ways a product of his experience of Rwanda and UNAMIR. Oz looks to three seminal legal lessons learned from the Rwanda operation. The first is the need for coordination and early – indeed pre-set - institutional cooperation in investigating mass atrocity. As he notes, intra-mission competition for resources, relevance, and mandate can (and in Rwanda did) lead to bureaucratic delay and loss of evidence. The second is the – ongoing – uncertainty that surrounds the interrelated matrix of use of force, RoE, and self-defence. The rise of Protection of Civilian mandates, and the need to educate the Secretariat as to the manner by which use of force is controlled by military contingents was – as other chapters in this book also note – a key consequence of the Rwanda mission. The third issue Oz deals with is detention operations – more specifically, the variety of detainee types that are encountered in UN operations, from criminal detainees through to people who wish to be detained for their own protection. The long operational and legal tail that the simple act of taking a detainee brings into play was, for Oz, one of the key insights he took away from UNAMIR, and one from which interfet operations in East Timor in 1999–2000 certainly benefited. His six legal lessons from Rwanda are as concise and practical an elaboration of pragmatic operations law concerns as one is likely to find.

Chapter 7 - Do Not Intervene: UNAMIR's Rules of Engagement from the Inside

Authors: Phillip Drew and Brent Beardsley

As with John Frewen and Bruce Oswald, Phillip Drew and Brent Beardsley were also on the ground during UNAMIR, Phil as the Canadian Intelligence Officer, and Brent as the Military Assistant to the UNAMIR Force Commander, Major-General Dallaire. In this joint chapter, Phil and Brent take up Ozzie's RoE theme and describe the UNAMIR RoE 'from the inside': process, content, uncertainties. As they observe, the UNAMIR RoE was vexed from the outset by a series of procedural and political pressures which proved insurmountable for UNAMIR in terms of establishing an agreed, approved, and accepted RoE profile. The first was the inability, incapacity – and indeed the unwillingness - of the Secretariat to agree, let alone approve, the draft RoE. This in turn meant that debates and uncertainties as to mandate scope and interpretation in relation to use of force, self-defence, and tasks and roles – the outcomes and resolution of which are often, but not always, expressed in RoE – were never resolved. These debates and uncertainties thus continued to dog UNAMIR, leading in effect to the legally incorrect, operationally nonsensical, and at a human level disastrous 'do not intervene' conclusion. Drew and Beardsley do not say that an approved, agreed, and accepted RoE would have solved everything: 'if a force does not have the capacity to perform a given task, then it is folly, and potentially dangerous, to provide it with RoE to do that thing'. Indeed, as they astutely note, in some ways the 'don't engage' approach may have (paradoxically) actually 'spared the tiny UN force from annihilation'. Nevertheless, the 'wilful neglect' of the UN in allowing uncertainty as to RoE – and so much else about UNAMIR - to continue played a clear role in the outcomes.

Part Two: The "G" Word

Chapter 8 - Defining Genocide

Author: Melanie O'Brien

Melanie O'Brien's article provides a vital element of the contextual background to Rwanda in 1994–1995, and to UNAMIR, naming and defining the fundamental horror that happened, and was allowed to happen, in Rwanda – genocide. She traces the origins of the term from Lemkin through to the Genocide

Convention, and through a number of iconic cases. O'Brien exposes for us some of the (still) unresolved tensions that have vexed the concept of genocide: The tension between broader cultural and existential approaches, and narrower physical and biological destruction approaches; and genocide as process or event. She also outlines some of the legal challenges that attend several of the key terms in the generally accepted definition of genocide: 'destroy', 'in part', 'groups', 'intent', and so on. She then concludes with an important and politically nuanced point essential to understanding the politics and afterlife of the Rwanda genocide – the 'weight of the "G" word'.

Chapter 9 - Rwanda, the Holocaust, and the Predictable Path to Genocide

Author: Phillip Drew

In his second piece, Phillip Drew – as noted previously, also a participant in UNAMIR as the Canadian contingent intelligence officer in mid-1994 - then leads us through much more of the harrowing detail surrounding the how and why of the genocide in Rwanda specifically. He does so by comparing the 'predictable path' to the genocide in Rwanda with the waypoints along the road to the Holocaust, identifying the indicia of parallel development. This comparative assessment is both possible and instructive, he notes, precisely because 'genocides don't just happen; rather they are the manifestation of planned and deliberate campaigns to bring about the destruction of an identifiable national, ethnical, racial or religious group.' Using Stanton's 'Ten Stages of Genocide' as his framework, Drew employs comparative touchstones – racism as ideology, perversion of law and normalisation of racism, impunity, hate propaganda, organised campaigns of extermination, and the bitter post-script of perpetrator escape and genocide denial – to illustrate the similarities in evolution as between these two genocides. He concludes that 'it is abundantly clear that post-1959 Rwanda was a society that was well-primed for genocide; all the hallmarks of a pending genocide were present'. The lost final chance to avert the crime – represented by the UNSC and key States failing to properly grasp the situation in Rwanda, and as a consequence consciously deciding to avoid a robust response – meant that none of 'the thousand early warnings that something appalling was about to occur in Rwanda' were heeded.

Chapter 10 - Moral Equivalence: The Story of Genocide Denial in Rwanda

Author: Linda Melvern

As an investigative journalist, author, and practitioner involved in the legal aftermath of the genocide, Linda Malvern builds on the foundations laid by O'Brien (the 'what went before' of the concept of genocide), and the Rwanda specific comparative analysis provided by Drew, and outlines the abhorrent – almost unbelievable – malignant afterlife of the genocide in the form of ongoing genocide denial. As Malvern observes, the Rwanda typology of genocide denial attempts to leverage a form of 'moral equivalence' between Hutu and Tutsi groups by claiming that both massacred each other and that, consequently, whilst Rwanda witnessed an abhorrent series of tit-for-tat mass killings, it was not a genocide. Consequently, this campaign –as Malvern indicates - does not focus on denying that mass atrocities took place; rather it is perpetrated through the artifice of re-casting the event as a series of iterative mass atrocity crimes on both sides, in an attempt to defang the particular moral opprobrium of the atrocity by removing the sting of the label 'genocide'.

Chapter 11 - Gendering Rwanda Genocide and Post-Genocide
Author: Adam Jones

Political scientist, Adam Jones, challenges us to think about the Rwanda genocide from a different perspective – that of gender: gendered anxieties, gendered agents, and roles, and gendercidal targeting. His chapter is a timely reminder that beyond its abhorrent nature and universally abhorrent consequences, genocide is as multi-dimensional as any other jus cogens level crime. Jones describes two broad typologies of genocide – 'gendercide', and 'root and branch genocide', which are 'distinguished by the different operations of the gender variable in each'. As Jones outlines, the Rwanda genocide evidenced broad range of gendered aspects – from leveraging ethnicised gender tropes, through the sometime employment of gender-based genocidal approaches (execution, rape), to the economic and social consequences (planned or not) that are the legacy of gendered genocide. 'The "gendering" of a given genocide', he concludes, 'therefore encompasses the cultural configurations that influence the mobilisation of perpetrators and the targeting of victims, as well as the sexed bodies that are damaged or destroyed in genocidal campaigns'.

Part Three: Prosecuting Genocide

Chapter 12 - The ICTR and Its Contribution to the Revivification of International Criminal Law
Author: Emily Crawford

Emily Crawford, a highly regarded and insightful scholar of loac and icl, explores one set of key institutional and legal responses to, and consequences of, the Rwanda genocide – the ICTR and the revival of icl that the ICTR and the

ICTY heralded. Tracing the development of the concept and institutions of ICL, Crawford observes how 'Beyond just their mere existence, the case law of the [ad hoc] tribunals, the ICTR in particular, were pivotal in progressively developing the international law of genocide, and the law of non-international armed conflict'. This is not least because the tribunals 'revived international criminal law as a discipline'; it is also because the jurisprudence of the ICTR was especially significant in the evolving jurisprudence in respect of genocide, and sexual violence as a means of genocide and as a war crime, the criminalisation of violations of both Common Article 3 of the Geneva Conventions and Additional Protocol ii, and the political leadership dimensions of command responsibility. 'While the record of the ICTR', she concludes ' was not without its problems, it nevertheless was an important institution, both for its own program of work, as well as for its contribution to re-establishing international criminal law as a distinct and permanent part of the international legal landscape'.

Chapter 13 - Post-Genocide Justice in Rwanda
Author: M.A. Drumbl

Crawford's chapter is neatly complemented by Mark Drumbl's equally compelling contribution on the domestic Rwandan legal and institutional response to the genocide. Drumbl notes the international (ICTR) and extraterritorial (genocide related cases in Canada, France, Belgium, and Germany) judicial responses to the genocide, but focuses his contribution on tracing the two main levels of Rwanda's judicialised domestic response to the genocide. He describes the foundations, operation, and legacy of organic criminal law and courts, and the employment of 'gacaca' – 'justice in the grass', a 'form of local dispute resolution' to adjudicate many genocide-related crimes. This multi-level approach was necessary, Drumbl notes, because the 'staggering number of genocide suspects… did more than, to draw from Hannah Arendt, "explode the limits of the law", they also exploded the capacity of whatever infrastructure that remained'. Drumbl takes some time to describe the utility of the gacaca in particular. He notes how – in a post-atrocity political context where no truth and reconciliation commission was established – this mechanism ('steeped in reconciliation, reconstitution, and reintegration', and empowered in order to 'attain both legal and extra-legal goals') nevertheless 'involved the local community sitting in judgment of persons having committed mass atrocity in the same community'. There was, as he concludes, a 'lack of congruence' between the nature and objectives of the international and Rwandan justice responses, and indeed also as between the two main Rwandan justice responses. But whether this is simply a valuable insight, or something more fundamental, is as yet undetermined, and to some extent hinges around his ultimate assessment that 'Whether the intense turn to criminal law in the aftermath of the Rwandan genocide… attained retributive, deterrent or expressive goals remains debated.'

Part Four: Rwanda's Legacy

Chapter 14 - Rwanda: Lessons Observed. Lessons Learned?

Author: Jane Boulden

Jane Boulden of the Royal Military College of Canada introduces the final section of the book – dealing with consequences and lessons learned/observed/ignored/unidentified – with a general survey of the shadow of UNAMIR, and the Rwanda operation, in terms of the UN. Boulden traces the assessments and outcomes of a select set of reports – broader UN, DPKO specific, and AU – in order to ask 'has peacekeeping changed since Rwanda?'. On one level, she concludes, it has not: There was no discernible UN turning away from 'continued use of peacekeeping as a tool since UNAMIR'; the UNSC has continued to authorise operations 'that address intra-state conflict'; and the many significant reports and doctrinal evolutions since Rwanda still tend to coalesce around the sacred nature of the three pillars of traditional peacekeeping – consent, impartiality, and minimum use of force. Boulden observes how these three pillars – and particularly 'impartiality' – have been subject to post-Rwanda debate and refinement, but indicates that this was in some ways the low hanging fruit. This is because it has proven – and continues to prove – much harder to deal with those other factors that this series of reports clearly agreed to be fundamental to the Rwanda context: The 'clear, grim picture of dysfunction, missed opportunities, and failure at almost every turn' that characterised the UN's engagement with Rwanda in the lead up to, during, and in the aftermath of the genocide. Accepting that there has been significant normative change flowing from these many analyses of Rwanda and peacekeeping more generally, the fact that the 15 years of reports between Brahimi and hippo 'overlap considerably in the points they raise and the recommendations they provide… demonstrates that not very much may have changed'.

Chapter 15 - Some Rules of Engagement Legacies of the 1999: Report of the Independent Inquiry into the Actions of the United Nations during the 1994 Genocide in Rwanda

Author: Rob McLaughlin

Rob McLaughlin then continues this analytical endeavour with his focussed examination of the 1999 Independent Inquiry Report into the UN and the

Rwanda operation, and the doctrinal legacies of that report in relation to UN RoE. McLaughlin traces the main findings of the Independent Inquiry Report with respect to UN RoE and associated doctrine, and then outlines the subsequent doctrinal and report-based see-saw between the traditionalist and progressive perspectives in terms of thinking around, and support for, robust RoE in peace operations. He concludes (along with Oswald, Drew, and others) that whilst progress is evident, the UN is still institutionally and doctrinally divided on the nature and role of RoE and associated doctrine for peacekeeping operations. This disconnect will continue to hamper operations until more clarity around issues such as self-defence, and use of force for mandate implementation, is achieved.

Chapter 16 - Rwanda and the Rohingya: Learning the Wrong Lessons?

Author: David J. Simon

David Simon, a political scientist, challenges us to think about the lessons learned, or not, from Rwanda through the prism of the current persecution and – as is before the icj as this book goes to press - genocide of the Rohingya. Simon assesses that the situation of the Rohingya exposes the 'hollowness' of the 'never again' post-Holocaust, post-Rwanda, post-Srebrenica assurances of institutional and communitarian lessons (not) learned, or indeed of learning the wrong lessons. As Simon outlines, there were in fact significant changes post-Rwanda to the international genocide prevention architecture; yet 'the nature of the changes to the international atrocity prevention regime that ensued, and then the global response to the genocide against the Rohingya in Myanmar… still falls short of what is necessary to prevent genocide'. The 'wilful ignorance', 'deception', 'cowardice' that dogged the unsc in 1993–1994, and the nature of the key proposed institutional and doctrinal solutions developed – organisational human rights actors and monitors, and R2P – have not functioned as hoped. Simon proposes that two factors – in particular – may help explain this. The first is that the unsc (particularly through use of the veto) can still remain wilfully ignorant when it wants to – and R2P does not and cannot prevent this. The second is the lack of internal coordination and unity of effort within and amongst the different actors and pillars of the evolved post-Rwanda atrocity prevention scheme, which can still hamstring the UN and international community's ability to identify pre-genocide indicators and warnings, and to halt genocides once they commence. 'In sum', he concludes, 'the core lesson from the UN's failure in Rwanda was not learned: that the current structure of the Security Council… is unlikely to authorise either a protection-driven intervention mission or a punitive procedure'.

Chapter 17 - Humanitarian Intervention and R2P

Author: Stacey Henderson

Finally, Stacey Henderson looks to the shadow of Rwanda in terms of the persistent – and persistently contested - concept of humanitarian intervention, and the evolution of the R2P doctrine. Tracing the 're-examination of the conceptualisations of sovereignty and the principle of non-intervention' that evolved after Rwanda, Henderson describes the long journey towards R2P, and assesses the legal, normative, and institutional challenges that still attend the attainment of its goals. This is not least due to continued associations of R2P with coercive measures, which – as Henderson notes - often tends to reanimate, rather than move on from, the baggage around humanitarian intervention. Ultimately, however, Henderson concludes her chapter, and indeed the book, on a note of cautious optimism: Although it is in no way a panacea, R2P - at the very least - 'raises the possibility that a greater range of measures may be taken in response to the commission, or anticipation of, atrocity crimes in the future. The legacy of Rwanda is the hope, reflected in R2P, that silence and idleness will never again be the international community's response to genocide'.

Conclusion

As stated above, this book deals with the context, the crisis and the consequences of a truly shocking time in the history of Rwanda and the lives of those that were in Rwanda in 1994. We hope that those who read this volume or dip into the specific chapters that follow will find that the richness of the personal accounts, comment and analysis has given them a better understanding of that shocking time. However, our ultimate hope is that every reader of this book comes away with a deeper commitment to do everything in their sphere of influence to condemn racism and other forms of intolerance, and ultimately, prevent another genocide.

PART 1

Rwanda, UNAMIR and the International Community

CHAPTER 1

Rwanda's Forgotten Years

Reconsidering the Role and Crimes of Akazu 1973–1993

Andrew Wallis

The official Independence Day celebrations that got underway on Sunday 1 July 1973 came as Rwanda teetered on the edge of an expected coup. Eleven years after independence the one party regime of President Grégoire Kayibanda was imploding. Hit by economic and political stagnation, notably the damaging failure to share the trappings of power with those outside his central regional support base, Kayibanda's future was bleak. During the previous months he had thrown his support behind the ethnic scapegoating of the Tutsi minority in an effort to deflect blame for his own regime failures. The tactic had worked when he first seized power, unifying the Hutu majority against the '*inyenzi*' threat. But times had changed. Kayibanda's fate and that of his regime was sealed by his failure to validate the vaulting ambitions of the northern officer corps in his army. He underestimated the danger posed by General Juvenal Habyarimana, his defence minister and head of the army and Habyarimana's close friends and allies from the Bushiru region in the north of the country: highly ambitious young officers like Major Aloys Nsekalije, Lieutenant Colonel Alexis Kanyarengwe, Major Sabin Benda, Major Laurent Serubuga, Major Laurent Simba, Major Théoneste Bagosora and Captain Elie Sagatwa.

Four days after Kayibanda's final speech to the nation given at the Independence Day event, his 11-year rule came to an abrupt end. On the evening of 4th July Habyarimana, allied with ten 'comrades',[1] launched a swift and decisive military coup. By the following morning Kayibanda had been arrested along with hundreds of his family, politicians and military, most from the centre and south of the country. Habyarimana, in a message to the nation, declared that 'enemies of peace' who had in previous times 'disturbed public order by sowing

1 The 11 were Major General Juvenal Habyarimana (Gisenyi), Lieutenant Colonel Alexis Kanayarengwe (Ruhengeri), Major Aloys Nsekalije (Gisenyi), Major Sabin Benda (Ruhengeri), Major Epimaque Ruhashya (Kigali), Major Fabien Gahimano (Gisenyi), Major Jean-Nepomuscene Munyandekwe (Gitarama), Major Laurent Serubuga (Gisenyi), Major Bonaventure Buregeya (Gisenyi), Major Bonaventure Ntibitura (Ruhengeri) and Major Aloys Simba (Gisenyi). Only one (Ruhashya) was a Tutsi, and only two (Ruhashya and Munyandekwe) were not from the northern prefectures of Ruhengeri and Gisenyi.

 | DOI:10.1163/9789004430129_003

discord and dividing the country into regional groups', had been overthrown. The National Guard, headed by Habyarimana, had taken control as it could no longer tolerate this atmosphere or 'keep its arms crossed'. Ending by announcing 'Long Live Peace and National Unity,' the new military regime set about establishing what was, for most Rwandans, a carbon copy of what had gone before during the past 11 years. The significant difference this time was that the ruling clique was a Hutu one from the north rather than the centre and south.

Born on 8 March 1936 to deeply religious parents – his father was a Catholic catechist at the imposing red brick parish church in Rambura, near Gisenyi – Habyarimana had initially been educated at Nyundo seminary before switching to medical studies at Lovanium University in Zaire. Unrest and anti-foreigner sentiment forced him to quit and return home where his impressive physical build and Hutu ethnicity led to his swift recruitment by the Belgian colonial authorities. In December 1961 Habyarimana passed out of military college as number 001, becoming the very first officer in what was to become the new Rwandan national army. A hard worker, with army discipline reinforcing his tough early life grafting in the fields with his father, Habyarimana spoke excellent French, dressed immaculately and was an imposingly tall and well-built figure. Never one to suffer fools gladly, and with an explosive temper, a major political and personal weakness was acute indecisiveness. His ambition for power and wealth was matched, like his predecessor Kayibanda, with a failure to act decisively to avert disaster. Ultimately though, his biggest strength was to become his greatest weakness: his family. In August 1963 Habyarimana's marriage to local girl Agathe Kanziga gave him what he needed most to succeed – a relationship with royalty. Her direct lineage to the Hutu Bushiru kings, allied with her father Gervais being both a former sub chief and now a wealthy owner of a textile business, was from the start a source of power and political strength. With Agathe came close family members: her brother Protais Zigiranyirazo, known as 'Monsieur Z', and cousins Elie Sagatwa and Seraphin Rwabukumba.

Habyarimana faced multiple challenges on seizing power. Despite promises to unify the nation regardless of ethnicity or region, the northern clique that backed the new president continued Kayibanda's anti-Tutsi discrimination. The former president's Parmehutu party was banned and Habyarimana's own single party, the MRND (National Revolutionary Movement for Development) took its place. It was not just a matter of having a new one party state: there was the need to make sure hearts and minds were quickly 'recalibrated'. The sole radio station, Radio Rwanda was given over to lengthy ballads rejoicing in the president's goodness and fatherly affection for his people as well as his hard work on their behalf. The press such as it was – the weekly regime newspaper *Imvaho* ('news') and Catholic weekly *Kinyamateka* – reported purely on state success stories and Habyarimana's accomplishments. All communes were instructed to hold weekly '*animation*' events. This significant propaganda tool was designed to push the Habyarimana brand into the lives of every citizen. The assembled populace would spend the afternoon dancing and singing, reciting poetry and stories with the sole aim of extolling the president and the state. Everyone was expected to wear a button lapel badge with Habyarimana's smiling face upon it. Catholic archbishop Vincent Nsengiyumva, who served on MRND's central committee, proudly wore his badge alongside his crucifix. It was difficult to know whether his loyalty was to his earthly saviour Habyarimana or his spiritual one.

As this 'social revolution' got into full flow in the mid 1970s, Habyarimana sent his ambassadors around the Foreign Ministries of Europe and North America to reassure the international community that Rwanda was very much open for business. His diplomatic envoys insisted the coup had been a necessary, but bloodless, event. Rwanda, under Habyarimana, could be relied upon as a peaceful, prosperous and steadfast ally. Unlike Kayibanda who avoided foreign travel where possible in favour of a quiet family life at his small residence outside Gitarama, Habyarimana and Agathe positively flourished when mixing with presidents and world leaders. Trips to Brussels and Bonn, Washington and Paris were to be fully enjoyed, with state banquets, shopping trips and a chance to relish the luxury living Rwanda was yet to welcome.

France rewarded Habyarimana with a new presidential plane and military pact. King Baudouin of Belgium and wife Queen Fabiola became firm family friends. Peter Molt from the Rhineland-Palatinate and Charles Jeanneret from Switzerland became high profile and highly paid presidential advisors. The World Bank and IMF were happy to throw money at the 'Switzerland of Africa' as it was regarded, with precious little analysis or due diligence. Outrages such as the World Bank's notorious GBK project that ran for seven very lucrative years from 1980–87 were allowed to take place.[2] Instead of protecting the last remaining natural forest in the centre and north west of the country and its indigenous inhabitants – many of them Tutsi and Twa – who had lived there for generations, the lavish new international funds were quickly 'repurposed'. Virgin forest was cut down, the local inhabitants expelled and huge cattle ranches carved out. Agathe, Z, Seraphin, Serubuga, Habyarimana and the regime clique were the beneficiaries.

2 See *Isibo*, 'Those who seized the Gishwati Project were aping Kinani', No. 70, 25 September 1992; World Bank, Project Completion Report, 'Rwanda, Integrated Livestock and Forestry Development', (Credit 1039-Rw), 12 April 1991.

On 21 May 1979 the effort to assert Rwanda's significance on a regional and indeed world stage was rewarded as the 6th Franco-African summit took place in Kigali. Habyarimana played host to 24 francophone leaders and the French president Giscard d'Estaing. There was a notable Rwandan absentee from this major event: Grégoire Kayibanda. Within days of his 'bloodless' coup Habyarimana had rounded up hundreds of the former president's supporters – diplomats, military, politicians, ministers and some of his family. Over the coming months they were tortured and brutally murdered. Kayibanda's wife Véridiane (Diane) died from a 'mystery illness' while under house imprisonment. On 15 December 1976 her husband was murdered in his own home, probably by Sagatwa and on orders from the presidency. There was no state funeral; the man who had presided over Rwandan's independence was swiftly and unceremoniously buried in a small plot in his own garden.[3]

The disappearance of such a number of high profile individuals failed to alert western allies to the far darker side of the regime they were feting with political and diplomatic plaudits and financial largesse. The Archbishop of Kigali, André Perraudin, a close friend and mentor to Kayibanda, along with some Rwandan bishops, made half-hearted requests to visit the political prisoners on behalf of their families. These were unsurprisingly rejected: the prisoners had long since been killed.

The speed with which Habyarimana's authoritarian regime was able to control and corrupt all aspects of Rwandan life can best understood by examining the political tracts that began to appear in Kigali in 1979, only five years after the coup. The first tracts accused Laurent Serubuga the deputy army chief of staff and Pierre-Celestin Rwagafilita, deputy head of the Gendarmerie, of breath-taking corruption, embezzling public funds, counterfeiting money, insatiable greed, wild ambition and 'hopeless and mediocre capabilities'.[4] Later tracts went further targeting Habyarimana for his greed, listing his recent and lengthy property, cash and luxury car acquisitions around the world. They questioned how the president had more offices of state than even the infamous ruler of the Central African Republic, the self-proclaimed Emperor Bokassa. Both *Umuganda* and *animation* were ridiculed, while the lavishing of funds purely on Habyarimana's northern homeland to the detriment of the centre and south was highlighted as highly damaging to national unity. It was

---

3 For accounts of Kayibanda's death see Andrew Wallis, *Stepp'd in Blood: Akazu and the Architects of the Rwandan genocide against the Tutsi*, Basingstoke, (Zero Books 2019), pp. 71–74.

4 The first tract appeared on 7 March 1979, and was in the form of an open letter from the National Bank's governor Jean Birara.

interesting to note the tract written by Kayibanda's former MDR-Parmehutu party attacked the president not just for personal abuses and also for being too soft on the Tutsi. Accordingly he should immediately to 'restore the values of the Muhutu before their anger bursts out.' In fact Habyarimana, despite promising ethnic unity, had moved to disenfranchise the Tutsi minority from all areas of public life to such an extent that during the late 1970s and 80s they were almost unnoticeable. They would be tolerated but nothing more. The only exceptions were businessmen like Valens Kajeguhakwa who were allowed to make money only because *Le Clan* could enrich themselves by effectively seizing a considerable part of the profits.

In April 1980, already under pressure from these unprecedented public attacks, an alleged coup attempt by two disgruntled military officers was uncovered. Former head of intelligence Théoneste Lizinde and the powerful ex interior minister Alexis Kanyarengwe were said to be trying to recruit others to overthrow Habyarimana. Lizinde had fallen out with Agathe, with his very public ambition coming into direct conflict with that of the first lady. There could only be one winner. Having failed to gain asylum at the Libyan, American and Vatican diplomatic missions, Lizinde was arrested. Kanyarengwe, who was tipped off, fled to Tanzania.

The stinking cells of Ruhengeri prison were soon filled with known and assumed enemies of the regime. Here in the '*cachot noir*' ('black coffins') the prisoners were held incommunicado, tortured by electric shocks and savage beatings, and left to rot. Show trials of those assumed to have written, published, read or seen the tracts or be part of the coup took place. Article 16 of the penal code, for those deemed to have 'incited people against the authorities,' was almost impossible to defend against – not least because there was no legal representation for the accused. The sight of Habyarimana's powerful brother-in-law Z sitting behind the judges passing notes as to how the proceedings should proceed was hardly reassuring. Lizinde was sentenced to death on 25 November 1981 though the sentence was not carried out after intervention from Amnesty International who heralded him as a prisoner of conscience.[5] Less fortunate were 43 'common' criminals whom the regime executed in September 1982.

The 1980s was a halcyon decade for *Akazu*. This term, which described the 'little house' or close family group around Agathe, did not come into common public usage until the late 1980s. However, *Akazu* as the pinnacle of a rhizomeous unofficial network was an actuality from the early days after the

5 There is some irony here, given Lizinde was personally responsible for widespread and appalling human rights abuses that took place during the mid 1970s in his role as head of the National Intelligence Services.

1973 coup. Known also as *Le Clan de madam,* it reflected Agathe's ambitions and that of her family to use the country as a private source of wealth, power and prestige. Brother-in-law Z, with no previous administrative experience, was made prefect of Kibuye shortly after the 1973 coup, and one year later, in November 1974, was handed the most lucrative of all state offices when he became prefect of Ruhengeri. Cousin Seraphin, despite his dire education record and no financial experience, was given the job of controlling foreign exchange at the National Bank of Rwanda, while Elie Sagatwa became head of intelligence and Habyarimana's shadow, patrolling and monitoring not just those who wanted to see or communicate with the president but also the president himself. Noel Mbonabaryi, Habyarimana's aged uncle, also known as 'the godfather,' became director general of employment. His nickname of *Conshoma* or 'give me a kiss' was extremely apt given his predilection for making young pretty girls 'earn' any employment they had come to him to request.

The State tea franchise OCIR was given to Michel Bagaragaza. This near neighbour of the presidential couple,[6] whose wife was related to Agathe, later explained to genocide investigators the methodology and makeup of *Akazu*. He described how *Akazu* relied on appointing others lower down the societal chain to carry out tasks that it was unable to do itself. To be recruited into this lucrative and powerful network was not down to intelligence, skills or ability, but a person's ethnic and regional background. Hutus from Bushiru and later, as the circle widened, from the northern prefectures of Gisenyi, Ruhengeri and Byumba, were the ultimate beneficiaries of this clientage. By May 1991 of the 62 directors of the main banks and public concerns, 42 came from this region. By contrast, the southern prefectures of Butare and Gitarama could boast only 4 directors each. Needless to say none were Tutsi or Twa.

Both inside and outside his prefecture of Ruhengeri Monsieur Z was the dominant figure, seeing to the appointment of loyal 'Zedist'[7] individuals who could be relied upon to reflect his decisions first, and those of president, people and country a distant second. To fall out with Z because he had taken a fancy to your wife or property or even for refusing to support his football team, Mukungwa FC, could prove fatal. Z surrounded himself with a number of

---

6 Bagaragaza lived 4 km away from the Giciye residence of Habyarimana, and only 2 km from Z's mansion.

7 This term was one used by Christophe Mfizi to describe the system of influence that Z established throughout all sectors of society including the military and intelligence services. See Mfizi, Christophe, 'The Zero Network, (B): Destroyer of the democracy and the Republic in Rwanda (1975–1994)', Consultation report written on the request of the Office of the Prosecutor General of the International Criminal Tribunal for Rwanda, 2006.

protégé's who would become vital links within *Akazu*: men like Ferdinand Nahimana at the University of Butare, which had a campus in Ruhengeri, Minister of Public Works, Joseph Nzirorera and Augustin Bizimana, head of the state Pyrethrum concern (OPYRWA).

The 'outer' rings of *Akazu* reflected every level and part of society, each owing allegiance to those above them in the structure up to the family itself. No part of society was free from its sinister influence. For example, to start a business, 'meant the need for a loan and to get such a loan you needed to pay off a member of this circle around the President with either shares in the company or a percentage of the profit or money up front.'[8] State enterprises were awarded not on the basis of past performance or business acumen but to those who could be trusted to funnel profits, foreign grants and influence back to those who put them in office.[9]

Members of the predominantly northern-based first officer batches that had trained with Habyarimana dominated the senior military ranks. Notable were Laurent Serubuga and Pierre-Celestin Rwagafilita, both intensely loyal to *Le Clan* and their own bank balance. Beneath them were individuals like Bushiru neighbour Colonel Aloys Nsekalije who became Education minister and the first Rwandan franc billionaire. Others such as Théoneste Bagosora, Anatole Nsengiyumva, Sabin Benda and Aloys Simba were equally ambitious to use their military careers to further their vaulting ambition. The state of the Rwandan army, the FAR, during the 1980s was a microcosm of all parts of society; its strength was fatally undermined from within by corruption, nepotism, regionalism and poor leadership that made it totally unsuitable for any combat operations.

During the late 1970s and 1980s the Rwandan people were controlled both by the one party authoritarian state of MRND/Habyarimana and by the unofficial parallel structure of *Akazu*. In 1974 Habyarimana had directed that the vital post of Bourgmeister (mayor) would from now on be one appointed by the president rather than the population in an individual commune as had been the case under Kayibanda. While Habyarimana may have officially selected the 143 bourgmeisters as a major conduit linking the regime with the mass of those they were meant to represent, with their remit to monitor, command and enforce presidential directives and desires, bourgmeisters such as

8 Katabarwa, André, interview with the author, June 2012.

9 For example, Alphonse Higaniro at SORWAL, Denis Ntirugirimbabazi at the National Bank (BNR) and Pasteur Musabe, the brother of Théoneste Bagosora, headed BACAR (Continental Bank).

Laurent Semanza (Bicumbi), Jean-Baptiste Gatete (Murambi) or Juvenal Kajelijeli (Mukingo), owed their far-reaching power and wealth to '*le Clan*.'

In the church, Archbishop Vincent Nsengiyumva became Agathe's personal confessor and would attend the presidential family at their residence daily. The bishops appointed by Habyarimana, all Hutu, were notable for their unrelenting support for the regime. During the 1980s the Rwandan bishop's conference made no mention of corruption, human rights violations or the ethnic and regionalist prejudice that disenfranchised large numbers of the population from jobs, education or state support. Instead they acted as a mouthpiece for the regime. The three Pastoral letters of 1990,[10] issued before the October invasion of that year, reiterate Rwandans should be grateful for the good things the regime has done for them such as giving the people roads, newspapers and MRND. The bishops take issue with those who complained that due to their ethnic origin, they had been refused a job or a place at school or that the judicial system had been unfair to them. It was a remarkable show of unity, not with the teachings of Christ, but with those of *Akazu*/Habyarimana.

In 1989 a public scandal shone a light on how ethnic prejudice had infiltrated the highest levels of the Catholic Church so that it had become merely another secular part of the regime's control over the country. The aged Tutsi bishop of Butare, Jean-Baptiste Gahamanyi, who had been appointed in 1961 just before independence, had put forward the intelligent, reserved and hard working fellow Tutsi priest Father Felicien Muvara to be appointed as his new assistant bishop. Those with deep-seated ethnic prejudices within the regime regarded the appointment with horror. Bagosora and the wife of Colonel Nsekalije intervened to insist to Habyarimana that such an appointment was impossible. All men might be equal in God's eyes, but to them Tutsi's were to be tolerated and exploited at best, and certainly not promoted. False rumours of personal impropriety were quickly spread about Fr. Muvara, allowing Archbishop Nsengiyumva to have the bishop-to-be called to Rome where he was pressured to 'resign' just days before his elevation to the episcopacy was due to take place. Soon afterwards, the rumours were shown to have been malevolently made up, though no apology was ever given to Muvara.[11]

The whole sordid affair illuminated how Church and State had become one in their ideology and rationale. Habyarimana, unlike his predecessor, had moved to ensure he had total control not just of the Catholic Church's

10 See the Episcopal letter issued in February 1990 entitled 'Christ our Unity,' and two further letters in May and August of that year.

11 Muvara returned home from this crushing disappointment to continue life working as a parish priest. He was murdered during the 1994 Genocide against the Tutsi.

leadership, but also over the Protestant churches in the country. The Anglican's, with Archbishop Augustin Nshamihigo, a former army chaplain in charge and the Presbyterians under Michel Twagirayesu, a member of the MRND prefectural committee in Kibuye, were both frequent visitors to the presidency and acted as loyal propaganda mouthpieces in their own churches for the regime, even during the 1994 genocide.

In an oral society where widespread illiteracy and poverty meant few outside the capital read a newspaper – and only a few thousand read one there – the pulpit represented the way 'news' came down to the peasantry. Control of the churches was of vital importance. When Pope John Paul II was persuaded to visit Rwanda in September 1990 – still the only time a pontiff has come to the country – it was an immense public relations coup for *Akazu*, and was treated by them as such. The Pontiff was treated to an audience with *Akazu*'s finest soon after his plane hit the Kigali tarmac, with endless photographs taken with Z, Noel, Sagatwa and Agathe. His presence was held as divine justification for the regime's hold over its people.[12]

The head of the state information bureau (ORINFOR) during the late 1970s and 1980s was Christophe Mfizi, who had the unenviable job of trying to put a positive spin on the regime that he served. He was replaced in December 1990 by Z's protégé Ferdinand Nahimana after years of being threatened by *Akazu*. Mfizi's highly acute, intellectual and analytical mind set him far apart from the bulk of those in power, most of whom had failed to finish secondary education. He had become highly disillusioned with *Akazu's* insidious and rampant corruption that was threatening to capsize the country by the late 1980s as famine and economic collapse took hold. In 1992, from the safety of Paris, he published an open letter to Habyarimana entitled 'The Zero Network'. He later told investigators: 'In about 1987 I got the first signs about the existence of a kind of well organised group of people in the top levels of Rwanda... I believe that their goal was to keep the power within the small group around the president and his wife... I called the group *Reseau Zero* (Network Zero) where the Z comes from Zigiranyirazo Proteus. I believe that this man played a very big role in this group. I do not know how big this *Reseau Zero* was. That depends on what level you look at. It was bigger than *Akazu* that is sure. I believe that different kinds of people were members of the *Reseau Zero*: businessmen, politicians, prefects, bourgmeisters, heads of governmental organisations and departments, journalists, military and even religious people and so on. I believe they all had some kind of importance, useable to the president's family at a certain level.'[13]

12 The visit of John Paul II was from 7–9 September 1994.
13 Christophe Mfizi interview with ICTR investigators, March 1996, Paris.

Mfizi's open letter informed not just Rwandans but the international community – especially regime supporters in France, Belgium, Germany and Switzerland and the Churches – that this network were effectively running the state for their own ambitions. He blamed 'a hardcore of people who have methodically pervaded the entire national life at the political, military, financial, agricultural, scientific, scholarly, family and even religious levels. This clique considers the country as a company which they can legitimately derive maximum benefit from, and this justifies all types of policies… it is the Zero Network that has stoked ethnic and regional divisions to hide its hidden agenda and interests'. In Mfizi's analysis, both Habyarimana and his MRND party were now just working tools of this 'Zero Network,' unable to function, reform or work to the benefit of the people they were meant to represent.[14]

Mfizi differentiated between *Akazu* as the small family group around Agathe, and the much wider, multi-layered 'Network Zero' that they had built throughout every part of society. Other contemporaries, such as Bagaragaza and Jean Kambanda, referred to the whole mafia-like group as *Akazu,* with its inner and outer core structures. 'Before that [multiparty politics that began in 1991] no one could dare mention it [*Akazu*] … can it be said that they knew? Yes, they knew. But at that time when they were still all-powerful, they were not called *Akazu* because no one coined the word yet. People only noted what they did. They didn't seek to conceal what they were doing. And people knew on what doors to knock to get favours from the regime. When the word '*Akazu*' was used with the advent of [multiparty] pluralism, they obviously were irritated… because it was not a word with a positive connotation. It was always associated with abuse so it didn't do them proud… it was like concentric circles. There is the very tiny circle that was the *Akazu*. But there were other circles around it'.[15]

Journalist Epimaque Habimana summarised the popular view about *Akazu* and its role in the country: 'The country's first lady, Agathe, at whom fingers are pointed, is indeed very family conscious. Her brother [sic] Colonel Sagatwa is the President's private secretary. The other is known more particularly by the letter 'Z' for to call him by his real name, 'Protais Zigiranyirazo' would make many a Rwandan tremble. So 'Z' and Seraphin Rwabukumba, the former's cousin, are the main actors in a vast network of political and financial racketeering that caused, in the year 1989–90 alone, a loss of state revenue to the tune of 5 billion Rwandan francs ($60 million). '*La Centrale*', which is a huge

14 Mfizi, Christophe, "'The Zero Network': Open letter to the President of MRND", (Kigali: Editions Uruhimbi, July–August 1992).

15 Kambanda, Jean, interview ICTR investigators, September 1997.

commercial company headed by Mr Seraphin Rwabukumba, alone holds more than 50 import licenses. Thus, it is at the centre of all the politico-financial scandals. A drug trafficking network involving J[ean] Pierre, the President's first son, and the Director of the tea board, Mr Michel Bagaragaza, thrives with the complicity of the customs department at Kigali airport. Boxes containing cannabis, labelled as tea for export, are regularly exported to patented agents in Europe or America under everyone's nose.'[16]

It was one thing for *Akazu* to generate and increase power and wealth. Of equal importance became protecting its assets from threats outside and inside the country. After Lizinde's 'coup' attempt failed – though in reality this had never amounted to any kind of real danger – *Akazu* took preemptive action during the 1980s against those it felt threatened their dominance or greed. The most notable casualties were all close to the president himself and suffered for being seen as possible rivals to Agathe's own family. The brutal murder of Habyarimana's close friend Colonel Stanislas Mayuya on 19 April 1988 came as the result of this officer being declared by the president as his 'dauphin'. Mayuya, a capable, hard working but above all moderate officer who was well respected within the army, posed a clear risk to Z's and Agathe's ambitions should he inherit power. His brutal murder was still being talked about years later – albeit in secret as to be heard mentioning the name of the former Colonel could lead to charges of treason. The contract killing was blamed on a number of scapegoated individuals, including three senior officers[17] accused of planning a coup. Though imprisoned, they were never brought to trial and were eventually released. Whether Habyarimana knew and was persuaded to action this murder by *Akazu* or whether Mayuya was murdered by them without his knowledge, the killing showed by 1988 the president had lost control of power, if indeed he had ever been fully in charge. Real power in the country lay elsewhere. The editor of Hutu extremist paper *Kangura* Hassan Ngeze explained at his later trial: 'in 1988… they [*Akazu*] have the bank. They have the money. They have the army; they have power… When Mayuya was killed by *Akazu*… It is just a small group, not only – not even from Habyarimana, just from his wife, just from his wife. Because Habyarimana – the wife of Habyarimana, the people who are close to Habyarimana's wife killed Mayuya.'[18]

16 Habimana, Epa, 'Vérité d'Afrique Impamo', No. 2, 26 August 1992.

17 Colonel Anselme Nkuliyekubona, Major Mathias Havugintore and Lieutenant Colonel Deogratias Ndibwami. For a full account of Mayuya's death see Wallis, *Stepp'd in Blood*, pp. 137–151.

18 Hassan Ngeze, witness examination, ICTR-99-52-T, 26 March 2003.

The murder of Dian Fossey, the American gorilla naturalist who had the temerity to try to block *Akazu's* attempt to exploit the Volcano National Park for their own considerable profit, showed a similar disregard for presidential authority. Habyarimana had made great public play about how his government fully respected the need to preserve this national resource. Fossey too, for several years, had tried to stop the exploitation of the gorillas and the park for commercial gain. Yet with the valuable growth of tourism to the area, as well as smuggling routes for drugs and minerals at stake, her murder in December 1985, with Z the chief suspect of future investigations,[19] was seemingly inevitable. A colleague within the gorilla preservation movement noted 'She was standing in the way of certain individuals making money. Whether it was because they were making money through the illegal bush meat trade or the gold smuggling trade or someone's aspirations to turn Karisoke into a tourist camp and make a lot of money that way, if you stand in the way of someone who is ruthless who wants to make a lot of money then it's not that surprising that she was killed'.[20]

A variety of regime critics also paid the price in the 1980s for questioning the rampant corruption, nepotism and regionalism of the regime. Abbé Silvio Sindambiwe, the editor of the Catholic newspaper *Kinyamateka* was threatened by the feared intelligence services, the SCR and warned to desist from publishing faintly critical articles. On 7 November 1989 he was murdered in a trademark road 'accident.' When Félicula Nyiramutarambirwa took her campaign for the rights of women, orphans and the mentally disabled to the World Bank, threatening a highly lucrative income from this body, she too was murdered. As was former health minister Francois Muganza who had unwisely fallen out with Habyarimana's family. Hundreds of members of religious minority groups, such as the Jehovah Witnesses, were rounded up and imprisoned for refusing to take part in *animation*. They were accused of state subversion and attempting to overthrow the regime.

Habyarimana's own brothers, Télésphore and older brother Mélane, who offered him important personal support away from Agathe and *le clan*, were both killed in car 'accidents' at the start and end of the 1980s respectively. Their independent advice to the president was a direct threat to *Akazu*. The result of their deaths, and that of Mayuya, left Habyarimana completely surrounded by

19 See, for example, Gordon, Nicholas, *Murders in the Mist: who killed Dian Fossey?* (London: Hodder and Stoughton), 1994.

20 Ian Redmond, interview in 'Gorillas revisited with David Attenborough', BBC television, transmission date 6 December 2012.

his wife and her powerful family with little, if any, independent support of his own to call on.

Even church critics, rare as they were, could not avoid the consequences of making enemies with *Akazu*. The Canadian priest Father Francois Cardinal had publicly questioned the flagrant embezzlement and corruption of *Le Clan*. His religious order, the Brothers of Christian Instruction, ran a college in Habyarimana's home village of Rambura. The Brothers were expelled from here on the excuse that foreign funding was be used to build a new school on their premises and they relocated to Kigali. In the event the foreign money for the school disappeared. Father Cardinal, who had made the scandal public, was murdered on 29 November 1992. Armed men, some in military fatigues, broke into the home of the religious and shot him dead. A later investigation[21] pointed to Sagatwa being behind the theft of the money and the killing. Fr. Cardinal's murder, and that of the nun Sister Antonio Locatelli, shot dead after telling Radio France International about genocidal massacres the regime was orchestrating in Nyamata, was greeted with silence by Habyarimana's international support base. The Canadian government, like that of Germany, Belgium, France, Switzerland and the IMF/World Bank, refused to launch any inquiry or stop funding a regime that was killing its own people.

By the late 1980s, a famine in the south of the country and the sharp decline in world coffee prices was having a devastating effect on the lower strata of society. For the first time the regime and its *Akazu* network were subject to critical voices, some in the European media and Rwandan diaspora, others in new journals like *Kanguka*, *Isibo* and *Umurangi*. In Germany, Jean Shyirambere Barahinyura, whose wife had been incarcerated in Ruhengeri prison after being accused of involvement in the 1979/80 tracts, published a highly damaging book entitled 'Juvenal Habyarimana: 15 years of tyranny and treachery.'[22] It was hardly a surprise to see Rwandan intelligence operatives operatives make the trip to Frankfurt to 'persuade' him to cease publication immediately, and he was granted German police protection as a result. Needless to say, inside Rwanda, to own the book or be known to have read it was regarded as a matter of high treason.

As the political and military threat to the regime became acute from late 1990, *Akazu* reacted by impressing on Habyarimana the need to keep his

---

21 Kinyamateka editor Fr. André Sibomana, interviewed in 'Hand of God, Hand of the Devil', Documentary by Téléfilms, directed by Yvan Patry, (Québec) 1995.

22 Barahinyura, Jean Shyirambere, *1973–1988 Le Major-General Habyarimana, Quinze ans de tyrannie et de tartuferie au Rwanda*, (Frankfurt: editions Izuba), 1988.

international backers on board at all costs. As with the early 1960s when '*inyenzi*' attacks had been fully exploited by Kayibanda for internal political gain, so the October 1990 RPF invasion was used to unify the Hutu majority that had splintered after years of regionalism and corruption had alienated vast parts of the southern and central population from MRND. The invasion gave the regime the excuse to arrest, disappear, imprison and kill those it felt threatened its power. From October 1990 the strategy was planned and targeted discrimination and dehumanisation of the Tutsi population, denouncing them *en masse* as 'enemies' of the country.[23]

One of the most disturbing aspects of *Akazu's* rise in the 70s and 80s was the failure of the international community, and especially those countries closest to the regime, to analyse and censure the regime for crimes, corruption and discrimination that were known to them. While the South African apartheid regime was regularly condemned at this time in the west and subject to severe restrictions due to its ethnic targeting and human rights abuses, the same system in Rwanda found those in power benefiting from regular foreign donor generosity. There was no pressure put on Habyarimana to remove ethnic-targeted quotas and anti-Tutsi rhetoric that grew exponentially after the 1990 invasion. On 9 January 1991 Belgian journalist David Coppi noted in *L'echo* that sources within the country had told him Habyarimana was moving towards eliminating the Tutsi population in a 'veritable genocide'.[24] This article was published soon after the massacres of Tutsi in Kibilira in October 1990 left hundreds dead. Three weeks after Coppi's report new genocidal massacres took place targeting the Bagogwe Tutsi.

During the coming three years Rwanda was riven by well organised, planned, financed and executed genocidal massacres that saw thousands of Tutsis murdered, women raped, homes burnt to the ground and possessions and cattle taken. During much of this time foreign money continued to pour into *Akazu*'s deep personal coffers, and into the regime, in effect allowing it to retain power. It was not until early 1993 that the World Bank curtailed its funding, much of

---

23 On 21 September 1992 army Chief of Staff Deogratias Nsabimana made public part of the findings from a commission set up by Habyarimana, and chaired by Bagosora, to identify the chief threats to national security. It reported that the enemy and its supporters were to be found among 'Tutsi refugees, Tutsi within the country, Hutu dissatisfied with the current regime, the unemployed within Rwanda and abroad and foreigners married to Tutsi women'. In effect, all Tutsi and moderate Hutu opposed to the regime. See: Bagosora Commission report, marked 'Secret: The Definition and identification of the enemy', undated, Military I, ICTR-98-41, prosecution exhibit 13.1, K1020477.

24 Coppi, David, 'Rwanda: Détenus politiques et étudiants suspects sous la menace d'un "plan d'éliminations" systématique', *L'écho*, 9 January 1991.

which Habyarimana had diverted to pay for a vast expansion of the army and continuation of the war and security clampdown. France continued to provide military personnel and trainers, weapons and finance to the regime up to and beyond 1994, while German, Swiss and Belgian assistance was on going until 1993. The Vatican meanwhile remained silent on the genocidal killings, with only a few dissenting clerical voices heard from within the ranks of the Rwandan bishops. Most, like Archbishop Nsengiyumva chose to ignore the killings altogether and laid the blame for the near anarchy reining in the country solely at the door of the RPF.

While such international supporters decided to deny or disregard the mounting evidence of state organised terror, a growing number of opposition journals inside Rwanda, despite constant threats and violence against them, made plain the state of the country. Numerous cartoons were published that vividly portrayed Agathe, Z, and *le Clan*, as well as Habyarimana, as bloodthirsty thugs, monsters or avaricious killers. A number of publications depict Habyarimana as a priest, his cassock covered in blood, giving communion or encouragement to 'his *Akazu*' as they murder Tutsi and political opponents. The satirical paper *Nyabarongo*, in one acutely observed cartoon, portrays Habyarimana standing at the head of a conference table, announcing 'I have done all I could.' Gathered around were those labelled '*Akazu*' – Agathe, Mathieu Ngirumpatse (MRND president), Joseph Nzirorera (MRND secretary general), Seraphin, Rwagafilita, Serubuga and Z. Underneath and around the table are hundreds of skulls labelled 'Tutsi'.[25]

One of the few international critical responses to the rapidly downward spiral Rwanda was on by autumn 1993 came when Belgian Senator Willy Kuijpers published an open letter to the Rwandan leader. It was the result of months of investigations he had undertaken, including visits to the country itself. The letter exposed 'the activities of an occult group called '*Akazu*' or '*Reseau Zero*'. The senator noted that 'In view of the serious allegations made against you (Habyarimana), with regard to the numerous instances of human rights allegations in Rwanda and the systematic plunder of Rwanda's meagre resources involving your family,' Habyarimana should 'make a commitment to stop perverting the democratisation process and put an end to political assassinations, persecution and other acts of intimidation of which leaders of the democratic opposition are victims.'[26]

With the very real prospect of losing power, wealth, position and possibly their lives, the stakes for *Akazu* from 1990 were clear. The fate of Kayibanda and

---

25 *Nyabarongo*, No. 13, March 1993.

26 Kuijpers, Senator Willy, 'Letter to President Habyarimana', 2 October 1993.

his supporters was not one Agathe and the family had any intention of sharing. Whereas during the 1970s and 80s the all pervasive security and intelligence services of Sagatwa, Augustin Nduweyezu and Pascal Simbikangwa had been able to quell dissent swiftly and quietly, the strategy and tools to remain in power changed markedly when faced with far more powerful internal and external threats in the early 1990s. The advent of the *interahamwe* and Hutu hate radio RTLM were products of their time. They heralded a new extremist strategy to head-off an extreme threat. With the military in the hands of Serubuga and Rwagafilita to 1992, and then, with its most powerful units coming under the control of *Amasasu* – Bagosora, Nsengiyumva, et al, the success of a peace process that would inevitably involve some form of compromise and power sharing was treated as treason.

Where was Habyarimana in all this? Never quite the fully paid up extremist of those around him, he was a president for the good times only, who delighted in the trappings of power and wealth, but failed to understand or adapt to the rapidly changing political and military pressure post 1990. He presents as a rather pathetic figure in his last years in office. He had taken part, with *Akazu*, in the planning and organising of the genocidal massacres that killed thousands of Tutsis, as the international commission of inquiry and the UN report of 1993 duly noted.[27] He had helped promote and fund both RTLM and 'his' *interahamwe* and publicly used his position to give them impunity from prosecution by the moderate multiparty government of Dismas Nsengiyaremye from April 1992. Yet Habyarimana ultimately was another victim of *Akazu*. His political and personal indecision, the breakdown of his marriage to Agathe after years of being bullied and overruled by her and her family, meant his final two years were filled with personal angst and depression. That Habyarimana wanted to find a way out of office – a comfortable retirement away from the enemies who surrounded him – was no secret. Nor was it a secret that he had been threatened by members of *Akazu* – including Bagosora – who demanded he refuse to sign the Arusha Accords and should stand down from office in favour of a far more acceptable leader: for example Z's ambitious protégé Joseph Nzirorera. By mid 1993 Habyarimana had lost the presidency of MRND, control of the military and most importantly, control of his own family.[28]

---

27 Report of the International Commission of Investigation [FIDH] on Human Rights Violations in Rwanda since 1 October 1990, Final report, (March 1993); United Nations, Commission on Human Rights, Report by Mr BW Ndiaye, Special Rapporteur, on his mission to Rwanda from 8 to 17 April 1993, (11 August 1993).

28 Mathieu Ngirumpatse replaced Habyarimana at the MRND summer conference 1993. The president gave up his post as Defence Minister as part of the power sharing deal, and his

Habyarimana became a pawn of a far more dynamic, extreme and unstoppable network. He was more use to *Akazu* dead than alive. From October 1993 the Hutu 'power' movement took the cynical ethnic divisionism that had been used by the regime as a means to unify the Hutu majority and turned it into a policy of extreme, universal, violence. No one who listened to speeches from Froduald Karamira on 23 October 1993 or Justin Mugenzi at Nyamirambo stadium in January 1994, could have any doubt that they saw the only solution to Rwanda's problems as power keeping – for their Hutu extremist 'Power' faction – not power sharing with moderates and the RPF as Arusha demanded. Retaining authority over the country would involve the elimination of those enemies and traitors (the Tutsi and moderate Hutu) who blocked their way. *Interahamwe* who had initially been recruited, trained and armed to defend MRND's interests against other political parties were now instructed to 'work' alongside these militias in the coming apocalypse. RTLM DJ's were recruited not because of previous broadcasting excellence, but because they were ambitious stooges willing and able to communicate the extremist views of Felicien Kabuga, Ferdinand Nahimana, Jean-Bosco Barayagwiza, Seraphin and Agathe to the population at large.

In the hours and days after Habyarimana's death on 6 April 1994, *Akazu* moved swiftly to put in place an extremist regime within which it could fully operate to facilitate its main objective – retention of power. While Agathe and Seraphin remained in the country only until the agreed transition of power to Bagosora and his client interim regime was finalised, other core members of the network were already in place to begin the twin tasks of genocide and winning the renewed war with the RPF. For the remainder of the summer Agathe worked hard from her new base in Paris with her existing political and diplomatic connections to support Bagosora, Bizimana, Kabuga, Nzirorera, army chief Augustin Bizimungu and others from the network. Arms deals were set up and finalised while diplomatic and financial support was sought from pro-regime leaders such as Moi (Kenya), Mobutu (Zaire), Omar Bongo (Gabon) Eyadema (Togo), Biya (Cameroon), Gaddafi (Libya) and Mitterrand/Chirac in France. That the planned re-invasion of Rwanda (September 1994–96) in the aftermath of the genocide did not happen was certainly not due to a lack of effort from the network and its international sympathisers. The ex-FAR and *interahamwe,* now based in the

position as head of the armed forces went first to Laurent Serubuga and on his forced retirement in 1992, to Deogratias Nsabimana. A number of visitors to the presidential residence commented on how Agathe and her family would lead discussions, debates and policy reviews with visiting guests even though Habyarimana was both head of the household and head of state and would have been expected to provide this role.

UN-funded refugee camps in Zaire and Tanzania, were rearmed and trained for the expected attack on the new Rwandan government. They were directed principally from Kenya where Agathe, Z, Kabuga, other *Akazu* and former senior regime figures had taken up residence.[29]

In their ruling of 15 February 2007, the Appeal Court of the French Refugee Commission [OFPRA] ruled against Agathe's attempt to gain refugee status in the country. In its damning findings, upheld later by the Council of State, it noted 'Mme Agathe Kanziga, widow Habyarimana, had an eminent role in the 'first circle of power' called *Akazu*; that she exercised a de facto authority between 1973 and 1994 but also beyond this date, keeping up privileged links with the caretaker government then with the Rwandan government in exile; that she evidently tried to conceal her real role and engagement in the country's political life; that her denial of the existence of massacres perpetrated by Hutu extremists on the Tutsi population as well as her denial of all ethnic tension in Rwanda before October 1990 need to be interpreted as the desire to hide her real awareness of the situation in her country; that she was at the heart of the genocidal regime responsible for the preparation and execution of the genocide that occurred in Rwanda during the year 1994; that she cannot therefore validly deny her support for the most extremist Hutu ideas, her direct links with those responsible for the genocide and her real influence on political life in Rwanda'. It noted 'the preponderant influence of the petitioner [Agathe] in the operation of political power as it was really exercised in Rwanda from 1973 to 1994, notably in her role as a hidden coordinator of different political, economic, military, and media circles, and to emphasize also the reality of her preponderant positioning within what has been designated as the *Akazu*, in the sense of a confraternity based on family, business, or other links and involved in the authoritarian exercise of power via structures of organised violence, and finally to decide that she was involved, within these different structures, in the development and preparation of massacres on an ethnic basis between April and June 1994'.[30]

Akazu changed and developed in the years from 1973 in terms of those who were part of the network and in its operational outcome: from its early years when it aimed at seizing power, wealth and control of every part of the state, to its post 1990 extremist incarnation with new recruits, organisations and structures put in place to protect at any cost the very wealth and position

29 See Wallis, *Stepp'd in Blood*, pp. 485–520.

30 French Republic, The Commission of Appeal for Refugees, (2nd Division), case No. 564776, Mme Agathe Kanziga, widow Habyarimana, 15 February 2007.

in the country it had so impressively grasped. However, it is during the years 1973–93, when it was able to establish itself throughout every part of the churches and state, military and administration that made possible the 'bringing of the apocalypse' to Rwanda in 1994. The crimes of *Akazu* during these two decades have almost entirely been forgotten and those responsible for the thousands of killings that took place then have gone unpunished. No international tribunal has ever looked at these crimes nor has the international community taken any interest in bringing to justice those responsible who now live comfortable lives outside Rwanda, often in the very countries whose assistance allowed *Akazu* to blossom during its formative years. Just as the Holocaust cannot be understood without reference to the rise of the Nazi party and its anti-semitic ideology and crimes during the 1930s, so the Rwandan genocide against the Tutsi can only be understood by reference to its perpetrators and their exercise of power pre-1994. In the present climate, as revisionists seek to revise, rework and often deny responsibility for *Akazu's* crimes committed during the 1994 genocide against the Tutsi, their twenty-year long history of devastation pre-94, which gave them the structure, finance and individuals to unleash the terror, should be afforded the prominent role it deserves.

CHAPTER 2

Rwanda: the Political Failure of the UN Security Council

Ambassador Colin Keating

In April 1994, the racial intolerance that had been smoldering in Rwanda for decades ignited into all-out genocide. Although the United Nations had a peacekeeping force in the country that had provided United Nations headquarters with warnings and credible evidence that genocidal violence was being planned, the institution did not move to either prevent the genocide from starting, or to stop it once it had started. This article discusses the role of the UN Security Council during the crisis in Rwanda in 1993/94. It focuses on the peacekeeping dimensions of the Council's involvement.

1 Why Is the Role of the UN Security Council Important?

In 1945, when the UN was established, the concept of peacekeeping did not exist. So, there is nothing about peacekeeping in the UN Charter. The Charter gave primary[1] responsibility for matters of peace and security to the Security Council.

In 1945 it was envisaged that the Council would work to prevent conflict using political tools[2] under Chapter VI of the Charter and, where this proved insufficient, the Council would decide on binding measures[3] or take collective military action[4] under Chapter VII, with the use of force being under the oversight of its Military Staff Committee.[5]

This model did not fare well in practice during the Cold War when the veto was often employed to frustrate Council action.[6] This experience, and the

1 United Nations Charter, Article 24(1).
2 Investigation under Article 34 of the United Nations Charter, calling for settlement of disputes under Article 33(2) or recommending procedures or methods for resolution under Article 36(1).
3 United Nations Charter, Article 41.
4 United Nations Charter, Article 42.
5 United Nations Charter, Articles 46 and 47.
6 Security Council Report, '*Chart comparing use of the veto during the Cold War and subsequently*', https://www.securitycouncilreport.org/atf/cf/%7B65BFCF9B-6D27-4E9C-8CD3-CF6E4FF96FF9%7D/SCR-veto-insert-2.pdf, accessed 1 June 2019.

 | DOI:10.1163/9789004430129_004

realisation that a neutral UN force could be helpful in preventing conflict or stabilising situations after a ceasefire, led to the innovation of peacekeeping as a new tool for the UN system.[7]

The first UN Peacekeeping Mission, UNTSO,[8] was an unarmed Observer Mission in the Middle East. It was approved by the Security Council in 1948 and is still operating today. The first armed peacekeeping force, UNEF I,[9] was established by the General Assembly rather than the Security Council. As the UN peacekeeping model evolved, it became the norm for the Security Council to decide on the establishment of a Mission, to specify the mandate and determine the size of the Mission.

The peacekeeping model developed on the basis that UN forces would only operate in a permissive environment i.e. where the parties gave consent. Force would not be used, except in self defence. UN forces would often be unarmed.

In a legal sense, Peacekeeping Missions are subsidiary bodies of the Security Council. Their composition, by custom, is left to the Secretary-General, as is the specification of the "Rules of Engagement" i.e. the conditions under which force might be used. Day to day oversight is also left to the Secretary-General.

The Charter also gave the General Assembly a role[10] in relation to international peace and security, particularly on matters not under action by the Security Council.[11] The General Assembly has also, very rarely, taken action where the Security Council was stalemated.[12] All matters involving financing for peacekeeping are the exclusive responsibility of the General Assembly.[13]

2 UNOMUR: the Trigger for Security Council Involvement in Rwanda

Security Council involvement in Rwanda started in early 1993, when France began canvassing informally with Security Council members a proposal for a UN Observer Mission on the border between Rwanda and Uganda. French diplomats explained to us that Paris was increasingly concerned about the civil

7 United Nations Peacekeeping, '*Our History*', https://peacekeeping.un.org/en/our-history, accessed 1 June 2019.

8 United Nations Peacekeeping, '*UNTSO Fact Sheet*', https://peacekeeping.un.org/en/mission/untso, accessed 1 June 2019.

9 United Nations Peacekeeping, '*First United Nations Emergency First UNEF I*', https://peacekeeping.un.org/en/mission/past/unefi.htm, accessed 1 June 2019.

10 United Nations Charter, Article 14.

11 United Nations Charter, Article 12.

12 Approval of mandate for UNEF I; see note 10 *supra*.

13 United Nations Charter, Article 17.

war that had commenced in Rwanda in 1990 between the Rwandan Government and the Tutsi led Rwandan Patriotic Front (RPF).

Under African Union leadership, a peace process was underway in Arusha, in neighbouring Tanzania. A ceasefire had been brokered, but it collapsed in early February 1993. Despite the presence of French troops fighting with the Rwandan Government forces, the RPF was achieving considerable military success against the Rwandan army. France wanted a UN presence on the border to help to stabilize the situation, believing that a UN mission could monitor and deter the movement of arms and RPF fighters across the border.

Letters quickly followed from Rwanda[14] and Uganda[15] formally requesting the Security Council to take action to establish such a mission.

The UN had been politically supporting the Arusha negotiating process. But putting Rwanda on the Security Council agenda was a major new step. There was hesitation from some major powers. But many in the Security Council were persuaded that the Rwanda issue now needed to be handled at the global level. An influential consideration was the concern, by some of us, that UN peacekeeping was overly focused on problems in Europe and that equally pressing problems in Africa were not being given their fair share of attention.

The intensified UN involvement seemed to help to stimulate agreement. On 7 March, in Dar-es-Salaam,[16] a new ceasefire was reached between the RPF and the Rwanda government. The Security Council moved quickly. On 12 March a resolution[17] was adopted requesting the Secretary-General to submit plans for a border observation mission and to begin work on a more substantial "humanitarian" and "protection of civilians" operation in Rwanda.

In May, the Secretary General recommended[18] that an observer mission should proceed on the Uganda side of the border. On 22 June the Security Council approved[19] the deployment of the mission, which was to be led by Canadian General Romeo Dallaire.

14 'Letter dated 93/02/28 from the Permanent Representative of Rwanda to the United Nations addressed to the President of the Security Council', UN Doc. S/25355.

15 'Letter dated 93/02/22 from the Permanent Representative of Uganda to the United Nations addressed to the President of the Security Council', UN Doc. S/25356.

16 'Note verbale dated 93/03/08 from the Permanent Mission of Rwanda to the United Nations addressed to the Secretary-General', UN Doc. S/25385.

17 United Nations Security Council Resolution 812 (12 March 1993) UN Doc. S/RES/812.

18 'Interim report of the Secretary-General on Rwanda', UN Doc. S/25810.

19 United Nations Security Council Resolution 846 (22 June 1993) UN Doc. S/RES/846.

3 UNOMUR (and the Security Council Involvement) an Apparent Success Story

Security Council involvement during 1993 seemed to be a success. It had generated ongoing political momentum for the negotiating process in Arusha. In particular it had helped to incentivise the President of Rwanda, Juvenal Habyarimana, whose military forces were under real pressure, to make the necessary political concessions for a successful peace agreement.

On 4 August a milestone peace agreement[20] was reached in Arusha. It involved wide ranging political change and power sharing in Rwanda. Transitional institutions of government were to be implemented in September.

On 10 September the Security Council[21] formally welcomed the Arusha Peace Agreement and signaled a readiness to consider a much more substantial peacekeeping involvement in Rwanda.

Encouraged by the Arusha peace agreement and the findings of a reconnaissance mission he had sent to Rwanda, the UN Secretary-General recommended that the Security Council establish a full peacekeeping mission. He proposed that it should assist with ensuring security in Kigali, monitor the ceasefire and investigate any non-compliance and that the border observation mission UNOMUR, be folded into the new operation.

The Secretary-General was upbeat about the underlying environment. He told the Council that "both sides seemed determined to achieve a durable peace through disarmament, demobilization and national reconciliation."[22]

As members of the Security Council we were surprised and impressed when representatives of the RPF and the Government came jointly to brief Council members on these developments. It was very unusual in our experience for recent combatant parties to be so cooperative. It reinforced the sense that positive progress being made in Arusha.

4 Negotiation of Resolution 872 to Establish UNAMIR

Most Council members were pleased with the Secretary-General's report. Many Security Council operations elsewhere were struggling because of intractable positions being taken by the combatant parties. UNOSOM in

20 Krok Institute for International Peace Studies, *'Arusha Accords'*, https://peaceaccords.nd.edu/accord/arusha-accord-4-august-1993, accessed 2 June 2019.

21 'Note transmitting statement by the President of the Security Council concerning the item entitled "The situation concerning Rwanda"', UN Doc. S/26425.

22 'Report of the Secretary-General on Rwanda', UN Doc. S/26488, para. 62.

Somalia[23] and UNPROFOR in Bosnia[24] were two such examples. It seemed as if Rwanda might offer the prospect of a successful UN peacekeeping mission which could make a positive difference.

Council members therefore immediately and energetically set to the task of negotiating a draft resolution to establish the Mission. But there was unexpected difficulty over the nature of the mandate and the expected cost.

First, US representatives began expressing concern about cost. The Republican controlled Congress was cutting US funding for peacekeeping. To all of the other Council members the cost of this new small operation seemed trivial in contrast to what was being spent elsewhere. Saving money, by reducing the force or delaying its full deployment, seemed unnecessarily risky.

Ultimately the US accepted much of what the Secretary-General had recommended, but subject to an unusual condition regarding the length of the mandate. Most UN peacekeeping operations had yearly mandates. In this case the US insisted that the operation be on a short leash. Ultimately a compromise was reached on six months, with a review after ninety days. Council members were told privately that this was the limit of financial flexibility that the US could accommodate.

Regarding the mandate, the debate centered on the possible use of force by the mission. Subsequent events proved that this debate was prescient. I argued in the informal consultations that, because the mandate included ensuring physical security in Kigali, which was recognised to be a flashpoint because of the close proximity in the city of Government and RPF forces, this necessarily implied an expectation that force could be used, if required. I maintained that the resolution needed stronger language.

There was also a similar and helpful argument from the US delegation. But eventually the US found itself conflicted on the issue. Concerns about cost did not sit well with support for a robust mandate. The US supported the New Zealand position for stronger wording in the operative paragraphs. But it opposed the resolution being under Chapter VII.

There was also wider opposition to formally adopting the resolution under Chapter VII. At that point in the history of UN Peacekeeping there was still a high level of political discomfort, especially but not only, in the Non-Aligned, about UN Missions using force. Many feared that this would undermine the

---

23 Department of Public Information, United Nations, '*Somalia – UNOSOM II*', https://www.un.org/Depts/DPKO/Missions/unosom2b.htm, accessed 5 June 2019. [Thereafter Somalia – UNOSOM II, 2019].

24 Department of Public Information, United Nations, '*Former Yugoslavia – UNPROFOR*', https://www.un.org/Depts/DPKO/Missions/unprof_b.htm, accessed 5 June 2019. [Thereafter Former Yugoslavia – UNPROFOR, 2019].

principles of impartiality and consent, which had been part of UN doctrine since the beginning of peacekeeping.

Some argued that the issue could be handled in the Rules of Engagement. Others thought that perhaps the resolution would be an example of a mandate under "Chapter six and a half". Some suggested that ambiguity didn't really matter because the Arusha process was going so well. New Zealand efforts to negotiate stronger language in the Rules of Engagement faltered in the face of opposition by the UK, which believed that Council members should not get involved in such matters. Eventually, the most that could be achieved was wording in the resolution[25] of a requirement on the parties for a "weapons secure area" in and around the city of Kigali.

Resolution 872 was adopted on 5 October 1993. It mostly followed the Secretary-general's recommendations. But there were two key weaknesses. First, for the reasons outlined above, the mandate was only for 6 months and US support was highly conditional. Secondly, the language about the robustness of the mandate was far too ambiguous. As events played out, these factors proved to be fatal flaws.

After the vote the US representative stated, ominously, that the US was deeply concerned about the increasing financial burden of UN peacekeeping and they would therefore look to "…reduce costs and personnel levels" of UNAMIR.[26]

5 Clouds on the Horizon

Despite the optimism in New York in late 1993, the situation in Rwanda was actually very precarious. President Juvenal Habyarimana had made significant concessions in Arusha to the RPF. The prospect, envisaged in the Arusha agreement, of the Transitional Institutions involving power sharing with the Tutsi, was incendiary to hardline Hutu extremist groups, who were growing in power. Violence against Tutsi and hate speech were becoming common. Habyarimana's control was eroding.

Hutu extremism was not new. Mass atrocities, akin to genocide, had been inflicted on Tutsi in Rwanda on previous occasions since independence. All

25 United Nations Security Council Resolution 872 (5 October 1993), UN Doc. S/RES/872, OP 3(a).

26 'Provisional verbatim record of the 3288th meeting, held at Headquarters, New York, on Tuesday, 8 October 1993', UN Doc. S/PV.3288, pp. 22–23.

this was well known to experts and to some Governments. But no experts were brought to give advice to the Security Council, not even the UN's own experts.

It is almost unbelievable, but the Council was never briefed on the fact that only a few months earlier, in April 1993, a UN expert, Special Rapporteur, Bacre Waly Ndiaye from the UN Human Rights Commission in Geneva, had visited Rwanda. His report[27] was issued in August, during the very period that the Secretary General was preparing his recommendations on the establishment of UNAMIR. Ndiaye reported recent massacres of Tutsi, death threats and political assassinations. He mentioned the hate propaganda on Radio Rwanda. He warned about distributions of arms to civilians. He described death squads with high level government involvement and plans to discredit the peace process. He recalled that past massacres of Tutsi could be considered genocide due to their ethnic motivation.

The siloisation of the UN machinery was clearly at fault. But it was not only the UN Secretariat that was so siloed. Most Council members had Missions in Geneva who would have received the Special Rapporteur's report. Most would have transmitted it back to their capitals. Yet no one joined the dots and thought that this alarming material should be brought to the attention of their Security Council teams in New York.

Moreover, some Security Council members also had Embassies in Kigali who would have been alert to the reality on the ground. Some were also participating in the Arusha process. If their reporting was made available to their teams in New York, this was never shared with the majority of their Council colleagues.

With hindsight, it may be easy to conclude that in late 1993 the Security Council was dangerously naïve regarding the risks in Rwanda and that its optimism was therefore really a case of wishful thinking. It is also easy to say that the Council was too hands off in its assessment of the political situation and of what might really be required for an effective peacekeeping operation.

It is true that the Council did absolutely no due diligence of its own. But that was the norm. The standard Council methodology regarding its peace operations was (and still is) very amateurish in nature. The Council relies almost exclusively on advice from UN officials whose resources and personnel for acquiring and collating information are often very limited.

Also, and in fairness to the UN and to the diplomats representing members of the Council, it should be remembered that Rwanda was far from the only issue confronting UN peacekeeping at this time.

27 'Extrajudicial, summary or arbitrary executions', UN Doc. E/CN.4/1994/7/Add.1.

In June 1993 the UN Peacekeeping Operation in Somalia, UNISOM II, comprised 28,000 personnel. After an attack on peacekeepers which resulted in 24 UN soldiers killed, the Security Council on 6 June put UNISOM onto what was effectively a war fighting basis.[28] In August, 4 US peacekeepers were killed, leading to the deployment of a large US Special Forces Group and an ongoing combat situation. In October, a major battle took place in Mogadishu, which subsequently became known as the "Blackhawk Down" incident, after a movie of the same name. 18 US soldiers were killed.[29] Some in the US blamed the UN for this failure. And it precipitated a huge political backlash in the US against UNISOM and against UN peacekeeping generally.

UNPROFOR, in Former Yugoslavia was also facing acute difficulties in late 1993 and early 1994.[30] This was an even larger peacekeeping operation, comprising up to 39,000 personnel. In March 1993 it became clear that Serb para military forces had massacred large numbers of civilians. In response the Security Council authorised[31] the use of force in the air to prevent breaches of the "no fly zone". It also established "safe areas" where force was authorised for the protection of civilians.[32] Throughout late 1993 and early 1994 the situations in Bosnia and Croatia lurched from crisis to crisis.

As if this were not enough, during the same period in late 1993 as the Council was considering the establishment of UNAMIR, the Council was also dealing with a crisis in Haiti, a major civil war in Georgia, a collapsing peace process in Mozambique, an active combat situation in Angola and the risk of war between Armenia and Azerbaijan.[33]

These situations occupied a huge amount of Security Council time and energy. Given the challenges elsewhere, it is not surprising that time for Rwanda was limited, especially when the information provided seemed to suggest that, by contrast to these other situations, peacekeeping in Rwanda would be a minor and benign project.

And a thought about the counterfactual is also appropriate. It is almost certain that, if there had been a full appreciation of the real risks in Rwanda, the US would never have agreed to establish UNAMIR in the first place.

---

28 United Nations Security Council Resolution 873 (13 October 1993), UN Doc. S/RES/873.

29 Somalia – UNOSOM II, 2019, note 25 *supra*.

30 Former Yugoslavia – UNPROFOR, 2019, note 26 *supra*.

31 United Nations Security Council Resolution 816 (31 March 1993), UN Doc. S/RES/816.

32 United Nations Security Council Resolution 836 (4 June 1993), UN Doc. S/RES/872.

33 UN Documents, '*Security Council Resolutions – 1993*', https://www.un.org/Docs/scres/1993/scres93.htm, accessed 3 June 2019.

6 Deployment of UNAMIR

Upon the adoption of Resolution 872, General Dallaire, who was commanding the observation mission on the Rwanda Uganda border, was appointed as commander of UNAMIR. An advance party was quickly deployed.

The authorised strength for the operation was 2,548 personnel. But in practice, deployment proved problematic. The initial headquarters did not become operational until 1 November 1993. Deployment of the UNAMIR battalion for Kigali was further delayed. It was not completed till the first part of December 1993. The Kigali weapons-secure area was only established on 24 December.

These delays in deployment resulted from an unwillingness by UN member states as a whole to respond the Secretary-General's appeal for troop contributions. This probably reflected what we Council members were seeing on many fronts at the time–a climate of peacekeeping fatigue. With so many very large operations requiring UN troops globally, most traditional peacekeeping countries military capacity was fully extended.

By the end of 1993 only Belgium, with a half a battalion of 400 troops, and Bangladesh with a logistical element of 400 troops, had offered personnel. It took five months to reach the authorized strength of 2,548.[34] By then the seeds of disaster had well and truly taken root.

7 The Descent into Genocide and the Security Council Response

On 30 December Council members received the first update from the Secretary-General on UNAMIR.[35] He said that UNAMIR was having a positive impact in Kigali, but the situation in much of Rwanda remained unstable due to the inability of the UN to fully deploy the authorised forces. He noted that several violent incidents had occurred and that the recent coup in neighbouring Burundi was accentuating tension.

On 6 January 1994 the Council completed the 90 day mandate review,[36] and adopted a resolution[37] which mostly accentuated the positive elements of the situation. It welcomed, the prompt establishment of the Transitional

34 United Nations Peacekeeping, '*Rwanda – UNAMIR*', https://peacekeeping.un.org/en/mission/past/unamirS.htm, accessed 6 June 2019.

35 'Report of the Secretary-General on the United Nations Assistance Mission for Rwanda', UN Doc. S/26927.

36 'Letter dated 94/01/06 from the President of the Security Council addressed to the Secretary-General', UN Doc. S/1994/14.

37 United Nations Security Council Resolution 893 (6 January 1994), UN Doc. S/RES/893.

Institutions and the progress being made, including the contribution by UNAMIR. It expressed concern the reported incidents of violence and the coup in Burundi, but decided that the correct response was to urge the early deployment of the second UNAMIR battalion.

Unbeknown to us in New York, at the same time as these discussions were taking place, General Dallaire in Kigali was dealing with alarming information. UNAMIR had received and corroborated information about a coordinated plan, by a large group of Hutu extremists known as "the Interahamwe", for the extermination of the Tutsi in Rwanda. On 11 January Dallaire sent an urgent code cable[38] to his superiors in New York reporting this intelligence and requesting permission to take pre-emptive action against the plotters. None of this information was relayed to the Security Council. Dallaire was denied permission to take forceful pre-emptive action.

This was an extraordinary development which completely undercut the optimistic assumptions under which the Security Council had been operating. Moreover it tallied exactly with the very similar warning given six months earlier by Special Rapporteur Ndiaye.

I have no evidence as to why the UN reacted in the way it did. However, my experience suggests that it is likely that UN Secretariat officials concluded that, with Rwanda at the Council table, it would have been impossible to share this intelligence and General Dallaire's proposal for a forceful response with the Council and keep it secret from the Interahamwe.

I also suspect that the denial of authority to use force was probably driven by concerns about the risks that the understrength UNAMIR would face and, in the absence of the second battalion, its capacity to carry out such a task. Also, the instruction to instead approach President Habyarimana and seek his intervention was in tune with the prevailing reluctance in the General Assembly for peacekeepers to act without host country consent. And it also, no doubt, reflected the acute awareness in the Secretariat of the knife edge on which UNAMIR was sitting in terms of US support. If UNAMIR began using force it would very likely precipitate a US demand for the termination of the operation.

But the net result was that Security Council Ambassadors were left in the dark and continued to proceed with an unrealistically positive appreciation of the situation in Rwanda.

38 United States Holocaust Memorial Museum, 'Genocide Fax: Part II', https://www.ushmm.org/confront-genocide/cases/rwanda/turning-points/genocide-fax-part-ii, accessed 5 June 2019.

A month later, by 17 February, the Council indicated concern[39] about delays in implementing the new transitional government in Rwanda and the deteriorating security situation in Kigali. It called for the parties to show greater cooperation. But it also reminded the parties of "..the consequences for them of non-compliance.."[40] – a veiled threat, inserted by the US, referring to the US position on the continuation of UNAMIR.

In terms of tactical management of a peacekeeping operation it is hard to imagine a more foolish position. This language would certainly have been understood by the extremists in Kigali as a clear indication that they did not need to worry about the UN frustrating their plans - all they had to do to get the UN to depart was demonstrate the collapse of the Arusha agreement.

The expiry of UNAMIR's sixth month mandate was due on 5 April. On 30 March the Secretary General recommended[41] that the mandate be rolled over for a further six months, notwithstanding the "political impasse" between the parties over setting up the Transitional Institutions, and the increased tension and insecurity. He concluded that a compromise was still possible.

But the US reacted strongly against the Secretary-General's recommendation. They were determined to radically tighten the leash on UNAMIR. After tough negotiations the US agreed to extend the mandate but only for four months,[42] until July, with a compulsory review in May. And there was now an explicit threat in the resolution that the UN would leave if the Arusha agreement was frustrated. All this, including the confidential internal dynamics in the Council which demonstrated the determined US opposition to UNAMIR, would have been faithfully transmitted by the Rwandan delegation to Kigali.

The next day the genocide commenced.

The Council was briefed on 7 April about the shooting down of President Habyarimana's plane as it approached Kigali. It was told of "the deaths of government leaders, many civilians and at least ten Belgian peacekeepers".[43] The Council strongly condemned "these horrific attacks and their perpetrators, who must be held accountable."[44]

France, with the assistance of the US and Belgium, immediately initiated a military operation to evacuate foreign nationals. France briefed the Security Council about this operation, but did not ask for Council approval.

39 'Statement by the President of the Security Council', UN Doc. S/PRST/1994/8.

40 Ibid., p. 2.

41 'Second progress report of the Secretary-General on the United Nations Assistance Mission for Rwanda', UN Doc. S/1994/360.

42 United Nations Security Council Resolution 909 (5 April 1994), UN Doc. S/RES/909.

43 'Statement by the President of the Security Council', UN Doc. S/PRST/1994/16, p. 1.

44 Ibid.

Shortly thereafter the US began pressing Council colleagues for UNAMIR to be withdrawn.

Belgium withdrew its soldiers from UNAMIR. They were the best trained and best equipped of the contingents. And the Belgian Government began to actively lobby[45] for the Council to terminate the Mission.

It is remarkable that there was nothing in the daily reporting to the Council from the Secretariat that suggested that what was unfolding in Rwanda might be genocide. This is despite the forewarnings of this from Special Rapporteur Bacre Waly Ndiaye and Force Commander General Dallaire.

Instead the Council was receiving misleading reporting from the Special Representative of the Secretary-General, J.R. Booh-Booh. He described the violence as a resumption of the civil war.[46] Given what we now know about General Dallaire's warning in January, it is hard to understand Booh-Booh's reports. They certainly had the effect of unnecessarily clouding the analysis. They also amplified the propaganda being shared in the Council by the representative of Rwanda.

The political dynamics in the Security Council became very tense. New Zealand and the Czech Republic quickly came to the conclusion that genocide was occurring. This was in part because both delegations sought briefings beyond the Secretariat. As President I reached out to the ICRC and MSF both of whom had personnel on the ground. As a result I received daily accurate advice about the situation which I then conveyed orally to the Council. The Czech Ambassador did likewise with information from Human Rights Watch.

We had support from Spain and Nigeria and Argentina and pushed for the situation to be named as a genocide, for the ambiguity in the mandate to be interpreted so as to allow General Dallaire to provide whatever protection could be offered and for UNAMIR to be reinforced as soon as possible. But we did not have the numbers to vote this through the Council and could not have overcome what seemed like a certain US veto.

Also we had to contend with the fact that UNAMIR was threatening to disintegrate. Belgium had withdrawn. Soon the Bangladesh Government began to demand that its contingent also be evacuated. As a logistics unit they had little in the way of training or weapons suitable for the changed situation. But the departure of these two substantial contingents meant that General Dallaire's options for protecting civilians were extremely limited.

45 As President of the Council I received urgent phone calls from Political leaders in Brussels to this effect.

46 Keating, 'An Insider's Account', p. 500.

There was also, sadly, ample scope for distraction. Just as the genocide began in Rwanda, Serb forces in Bosnia began an attack on the "safe area" of Gorazde.[47] This crisis diverted Council energy considerably. It led the Council to initiate the use of air strikes against Serb forces. For the first two weeks of the genocide a real frustration for me, as President of the Council, was the failure of the media to give any real attention at all to the Rwanda situation. They only wanted to question me about Bosnia and the attack on Gorazde.

Obstruction was also a factor because of the presence in the Security Council of the Rwandan Ambassador, recently elected by the General Assembly.[48] He was a representative of the Hutu regime and he sat at the very heart of the Security Council's private discussions in April and May, pursuing a very partisan interest. He was able to obfuscate and also, on several occasions, to use the consensus rule of the informal consultations to obstruct.

For a time in mid-April, with the departure of the Belgian and Bangladeshi contingents, it seemed possible that UNAMIR might just collapse. However, Canada, Ghana and Senegal were steadfast and continued to allow their personnel to be used to protect whatever civilians they could. Particular bravery was shown by UNAMIR personnel protecting hundreds of Tutsi civilians in the Kigali Stadium.

Instead of UNAMIR being closed down in April – as the US wanted – it actually survived. The Security Council resolution[49] to reduce the force has been rightly criticised. UNAMIR should have been reinforced, as some of us were arguing. But it needs to be understood that, at that moment, the reduction reflected a practical reality. As a result of the departure of troop contributors such as Belgium and Bangladesh, the force was already substantially diminished. The resolution also reflected a critical political reality. In order to turn around the pressures for complete closure, a deal had to be struck with the US and others who were arguing that the mission should just be abandoned.

Having preserved the existence of the operation, it was possible to take the next step in the strategy to get to a decision to reinforce it. To me, it seemed clear that private diplomacy was getting nowhere. The best hope for Rwanda was to generate a surge of public concern that would embarrass diplomats and politicians into supporting a reinforcement of UNAMIR. To do that, as

---

47 'Gorazde panic as Serbs enter safe area', *New York Times*, 18 April 1994, https://www.nytimes.com/1994/04/18/world/conflict-balkans-overview-gorazde-panic-serbian-forces-enter-safe-area.html, accessed on 5 June 2019.

48 See United Nations Security Council, 'Elected members of the Security Council by year', http://www.un.org/sc/searchres_sc_year_english.asp?year=1994, accessed on 4 June 2019.

49 United Nations Security Council Resolution 912 (21 April 1994), UN Doc. S/RES/912.

President, I reached over the top of the Council Members, speaking to the media sometimes several times a day.

Also, it seemed that an initiative to name the violence as genocide would help galvanize public opinion significantly. New Zealand therefore presented a draft resolution specifically naming the situation as genocide. This resulted in the adoption on 30 April of a Council Statement[50] which focused for the first time on the mass atrocities that were happening in the towns and villages across Rwanda.

It was not possible to get agreement on the use of the word "genocide". China at the time, for ideological reasons, opposed any reference in the Security Council to human rights. It mistakenly characterised the Genocide Convention[51] as a human rights instrument. China, therefore, for several weeks, spoke against any reference by the Council to the violence in Rwanda as genocide. The UK, for different reasons cautioned against recognising the situation as genocide. Some of the Non-Aligned countries on the Council were also resistant, out of a reluctance to name and shame. And the US, a long-time sceptic about the Genocide Convention,[52] also resisted. However, the statement did use the exact words of the Genocide Convention in describing the situation.

The initiative had a decisive impact in terms of changing the atmosphere in the Council. One week later New Zealand and Nigeria presented draft resolutions to reinforce UNAMIR and give it a clear robust mandate to prevent further atrocities and protect civilians.

Within ten days of these drafts, agreement was reached on 17 May on a new resolution. The Council decided[53] to significantly expand UNAMIR and give a new Chapter VII mandate with explicit language authorizing the use of force for protection of civilians. (Indeed, the provision on protection of civilians in resolution 918 became the model for future protection of civilians' mandates).

But at US insistence, resolution 918 required, unusually, a supplementary authorisation for actual deployment, once the Secretary General had been able to procure the necessary contingents. It is true that the Secretary-General struggled to secure commitments. But US opposition was clearly influencing the situation. The US continued to block authorisation for deployment until

50 'Statement by the President of the Security Council', UN Doc. S/PRST1994/21.

51 UN General Assembly, *Convention on the Prevention and Punishment of the Crime of Genocide*, 9 December 1948.

52 The US delayed ratification of the Genocide Convention for 40 years, and even now maintains formal legal reservations.

53 United Nations Security Council Resolution 918 (17 May 1994), UN Doc. S/RES/918.

the genocide and the fighting between the RPF and the Rwandan army was over.

Without doubt there was a problem of lack of peacekeeping contributions. But twice in 1994 major powers were able to galvanise robust military forces, equipment, airlift and financial resources to intervene in the Rwanda crisis. First was the operation in April to evacuate foreign communities.[54] Secondly, an even larger operation was organized in July 1994 to provide humanitarian care for the Rwandan Hutu refugees, after their retreat to Goma in the DRC.[55] It is clear, that there was never any real lack of resources. For the victims of the genocide – when resources were required for reinforcement of UNAMIR for prevention and protection – what was really lacking was political will.

It is important to record that there was not complete paralysis. Following the initiative to name the genocide, New Zealand and Spain pressed for the Council to establish the International Tribunal for Rwanda[56] (ICTR) and quickly got wide support in the Council. (It needs to be noted that, in contrast to its position on the deployment of reinforcements for UNAMIR, the US played a positive role in the negotiations on the Tribunal.) The ICTR subsequently had some success in holding accountable many of the senior figures responsible for genocide. It has also helped, to some extent, to build international acceptance of the truth about the crimes that were revealed.

8 The Underlying Cause of the Security Council Failure

As the above analysis shows, there were many factors that contributed to the failure of the Security Council. But the most important was the position of the United Sates. It is important to record, however, that President Clinton subsequently and courageously went to Rwanda[57] and apologized for the mistakes that led to the US decisions.

Three issues lay behind the US position. Because they all relate to peacekeeping aspects, it is worth exploring them in more detail. The first was the so called "Mogadishu factor". As we have seen above, only six months earlier, US

54 Department of Public Information, United Nations, '*Rwanda – UNAMIR*', https://www.un.org/Depts/DPKO/Missions/unamir_b.htm, accessed 2 June 2019.

55 Ibid.

56 United Nations Security Council Resolution 955 (6 November 1994), UN Doc. S/RES/955.

57 Charles Krause, 'Promoting Peace in Rwanda', *PBS*, 25 March 1998 https://web.archive.org/web/20120225223441/http://www.pbs.org/newshour/bb/africa/jan-june98/rwanda_3-25a.html, accessed 19 May 2019.

peacekeepers had suffered a humiliating defeat in Mogadishu.[58] False claims were made in the US, blaming the fiasco on UN peacekeeping systems. Opposition in Congress to UN peacekeeping was strengthened and US policy shifted against robust UN peacekeeping.

Secondly, as we have also seen above, the US Congress was pushing the Clinton Administration to reduce US contributions to UN peacekeeping.[59] US representatives told me that they needed to make an example of a peacekeeping operation and close it down. UNAMIR became such a target. By insisting on funding UNAMIR only for short mandates,[60] the US failed to appreciate the impact on the ground. This position actually incentivised bad behavior by the party that wanted the UN Mission UNAMIR out of the way.

The third factor that influenced the US position was very specific to the role of UN peacekeeping. The US had been undertaking a review of its policy regarding peacekeeping. It was a well-intentioned exercise designed to help secure wider domestic support in the US for UN peacekeeping. The outcome was Presidential decision PDD25.[61] One of its key conclusions was that, in future, the US in deciding whether to vote in favour of future UN peacekeeping operations should place weight on whether a peace agreement was in place and being observed. In parallel, although unconnected, there were negotiations in the Security Council in March, April and May 1994 on a Council statement on peacekeeping. It is not surprising that US negotiators in these discussions argued, in terms similar to PDD25, that future UN peacekeeping should take place only in situations where there was a benign environment. Robust mandates, requiring assertive military action, should be left to coalitions of the willing. The eventual Security Council statement did not go so far as PDD25, but, like PDD25, it did contain language favouring UN operations where a "cease fire exists".[62]

The manifest absence of a ceasefire in Rwanda at the time the genocide commenced seems to have contributed heavily to the US analysis that

58 See PBS, 'Synopsis' in 'Ambush on Mogadishu', 29 September 1998 http://www.pbs.org/wgbh/pages/frontline/shows/ambush/etc/synopsis.html, accessed on 19 May 2019.

59 See for example bills drafted by Congress during the Clinton era which sought to limit funding to UN peacekeeping operations. Michael Renner, 'Peacekeeping and the United Nations', *Foreign Policy in Focus*, 1 December 1996, http://www.fpif.org/reports/peacekeeping_and_the_united_nations, accessed on 19 May 2019.

60 United Nations Security Council Resolution 909, adopted on 5 April, the very eve of the commencement of the genocide, warned at US insistence that the Mission would be closed unless specific benchmarks were met. Note 44 *supra*.

61 See Presidential Decision Directive 25 (PDD-25) (6 May 1994) at http://www.fas.org/irp/offdocs/pdd25.htm, accessed on 1 June 2019.

62 'Statement by the President of the Security Council', UN Doc. S/PRST/1994/22, p. 2.

UNAMIR should be closed down and the position that they later adopted blocking implementation of Resolution 918 which would have allowed more effective action by the UN to respond to the genocide.

9 Lessons Learned: Has the Security Council Learned Lessons from Its Rwanda Experience?

The UN conducted major reviews[63] after the failures in Rwanda, as well as in Somalia and Bosnia. At an operational level the UN Secretariat began a programme of steady improvement of its doctrine, planning and logistics capability.

As outlined above, two key lessons from the Council's Rwanda experience relate to the unintended impact of unreasonably short mandate periods and the consequences of not explicitly authorizing peacekeepers to use force when necessary for the protection of civilians. I think there is now considerable evidence that both of those lessons have been well understood.

But in other areas, such as ensuring good information, collectively undertaking due diligence and giving appropriate practical and political oversight, there is still a great deal of weakness. And the past few years have shown that, in the prevailing international climate, there is a distinct retreat from the political will to use the powers of the Council to good effect.

In the years immediately after the Rwanda genocide the political appetite for any new United Nations peacekeeping to protect vulnerable populations from atrocities evaporated. New tragedies unfolded, especially in Africa. The presence of the Rwandan "genocidaires" in the DRC became a major element in a civil war[64] in the DRC that eventually cost three million lives – most of them civilians. Conflicts in Sierra Leone and Liberia continued the horrific pattern of atrocities against civilians. However, the only lesson that seemed to matter to the Security Council at that time was that the UN peacekeepers should keep away and that solutions, if any, should be left to regional powers.

In the late 1990s there was a change. Public opinion and NGO pressure began to have an effect. These new wars were having a terrible impact on civilians

63 'Report of the Independent Inquiry into the Actions of the United Nations during the 1994 Genocide in Rwanda', UN Doc. S/1999/1257; 'Identical letters dated 2000/08/21 from the Secretary-General to the President of the General Assembly and the President of the Security Council' (The Brahimi Report), UN Doc. S/2000/809.

64 'DRC: Attacks prompt UN to boost patrols in east Congo', *Reuters*, 12 January 2004.

generally, and on women and children[65] in particular. The recruitment and exploitation of child soldiers[66] also helped to galvanise a new sense of public urgency. This began to be reflected in a renewed willingness in the Security Council for robust UN peacekeeping to be reactivated.

The Council also began to develop normative principles about protection. This thematic programme included:

- In June 1998 the Security Council adopted a landmark statement[67] on "Children in Armed Conflict".
- In February 1999 an equally historic statement[68] was approved on the "Protection of Civilians" in which the Council called for a "comprehensive and coordinated approach" to "address the problem of protection of civilians in armed conflict".
- In August 1999 the Council adopted its first resolution[69] on the protection of children, in particular condemning the targeting of children
- In September 1999 the Council adopted a resolution[70] on protection of civilians condemning targeting of civilians, reinforcing international humanitarian law, threatening specific measures against violators and confirming the protection role for peacekeeping missions.
- In August 2000 there was a resolution[71] on children in armed conflict
- In September 2000 another landmark resolution,[72] this time on women peace and security, focused on the disproportionate impact in conflict on women and girls

This thematic progress was also reflected in renewed political will to apply lessons from Rwanda, Bosnia and Somalia. Responding to the conflicts in Sierra Leone[73] and the DRC,[74] the Council gave robust mandates to use force to protect civilians – ironically picking up the language that had been developed by New Zealand and Nigeria for Rwanda in May 1994 in resolution 918, but tragically never used.

---

65 'Violence against women in the family: report of the Special Rapporteur on violence against women, its causes and consequences, Radhika Coomaraswamy, submitted in accordance with Commission on Human Rights resolution 1995/85', UN Doc. E/CN.4/1999/68.

66 'Impact of armed conflict on children: note by the Secretary-General', UN Doc. A/51/306.

67 'Statement by the President of the Security Council', UN Doc. S/PRST/1998/18.

68 'Statement by the President of the Security Council', UN Doc. S/PRST/1999/6.

69 United Nations Security Council Resolution 1261 (25 August 1999), UN Doc. S/RES/1261.

70 United Nations Security Council Resolution 1265 (17 September 1999), UN Doc. S/RES/1265.

71 United Nations Security Council Resolution 1314 (11 August 2000), UN Doc. S/RES/1314.

72 United Nations Security Council Resolution 1325 (31 October 2000), UN Doc. S/RES/1325.

73 United Nations Security Council Resolution 1289 (7 February 2000), UN Doc. S/RES/1289.

74 United Nations Security Council Resolution 1291 (24 February 2000), UN Doc. S/RES/1291.

For Kosovo[75] and East Timor,[76] the Council gave the UN both forceful mandates and unique roles in managing the administration of the territories – in effect assuming the sovereign responsibility of protection and governance.

The evolution of the new doctrine of "Responsibility to Protect"[77] (R2P) also drew significantly on the Rwanda experience. Both R2P and the Security Council's thematic approach were given a boost at the United Nations World Summit in 2005. The Summit agreed to take action multilaterally via the Security Council to protect threatened populations from mass atrocities. This was reinforced at the UN General Assembly in 2009[78] in its debate on "Responsibility to Protect" and again in 2010 at a General Assembly "Informal Interactive Dialogue",[79] which focused on the issue of "early warning".

The idea that lessons were being learned also seemed to be reflected in a growing interest by the Security Council in the related concepts of preventive diplomacy, mediation and non-coercive measures for the prevention of conflict as well as the protection of civilians.[80] The critical link between good governance, development and security and the importance of collective action for preventing war and mass atrocities was highlighted in this context.[81]

The establishment of a Peacebuilding Commission[82] in 2005 seemed, at least initially, to offer exciting prospects for a partnership with the Security Council on prevention and post conflict restoration.

Further new peacekeeping operations with robust protection mandates were established in Cote d'Ivoire (UNOCI)[83] South Sudan (UNMISS)[84] and

---

75 United Nations Security Council Resolution 1244 (10 June 1999), UN Doc. S/RES/1244.

76 United Nations Security Council Resolution 1264 (15 September 1999), UN Doc. S/RES/1264.

77 Report of the International Commission on Intervention and State Sovereignty; "The Responsibility to Protect"; December 2001, International Development research Centre, Ottawa.

78 United Nations General Assembly, 'Official Records of the 63rd Session', Plenary Meetings 97 – 101 (UN Doc. A/60/PV.97 – PV.101), 23–28 July 2009.

79 International Coalition for the Responsibility to Protect, 'GA dialogue on Early Warning, Assessment and the Responsibility to Protect', http://www.responsibilitytoprotect.org/index.php/component/content/article/35-r2pcs-topics/2914-general-assembly-debate-on-early-warning-assessment-and-the-responsibility-to-protect-, accessed on 7 June 2019.

80 'Security Council, 65th year: 6389th meeting, Thursday, 23 September 2010, New York', UN Doc. S/PV.6389.

81 Security Council, 65th year: 6427th meeting, Monday, 22 November 2010, New York', UN Doc. S/PV.427 Resumption 1; 'Security Council, 66th year: 6479th meeting, Friday, 11 February 2011, New York', UN Doc. S/PV.6479.

82 United Nations Peacebuilding, '*United Nations Peacebuilding Commission*', https://www.un.org/peacebuilding/commission, accessed on 2 June 2019.

83 United Nations Security Council Resolution 1528 (27 February 2004), UN Doc. S/RES/1528.

84 United Nations Security Council Resolution 1996 (8 July 2011), UN Doc. S/RES/1996.

Central African Republic (MINUSCA).[85] New drivers for robust UN peacekeeping have emerged. In Mali[86] UN peacekeepers are involved in a major anti-terrorism operation, MINUSMA.

10 Conclusion

It is fair to say that lessons learned from the Security Council's experience on Rwanda have contributed to some important positive developments, especially in the first decade of the twenty first century. Other peacekeeping failures from the 1990s, in addition to the Rwanda case, no doubt also contributed to these developments. But it is important to acknowledge the emergence of the Security Council's thematic agenda, outlined above, as a step towards improving the overall political framework for peacekeeping and providing political support for a more principled protection focus by peacekeepers. Similarly, the fact that there have been a number of positive and relatively successful examples of robust peacekeeping over the past decade, suggests that some lessons have been learned.

But my experience, from involvement in New Zealand's most recent term on the Security Council, in 2015–16, suggests that the Security Council has still not internalised all the necessary lessons. Looking at the situation today, I find it difficult to escape the conclusion that much of what should have been learned by the Security Council from the Rwanda tragedy is either absent or eroding.

There is increasing pressure, primarily from Russia and China, but also more recently the US as well, to roll back some of the thematic agenda.[87] The overall deterioration in the state of global relations over the past decade is also a contributing factor to this conclusion. Current tensions between the major powers seem to be undermining the implementation of the lessons from the past and putting at risk the improvements in peacekeeping achieved over the past two decades.

There is a growing absence of political will in the Security Council to implement the doctrine of "Responsibility to Protect". This is manifested in reluctance to undertake more intensive preventive work under Chapter VI, or to take effective Chapter VII action.

85 United Nations Security Council Resolution 2149 (10 April 2014), UN Doc. S/RES/2149.

86 United Nations Security Council Resolution 2100 (25 April 2013), UN Doc. S/RES/2100.

87 "How a UN bid to prevent sexual violence turned into a spat over abortion" Foreign Policy 23 April 2019, https://foreignpolicy.com/2019/04/23/united-nations-bid-end-sexual-violence-rape-support-survivors-spat-trump-administration-sexual-reproductive-health-dispute-abortion-internal-state-department-cable/.

As far back as 2012 Russia laid out its position very bluntly, warning that its policy would be "… decisively countering attempts to use the UN Security Council for legitimizing external interference, including military interference, in the internal affairs of states in circumvention of the UN Charter and putting political pressure from the UN Security Council on "unwanted" regimes, including under the pretext of protecting civilians."[88]

The experience resulting from the crisis in Libya in 2011 seems to have played an important role in the pushback. Protracted instability and violence followed the Security Council authorised[89] use of force in Libya in 2011 and the resulting collapse of the Gaddafi regime. This violence and instability have continued for over 8 years. The Security Council action in 2011 was based at least in part on the R2P principle. It seems that the Libya experience has intensified opposition to robust action to protect civilians and has contributed to the Russian and Chinese determination to oppose the practical implementation of R2P in other cases.

The repeated failure of the Security Council, for over 8 years, to take meaningful action in respect of the crisis in Syria, is also linked to this absence of political will. And the wider chill in relations between Russia and the western Permanent Members contributed to Council failures over the Russian invasion of Crimea and the war in Ukraine.

Even the management of otherwise uncontroversial peacekeeping operations has become infected by the deterioration in the climate of major power cooperation in the Security Council, as shown in the political difficulties in the Council in 2018 over the peacekeeping mission in Central African Republic, MINUSCA.[90]

But the current weakness of the Security Council is also caused in part by a systemic institutional failure – a failure that was also apparent in 1994. The Council's working methods are archaic and not well adapted to the needs of the complex situations of today, nor to the high expectations of global public opinion and the international media.

There has always been a deep reluctance on the part of the Permanent Members of the Council to undertake meaningful reform of Security Council

88 "On Russia's position at the 67th Session of the UN General Assembly"; Permanent Mission of the Russian Federation to the United Nations; http://russiaun.ru/en/general_assembly/glavnyj_blok__2.

89 United Nations Security Council Resolution 1973 (17 March 2011), UN Doc. S/RES/1973.

90 Richard Gowan, '*What the U.N. Peacekeeping Mission in CAR Reveals About Security Council Gridlock*', World Politics Review, https://www.worldpoliticsreview.com/articles/26785/what-the-u-n-peacekeeping-mission-in-car-reveals-about-security-council-gridlock, accessed on 4 June 2019.

working methods[91] in ways that that might significantly improve the Council's performance in managing robust and difficult peacekeeping operations or undertaking Chapter VI prevention work.

So, it is hardly surprising, in the current state of global relations, that there is still almost no independent effort by the Security Council to collectively ascertain the facts. Mandating remains a major issue. There is still no effective Council process for detailed oversight of operations once they have commenced and no counterpart for peacekeeping operations of the Military Staff Committee envisaged in the Charter.[92]

An arm's length policy towards peacekeeping management by the Security Council may have been appropriate in the context of the early days of peacekeeping. But the case of Rwanda proved in 1994 that traditional peacekeeping was not really suitable for such a complex situation. Complex civil wars required more due diligence, more Council involvement in peace processes, better mandates and better working methods for proper oversight of evolving situations.

And there has been significant regression in some areas of the Councils working methods. Under today's restrictive procedural practices, it would no longer be easy for elected members to do what New Zealand and Nigeria did in May 1994 to bring forward their own resolutions to reinforce UNAMIR.[93] No longer would it be possible for a Council President to act as I did in 1994 to lead by reaching out to the media and global public opinion. Today the Council operates a much more restricted control of the President's discretion, including by insisting that media lines be agreed collectively.

This reinforces my conclusion that the Security Council, more than twenty years after the Rwanda genocide, is still far from learning all the necessary lessons.

---

91 Security Council Report, '*Security Council Working Methods: Provisional Progress*', https://www.securitycouncilreport.org/research-reports/security-council-working-methods-provisional-progress.php, accessed on 4 June 2019.

92 Security Council Report, '*Is Christmas Really Over? Improving the Mandating of Peace Operations*' https://www.securitycouncilreport.org/atf/cf/%7B65BFCF9B-6D27-4E9C-8CD3-CF6E4FF96FF9%7D/research_report_council_mandating_february_2019.pdf, accessed on 4 June 2019.

93 "Penholders and Chairs", Security Council Report; 10 July 2019, https://www.securitycouncilreport.org/un-security-council-working-methods/pen-holders-and-chairs.php.

CHAPTER 3

Wilfully Blind: the Security Council's Response to Genocide in Rwanda

Tamsin Phillipa Paige

1 Introduction

The Civil War and genocide in Rwanda represent a significant moment in the Security Council's history. Perhaps the most significant aspect of this is how the Security Council's response shaped mainstream international law, with the establishment of the ICTR and the solidification of the notion of individual criminal responsibility for *jus cogens* violations that came with that establishment. While the repercussions of the creation of the ICTR on international law and international relations have been extremely significant, perhaps more important to understanding the role that the Security Council played in the Rwanda genocide is the fact that the Security Council reversed its position on Rwanda and a 'threat to the peace' finding between 21 April and 17 May 1994. While the details of the justifications for this reversal are addressed as the focus of this article, in summary, when the genocide commenced, the Security Council initially opted to treat the situation as an internal matter for Rwanda to address (mostly at the behest of the French but supported by the P5 as a whole), drastically reducing UNAMIR forces and reducing their mandate to facilitate a political ceasefire between the parties involved (in a manner that was tantamount to a withdrawal of UN peacekeeping in the region).[1] Four weeks later, the Security Council reversed this position, which led to a finding of 'threat to the peace' and the deployment of a peacekeeping force under Chapter VII.[2] While we cannot be sure what would have happened if the Security Council had not initially treated the genocide as an internal Rwandese matter, the evidence

1 Resolution 912 (1994) 1994 (UN Security Council); United Nations Secretary-General, 'Special Report of the Secretary-General on the United Nations Assistance Mission for Rwanda' (United Nations 1994) S/1994/470 15–18.

2 Resolution 918 (1994) 1994 (UN Security Council).

 | DOI:10.1163/9789004430129_005

suggests that the Security Council was aware,[3] at the very least, that a genocide was a real possibility and it chose to withdraw peacekeeping forces despite this knowledge. This makes them inadvertently complicit in the genocide. In this article I will explore how the Permanent Five Members (P5) of the Security Council discussed Rwanda (with a focus on whether there was a 'threat to the peace') in order to make their initial decision to withdraw peacekeeping forces, and then their decision to intervene in order to halt the genocide.[4]

2 Context of the Security Council Meeting Statements

The Arusha Accords establish the backdrop to all of the information that was put to the Security Council when debating if and how they should act. The Arusha Accords were finalised on 3 August 1993,[5] but negotiation started with the amendment of the N'sele Cease-fire Agreement on 12 July 1992.[6] Of particular note in the N'sele Cease-fire was Article V, which contained provision for Rwanda moving forward with a democratically elected government and a military that was made up of members from both sides of the civil war.[7] Following the amending of the N'sele Cease-fire, the Arusha Accords set out a framework and details for implementing the peace between the government and the Rwandese Patriotic Front (RPF) which were finalised on 30 October 1992.[8]

The Security Council considerations of Rwanda began with the letter of request (containing the ceasefire agreement) from the Rwandese Government to assist in implementing the peace accords.[9] This request was supplemented by a briefing from Rwanda regarding the Civil War's effect on the country. Rwanda

3 The decision to only use evidence put before the SC instead of including national internal intelligence on the matter was two-fold: 1] It ensures that all of the information being used to analyse the P5 statements are on public record and thus verifiable; 2) By using the same base line context information for analysing the responses and statements of the P5 it assists in ensuring that the analysis is as free from bias as possible. Tamsin Phillipa Paige, *Petulant and Contrary: Approaches by the Permanent Five Members of theUNSecurity Council to the Concept of 'threat to the Peace' under Article 39 of theUNCharter* (Brill Nijhoff 2019) 33–36.

4 This is an expansion and refocusing of the chapter addressing the Rwandan civil war and genocide in: ibid 132–140.

5 Peace Agreement between the Government of the Republic of Rwanda and the Rwandese Patriotic Front 1993 4.

6 ibid 5.

7 ibid 7.

8 ibid 9–36.

9 Corneille Munyampeta, 'Letter Dated 4 March 1993 from the Charge D'Affaires A.I. of the Permanent Mission of Rwanda to the United Nations Addressed to the President of the Security Council.' (1993) S/25363.

highlighted that the 'particularly atrocious war' commenced on 1 October 1990, with ceasefire agreements put in place on 17 February 1991, 16 September 1991 and 12 July 1992. Rwanda also noted recent ceasefire violations on 7 and 8 February 1993. Rwanda noted that numerous international humanitarian law (IHL) violations had occurred, as well as large flows of displaced persons:

> Many civilians are still being killed and others mutilated, not to speak of the thousands who are being displaced and haunted by the spectre of death. National and international public opinion are greatly concerned by the 1 million who have been displaced ...
>
> Please allow me to offer—if only briefly—a few examples of the atrocities that exacerbate the situation: calling farmers to a meeting before massacring them with machine gun fire; shutting up scores of people in a house before killing them with grenades or explosives; disembowelling women and old people; shootings in the displaced persons camps; dismemberment, gouging out of eyes and cutting off the breasts; binding people hand and foot; and so on.[10]

Because of these atrocities and continued ceasefire violations, the Rwandese Government requested assistance on 12 March 1993, in the form of 'a multipurpose international force' to guarantee the safety of displaced persons in a demilitarised zone, and help guarantee the ceasefire:[11] 'May the Rwandese nation's distress and its call for help be worthy of the compassion of the Security Council, the last hope for the triumph of reason over the arguments of the gun.'[12] *Resolution 812 (1993)*, requesting that the Secretary-General investigate the role the UN could play in supporting the peace process in Rwanda, was unanimously passed at the end of that meeting.

From the commencement of the Secretary-General's involvement until the outbreak of violence on 6 April 1994, the factual situation that informed the Security Council's decisions was presented in reports by the Secretary-General. The initial report suggested deploying an observer mission to help facilitate the peace process and provide humanitarian assistance while overseeing the continuation of the ceasefire.[13] This was supported by the unanimous

10 United Nations Security Council, 'Security Council, Forty-Eighth Year: 3183rd Meeting (S/PV.3183)' 6.
11 ibid 7.
12 ibid.
13 United Nations Secretary-General, 'Interim Report of the Secretary-General on Rwanda' (United Nations 1993) S/25810 paras 19–23.

passing of *Resolution 846 (1993)*, creating the United Nations Observer Mission Uganda—Rwanda (UNOMUR).[14] The primary mandate of UNOMUR, a mission comprised of around 100 personnel from military and civilian backgrounds, was to prevent the flow of weapons to the RPF over the Ugandan border.[15] Because this mission was relatively unsuccessful at having a meaningful impact on circumstances in Rwanda, this was followed by the recommendation to deploy a full UN mission to Rwanda to help facilitate the peace process in a demilitarised zone,[16] resulting in the unanimous passing of *Resolution 872 (1993)*, establishing United Nations Assistance Mission for Rwanda (UNAMIR).[17] UNAMIR contained around 2,500 military personnel and was mandated to, among other things, ensure that Kigali was a demilitarised zone, provide assistance to displaced persons, coordinate humanitarian assistance to the region, and facilitate the power-sharing arrangements contained within the Arusha Accords.[18]

The next report put before the Security Council, on 30 December 1993, emphasised that reducing the force numbers of the observer mission could jeopardise the peace process,[19] and that while the ceasefire was holding for the most part (minor violations were noted), both sides were being relatively inflexible in negotiating a long-term peace deal in spite of negotiations taking place in relative good faith.[20] Further, the reports made consistent note of rising ethnic tensions in conjunction with the heavy influx of, and easy access to, weapons in and around refugee camps in the DMZ, southern, and northwestern regions of the country.[21] Just prior to the resumption of widespread violence in April, in conjunction with the plane crash that killed the presidents of Rwanda and Burundi, the Secretary-General's reports noted increased political violence and ethnic-based violence.[22]

---

14 United Nations Security Council, 'Security Council, Forty-Eighth Year: 3244th Meeting (S/PV.3244)' 3–5.

15 RA Dallaire and B Poulin, 'UNAMIR: Mission to Rwanda' (1995) Spring 1995 Joint Forces Quarterly 66.

16 ibid; United Nations Secretary-General, 'Report of the Secretary-General on Rwanda' (United Nations 1993) S/26488 para 63.

17 United Nations Security Council, 'Security Council, Forty-Eighth Year: 3288th Meeting (S/PV.3288)' 19.

18 Dallaire and Poulin (n 15) 66–67.

19 United Nations Secretary-General, 'Report of the Secretary-General on the United Nations Assistance Mission for Rwanda' (United Nations 1993) S/26927 para 30.

20 ibid 28.

21 ibid 16 & 29.

22 United Nations Secretary-General, 'Second Progress Report of the Secretary-General on the United Nations Assistance Mission for Rwanda' (United Nations 1994) S/1994/360 paras 26(f)-27 & 36.

Following the plane crash and death of the presidents of Burundi and Rwanda, the Secretary-General, at the request of the Security Council, issued a special report outlining the conditions in Rwanda and three alternate strategies that the Security Council could adopt. The report noted that in the wake of the plane crash, the ceasefire had ended, resulting in mass violence throughout the country that was both political and ethnic in nature.[23] The alternatives the Secretary-General offered for the UNAMIR mandate were as follows. Alternative one proposed a massive increase in force deployment, changes to the mandate to place it under Chapter VII and allowing peacekeepers to use force in an effort to enforce peace in the region. This was the option requested by the governments of Rwanda and Uganda.[24] Alternative two suggested a reduction in UNAMIR's numbers to a barebones security force mandated only to protect the force commander, who was to continue attempting to broker a ceasefire between the parties.[25] Alternative three was the complete withdrawal of UNAMIR.[26] While the report strongly inferred a recommendation for alternative one, the Security Council unanimously passed *Resolution 912 (1994)*, adopting alternative two from the Secretary-General's report.[27]

Four weeks after the mass killings had commenced, the Secretary-General issued another report updating the Security Council on the situation in Rwanda. The report noted that heavy fighting was occurring and that militias were engaging in the mass killing of civilians throughout the country.[28] It also noted that there were now around two million displaced persons as a result of the resumed fighting.[29] The report proposed a new force of approximately 5,500 troops, with constabulary rules of engagement (UNAMIR II), and a mandate to provide humanitarian assistance and civilian safe zones.[30] *Resolution 918 (1994)*, which created UNAMIR II and an arms embargo under Chapter VII for Rwanda (at Russia's insistence, given the absence of a ceasefire), was passed, with Rwanda voting against the Chapter VII arms embargo contained in section B of the resolution.[31] Rwanda justified this vote on the basis that the weapons fuelling

23 United Nations Secretary-General, 'Special Report of the Secretary-General on the United Nations Assistance Mission for Rwanda' (n 1) paras 1–3.

24 ibid 13–14.

25 ibid 15–18.

26 ibid 19.

27 United Nations Security Council, 'Security Council, Forty-Ninth Year: 3368th Meeting (S/PV.3368)' 6.

28 United Nations Secretary-General, 'Report of the Secretary-General on the Situation in Rwanda' (United Nations 1994) S/1994/565 para 3.

29 ibid.

30 ibid 11–15; also see Chapter 7 of this volume by Drew and Beardsley for more detail.

31 United Nations Security Council, 'Security Council, Forty-Ninth Year: 3377th Meeting (S/PV.3377)' 10–11.

the conflict and genocides were being supplied to the RPF by Uganda and that the arms embargo should be thus directed at Uganda rather than Rwanda.[32]

3 The Statements by the P5 in Response to the Civil War and Genocide

Until *Resolution 918 (1994)*, the P5's justificatory discourse hinged very strongly on peace through political negotiation without external interference. This position was most strongly vocalised by France, which opted to make statements in more meetings than any other member of the P5 on this issue.[33] The decision to make a finding of 'threat to the peace' was generally justified by the P5 on the basis of trying to foster the conditions necessary for a peaceful settlement to the conflict in the face of the humanitarian crisis.

China opted to make statements about Rwanda on two separate occasions, the first being after the passing of *Resolution 872 (1993)* creating UNAMIR under Chapter VI of the Charter. The second was before voting on *Resolution 918 (1994)*, which resulted in the creation of UNAMIR II and the finding of 'threat to the peace' under Chapter VII. With the initial UNAMIR mission, China argued that the peace process in Rwanda was at a crucial stage that relied upon the continued ceasefire and stability to proceed. China called upon both parties to 'start forthwith the cantonment and demobilisation of their troops so as to create necessary conditions for the establishment of the transitional institutions and the holding of general elections on schedule'.[34] Further, China noted that support for creating UNAMIR was entirely grounded in the mandate of the mission to promote compliance with the peace agreements in conjunction with the request of both parties for such support from the UN.[35]

Before voting on *Resolution 918 (1994)*, China stated that

> the conflicting Rwandese parties should cease forthwith massacring each other and agree to an effective and lasting cease-fire so as to create the conditions necessary for an improvement in the humanitarian situation and the settlements of the conflict through negotiation.[36]

---

32 ibid 6.

33 Why France chose to speak so frequently on Rwanda in the Security Council compared with the rest of the P5 is unclear.

34 United Nations Security Council, '3288th Meeting' (n 17) 24.

35 ibid.

36 United Nations Security Council, '3377th Meeting' (n 31) 9.

Following this statement, China made it clear that support for *Resolution 918 (1994)* was '[b]ased on humanitarian considerations'[37] and 'sincere desire to create conditions for the early restoration of peace and security in that country'.[38] Finally, China argued that the already agreed-upon peace accords was the framework to which both parties should adhere when establishing peace and new government within the country.[39]

Russia's statements on this issue mirrored China's—it opted only to articulate their position after the passing of *Resolution 872 (1993)*, and before voting on *Resolution 918 (1994)*. In relation to the creation of UNAMIR, Russia argued that the mission and its mandate should assist both parties in Rwanda to comply with the peace agreements to assist in facilitating lasting peace for the nation.[40] Russia also stated that it believed the Security Council's role in situations such as this was to support the effort of regional organisations to end conflict.[41] Its support for UNAMIR's creation under Chapter VI was grounded in these positions.

Before voting on *Resolution 918 (1994)*, Russia argued that the gravity of the situation in Rwanda since the fighting had resumed demanded a Security Council response. Russia stated that it supported the expansion of UNAMIR's mission under the new UNAMIR II tag because of the 'severe humanitarian crisis' that was now underway in Rwanda.[42] Further, Russia's support for the peacekeeping mission was based on the fact that the draft resolution now addressed its concerns about taking into account the basic criteria for carrying out peacekeeping operations (Russia was unclear on what criteria it was referring to), which the Security Council had confirmed by presidential statement on 3 May 1994.[43] Further, Russia insisted upon imposing an arms embargo, necessitating the finding of a 'threat to the peace' and Chapter VII action by the Security Council.[44] It further argued that this would help foster the necessary conditions for a successful peacekeeping operation.[45] In spite of this, Russia

37 ibid.
38 ibid.
39 ibid.
40 United Nations Security Council, '3288th Meeting' (n 17) 26.
41 ibid.
42 United Nations Security Council, '3377th Meeting' (n 31) 9.
43 ibid 10. Interestingly, the Presidential Statement in question (S/PRST/1994/23) made in relation to Bosnia and Herzegovina made no direct mention of peacekeeping criteria. It is possible that Russia were referring to statements regarding aerial surveillance and the use of force to be used against safe zone violators.
44 ibid.
45 ibid.

highlighted the importance of the 'unconditional cooperation of both Rwandese parties' if the peacekeeping mission were to be successful.[46]

The UK's only statements on this situation were made after voting on Resolutions 872 (1993) and 918 (1994). In relation to the initial deployment of UNAMIR, the UK argued that the UN's role in Rwanda was that of facilitator, and that peace would only be achieved when 'an African solution was found to an African problem'.[47] On this note, the UK contended that the responsibility for ending the protracted conflict and creating an atmosphere that allowed displaced persons to resettle within Rwanda lay with the Rwandese Government and Rwandan Patriotic Front (RPF).[48] After making these positions clear, the UK noted that it was strongly in favour of the international community providing support for these endeavours.[49] This position of supporting the RPF and the Rwandese Government to end the violence in the Rwandan conflict continued in the UK's statement after the passing of *Resolution 918 (1994)*:

> The world has been appalled by the scale of tragedy which has occurred in Rwanda. It is not tragedy to which there is an easy international response. The United Nations cannot impose an end to bloodshed. But neither can it stand idly by ... The focus of this expanded United Nations operation will rightly be humanitarian.[50]

The UK then proceeded to state that the only way to end to bloodshed and establish peace was for the parties involved to take responsibility for their actions and resume a politically negotiated settlement: 'The Arusha Agreement remains the only viable basis for national reconciliation in Rwanda.'[51]

The US position throughout this situation was that the responsibility for establishing peace in Rwanda lay with the Rwandese people, in particular those who were parties to the conflict. When making statements after the passing of *Resolution 872 (1993)*, the US highlighted that its support for deploying UNAMIR was grounded in the fact that 'it will advance the goals of peaceful conflict resolution and democratization, and allow the return of hundreds of thousands of those that fled their homes'.[52] After emphasising this basis for action, the US expressed its concern at the burden the Security Council was

46 ibid.
47 United Nations Security Council, '3288th Meeting' (n 17) 21.
48 ibid.
49 ibid.
50 United Nations Security Council, '3377th Meeting' (n 31) 12.
51 ibid.
52 United Nations Security Council, '3288th Meeting' (n 17) 22.

shouldering, noting that it was important to ensure the mission remained focused on a narrow mandate.[53] Regarding the question of peace within Rwanda, the US stated that it was 'up to the Rwandese themselves to ensure that the transition to democracy moves forward'.[54]

Just prior to the resumption of violence on 6 April 1994, the US raised its concerns over delays by the parties involved in terms of implementing transitional institutions, noting that the Secretary-General suggested that such delays posed a threat to peace and security in the region.[55] The US argued that its support for Chapter VII action in *Resolution 918 (1994)* was premised upon the basis that '[t]he sheer magnitude of the humanitarian disaster in that tragic country demands action. This Council has struggled to formulate a response that is both appropriate and effective'.[56] While supporting Security Council action on the basis of the disaster's magnitude, the US was clear in its position that 'whatever efforts the United Nations may undertake, the true key to the problems in Rwanda is in the hands of the Rwandese people'.[57] Finally, the US stated that continued international assistance in Rwanda was contingent upon both parties to the conflict demonstrating a willingness and ability to cooperate with the peacekeeping forces and bringing about an end the violence.[58]

France opted to speak in every meeting leading up to the finding of a 'threat to the peace' regarding this situation. The core of its argument throughout these statements was that the only way to achieve peace in Rwanda was through a politically negotiated settlement between the parties to the conflict.[59] France asserted that the UN should support these processes, but that the majority of the work had to be performed by the Rwandese Government and the RPF.[60] After the passage of *Resolution 872 (1993)*, France stated that it only supported establishing UNAMIR because it was being done with the cooperation of both parties to the conflict.[61] Before UNAMIR troops were withdrawn in the wake of resumed conflict on 6 April 1994, France argued that the 'continuation of United Nations action in Rwanda depends directly on the

53 ibid 23.
54 ibid 22.
55 United Nations Security Council, 'Security Council, Forty-Ninth Year: 3358th Meeting (S/PV.3358)' 6.
56 United Nations Security Council, '3377th Meeting' (n 31) 12.
57 ibid 13.
58 ibid.
59 United Nations Security Council, '3244th Meeting' (n 14) 4–5; United Nations Security Council, '3358th Meeting' (n 55) 6.
60 United Nations Security Council, '3183rd Meeting' (n 10) 15.
61 United Nations Security Council, '3288th Meeting' (n 17) 20.

efforts [that the RPF and the Rwandese Government] are prepared to make to restore peace definitively to Rwanda in the wake of a conflict that has, alas, claimed all too many victims'.[62] This position proved relatively accurate given the passing of *Resolution 912 (1994)*, which significantly reduced the scope of the mandate and UNAMIR force numbers. France again used this opportunity to restate its position that there was no military solution possible in Rwanda, and that only a political solution could bring about peace in the region.[63] France also reiterated its conviction that should the parties not agree to a ceasefire, the UN would have to reconsider UNAMIR having a continued presence in Rwanda at all.[64]

After the finding of 'threat to the peace' in *Resolution 918 (1994)*, France justified support for Security Council action on the basis of the gravity of the humanitarian situation further unfolding in Rwanda: 'Faced with a humanitarian catastrophe on such magnitude, the international community could not fail to react'.[65] France also opted to defend its vocal support for withdrawing the majority of UNAMIR after fighting had resumed, arguing that the Security Council was 'compelled to make troop reductions'[66] and 'took that decision reluctantly'.[67] Given France's previous threats that continued UN support in Rwanda depended upon the Rwandese people making progress in the peace process, such justifications regarding UNAMIR's withdrawal seem disingenuous at best. France closed its statements by arguing that UNAMIR II's mission was to protect the civilian population and deliver humanitarian assistance, as peace in Rwanda could only be attained by resuming the peace process that had already been politically agreed upon.[68]

4 Conclusion

While it is clear that all of the P5 eventually supported a finding of 'threat to the peace' in an effort to end the genocide in Rwanda, the P5 (with France as the most vocal advocate) created the conditions that allowed the mass

62 United Nations Security Council, 'Security Council, Forty-Ninth Year: 3326th Meeting (S/PV.3326)' 11.
63 United Nations Security Council, '3368th Meeting' (n 27) 7.
64 ibid.
65 United Nations Security Council, '3377th Meeting' (n 31) 11.
66 ibid.
67 ibid.
68 ibid.

killings to be so widespread and intense. They achieved this through their insistence upon the drastic reduction of UNAMIR after the resumption of hostilities on 6 April 1994. At the time, France justified this as a consequence for both sides of the conflict because of their inability to negotiate a peace and abide by the ceasefire agreements. However, France later suggested that the withdrawal of the majority of UNAMIR was taken with great reluctance, and that the Security Council was forced into the situation. What is also clear is that prior to the withdrawal of UNAMIR the Secretary-General through his reports had made it clear that the conditions existed for the genocides to occur. This was stated in his reports, where he noted relative instability, and high levels of weapons flow to refugee camps around the country. When all of this is considered the only reasonable conclusion that we can reach is that the Security Council, at the behest of the French, was complicit through its inaction in the Rwanda genocides. While will never know if maintaining or increasing the UNAMIR presence within Rwanda would have prevented the genocides, it is clear that decision by the Security Council to withdraw that peacekeeping force created conditions that allowed mass killings to occur relatively unchecked.

CHAPTER 4

Underpowered and Mostly Unwanted

A Short History of UNAMIR

Jean Bou

Created in 1993 and disestablished in 1996, the United Nations Mission in Rwanda (UNAMIR) led a brief and mostly unhappy existence. Established to help end a civil war, its purpose became irrelevant in April 1994 when the outbreak of the Rwandan Genocide, and the accompanying resumption of the Rwandan Civil War, meant that achieving its mission of helping a country achieve peace became impossible. Reduced to a rump force, unable to halt the genocide and limited to *ad hoc* roles the mission became, along with failures in Somalia and the former-Yugoslavia, symbolic of the mid-1990s nadir of UN peacekeeping. Traditionally a mission being unable to do its job might have led to its withdrawal, but the horrible events of 1994 meant the international community had to react and in May–June 1994 UNAMIR II was recreated. Backed by new mandates and troop contributors, its mission-crafted as the genocide was ongoing – was to provide security and help ameliorate the effects of genocide and war. It was several months before the revitalised force took the field, however, and in the meantime the situation in Rwanda had moved on. The victory of the rebels over Rwanda's genocidal regime greatly diminished the killing and brought a degree of stability to the country, but it also meant that UNAMIR now had to get on with an immature government and army that had its own objectives and which was not well disposed toward the UN mission. The Rwandans grudgingly accepted UNAMIR but grew increasingly critical of it, and by early 1995 they wanted to be rid of it. By April of that year there were fears that UNAMIR forces and their Rwandan hosts would come to blows and the UN mission increasingly looked as if it was on borrowed time. Again, UNAMIR's mandate was not well aligned to its circumstances and once more it could only stand by when more blood was shed by the country's new rulers when they moved to forcefully close an internally displaced persons camp in southwest Rwanda.[1]

1 This chapter is based upon the Rwanda chapters published in Jean Bou et al., The Official History of Australian Peacekeeping, Humanitarian and Post-Cold War Operations, volume 5, *The Limits of Peacekeeping; Australian Missions in Africa and the Americas, 1992–2005* (Cambridge University Press, 2019). Though it will undoubtedly frustrate the present reader, in the interests of brevity citations in this chapter have been kept to a minimum and readers are directed to the longer source for a deeper analysis and the full listing of primary and secondary sources that underpin it.

 | DOI:10.1163/9789004430129_006

1 The First Birth and Death of UNAMIR

Rwanda's process of gaining independence from Belgium, attained in 1962, had been accompanied by a rise in tension between the country's traditional ruling caste/ethnicity, the Tutsis, who made up perhaps 15 per cent of the population, and the traditional lower caste, the Hutu.[2] The Hutu majority, or maybe more accurately its most adroit political players, had prevailed and their assertion of primacy, along with several associated waves of violence, led to Tutsis leaving for neighbouring countries. Many of them, particularly those who went to Uganda, where they were not particularly welcome and got caught up in that country's civil wars, maintained a desire to return to Rwanda.

This 'right of return' was long asserted, but apart from a failed foray from Burundi in the early 1960s, action was lacking until 1990 when the Tutsi-dominated Rwandan People's Front (RPF), through the agency of its military wing, the Rwandan People's Army (RPA), invaded Rwanda from across the northern border with Uganda. Built upon Tutsi members who had previously fought for Yoweri Museveni's National Resistance Army in Uganda's civil wars, the RPA force had some military experience, and enough manpower and equipment, to undertake the invasion, though not enough to succeed. The RPA's commander was killed – probably in a quarrel with a subordinate – and the Rwandan Army, with some support from Zaire and France (Rwanda's major external backer), soon had the upper hand. The RPA, now led by Major Paul Kagame, withdrew into Uganda and then sought refuge in the highland forests of Rwanda's north-west. Here the porous Ugandan border offered a route for supplies and a bolt-hole if needed. After a pause to gather themselves, the RPA commenced a guerrilla war against their Rwandan Hutu opponents in 1991.

The war continued into 1992 when the dictatorial Rwandan government of Juvénal Habyarimana, under French and American post-Cold War pressure to liberalise Rwanda, agreed to negotiate with the RPF. These talks continued for about year and in August 1993 the final peace agreements were signed in Arusha, Tanzania, whereby they became known as the Arusha Accords. Habyarimana had been coy and non-committal for much of the negotiations and likely only signed the final agreements because of external pressure. Within Rwanda itself there was much opposition to the peace agreements, particularly from more vociferous Hutu groups who wanted no accommodation with

2 The Tutsi-Hutu divide is usually described as an ethnic one, but given they spoke the same language and lived in an interconnected community the relationship has been more accurately described as 'caste-like'.

a Tutsi-dominated rebel army. These negotiations and the attempt to implement the Arusha Accords took place at a time when Rwanda was increasingly tumultuous, and its Hutu majority was being primed and organised to undertake what would become known as the Rwandan Genocide.

Aside from external pressure on the two parties to the Rwanda Civil War to reach an agreement, there had also been attempts to facilitate the peace via the creation of successive bodies to aid and oversee developments. The first of these had been the Organisation of African Unity's (OAU) July 1992 creation of a Neutral Military Observer Group (NMOG I) to keep an eye on the Ugandan-Rwandan border. Despite this the Rwandan Government was wary of the RPA's links to Uganda and accused Kampala of providing arms to the RPA, an accusation it denied. Unable to defuse the tensions both governments approached the United Nations seeking the establishment of a border observer force that would prevent supplies crossing the border. In April 1993 a United Nations 'technical mission' travelled to the region and soon after the UN Secretary-General, Boutros Boutros-Ghali, recommended that the observer mission be established. In New York there followed 'weeks of quibbling…on the details' between the French and American delegations.[3] Only the French, thanks to their close links to Kigali and keen interest in the region, were wholly in favour of the mission, and they were the only delegation in to speak in the Security Council when the necessary resolution was finally passed on 22 June 1993.

This resolution created the UN Observer Mission Uganda–Rwanda (UNOMUR) and the Chief Observer was a Canadian officer, Brigadier General Roméo Dallaire. Because the border was mostly controlled by the RPA, UNOMUR was to operate on the Ugandan side and was based in Kabale in southern Uganda. As this mission was being established the Arusha Accords were signed, which led to a further development when the Rwandan Government asked the United Nations for help in implementing them. As this was considered in New York the OAU created NMOG II as an interim arbiter while the hoped for UN-backed 'neutral international force' was arranged for Rwanda.[4]

Once more the United Nations despatched a technical mission to Rwanda and in New York the French delegation was again keenly promoting the idea that the UN should get involved in the Rwandan peace process. Paris wanted a strong force, while the Americans, with an eye on the expenses and the United

3 Australian Department of Foreign Affairs [hereafter DFAT] cable UN58955, New York to Canberra, 22 June 1993, National Archives of Australia (NAA:), 93/060599; UN Security Council Resolution 846, 22 June 1993.

4 United Nations, The *Blue Helmets*, 3rd ed. (United Nations, 1996), 342–3.

Nations parlous finances, initially wanted no new force at all and then tried to keep a cap on the numbers to about 500. Boutros-Ghali eventually sought a force of 2500 personnel who would; oversee the ceasefire; separate, canton and then integrate the opposing armies; would secure the Rwandan capital of Kigali; and ensure security in the lead up to free elections. Boutros-Ghali and the French got their way and 5 October 1993 Security Council Resolution 872 established the UN Assistance Mission in Rwanda (UNAMIR). This new force of 2500 personnel, including civilian police and military observers, had a six-month mandate and was to incorporate the NMOG II and UNOMUR missions, though the latter eventually stayed technically separate. Dallaire, promoted to major general, was to be the force commander, while the former Cameroon Minister for External Relations, Jacques-Roger Booh-Booh was appointed the Secretary-General's Special Representative.

The new mission's objectives roughly accorded with what Boutros-Ghali had suggested and were intended to support the implementation of the Arusha Accords. The tasks included bolstering security around Kigali, observing and reporting on the ceasefire, monitoring the security situation during the transitional period to a new government and monitoring the repatriation of refugees.[5] That UNAMIR might be able to achieve all this was made difficult by the unwillingness of countries to offer their troops to serve with the UN mission. Belgium, the former colonial power, provided 400 paratroopers and Bangladesh another 400 logistic troops, but other countries were slower to contribute and delays in deployments meant that it took five months for the force to get up to its mandated strength.

In the meantime, while there was great international optimism that the Arusha Accords would provide a basis for a lasting peace, the situation inside Rwanda was not encouraging. The legacy of Hutu hatred towards Tutsis, built on decades of anti-Tutsi propaganda, whipped up by increasingly strident Hutu-dominated media and the tumult of the civil war led to a climate of great opposition to the peace agreement. This was most evident from more extreme Hutu groups and politicians who soon regarded the Habyarimana regime, despite its pedigree of anti-Tutsi attitudes and behaviour, as too moderate. Indeed, while the country was riven by the Hutu-Tutsi divide, there was also increasing competition between various Hutu groups for control of the country, which further complicated the situation.

In early February 1994 Habyarimana was sworn in as the country's interim president, but the establishment of the transitional government was no closer as Habyarimana and others used various tactics to stall progress in the coming

5 UN Security Council Resolution 872, October 1993; United Nations, *The Blue Helmets*, 343–4.

months. Violence was spreading too, and that February two senior politicians were killed by mobs of their political opponents. UNAMIR was also getting information that weapons were coming into the country to arm the Hutu militias that Habyarimana's government and the Hutu-extremist Coalition pour la Défense de la République (CDR) were fostering, and then, via an informant, heard of a plan for those Hutu militias to exterminate Rwanda's Tutsi minority. The informant also passed on that a number of UNAMIR's Belgian peacekeepers would be killed so as to force that contingent's withdrawal and hobble the UN force. Dallaire asked New York for more peacekeepers and the power to search for and seize arms caches, but found that neither Boutros-Ghali nor any of the members of the Security Council wanted to grant a more robust mandate to create a more interventionist UNAMIR – cooperation with the parties in Rwanda and the Arusha Accords remained paramount.[6]

Nevertheless, the delays and challenges in Rwanda were causing some vexation in New York and elsewhere, and soon leading to louder international calls for more progress on establishing the interim government. Following several missed handovers by Habyarimana, Boutros-Ghali reported to the Security Council on 30 March that there were significant concerns about the implementation of the Arusha Accords, but given the ceasefire was holding and both sides were still supporting the accords, that continued efforts were worthwhile.[7] Hence, despite the international misgivings, on 5 April the Security Council extended UNAMIR's mandate for a further four months.

The efforts of the United Nations and UNAMIR meant little when, on the following day, a plane carrying Habyarimana and Cyprien Ntaryamira, the President of Burundi, back from a meeting in Dar es Salaam was struck by two surface-to-air missiles as it approached Kigali airport. The event was a trigger for a well-planned political take over and wave of genocidal violence. Prominent Hutu figures quickly established an 'interim government', road blocks sprang up around Kigali and elsewhere, and the Hutu militias began their terrible work of killing. Making use of the lists that had been long compiled, and guided by Rwanda's extremist radio stations, the militias targeted country's Tutsi minority, Hutus thought to moderate, politicians deemed unpalatable and Rwanda's Twa people. The Rwandan Genocide, as it soon became known was, by best estimates, to claim the lives of some 850,000 people.[8]

---

6 Turid Lagrid, 'UN Peacekeeping in Rwanda', in Howard Adelman & Astri Sukre (eds) *The Path of Genocide* (Transaction Publishers, 1999), 233–4; UN, *The United Nations and Rwanda* (UN Department of Public Information, 1996), 1–2.

7 UN*The United Nations and Rwanda*, 35–6.

8 Gerard Prunier, *The Rwanda Crisis* (Columbia University Press, 1995), 252–3.

The height of the genocide was from the second week of April through to about the third week of May. Adding to an already complex situation, Rwanda's civil war immediately restarted and the Tutsi-dominated RPA advanced into the country from its side of the Arusha-agreed ceasefire line. Among its goals was the relief of an RPA battalion that had been stationed inside Kigali as part of the Arusha settlement and which was soon besieged by Hutu forces.

During these weeks the situation for UNAMIR became increasingly grim. Upon Habyarimana's death the UN force had only just reached it full operating strength. As foreshadowed by the informant, ten Belgian peacekeepers, who had been guarding Agathe Uwilingiymana, the moderate-Hutu interim Prime Minster, were taken away, disarmed and killed. As intended this soon led to Brussel's withdrawing it troops, though that county's diplomats, possibly as a face saving measure, were soon saying that UNAMIR's mandate had been too weak.[9] The force's Ghanaian battalion was isolated in northern Rwanda by the renewed civil war while the Bangladeshi unit, probably acting on orders from home, became inactive, and in Kigali Dallaire had to rely on a single Tunisian company.[10] The force's logistic lifeline, Kigali airport, was an intermittent battlefield and when it was open evacuating foreigners proved the most pressing task for the international community.

The force's role in the circumstances was also unclear. Though it continued to be invoked as some sort of diplomatic and political touchstone, the Arusha Accords were being ever more shredded by the genocidal reality in Rwanda. Rwanda's interim government, the Rwandan Army and the Hutu militias tended to view UNAMIR as the distained agents of the unwanted Arusha settlement and an impediment to their genocidal program. They only softened this position as the civil war started to go against them and they the idea of outside intervention forces gained some appeal. For its part, while the RPF/RPA developed a strong dislike of Booh-Booh and became vocal critics of the UN force's inability to stop the genocide, they were willing to tolerate UNAMIR's presence as long as it did not get in the way of their attempt to conquer the country, which quickly became its main goal. Moreover, undoubtedly enraged by the genocide, and no doubt sensing its growing battlefield advantage, the RPF refused to negotiate with those responsible for the genocide which, together with the Hutu elite's matching intransigence and untrammelled violence, meant that UNAMIR facilitating a negotiated settlement was impossible. Unable to affect a peace that neither side wanted and lacking the strength,

9 DFAT cable BS2035, Brussels to Canberra, 9 May 1994, NAA: A9737, 93/060859, pt 3.

10 Romeo Dallaire, *Shake hands with the Devil* (Carrol & Graf, 2005), 302; Laegrid, 'UN Peacekeeping in Rwanda', 237.

mandate and political backing to stop the genocide, UNAMIR was limited to the significant but *ad hoc* roles of protecting the few people it could, exhorting the belligerents to talk and, perhaps most importantly, reporting on the atrocities around them.

This reporting fell on mostly deaf ears for the first few weeks, however. In New York the UN Secretariat was soon passing on the reports to the Security Council and national missions, but there was an air of disbelief as to their accuracy. It was not until late April that the US mission in New York started to pass on its supportive intelligence assessments and this, together with the international media's belated realisation of what was happening in Rwanda, finally brought on some sense of urgency.[11] By now the focus in New York was on what to do with UNAMIR. With its purpose unclear and its safety in doubt, on 20 April Boutros-Ghali had provided the Security Council with three options: first, that it be reinforced and given a mandate to effect a ceasefire; second, that it be reduced to a rump force to help the Special Representative and Force Commander act as intermediaries; or third, that that it be completely withdrawn. The Secretary-General had advised against the final option and with nobody on the Council interested in an expanded and combative UNAMIR, on 21 April it voted to reduce the force to fewer than 300 personnel to support Booh-Booh and Dallaire in restoring the Arusha process.

2 The Second Birth of UNAMIR

In early May the Council sought further ideas from the Secretary-General. Boutros-Ghali, following advice from Dallaire, proposed establishing a 5,500-strong peacekeeping mission that would fan out from Kigali to secure safe havens and distribute aid, but the idea met a cold response. The United States, recently bruised in Somalia and limited by the freshly produced Presidential Directive Decision 25 (PDD-25), which put distinct boundaries on American involvement in and support of UN peacekeeping missions, wanted nothing to do with any potentially combative peacekeeping force. This, combined with the testy relationship between the United States and Boutros-Ghali, proved a major sticking point in developing a response. Conversely others on

11 DFAT cable UN61930, New York to Canberra, 27 April 1997, NAA: A9737,93/60859 pt 2; New Zealand Ministry of Foreign Affairs and Trade (MFAT) cable, C04387/NYK, New York to Wellington, 29 April 1994, NAA: A9737, 93/060859. pt 2. New Zealand was serving on the Security Council in 1994 and at that time was its President. New Zealand shared many of its New York diplomatic cables with Australia in this period, keeping Canberra very well informed.

the Council, notably France and its then president New Zealand, wondered how a force with a limited mandate would be able to work in such dangerous circumstances and do something about the genocide.

The result was that after more haggling the Security Council passed Resolution 918 on 17 May 1994. This authorised the expanded 5,500-strong mission but limited it to a Chapter VI mandate (geared to the pacific settlement of disputes) rather than a more robust Chapter VII one (which is about threats to peace and facilitates strong military action). Despite this limitation the mandate, which was expanded upon a few weeks later with Resolution 925, also uniquely set out that the force was to 'contribute to the security and protection' of people at risk in Rwanda as well as provide security for the distribution of humanitarian aid. Aimed at protecting Rwanda's civilians it enlarged the concept of 'self-defence' to include any persons threatened in 'protected sites and populations'.[12] It was an incongruous proviso for a Chapter VI mission and at the time some called it a 'Chapter VI plus' mission – it would prove to be neither fish nor fowl.

This resolution led, eventually, to the recreation of UNAMIR from the rump force it had been reduced to the previous month to a much larger one with much larger responsibilities (though often called UNAMIR II, this was never the reconstituted mission's title). The revitalised mission had many obstacles in front of it, however. In the first instance Kigali airport was still being fought over, which would forestall any deployment through there. This problem was overcome a few days later when it was secured by the RPA. This made the Dallaire/Boutros-Ghali plan viable and what had until now been a rather woolly 'concept of operations' started, after more planning, to become a workable plan. The Americans, who had continued to criticise the scheme, were now mollified enough that they were willing to offer logistic and other support to get the mission in place. Who was to deploy, however, was a still a mostly unsolved problem and donor nations were, despite the international horror at events, scarce in the face of a deployment to into a genocidal civil war. The Americans were never interested, and European countries were either unacceptable (France), too committed elsewhere (UNAMIR had become the UN's 16th operational peacekeeping mission when it was established) or made their excuses. Canada, under pressure to back Dallaire, offered a signals squadron and became the first western country to get involved since the Belgians departed. African countries started filling in the gaps, but most of these contingents needed equipment, logistics or training to take the field and finding the necessary support proved time consuming, and a stretch for the UN's parlous

12 UN Security Council Resolutions 918 and 925, 17 May and 8 June 1994.

finances and sclerotic bureaucracy. This led to further delays and in early June there were fewer than 500 peacekeepers in Rwanda.

As UNAMIR slowly built up – it was August before it reached something like the authorised strength – two major events occurred which were to have a profound effect on its future. First the French, with Security Council authorisation, intervened in Rwanda with its Opération Turquoise. Considering France's venture into Rwanda in 1994 is beyond the scope of this chapter, but it affected UNAMIR in the short term by causing it to unexpectedly scramble to factor the intervention into its limited operations, and in the longer term by the consequent creation of a French-sponsored 'safe humanitarian zone' in southwest Rwanda. This zone was created in early June and given the French desire to keep the RPA away from it, it seemed at the time as though it might have been created as a last-ditch effort to prop up the faltering Rwandan interim government and its army. If that was the intention Paris failed as both were soon making their way into refuges across Rwanda's borders. The 'safe humanitarian zone' became, however, the place where the mass of Rwanda's Hutu 'internally displaced persons' (IDPs) took shelter from the advancing Tutsi-dominated RPA. By late 1994 the zone hosted nearly 40 IDP camps and perhaps 350,000 IDPs.[13] Getting these people to return to their home communes would prove to be one of the greatest challenges to face UNAMIR and other agencies in 1994–95.

The second major event to affect UNAMIR in mid-a994 was the RPA's victory in the Rwandan Civil War. Despite the strength of the Rwandan Army it proved completely unable to counter the RPA. Since April the rebel army had advanced from north-east Rwanda to take, first the eastern portion of the country, then Kigali, and then, through June, central Rwanda before moving into the west and south-west. There it ran into the French forces deployed for Turquoise and, due to quiet negotiations with the French and under international pressure, it stopped its advance. By mid-July it was the master of the country and justifiably counted itself as the agents of the end of the genocide. With a nod to the Arusha settlement it established the intercommunal Broad-Based Government of National Unity (BBGNU), but as the only large-scale organised element in the country, and the possessor of all the military power, it was quickly

13 'Report of the independent internal commission of inquiry on the events at Kibeho, April 1995, 4, attached to DFAT fax UN5061, New York to Canberra, 19 May 1995, NAA: A9737, 93/060859 part 38; UN Rwanda Emergency Office figures, cited in Prunier, *Africa's World War*, 38. In August the UN thought there might have been 2 to 2.5 million IDPs in southwest Rwanda, DFAT cable NA958, Nairobi to Canberra, 10 August 1994, NAA: A6721, 23170 part 1.

realised that the RPA and its commander, Paul Kagame (now a major general and vice president), were the country's key power brokers.

For UNAMIR this meant several things. First, despite its mandate, its role transformed from trying to implement the Arusha Accords into an *ad hoc* one of assisting a new and immature government in a destabilised and traumatised country. Its relationship with the new government and the RPA became key to its future and its ability to do it job. However, the RPF/RPA's international position as Rwanda's 'good guys', its capriciousness, its ambivalence towards UNAMIR and its own violent tendencies were to, once again, make the UN mission's time in Rwanda challenging. Second, with the RPA's victory Rwanda now seemed *relatively* stable. Countries that had been hesitating over committing peacekeepers, such as Australia and Great Britain, now proved willing to offer them.[14]

3 Increasingly Unwelcome Guests

By late August 1994 UNAMIR' personnel strength was starting to build and operations commenced. It also had a new force commander. Dallaire, by his own later admission, was exhausted and traumatised by what he had witnessed and asked to go home. He thought his Ghanaian deputy, Brigadier General Kwami Anyidoho, should replace him, but Boutros-Ghali overruled him and insisted on seeking another Canadian. Hence, Major General Guy Tousignant took over the appointment on 19 August. One of Dalliare's last acts had been an attempt to have UNAMIR's mandate altered so it could operate along and across Rwanda's borders to counter possible 'subversive activities' by the former-Rwandan government forces. As one diplomat noted, in the aftermath of Somalia picking sides 'to go after the bad guys' did not seem wise to many and with African troop contributors also being cool on the idea, the plan got nowhere in New York.[15] Dallaire, who had been active and vocal about the need to act during the genocide, had also seemingly worn out his welcome with New York and when Tousignant arrived in Kigali he did not know that he was carrying a letter that ordered Dallaire's *immediate* relief – there was no staged 'handover'.[16]

14 For an examination of the interactions of various forms of internal and external pressure, and the situation in Rwanda, on Australia's UNAMIR contribution, see Bou et al., *The Limits of Peacekeeping*, 221–9.

15 Bou et al., *The Limits of Peacekeeping*, pp. 238–9 for a more detailed summary of Dallaire's plan and its rejection.

16 Author's interview, Guy Tousignant, 22 April 2016.

Tousignant and the new Special Representative, Pakistan's Shaharyah Khan, thus were limited to utilising the extant mandates, which was to prove increasingly difficult. Lacking coercive powers under the Chapter VI mandate, UNAMIR was nevertheless responsible for protecting threatened sites and populations. This provision acted as a diplomatic balm in New York during the civil war and genocide, but the RPA's conquest of Rwanda transformed it into a profound complication in Africa. Instead of acting as an independent arbiter between Rwanda's warring parties, UNAMIR now had to work in a country with a new and inexperienced government that in the circumstances was soon widely recognised as the legitimate government, and with a victorious recent rebel army whose own bloody tendencies were to become increasingly apparent. New York wanted co-operation with the new Rwandan government and the RPA, and UNAMIR's ability to stay in the country required their acquiescence, but the mandate technically required the UN force to hold them to account for their actions. This paradox meant the mandate and the reality were not in sympathy and Tousignant quickly found that navigating the space between the two was his greatest challenge. After just a few weeks he concluded the mandate was nearly meaningless in Rwanda and it was simply a case of making the best of the situation.[17] The problem could not be escaped, however, and its tensions were to play out in 1995.

The RPA remained ambivalent about UNAMIR's presence in 1994, or at least it attempted to conceal its contempt, but by early 1995 it was becoming more obviously hostile. It saw itself as the civil war's victor and justifiably claimed to have ended the genocide. It was also anxious to cement its control of the country and about the possibility that their former enemies might restart the war from across the borders. The RPA's attitude to UNAMIR partly stemmed from its criticism of its failures during the genocide, but while this was frequently used as a stick to beat the force and the United Nations for its ineptitude, a more proximate cause for the animus was that the Security Council's mandates made the UN force responsible for the safety of Rwanda's people. For elements of the BBGNU and the RPA this was a direct impingement on the new government's ability to rule Rwanda and probably the key factor in its turn against UNAMIR in 1995.[18]

The biggest problem in UNAMIR–Rwandan relations by late 1994 was what to do with about Rwanda's refugee problem, particularly the IDPs in the southwest. Returning them to their 'home communes' was central plank of Rwanda's 'normalisation' and the new government was also keen to weed out the

17 Author's interview, Guy Tousignant, 22 April 2016.
18 Bou et al., *The Limits of Peacekeeping*, 296–7.

genocidaires sheltering in the camps. A factor in this was the continuing fear of resurgent civil war and the possibility that the IDP camps might became bases for the old regime. Hence in late 1994 the BBGNU, UNAMIR and nearly every international agency in Rwanda combined to execute Operation Retour (Return), which aimed to encourage the IDPs to leave the camps and go home. Unfortunately, it failed completely when the IDP camps' Hutu inhabitants proved mostly unwilling to leave them. This was partly due to NGOs refusing to stop supplying the camps to help Retour, but more important was the real threat of Tutsi reprisals outside the camps, the Rwandan government's arbitrary detention of tens of thousands in overcrowded pestilential jails, and the increasingly apparent violence perpetrated by the RPA in pursuit of its objective of controlling the country. At Busanze IDP camp, near Runyombyi, in January 1995, for example, the RPA opened fire one night in an attempt to close the camp. In doing so they killed about a dozen people and wounded another 35.[19] They succeeded in closing the camp, but the event blended with other stories of RPA violence to confirm the fears of Hutu IDPs and contributed to Retour faltering.

Retour's failure heightened the tension with UNAMIR as the RPA increasingly looked as though it would unilaterally move to close the camps, possibly by force. Tousignant enquired of UN Headquarters at the end of March what UNAMIR should do if this happened given that his mandate specifically charged him to protect Rwanda's people. He was told that UNAMIR could not and should not stand in the way of forcible closure of the camps.[20] As one of Tousignant's national contingent commanders noted in his diary at the time, this seemed 'somewhat at loggerheads with our mandate'.[21] This direction had consequences a few weeks later when, on 19 April, the RPA arbitrarily moved to close four large IDPs in southwest Rwanda. In most instances these closures occurred with a minimum of violence, but at Kibeho the RPA lost control of the situation and itself, killing possibly thousands of IDPs.[22] The Zambian and Australian peacekeepers that were present, partly due to the orders passed

19 Bou et al., *The Limits of Peacekeeping*, 307.

20 Commander Australian Continent [Colonel Peter Warfe] diary entry, 31 March 1995, Australian War Memorial record series (AWM) 323, 46; Author's interview, Guy Tousignant, 22 April 2016.

21 Commander Australian Continent [Colonel Peter Warfe] diary entry, 31 March 1995, AWM323, 46.

22 The death toll was and remains unclear, though UNAMIR went with an informed guess of 2000 at the time. See Bou et al., *The Limits of Peacekeeping*, 321–25, for a consideration of the number killed.

from New York in March, were unable to intervene.[23] While the incident was partly a one-off caused by the RPA unit at Kibeho, it was also part of broader pattern of violent and repressive behaviour by the RPF/RPA in its quest to secure control of the country.

Kibeho was the violent highlight of the paradox of UNAMIR having to police and be reliant on the same people at the same time, but the relationship was increasingly rocky. Partly due to the failure of Retour the Rwandans had been ever more critical of UNAMIR in the first months of 1995. In the lead up to the first anniversary of the genocide, government orchestrated anti-UNAMIR demonstrations had become common and both BBGNU and RPA representatives made it increasingly clear that the UN force was no longer welcome. There were increasing fears that the would be a UNAMIR–RPA clash and, given the hostility and the lack of cooperation from his hosts, by April Tousignant had concluded that his force had outlived its usefulness. The tensions remained high through May, but in June the new Rwandan government got what it wanted at the Security Council, where UNAMIR's mandate was scaled back in early June (Resolution 997), stripping it of its security role. From this point the Rwandans mostly ignored the peacekeepers and Tousignant was reduced to seeking the assistance of the German or US ambassadors to achieve anything. Unhappily he stayed on until December 1995 when India's Brigadier Shiva Kumar took over and supervised the closing of the mission in March 1996.[24]

---

23 For a detailed examination of the Kibeho massacre and its context see Bou et el., *The Limits of Peacekeeping*, 302–39.

24 Bou et al., *The Limits of Peacekeeping*, 296–98.

CHAPTER 5

Rwanda Revisited: UNAMIR II

Australian Reflections on the Mission and the Mandate

Lieutenant-General J.J. Frewen

1 Introduction

All military missions are unique in their own way. For the majority of the Australians, including me, the second United Nations Assistance Mission for Rwanda (UNAMIR II) was our first deployment. We had no previous operational experience to draw on and no context for what we would see. We were also rapidly assembled and deployed. Little was really known about what was actually occurring inside Rwanda. Therefore our training was unavoidably inadequate for what we encountered. I have since served on many missions in conflict zones around the world, from the Pacific to the Middle East. None of those other missions has presented such a profound range of moral, ethical and legal dilemmas as my service with UNAMIR II. These sometimes traumatic experiences, as a young Captain, have served me well in subsequent commands.

Over roughly 12 months during 1994 and 1995, Australia deployed approximately 600 peacekeepers in two contingents in support of UNAMIR II. I was a member of the first of these contingents which encountered the immediate aftermath of the Rwandan genocide and rising tensions with the Rwandan Patriotic Army (RPA). Members of the second Australian contingent would be present at the Kibeho massacre perpetrated by the RPA on Rwandan citizens. The Kibeho massacre still haunts those soldiers who question whether they could have done more to save lives.

While proud of what we did achieve in our specific roles, it is still hard to fathom whether we – and the UN – could have achieved the UN's stated goals. UNAMIR I imploded impotently in the face of the Hutu-driven genocide against the Tutsi. UNAMIR II could not avert the Kibeho massacre. Both missions failed the grand ideals of humanitarian intervention assigned them. The mandate which evolved through these missions is key to why the UN in Rwanda remained underwhelming throughout.

The mandate for UNAMIR II was a topic of debate throughout our time in Rwanda. Were we peacekeepers or peacemakers? What precisely was our relationship to the transitional Rwandan government – a government that had

 | DOI:10.1163/9789004430129_007

seized power through military force but was as yet unelected – and was itself engaged in violence against its own citizens? Did the UN mandate permit the use of force to protect Rwandan citizens from their own government? Would the UN or our own governments support our use of force? Was it ethical or moral to not respond to violence being inflicted upon others because of a UN mandate? Many of these questions are still unanswered.

This paper will describe some of the background to UNAMIR that is relevant to how the mandate took shape and how the mission unfolded within a broader international context. It will then outline the Australian contribution, The Medical Support Force (MSF), and some of its challenges, including rising tensions with host nation RPA. I will highlight some personal experiences from Rwanda which had a lasting impact on me, and offer lessons that have shaped my thinking and operational service since Rwanda.[1] Finally, I will reflect on how effectively UNAMIR II's mandate served the people of Rwanda.

2 The UN Mandate

The UNAMIR mission was established under UN Security Council Resolution 872 on 5 October 1993. Its aim was to facilitate the Arusha Accords including: enhancing the security of the city of Kigali; monitoring the cease-fire agreement; monitoring security in the lead-up to elections; assistance with mine clearances; investigation of alleged non-compliance; monitoring the process of repatriation of Rwandese refugees and resettlement of displaced persons; the coordination of humanitarian assistance activities in conjunction with relief operations; and investigation and reporting on incidents regarding the activities of the gendarmerie and police.

The UN initially struggled to attract contributors, perhaps due to donor fatigue, the United States' recent debacle in Somalia, and a broader debate about the efficacy of UN peacekeeping.[2] Notwithstanding, the UN force gradually reached its target size of 2,500 civilian police and military forces by early April 1994.[3] When widespread violence broke out the UNAMIR Commander, Canadian Major General Romeo Dallaire requested immediate reinforcement but was denied. In the face of chaos and danger – including the murder of 10

1 The majority of my recollections in this paper are from memory or from the personal daily diary that I maintained throughout the tour.

2 The US actively discouraged involvement in accordance with Clinton's Presidential Decision Directive/NSC-25 which set strict criteria for US involvement in peacekeeping operations in the aftermath of Somalia.

3 UN; *Blue Helmets*, 1996, pp. 343–4.

Belgian UN soldiers,[4] – the Security Council voted to reduce the number of troops from 2,500 to 270 personnel on 21 April 1994.

Thereafter, the UN largely became a bystander to the ensuing carnage. In one of Dallaire's parting cables, he wrote: "the [UN] force has been prevented from having a modicum of self-respect and effectiveness on the ground."[5] The lack of international resolve was partly to blame but confusion about UNAMIR's mandate had also contributed to this calamity. Using force to beget humanitarian behaviour was a bridge too far. The UN failed to stem the violence in any meaningful way and its reputation suffered accordingly.

Once the true extent of the genocide became more widely understood, international impetus grew – albeit reluctantly – to return to Rwanda. On 17 May 1994, the Security Council expanded the original UNAMIR mandate and size to include the security and protection of displaced persons, refugees and civilians at risk in Rwanda – including through the establishment and maintenance, where feasible, of secure humanitarian areas; and security and support for the distribution of relief supplies and humanitarian relief operations. This new force was renamed UNAMIR II and called for nearly 5,500 troops.

Contingents of UNAMIR II began arriving gradually from early June 1994 but could not immediately deliver significant effect. The precise nature of the mission also remained unclear. The new mandate was stronger in intent but UN resolutions remained unclear on the right to use force in stopping violence, and all action was contingent on agreement between the opposing parties and the forces available to the UN.[6] This last concession alleviated the nervousness of some UN contributors about likely risks to their troops. Equally, it gave the RPA leeway to prosecute their own aims free of UN interference. This would become increasingly problematic for UNAMIR II as the malignant nature of the RPA became apparent.

One fact in particular caused consternation among UN troops, concerning the nature of their mandate. Significantly, the UNAMIR mission was authorised under Chapter VI of the UN Charter which bound UN troops to peacekeeping activities with concurrence of the parties in Rwanda. This mandate did not support independent or pre-emptive enforcement actions by the UN such as those permitted under Chapter VII of the UN Charter. The key difference is that Chapter VI is typically associated with peacekeeping, keeping

4 The day after the President's assassination, ten Belgian peacekeepers were surrounded then tortured and killed after being ordered by UN headquarters to surrender their weapons.

5 Power, 2002. pp. 329–390.

6 On 19 June, the UN passed Resolution 925 which confirmed that UNAMIR II would not act to separate the two sides in Rwanda.

antagonists apart. Chapter VII infers peacemaking – the authority to actively intervene to influence events or to compel antagonists to comply.

The UNAMIR II mission would never sit neatly on either side of these requirements.

The mission did not require the traditional notion of 'blue helmets' to establish a buffer zone between warring factions, but would require more than the traditionally passive role under Chapter VI mandates. This fact shaped the tone of UNAMIR II and was to confuse and confound UN operations right through to the massacre in Kibeho.

3 The Australian Contribution

Australia did not initially see a national interest in helping Rwanda, and government departments could not agree on a position. The Australian Government opted to send a reconnaissance team and to make a decision based on the findings of their report. The team concluded that UNAMIR II lacked a medical element to support the UN troops, and that the risks associated with such a task in Rwanda were manageable. After months of prevaricating, on 25 July, Australia committed 300 personnel, comprising a military field hospital and an infantry protection element and other supporting capabilities. This decision was born amidst rising public pressure to act and greater surety around the security situation in Rwanda.

The first Australian contingent's preparations were rushed. We would deploy in less than a month, having been drawn from a diverse and disparate range of the three services and units across the Australian Defence Force (ADF). The primary mission was to provide medical support to the UN force, including a surgical capacity. Humanitarian support would also be provided, within 'spare capacity'. For reasons that remain unclear, the health element was assembled *ad-hoc* rather than drawn from a formed field hospital. The security and support elements were drawn from the Army's high-readiness brigade. As with any rapidly formed group, they would commence operations without the tight cohesion and mutual understanding forged within standing organisations.

The force was bespoke and a unique model for the Australians. The nature and mandate of the mission was also, at the least, new ground – and at worst unclear. Training time was limited and other aspects needed attention – in addition to the critical 'rules of engagement' that determine how force may be used. Members of the force progressively converged on Townsville in northern Queensland, eager to learn what their mission would be, what the environment was like, and who they would be working with. Preparations under pressure can help bring people together. In this case confusion around the mission, and the complexities of providing logistics to a new force distant from the contributing units, did not foster immediate harmony.

In particular, tension arose between the medical element – the reason for the contingent – and the infantry force protection element, which was from a rapid-response formation. Tactical command of the medical support force was assigned to the infantry commanding officer, given the security situation. A senior Australian medical officer, attached with a small group of staff officers to the UN Headquarters in Kigali, was the UN Force Medical Officer and the overall Australian contingent commander. This command arrangement also created friction among the Australians. Strained relations would linger and add to the complexity of dealing with challenges later in the mission.

It is reasonable to say that during the pre-deployment training the medical personnel were less focussed on the 'rules of engagement' than the security personnel. The medical team had the additional challenge of forming working units and developing operating methods and procedures for delivering care. Security forces were tasked – above all – to provide protection and were principally interested in threats and the legal use of force. The two elements would continue throughout the mission with these distinct purposes – each not fully understanding the other, and questioning the other's decisions and behaviours from time-to-time.

I arrived in Rwanda on the night of 7 August with the infantry and medical advance party tasked with preparing accommodations and the hospital for arrival of the main force on 21 August. We occupied the Kigali Central Hospital initially and expanded into the lines of the nearby military academy. The sense of the recent chaos was palpable. There was evidence of recent bloodshed everywhere. Unexploded munitions littered the grounds of the hospital. Our new accommodations were filthy, including human excrement and remains. The clean-up task was dangerous and confronting. At the same time, we were dealing with casualty incidents and deaths – many of us for the first time. No running water, sewerage, or electricity were available; even when the main contingent arrived a few weeks later.

The first contingent got about its work efficiently and was soon learning the ways of UN missions. The hospital began receiving UN patients immediately. Minor illnesses mainly. Occasionally, something more serious caught our attention – such as a British soldier who had lost a leg to a mine while repairing a bridge. Although, our Health Company was intended to service UN personnel, we were advised that under the agreement between the UN and the Rwandan Government we also had to provide treatment to their officials, as required.

This was not too problematic short of the occasional misunderstandings and rude behaviour that confronted our medical staff. It is typical of Australian troops – and of specialists (particularly surgeons) – to keep busy and to help others as best they can. This led to a growing number of civilian patients passing through our care, within our 'spare' capacity.

Our primary purpose was supporting the UN itself but demand in this regard was not high. Support to civilians became the mainstay of our hospital and magnificent work was done helping innocent victims of violence. The Australian hospital, and our detachments outside of Kigali, helped hundreds of people with the most horrendous wounds. Mines, machetes, burns and vehicle accidents featured prominently. Tropical diseases also presented that our doctors recalled learning about at medical college with the proviso that, 'they would never see them in the modern age.' Our medical staff worked at a rate and intensity not seen since the Vietnam War. These patients were not the main reason Australia joined the mission, but they were where we did the most good. We filled a void 'within surplus capacity' to the benefit of ordinary people. We provided hope to many and felt, in this regard, we had made a real difference.

Even in humanitarian medical support there were sometimes interesting ethical challenges. It was natural to question what priority a suspected murderous member of a militia should receive for medical treatment.[7] Equally, when the RPA insisted a terminal patient be kept alive, consuming scarce resources and energy. Through all this, the medical staff remained professional and consistent regardless of who they treated, as should be expected. If anything, the medical support to the many civilian Rwandans who passed through our hospital was the Australian's most lasting legacy from UNAMIR II.

The Australians were also drawn into other projects beyond our particular UN medical mandate. We supported a campaign of inoculation for children in remote areas. We supported the distribution of the new Rwandan currency across the land (intended to deny those in exile their reserves of the former currency). We provided legal advice that sought to restore the devastated justice sector from root to branch. And, we participated in the UN's *Operation Retour* to return internally displaced persons (IDPs) from the large camps to their home villages. Yet all of this compassionate contribution to the well-being and future of Rwanda was not enough to win the affection of the RPA. Within weeks of our arrival, a cautious and strained relationship had taken shape with the RPA. This was not what we expected.

7 I learned in Rwanda that you can identify a killer by their eyes. Even in a crowd, there was an intense stare that typically belonged to a militia member with a murderous past.

4 Tensions with the RPA

Our assumption prior to arrival was that we would be regarded as altruistic and impartial. The true situation, as with any conflict zone, was complex and opaque. As we adapted to our new surrounds, we began to get a sense of the UN – of who was useful and who was not. We grew increasingly aware of non-governmental organisations (NGOs) – and which were effective or otherwise. We built the relationships essential to operating effectively. Despite friendly attempts, however, we never established an easy rapport with the RPA.

Australian soldiers naturally seek to form amiable bonds with others without dropping their guard. They use humour to establish relationships while avoiding becoming a soft target. In danger they typically respond aggressively. In these new circumstances, and with the recent fate of the Belgians in our minds, our security posture was robust and intended to deter. This was appropriate but we misjudged two things initially. The RPA's true intentions and their perceptions of us.

From the beginning, the RPA's attitude toward us swung from begrudging acceptance to outright hostility. We were slow to comprehend, and optimistic we could win them over. Their attitude was part annoyance at the UN's presence and part bristling at the perceived arrogance of Western forces who had not, as they had, recently liberated Rwanda. In their minds, we were not suitably deferential, and an impediment to their future designs. Adding salt to wounds were our armoured personnel carriers (APCs) that gave them the impression of an occupying force determined to outmatch their lightly armed forces. To them we were an unwelcome, if not overbearing, imposition.

We believed our mandate had taken us to Rwanda to help the new nation, and were frustrated that the RPA was inhibiting us from doing so. Relations with the RPA could be cordial but they frequently held us up seemingly randomly at checkpoints (despite the UN's agreed right to free access). Occasionally they threatened us, brazenly pointed weapons at us, and more rarely seized our vehicles or equipment. Grievances over perceived slights were overblown and public. We were agog that this was how they treated a UN assistance mission. Increasingly, we regarded them with suspicion and caution.

Neither peacekeepers nor peacemakers, we had become a complicating part of an ecosystem still ridding itself of the anti-bodies from a genocide and a civil war. The RPA was preparing itself to become an independent, albeit Tutsi-dominated, new nation. Our mission was deployed into this environment without clarity on what should be done. The two parties to the dispute were a self-appointed rather than elected government – and a defeated government with its armed elements now either dispersed through IDP camps or in self-imposed exile in neighbouring countries. It also soon became apparent to us that the RPA had unfinished business with its former foes and adversaries.

Although the civil war was over, the violence continued. Groups such as the *Interahamwe* acted violently within the IDP camps and struck out into the surrounding countryside. The RPA settled scores and extracted extra-judicial revenge for these incursions. We began to understand that the RPA were neither welcoming nor benign. Increasingly, the RPA hampered our operations both routinely and for nefarious reasons. We became increasingly involved in circumventing RPA and Rwandan Government excesses, while their resistance to our presence grew.

The problematic relationship, and confusion about our mandate, played out in many ways. Could, or should, we force our way through an RPA checkpoint that explicitly contradicted our UN mandate? How tolerant should we be in the face of threats from the RPA, including having loaded weapons pointed at us? Should we hand over militia members suspected of abhorrent crimes to the RPA when we could not expect them to receive fair trial? Many questions such as these were referred to our higher headquarters, and often then on to UN headquarters. Most commonly the answer was down the path of least resistance, typically avoiding conflict in favour of the RPA. Ultimately, this would come to a shocking head at Kibeho in April 1995.

5 Formative Experiences

Regardless of which contingent we served with, Rwanda proved a profound experience for the Australians who served there. We learned many lessons about ourselves, about the nature of operational service, and about how UN missions function. As I mentioned earlier, these lessons have stayed with me throughout my career.

UN contingents are a diverse family and in Rwanda many national sensitivities were managed in-house. As a general observation, I was surprised to find that not all UN contingents approached the mission in the same way. I was shocked to learn that some UN contingents appeared to have little interest in the mandate and were happy to bide their time without incident, collecting UN allowances and passing the time as best they could. Occasionally, we suspected or witnessed confronting behaviours among other UN elements including paedophilia and brutality. These actions were reported to higher headquarters but, typically, no response was forthcoming but it was not possible to know whether the perpetrators were actually punished.

In the humanitarian domain, I witnessed NGOs doing remarkably selfless and compassionate work. I also saw the opposite. Not all NGOs welcomed our presence or support. Some fiercely protected their independence and neutrality. Others were concerned that we might somehow move into their patch and undermine their relevance. More than once I encountered individuals more concerned about their own inadequate conditions than delivering aid. Such manifestly different motivations among Australian troops and NGOs was a disconcerting revelation to me but I became less naïve. Three particular incidents left more profound impressions on me.

6 Dealing with Horror

During my time in Rwanda I confronted horror or managed troops who had been exposed to traumatic events. On arrival, the advance party discovered the evidence of terrible crimes. We had to remove human remains, scrub bloody hand-prints from walls, and disinfect an entire hospital returning it to operations from an abhorrent state. Later I visited the massacre site at the Ntarama Church (also detailed by Bruce Oswald in his article). There, well-dressed human remains lay intermingled among church pews. The bodies of those who had attempted to flee the church lay as evidence of the sadistic execution by machete.

Elsewhere, some of our soldiers responded to an emergency call and discovered a recently murdered family in the dark evening. I was involved in supervising our troops recovering a body from a well which came apart while being raised by grappling hook and ropes.

The most harrowing for me was the clean-up of the morgue at the Kigali hospital by a small group of soldiers. This was the advance party's third day in-country, (we handled a mass-casualty incident of nine victims the following day). Two adult bodies had been left in the small morgue without power. In the African heat, they had decomposed in their trays. The smell was revolting and the remains sloshed about onto our boots and clothes. Most of us vomited at least once. Later we had to hand-scrub the stench from clothing. Most distressingly, we found a small elaborate sarcophagus which contained an infant child. The obvious care for the remains stood in stark contrast to the evil brutality that marked the surrounding area. It was striking and hard to reconcile – but it reinforced to how fragile civilisation is and how quickly and deeply it can sink.

We were ill-prepared psychologically for Rwanda and had inadequate support while deployed. Our Army has learned much since then but this was too late for many of our contingent. As a result of Rwanda, I have a sure sense of what soldiers should, and shouldn't, be expected to do without adequate training or equipment. I understand the damage that wrong decisions can cause. On more than one subsequent mission, I have barred my soldiers from being involved in the extraction of human remains (even those who volunteered). In each case I insisted that appropriately trained and equipped specialists be employed for the task. Despite the friction this caused, I am confident I have saved soldiers from unnecessary trauma and debilitation.

I also learned how to do first-aid debriefing of a critical incident. This involves having individuals share what they saw and felt as soon after an event as possible to bring context to their own reactions. I had not spoken of my emotions during the first week in Rwanda and experienced recurring disturbing images in dreams. Without good training, the desire to not appear weak was an overwhelming one that did more harm than good. Again, on numerous occasions since, I have employed this method after traumatic events with, I believe, good effect in helping soldiers to avoid deeper adverse reactions. These were hard won lessons but in time they helped me to be a better leader.

7 Why Discipline Matters

As I have described, we experienced frustration (and sometimes anger) in our dealings with the RPA. Their behaviour towards us included dangerous provocations that could have warranted force in return. Pleasingly, the Australians never responded with force even though some circumstances might have justified it. One example is when an RPA soldier – after a heated exchange at a checkpoint – fired at, and struck, an Australian vehicle as it departed. The young Australian soldier trained his weapon on the Rwandan soldier but had the composure to decide that the Rwandan was aiming at a tyre, not the passengers. If the rifle had been parallel to the ground, our soldier would have shot him and unleashed certain other chaos.

Two 'Mexican' style stand-offs occurred between the RPA and Australians during the first contingent. I was involved in both. The latter occurred at the front-gate of our barracks in Kigali toward the end of our six-month tour. It concerned our Commanding Officer and an irate Rwandan Officer who claimed the Australians had deliberately collided with his vehicle. This resulted in an Australian vehicle and equipment being seized by the RPA (supported by the direction of UN Headquarters). These were not returned for some days and increased our frustration both with the RPA and the true nature of our mandate. Fortunately, despite loaded weapons and high tension, the incident was resolved peaceably through some tense negotiation.[8]

Earlier in the tour, I was called from a meeting in the small UN Headquarters in Butare by an Australian Corporal. The Corporal indicated that Australian soldiers had brought a Zambian UN soldier to the compound for safety after he had accidentally struck and killed an RPA pedestrian with his truck. The Australian Section had witnessed the incident and had made a quick decision to grab the Zambian and bring him to safety. But by now the RPA had discovered the Zambian's location and were clearly baying for vengeance.

When I arrived at the gate of the walled UN compound, I discovered an Australian Infantry Section lined across the front of the gate with their rifles aimed at a larger force of RPA across the road. They were lined out also, with many more weapons including machine guns (and at least one rocket propelled grenade) pointed back at the Australians. The RPA soldiers looked poorly trained and the weapons appeared in a poor state of maintenance (a combination more likely to result in an accidental discharge). The Rwandan in-charge was furious and threatening to open fire if we did not accede to his demands.

This was a highly dangerous and volatile situation. I immediately ordered the Australian Corporal to have his men apply their safety-catches, lower their weapons, and march 100m down the hill. He hesitated, but did as directed. This placated the Rwandan officer and, after urging, he had his men also lower their weapons.

I made a deal with the RPA then headed down to the Australians to reassure them that they had acted under my orders and that they should not feel humiliated. One soldier obviously disagreed, having not unloaded his weapon as directed. He was admonished by the Corporal then and later disciplined. Fortunately, he had not resisted more stridently and made the situation worse. The incident underscored the importance of military discipline. That it must, in some situations, be total and immediate despite adrenalin or anger. It also accentuated the role of young officers, who through selection and training must bring an additional layer of judgement and context to that of the soldier.

8 Kibeho–a Mandate Gone Wrong

The second Australian contingent's mission and mandate remained the same as the first's. Unlike the initial contingent, they had more time to prepare and

8 For an interesting legal perspective, see also Bruce Oswald's account of his role in this incident in "UNAMIR: A Deployed Legal Offi cer's Retrospective" pp. 95–115.

to build a cohesive team and identity. They came to Rwanda better prepared and – reasonably – determined to avoid repeating the mistakes of their predecessors. They wore different headdress to the first contingent – baseball caps instead of slouch hats – specifically to let the Rwandans know that they would take a different approach. The second Australian contingent sought to establish better relations with the RPA and to be more gracious guests in Rwanda. While this may have been positive in the short-term, events at Kibeho revealed the true nature of the RPA all too vividly in April 1995. Neither goodwill nor a mandate could avoid the calamity at Kibeho.

I had visited Kibeho many times during my tour.[9] At its height, we estimated 140,000 Rwandans sought refuge there.[10] Despite RPA exhortations to leave, by April 1995 there was still an estimated 50,000-strong population. One explanation suggested a fabled appearance of the Virgin Mary at Kibeho in 1981 had caused people to flock there during the genocide. Opponents of the RPA coerced refuge-seekers to stay to maintain the sanctuary within which to hide.

I returned to Australia in late February 1995 once the second contingent had arrived. I was saddened, but not surprised, at news that a massacre had occurred at Kibeho on 22 April. A few days earlier, amid rising tensions, 32 Australians had arrived at the camp to reinforce the small Zambian contingent there.

Two battalions of RPA had surrounded the camp and began a cordon-and-sweep clearance including the indiscriminate use of machine guns. Once the killing started in earnest, the Australians – who had been expressly ordered by their own national command not to use force – did their best to help. They were massively out-numbered and out-gunned and acted heroically in the face of a murderous RPA who demanded they not intervene. They saved many Rwandans but were horrified by what they witnessed, and distressed at their powerlessness to stop the RPA.

I spoke to one Australian veteran by phone from Australia shortly after he returned to Kigali from Kibeho. He said during the aftermath Australians had counted 4000 bodies with pace-counters. He believed they were only half-way through the camp when the RPA removed the remaining bodies. His estimation was that 8000 Rwandans had perished. A later UN report would conclude that only a few hundred had been killed. The discrepancy is hard to reconcile and has compounded the suffering of the Australians present at Kibeho. It's difficult not to conclude that the UN response to the massacre was another

9 Kibeho is around a 2.5 hour drive South-West from Kigali.
10 Captain J.J. Frewen, Personal Diary, Rwanda 1994–5.

example of shying away from hard and direct criticism of the transitional Rwandan government and its troops.

It has been argued that Australian troops at Kibeho were lawfully authorised to use proportionate force against the RPA to protect innocent civilians. However, precisely where the UN stood in relation to the RPA was unclear at this time. As it was, it was not only the oblique UN mandate that prevented aggressive Australian action at Kibeho. In fact, it was a direct order of the commanding officer of the second contingent that expressly forbade them to do so. Notwithstanding, the Australians saved many lives under fire that day without using their own weapons. Four of the 32 present were to receive gallantry awards – the first Australians to be recognised in this way since the Vietnam War. Confusion as to whether the UN mandate or UN politics had a hand in the decision to not react with force avoids the grim reality that Australian forces at Kibeho were massively out-numbered and out-gunned. And, that any use of force by them would almost certainly have led to their own extermination. How did Australian troops come to be in this situation?

In early February 1995, a UN Tactical Headquarters (TAC HQ) in Butare was coordinating UN efforts to empty out the IDP camps across the South-West of Rwanda know as *Operation Retour*. I was then commanding an Australian detachment of medics, logisticians and infantry in support of this operation. Each day we would visit camps such as Cyanika, Rukondo and Kibeho. Our role was to provide medical and dental screening of IDPs to ensure they were fit to be transported back to their villages. Our work was carried out under the watchful eye of RPA soldiers. We would check individuals, conduct minor medical and dental procedures where appropriate and issue medicines. Occasionally, the RPA would detain and remove individuals who they had an interest in. This was disconcerting but it was not our role to intervene. At best, we were uncertain of their fate.

Operation Retour was being undertaken to disestablish the camps which had appeared during the French *Operation Turquoise*.[11] These camps were considered eyesores and an international embarrassment by the RPA. They also knew that their enemies were hiding within them. *Operation Retour* made slow progress repatriating the IDPs. Many IDPs were wary of returning to their

11 As UNAMIR II took shape, the French launched *Operation Turquoise*. Portrayed as a humanitarian intervention, ulterior French motivations were unclear and international reception was mixed. The US supported the move as it delivered a credible military force to the crisis. The RPA were wary of French meddling and denounced the intervention. Despite concerns, the UN granted the French a Chapter VII resolution on 22 June (UN Resolution 929). This intervention led to the establishment of camps such as Kibeho in the safe-haven created in the South West of Rwanda.

villages due to rumours of revenge fuelled violence. Some would return but then walk back to the IDP camps (sometimes 20–30 kilometres or more) where food and water, and perhaps medical support, was assured. Return journeys to the camps made the numbers of repatriated people seem more impressive impressive due to double-counting. Some camps closed but others, most notably, Kibeho, remained.

Complicating progress was the fact that some NGOs cooperated with the UN plan but others, such as the International Community of the Red Cross (ICRC), did not. The ICRC wished to remain independent. They also appeared to need supplies moving at scale. This undermined the UN's intent to progressively cut aid to the camps as an incentive to return home. Slow progress increasingly frustrated the RPA. On 8 February at the TAC HQ in Butare I was told by an agitated senior RPA officer that if the UN did not close the camps before the wet season commenced that they would use, "all means at their disposal" to do so. I reported this thinly veiled threat to my own headquarters as its intent was clear. I returned to Australia soon after.

The RPA had made their intention clear some months before. The UN had chosen either to not take this seriously or had failed to position adequate forces to fulfil the May 1994 resolution to provide, "…security and protection of displaced persons, refugees and civilians at risk…" Australian troops at Kibeho had a right to intervene to protect the innocent but not the means. Sensibly, they had been ordered not to place themselves in futile risk. The mandate of UNAMIR II foresaw a threat to IDPs and civilians but the UN had not carried through on it. Additional UN infantry could have been deployed to Kibeho as a deterrent to the RPA (for example, UNAMIR II had infantry battalions from Ghana, Ethiopia and Zambia among other combat troops available). I do not know why they were not, but suspect the awkward accommodation of the unelected Kagame government and the broader reluctance of the international community to use force were both at play. The mandate might have made a difference but, for whatever reasons, the will did not exist.

This sad episode reinforced the importance of discipline in carrying out orders. It also heightened my admiration for the troops who were forced to swallow such a bitter pill. What it taught me most of all is an abiding scepticism as to how controversy is managed at a strategic level. This has served me well in resolving multi-national incidents on other operations. It has also made me acutely aware of the need to understand the precise implications of the letter and spirit of a mandate. It is something I have sought to thoroughly test in predeployment training scenarios ever since.

9 Did UNAMIR II Succeed?

Timing and context conspired to undermine UN efforts in Rwanda. UNAMIR I had failed to avoid the 1994 genocide and disintegrated in ignominy. It lacked the mandate and forces to check a rapidly declining situation – and no reinforcements were forthcoming. Western powers were torn over the relevance of Africa, the dangers of missions like Somalia and Bosnia, and what should or could be achieved in Rwanda. In particular, the US actively petitioned to avoid the UN assembling a subsequent response but other States were also slow to react and there was an inherent lack of will to respond with force.[12]

UNAMIR II, though well intentioned, arrived too slowly to be relevant to a Rwanda by then settling into its new phase of existence. The victims of the genocide and subsequent violence were doubly unlucky. (Western) ghosts of Somalia contributed to both the lack of a timely rescue and the reluctance to intervene strongly. Notwithstanding Rwanda's current status as a thriving African society – under the apparent President-for-life, Paul Kagame – the journey there has been marred by scandalous behaviour by all parties. Those who acted evilly and those who looked away. Like UNAMIR I, UNAMIR II was to become little more than a bystander to the terrible drama playing out before them. The UN, the RPA, and the global context shared responsibility for this state of UNAMIR IIs semi-paralysis.

Even with limited US support, a case can be made that the UN and contributing countries could have reacted more effectively to the genocide and the civil war in Rwanda 1994. *Operation Turquoise* is an example of how even a relatively small, but determined, force can make a difference. The force the UN eventually assembled under UNAMIR II could have acted more robustly within the resources and mandate it had. The UN could have legally placed a larger and more determined force at Kibeho to act as a deterrent, if it had chosen to do so. A reluctance to act in this way remained evident throughout the UNAMIR II. We helped Rwanda where we could, and where they would let us – as neither peacekeepers nor peacemakers in the traditional sense. In retrospect, I feel that we acted more as representatives of peace, where no true peace had yet settled. And, that we only did this to the extent permissible to the UN and the RPA.

Symptomatic of the inherent ambiguity within the mission was that an earlier UN decision to extend the UNAMIR mandate (to 29 July 1994) was

12 The exception was the French, whose decisive actions under a Chapter VII mandate would unintentionally sow the seeds of the atrocity at Kibeho.

made despite serious reservations. The UN expressed "deep concern at the delay in the establishment of the broad-based transitional Government and the Transitional National Assembly" and "concern at the deterioration in security in the country, particularly in Kigali." Neither of these had improved by the end of 1994 nor had the UN's ability to influence them. At the strategic level, the UN was ineffectual in bringing the Rwandan nation forward in a manner that pleased or comforted them. At the tactical level, they were doing what they could but in-spite of the nation they were trying to support.

10 Conclusion

The transitional Rwandan government could have been more benevolent and lawful in its treatment of its own citizens. It chose not to be. Some of the RPA's poor behaviour could have been constrained by UNAMIR II if the UN had resolved to do so. Again, the UN did not. Choices were made by both parties within the broader political context. This draws on the privilege of hindsight but debate to this effect was alive among members of the Australian contingents of UNAMIR II at the time. Regardless of whether UNAMIR II was established under Chapter VI or Chapter VII of the UN charter in 1994, the international will did not exist to enforce either to their full extent. As Australians with UNAMIR II, we understood our mandate but we also understood it would not be fully enforced. In the geo-political context of the time, this was probably as good as we could expect.

The experience of UNAMIR II was intense and formative. Like many fellow UNAMIR II veterans, damage was incurred personally, but – for me – the ultimate result was beneficial to my ongoing military service. I prefer to consider my outcome as post-traumatic growth. For others, the outcome was not so positive and I understand their grief. Fortunately, I have been able to take lessons from this troubled operation that have contributed to better outcomes in other areas of conflict, and have helped avoid unnecessary damage to my soldiers. Of course, we were there, above all, to assist innocent Rwandans, Hutu and Tutsi.

Tragically, for the victims of Kibeho, and the countless other Rwandans who suffered, UNAMIR II came with too little, too late, and without the resolve to intervene decisively. How might the world and the UN react to the same circumstance in central Africa today? Recent and ongoing events in the Ukraine, South Sudan, Libya and Syria do not give cause for comfort. If anything, these conflicts suggest that the civilised world is still to find an effective collective response to violent humanitarian crises. Some humanitarian situations will require the use of force to resolve. Some will require risk to life and limb – beyond limited national interests – and in pursuit of a more noble causes. I learned in Rwanda that having a mandate is one thing – but having the collective will to use it is another.

CHAPTER 6

UNAMIR: a Deployed Legal Officer's Retrospective

Bruce 'Ossie' Oswald

1 Introduction*

This paper focuses on three legal issues that I dealt with during my deployment to Rwanda which have had an ongoing impact on my practice as a military lawyer, as well as my research and writing as an academic.[1] These issues are: (1) investigating the mass grave site at Ntarama; (2) the use of force in defence of the mandate and individual self-defence; and (3) detention. One of my primary aims in writing this paper is to explain how tactical issues often unfold and take on legal dimensions.

2 Investigating the Mass Grave Site at Ntarama

On 14 September 1994, I was called to the office of the Commanding Officer of the Medical Support Force (MSF), Lieutenant Colonel Pat McIntosh, to be briefed on an alleged mass grave site about one hour away from Kigali, in a village called Ntarama. At that time, I was serving in Rwanda as a legal officer to the Medical Support Force (MSF) and in that capacity appointed to the Headquarters (HQ) MSF. The briefing Officer explained to me that UNAMIR had been notified that a mass killing had occurred in and around Ntarama and the UN wanted a report on the following matters:

1. Confirmation that there had been a mass killing in Ntarama,
2. Information about the victims,

* Unless otherwise stated, the primary source for the material in this chapter is from the diary that I kept while serving in Rwanda.

1 I deployed to Rwanda on 20 August 1994 and left Rwanda to return to Australia on 20 February 1995. I served as the legal officer to the Medical Support Force (MSF) and in that capacity appointed to the Headquarters (HQ) MSF. For a more detailed history and analysis of the MSF and the Australian contingents that served in Rwanda see Jean Bou, Chapters 8–11 in Jean Bou, Bob Breen, David Horner, Garth Pratten, and Miesje De Vogel, *The Limits of Peacekeeping: Australian Missions in Africa and the Americas*, 1992–2005, Volume IV (Cambridge, 2018). [Thereafter Official History].

 | DOI:10.1163/9789004430129_008

3. Information about those that had committed the mass killing,
4. Information as to why the mass killing had been committed, and
5. Information about the current and potential health risks for the community living in and around Ntarama.

To complete the task, UNAMIR Headquarters (HQ) decided to send the UNAMIR HQ health officer (an Australian Army Captain), the Australian Intelligence Officer, two officers from UNAMIR HQ and myself. We were accompanied by an infantry protection party consisting of a section of Australian Infantry.

We drove to Ntarama on 15 September and arrived around mid-morning. A couple of the villagers spoke English and explained to me that on or about 8 April either the Interahamwe or the Rwandan Government Forces (RGF) entered the village and started to separate the Tutsis from the Hutus. They told the Hutus that they were free to go and told the Tutsis to gather in the Ntarama chapel. They recounted that after the separation had occurred the Tutsis were massacred in the chapel and those that had tried to escape were hunted down and killed. One of the witnesses walked with me to the chapel.

The closer I got to the chapel the more obvious it became that there were a great many decomposing bodies in the vicinity. Between where we were parked and the chapel I counted close to a hundred bodies. On entering the chapel, I saw that bodies were in a high state of decomposition. I noted the following:

> The ages of the victims ranged from young children to adults and consisted of both sexes. Clearly in places there were family groups.... There were at least 300 bodies in the church. The only way to traverse the church was to walk from pew to pew, as the bodies were piled up to at least the height of the pews. There were many bodies piled up around the altar. Most of the victims appeared to have been attacked with machetes or clubs. Very few bullet holes were in the building structure. Many of the victims appeared to have been decapitated...other wounds included the loss of limbs and trauma to the chest area.

At the same time, we were carrying out our investigations Scott Peterson, an international journalist, was also gathering material to write a story about what had happened at the Ntarama. Scott wrote:

> The bodies were packed between the bench pews. Two feet deep, 300 or so...[c]hildren stood at the door, inspecting the bodies too, and played outside, numbed by months of watching the decay. Every day they played here. The stinking air stuck in their mouths, and they spit often. Inside, a

> useless rosary hung from a desiccated wrist. There was no one to bury the bodies – every family member had been killed.[2]

It was difficult to move in the chapel without standing on bodies. I resorted to jumping from one pew to another. The other officers carrying out their investigation also found it difficult not to crunch 'bones underfoot as they took photographs and diagrammed the site. They couldn't help it.'[3]

Our protection party of infantry soldiers found the chapel and its surrounds difficult to deal with. The Section Commander came up to me after some time and asked if he could take his soldiers outside the village to set up an outer protection cordon. He said his soldiers had had enough of the sight of dead bodies and smell of decomposing flesh. Of course, I gave him permission to redeploy his soldiers.

Before leaving the site, I felt it was important for all of us to spend a few moments in thought and prayer about what we had experienced by entering Ntarama. Scott recorded some of what I said:

> Lord…[t]hese people obviously sought sanctuary in your house and it was not provided to them. May the spirit of their souls rest in your Heavenly abode forever…[a]lso we ask that you provide us with understanding, so that when we go away we will know how this can be your will…'[4]

On my return to Kigali I completed my report and submitted it to UNAMIR HQ recommending that UNAMIR, in conjunction with the Office of the UN High Commissioner for Human Rights and national Rwandan authorities, carry out a more detailed investigation of the site to find the perpetrators of the massacre.

A few days after handing in my report, McIntosh told me that he had received a call from UNAMIR HQ telling him that UNAMIR were not going to undertake any more investigations of mass grave sites in Rwanda. I was perplexed as to why the HQ had taken this approach. On my next visit to the HQ, I made some inquiries concerning the report and was told that the Office of the High Commissioner for Human Rights (OHCHR) had complained about UNAMIR doing the report. OHCHR considered it within their mandate and not within the mandate of uniformed peacekeepers. I responded by emphasising that

2 Scott Peterson, *Me Against my Brother: At War in Somalia, Sudan and Rwanda* (Routledge, 2000), p. 320.

3 *Ibid.*

4 *Ibid.*

gathering evidence of mass atrocities like the one in Ntarama was important and needed to be done as soon as possible, including by peacekeepers if necessary. I remember feeling quite upset with the approach taken by the OHCHR.

Once the word got out about Ntarama several people in the Australian contingent and at UNAMIR HQ asked if they could visit the site. McIntosh firmly forbade such visits 'on the grounds that it was grisly tourism and that, given that they had arrived in the recent aftermath of the genocide, there was plenty of death to see in Rwanda anyway.'[5] I understand that the Commanding Officer of the contingent that followed us did not have a similar attitude. The official history of Australian peacekeeping published by the Australian War Memorial records that 'Roche [CO of the 2nd contingent] six months on, [thought that such visits]...was a way of developing an understanding of events among his contingent members.'[6]

Today Ntarama is a Genocide memorial and a tourist site. The Visit Rwanda website explains:

> The Ntarama church was converted into a genocide memorial on the 14th April 1995 and was dedicated to over 5000 people who lost their lives in this place. Ntarama which is one of the six national Genocide memorial sites contains human clothing's, remains and artefacts which belong to those who were killed at the church, these items have remained at display all times. During the Genocide, the Tutsis persecuted much of the population who sought sanctuary in the catholic churches believing that they would be protected and safe there. It's also thought that church leaders informed the Hutus of the secret mass of Tutsis who were in the churches, and the Hutus stormed the churches and killed all the people.[7]

I am unsure where the reference to 5000 people stems from but accept that my investigation did not extend to visiting other buildings in the village.

3 Looking Back

Since my visit to Ntarama there are two matters I have reflected on. First, is the importance of ensuring that soldiers are prepared to deal with visiting sites

5 Official History, n 1, p. 288.

6 *Ibid.*

7 Visit Rwanda, Ntarama Genocide Memorial https://www.visitrwandaguide.com/rwanda-safari/ntarama-genocide-memorial-rwanda/ accessed 29 January 2019.

of mass trauma, and that they can speak to others to process what they have seen. In some senses we were akin to police officers, fireman and paramedics who deal with mass trauma as a part of their work. Clearly, we had a job to do and that job necessitated not only visiting Ntarama but undertaking the investigation.

There is a difference in visiting such sites because you have a job to do, as opposed to visiting them as a tourist. I have often wondered how a tourist gains a better understanding of what occurred by visiting a mass grave site. Perhaps, if I visited Ntarama today I too would feel like Scott when he returned to visit another mass grave site in Rwanda:

> When I returned [to Nyarubye] one year after the killing, when Nyarubuye was a must-see site for "body tourists," I was disappointed. The impact had diminished with the passage of time...The evidence of sacrilege was disappearing, something I found difficult to accept.[8]

For those who were with me in Ntarama, it might be consoling to know that the International Criminal Tribunal for Rwanda sentenced Mr Franqois Karera in 2007 to imprisonment for the rest of his life for, among other crimes, genocide. The Tribunal found him guilty of being present during the attack on the Tutsis in the church, for encouraging the attack, and for participating in the attack.[9]

The second matter that I reflect on is whether it was appropriate for me to do the first investigation of the events that unfolded in Ntarama. Put another way, was it appropriate for the OHCHR to insist that they were the appropriate body to carry out the investigations? As a lawyer I know that gathering evidence must be left to experts. However, at the time I was concerned to act swiftly, so that the evidence would not deteriorate to the point where it would be useless to anyone seeking to prosecute those who had committed the mass killings. At one level, it would have been unforgiveable to know of the crimes committed in Ntarama and not to investigate what happened there as soon as possible. At another level, I can understand the OHCHR's perspective of ensuring that the investigations were done consistently and thoroughly.

In any case, on 15 October 1994, the UNAMIR Force Commander issued a directive entitled *Force Commander's Directive on Mass Graves and Alleged Massacre Site Registration, Investigation and Handling*. In that directive he outlined UNAMIR's policy on registration and handling of mass graves; and

8 Peterson, n 2, pp. 320–21.

9 *The Prosecutor v Franqois Karera*, ICTR Case No. ZCTR-01-74, 7 December 2007.

emphasised that human rights bodies and the Rwandan Broad Based Government of National Unity (BBGNU) had the responsibility to investigate mass grave sites. He made it clear that UNAMIR personnel were not to investigate such sites unless specifically ordered to do so by his HQ.

Rather than banning UNAMIR forces from undertaking investigations of mass grave sites, particularly given that they were often the first to arrive at such sites, UNAMIR could have developed better guidance for its forces. For example, UNAMIR with OHCHR could have developed a directive which encapsulated the relevant UN standards and guidelines, and best practice for gathering evidence of mass grave sites. The OHCHR later issued such guidance for the International Force East Timor (INTERFET).[10] That note dealt with basic principles and measures to preserve physical evidence so that it could be used by tribunals and courts. The need to preserve the chain of custody was one of the key points made by the note. This is perhaps an example of how learnings from peacekeeping missions such as Rwanda have been able to inform practices in future missions.

4 Use of Force and ROE

UNAMIR's mandate (pursuant to Security Council resolution 918) was:

> 3 (a) To contribute to security and protection of displaced persons, refugees and civilians at risk in Rwanda, including through the establishment and maintenance, where feasible, of secure humanitarian areas;
> (b) To provide security and support for the distribution of relief supplies and humanitarian relief operations.[11]

Based on this mandate UNAMIR peacekeepers were expressly authorised to use force to:

(1) protect three categories of persons: internally displaced persons (IDPs), refugees and civilians at risk;

10 Office of the High Commissioner for Human Rights, *Note on Guidance for multinational peace-keeping force in East Timor on preservation of evidence*, 28 September 1999 reprinted in Australian Defence Force Military Law Centre, *Law and Military Operation in East Timor Sep 1999 – Feb 2000: Lessons Learnt for Legal Officers* (inhouse publication, undated).

11 United Nations Security Council (UNSC) Resolution 918 of 7 May 1994, S/RES/918 (1994) operative para 3.

(2) establish and maintain secure humanitarian areas to enhance the security and protection of IDPs, refugees and civilians at risk; and
(3) protect the distribution of relief supplies.

When interpreting the justification for the use of force to protect individuals, relief supplies and humanitarian areas, the Security Council used the doctrine of self-defence by recognising that:

> UNAMIR may be required to take action in self-defence against persons or groups who threaten protected sites and populations, United Nations and other humanitarian personnel or the means of delivery and distribution of humanitarian relief.[12]

When interpreting the above quoted paragraphs, there was some confusion at UNAMIR HQ as to whether the right to use force to protect civilians stood separate to the doctrine of individual self-defence. There were some at UN HQ who disagreed that the provisions enabled the use of force, and who argued that the doctrine of individual self-defence did not extend to allow forceful protection of non-UN personnel, and more importantly, forceful protection of civilians from the Rwandan Patriotic Army (RPA). This narrow approach was taken on the basis that resolution 918 was a Chapter VI operation rather than a Chapter VII operation[13] (because the resolution did not state that it was passed pursuant to Chapter VII)[14] and therefore a narrow interpretation of the use of force in self-defence should be adopted. This interpretation was narrower than the interpretation I argued for at the time.

The debate concerning a broader approach to acting in individual self-defence to protect any person who was attacked or threatened was won when the UNAMIR Force Commander, Major-General Tousignant issued rules of engagement (ROE)[15] to the force which permitted UNAMIR personnel to use deadly force:

(1) In self-defence...against persons committing a hostile act or exhibiting a hostile intent;

12 *Ibid.*, operative para 4.

13 The term 'Chapter VI' operations as used here refers to Chapter VI of the UN Charter and is shorthand for saying that UN peacekeepers may only use force in self-defence of themselves and other peacekeepers.

14 The term 'Chapter VII' as used here refers to Chapter VII of the UN Charter and is shorthand for saying that UN peacekeepers may use force not only in self-defence but also to achieve the mandate and to protect civilians.

15 Section 9: Operational Directive No. 02: Rules of Engagement, 6 October 1994. [Thereafter ROE].

(2) To protect from damage or destruction, property or installations belonging to or under the protection of UNAMIR, including protected sites and means for the distribution and delivery of humanitarian relief:
   a. Which have been designated by the unit Commanding Officer, in consultation with Force Commander, as essential to the success of the UNAMIR mission,
   b. Which justify protection through the use of deadly force, and
   c. Where there is no way to prevent damage or destruction;
(3) To overcome forcible attempts to prevent UNAMIR Force discharging its duties, when authorised by the Force Commander;
(4) To resist armed attempts to disarm, abduct or detain UNAMIR military or civilian personnel;
(5) To resist armed attempts to compel UNAMIR personnel to withdraw from protection areas they were ordered to occupy by the Force Commander or his delegate; and
(6) To resist armed attempts to cut off a UNAMIR force.[16]

It was a tougher battle to convince UNAMIR HQ that force could be used by UNAMIR personnel to protect anyone being attacked by the RPA. It had been noted, certainly by the Australian contingent, that the real threat to the UNAMIR force and to the local population was from the RPA and not other hostile individuals or other forces. General Tousignant however was not convinced that UNAMIR could act against the RPA:

> He [General Tousignant] felt that the letter of the mandate was genuinely meaningful only for the first few weeks he was in Rwanda...[and] instructions from New York made it clear...that they wanted him to cooperate with his hosts rather than challenge them. UNAMIR's Force Commander hence found himself in charge of a mission where the mandate had little real meaning and implementing it had no great support from UN New York, whatever the Australians' legal advice.[17]

The Official Australian history of UNAMIR concludes that:

> There was an undoubted moral and legal case for challenging the RPA and the Rwandan Government, but doing so would have had consequences, including for the safety of the UN force that might have to confront the army of their hosts, or for the longer-term ability of UNAMIR to carry out any of its work.[18]

16 *Ibid.*, para 8b.
17 Official History, n 1, p. 262.
18 *Ibid.*

However, by November 1994, after several incidences where the RPA carried out hostile acts or demonstrated hostile intent against UNAMIR and the local population[19] Tousignant recognised that the RPA had to be stopped from detaining UN personnel and Rwandan Nationals. To this end he issued a directive setting out the extent to which UNAMIR personnel could resist attempts by the RPA to unlawfully detain UNAMIR personnel and Rwandan nationals.[20]

One case where the RPA stretched their relationship with the MSF by demonstrating hostile intent occurred on 15 February 1995. The incident involved the RPA blocking the entrance to the Australian barracks in Kigali with one of their vehicles. The pretext for the blocking was that one of our vehicles had collided with the RPA vehicle when driving out of the barracks. My diary notes that matters escalated very rapidly with the RPA calling for support. The increase in RPA members led to the Australians military numbers also increasing. The RPA were on one side of the road, McIntosh and I were negotiating with an RPA in the middle of the road, and the Australians were on the other side of the road – some on the edge of the road near the barracks front gate, and some were inside our barracks. While we were negotiating with the RPA one of the Australian soldiers saw an RPA soldier go to "instant" with his pistol (i.e. cock his pistol and take the safety catch-off, so that all he had to do was squeeze the trigger to fire). With that demonstration of hostile intent, the Australians also escalated by going to "instant". McIntosh, realizing that the risk of shots being fired was very real, ordered the Australian soldiers to "unload" (i.e. uncock the weapon, eject the round from the weapon, and put the safety catch on safe). Some of them did not, and so he ordered them to unload again. Afterwards, when we did our de-brief he asked me why the soldiers had not unloaded when he first issued the order to unload. We concluded that disobeying his command to unload stemmed from the soldiers believing that they had an 'inherent right to self-defence' and therefore could not be ordered to unload.

5 Looking Back

I have argued that for the purposes of interpreting a mandate there are two matters to consider: first, what is expressly authorised by the Security Council, and the second, what may be authorised by implication by the Security

19 For a detailed description of some of these incidents see Official History, n 1, pp. 262–264.

20 See discussion below under the heading 'Detention'.

Council. In my view resolution 918 explicitly authorised peacekeepers to protect IDPs, refugees and civilians at risk. The resolution also authorised the use of force to protect relief supplies and humanitarian areas. The protection of UNAMIR forces and assets was expressly authorised under the doctrine of self-defence. Furthermore, use of deadly force was implied by the terms to 'contribute security and protection'[21] and 'provide security'[22] There was no caveat which restricted UNAMIR from using force to protect either civilians or UNAMIR forces from the RPA. The fact that resolution 918 did not expressly state that UNAMIR was authorised to undertake its mandate pursuant to Chapter VII seems irrelevant to me when the terms of the Resolution explicitly (or at the least, impliedly) provided for the use of force. This approach now seems to be accepted in UN doctrine which provides that the use of force is governed by the specific mandate given to peacekeepers.[23]

Another interesting matter arising from the use of force mandate for UNAMIR as described by resolution 918 was whether the protection of civilians falls within the doctrine of self-defence. The traditional UN approach to the use of force by peacekeepers limited the use of force in self-defence to the protection of peacekeepers and UN personnel.[24] This traditional approach is narrower than the domestic law of individual self-defence, which does not distinguish between self-defence of oneself and self-defence of others. The protection mandate in Rwanda was in my view closer to the domestic law doctrine of

21 S/RES/918, n 11, operative para. 3(a).

22 *Ibid.*, operative para. 3(b).

23 United Nations, 'United Nations Peacekeeping Operations: Principles and Guidelines',2008, 31–4. (Thereafter UN Principles and Guidelines, but also known as the 'Capstone Doctrine') pp. 14 and 35; and Department of Peacekeeping Operations/Department of Field Support, Guidelines: Use of Force by Military Components in United Nations Peacekeeping Operations, 1 February 2017.

24 See for example in relation to the United Nations Emergency Force I, Report of the Secretary-General, Summary study of the experience derived from the establishment and operation of the Force, UN Doc. A/3943, (October 1958, paras 70, 178 and 179; Organisation des Nations Unies au Congo (ONUC), Operations Directive No. 1, para. 4, reprinted in Trevor Findlay, *The Blue Helmet's' First War? Use of Force by theUNin the Congo, 1960–64* (Canadian Peacekeeping Press, 1999) p. 172; and UN Peacekeeping Force in Cyprus (UNFICYP), Report of the Secretary-General on the United Nations Operations in Cyprus, UN Doc. S/5950, 10 September 1960, paras 7(c) and 232(b). For a more detailed discussions concerning my views regarding the evolution and application of the doctrine of individual self-defence in UN peacekeeping see: Bruce 'Ossie' Oswald, 'Robust Peacekeeping and Self-Defence', Proceedings of the 113th Annual Meeting, American Society of International Law (Cambridge University Press, forthcoming); and Bruce Oswald, 'Soldier Self-Defence Symposium: The Evolution of the UN Doctrine of Self-Defence in UN Peacekeeping, http://opiniojuris.org/2019/05/01/soldier-self-defense-symposium-the-evolution-of-the-un-doctrine-of-self-defence-in-un-peacekeeping/ accessed at 11 June 2019.

self-defence and consequently, I had no difficulty supporting the ROE that Tousignant issued in October 1994. More recent UN mandates on the use of force seem to have separated the protection of civilians from the doctrine of individual self-defence.

Turning to the issue of whether peacekeepers have an "inherent right of self-defence", my experience during the road block incident made me reflect on whether self-defence is an "inherent right" and to what extent self-defence may be subject to military command. Using Australia as a case study, all ADF members are subject to *Australian Defence Force Discipline Act 1982* (Cth) and the *Criminal Code Act 1995* (Cth) (the Criminal Code). The Criminal Code defines self-defence in the following terms:

> (1) A person is not criminally responsible for an offence if he or she carries out the conduct constituting the offence in self-defence.
> (2) A person carries out conduct in self-defence if and only if he or she believes the conduct is necessary:
> (a) to defend himself or herself or another person; or
> (b) to prevent or terminate the unlawful imprisonment of himself or herself or another person; or
> (c) to protect property from unlawful appropriation, destruction, damage or interference; or
> (d) to prevent criminal trespass to any land or premises; or
> (e) to remove from any land or premises a person who is committing criminal trespass; and the conduct is a reasonable response in the circumstances as he or she perceives them.
> (3) This section does not apply if the person uses force that involves the intentional infliction of death or really serious injury:
> (a) to protect property; or
> (b) to prevent criminal trespass; or
> (c) to remove a person who is committing criminal trespass.[25]

....

There are three points to be made about this definition. First, the doctrine of self-defence is a justification that recognises the defendant's responsibility for the 'harmful conduct but contends that it was done in circumstances which made the conduct rightful in the eyes of society...the actor therefore deserves

25 *Criminal Code Act 1995* (Cth), s. 10.4, Self-defence. While it is true that the Criminal Code was in effect at the time we served in Rwanda, the principles articulated in the section reflect those we were bound by.

praise rather than blame.'[26] Second, it is a claim that can arise for all criminal acts but only after a violent offence has been committed. Third, the claim is not an immunity from prosecution, nor is it a right in the sense that once making the claim the defendant need do no more to demonstrate his or her innocence. The practical effect for all those who rely on self-defence therefore, is that they may claim the defence when charged for an offence, but it is for the tribunal, court or another appropriate decision-making body to decide whether the claim of self-defence is justified in the circumstances. The Australian High Court has stated that '[i]t is only after the circumstances of the attack and the defendant's responses are evaluated that a court can determine whether the person was exercising the right of self-defence.'[27]

In the context of military operations, a further issue must be kept in mind: the use of force is always controlled. Consequently, it must be for the commander to decide whether the use of force in a circumstance is justified. McIntosh recently reminded me that he believed that our soldiers had no right to got to "instant" simply because an individual RPA soldier cocked his pistol. In his view the RPA member cocking his pistol was not enough of a reason for our soldiers to escalate to "instant". He has said: 'given that we had no knowledge of the weapon state of the RPA soldiers we encountered in the absence of an RPA soldier being seen to go to "instant" and then aiming the weapon with intent, our soldiers had no right to escalate. That mass cocking of weapons could have had fatal consequences, especially for the two of us [McIntosh and myself] who would have been caught in the cross-fire.' This example is a stark reminder why commanders quite rightly believe that in some circumstances it is for them to judge, rather than their soldiers, when to escalate the use of force. The control of force by commanders is what, in my experience, separates a professional military from a rabble.

If UNAMIR existed today its work with the RPA would most likely be governed by the UN Human Rights Due Diligence Policy (HRDDP).[28] This policy ensures that when UN peacekeepers and other UN entities support non-UN entities, such as local military forces, the support 'must be consistent with the… [UN's] purposes and principles…and with its obligations under international

26 Stanley Yeo, *Unstrained Killing and the Law* (Oxford University Press, India 1998) p. 168.

27 *Taikato v R* [1996] HCA 28.

28 Identical letters dated 25 February 2013 from the Secretary-General addressed to the President of the General Assembly and to the President of the Security Council, UN Doc A/67/775-S/2013/110, 5 March 2013. [Thereafter HRDDP]. The HRDDP is annexed to the letter. The UN has also published a guidance concerning the application of the HRDDP: 'Guidance Note: Human Rights Due Diligence Policy on UN Support to Non-UN Security Forces', 1 July 2014.

law to respect, promote and encourage respect for international humanitarian law, human rights and refugee law.[29] Pursuant to the HRDDP, UNAMIR would have been obliged to undertake a risk assessment of providing support to the RPA; be transparent with the RPA about UNAMIR's international law obligations; and assess the risks involve in providing support to the RPA. Furthermore, UNAMIR would have had a framework for ensuring that the support it provided the RPA and the Rwandan Government more broadly would meet the UN's obligations.[30]

6 Detention

Very early on in the deployment it became obvious to me that there was insufficient direction as to how UNAMIR was to deal with detainees. On numerous occasions in our first few weeks in Rwanda MSF personnel faced situations where Rwandan nationals sought protection from the RPA. In broad terms the circumstances always seemed to follow a theme: a Rwandan would approach a member of MSF, state that they needed protection from the RPA, and that if they did not receive the protection they would be beaten or killed by the RPA. The RPA narrative was that the Rwandan had committed genocide and that the RPA was taking them into custody. In such circumstances, the issue was whether UNAMIR was permitted to provide protection to the Rwandan, and if they did, how were they to handle the Rwandan?

In other circumstances, UNAMIR peacekeepers found themselves in situations where they were required to take detainees because the detainees were accused of committing a variety of offences ranging from stealing to committing murder – hardly surprising considering the incredible destruction of community and personal values that occurred through the genocide.

The authority to detain was provided for in the ROE in the following terms:

> 10. Individuals shall only be detained if they commit a hostile act, display hostile intent or carry out any activity which would require that force be used against them…
>
> 11. Once detained, only minimal non-deadly force is authorized to prevent the escape of a detainee, unless there is a necessity to act in self-defence, in which case, minimum force, up to and including deadly force, is authorised. However, if the individuals flee and the threat of their use

29 *Ibid.*, para. 1.

30 *Ibid.*, para. 2.

> of force has thus been removed, further force of any kind shall not be employed to apprehend them.
> 12. Any individual detained shall be turned over as soon as possible to appropriate civilian police authorities as designated by the Force Commander. Any weapons seized from detainees shall be confiscated or rendered militarily ineffective.
> 13. Detainees shall not be subject to intimidation, deprivation or humiliation. Medical care and attention of medical personnel shall be provided when required. Detainees shall be given rations and shelter equivalent to that of UNAMIR personnel.[31]

Clearly the above standards for dealing with detainees complied with legal standards and made operational sense. What the ROE did not address was what to do with detainees accused of committing crimes such as genocide, murder, rape, and theft. To deal with UNAMIR handling criminal detainees the Force Commander issued a directive on 8 September 1994 entitled 'FC [Force Commander] Directive for the Disposal of Criminals.' That directive authorised UNAMIR peacekeepers to 'apprehend suspected criminals.' The term "suspected criminals" was defined 'as a person who is suspected of an act of sabotage, subversive activity, or assignation or banditry.' The directive also outlined the procedures for dealing with suspected criminals which included providing a 'safe and secure place…as a temporary place of custody', and 'transport to be arranged in order to evacuate suspects to the appropriate regional authority or Kigali….' The directive did not however provide detail concerning how handovers of detainees to the Government of Rwanda were to occur, and it did not deal with those accused of committing serious crimes such as genocide, murder or rape.

After much discussion with the Force Headquarters, the International Committee of the Red Cross, and the Office of the High Commissioner for Human Rights, I wrote (with the permission of McIntosh) a draft directive for Tousignant outlining the legal framework applicable to UNAMIR personnel for detaining individuals (regardless of whether they were Rwandan or foreign nationals). Based on UNAMIR experiences of the RPA seeking to detain UNAMIR personnel the draft also dealt with the circumstances in which UNAMIR might handover UN personnel to the Rwandan authorities. The draft had several annexes which dealt with, among other things, procedures for handing over Rwandan Nationals to the Rwandan Office of Prosecutions, and a proforma to

31 ROE, n 15, para. 9.

be completed by the UNAMIR peacekeeper responsible for the handover and the Office of the Prosecutor to whom the detainees was being handed to.

On 3 November, Tousignant issued his directive entitled 'FC [Force Commander] Directive on the Legal Jurisdiction Applicable to UNAMIR and Rwandan Authorities.[32] This directive dealt with three of my primary concerns relating to the taking and handling of detainees by UNAMIR. First, it made it clear that UNAMIR civilian personnel must not be handed over to Rwandan authorities without the express authority of the Special Representative of the Secretary-General; military personnel must not be handed over without the express authority of the Force Commander; and where Rwandans were under the protection of UNAMIR they must not be handed over unless permitted by the Force Commander. Second, UNAMIR troops were authorised to use force in accordance with their ROE in situations where Rwandan authorities used force or threatened to use force to take UNAMIR civilians, UNAMIR military personnel or Rwandans under the protection of UNAMIR into custody. This clear authorisation to limit the power of the RPA to interfere with UNAMIRs ability to protect its personnel and Rwandans was essential in ensuring that UNAMIR maintained its protection mandate. Third, the directive created a formal process for handing over detainees taken by UNAMIR troops. Two key components of that process were the requirement that detainees must be handed over to the Office of the Prosecutor (rather than the RPA);[33] and that the ICRC be present at the time of hand over so that there would be an independent witness to the handover. Over the period of my deployment I know that UNAMIR at least 100 detainees and handed them over to the Prosecutors office, sometimes with the ICRC present. It was only at the end of my deployment, when I visited the Kigali Prison, that I realised that handing over detainees to the Prosecutor's Office did not mean that the detainee would receive due process.

On 7 and 13 February 1995 I made two visits to the Kigali Prison. On my first visit I was accompanied by two Human Rights monitors. On my second visit I was accompanied by members of the UNHQ. After both visits I reported to the Force Commander that the conditions in which I saw prisoners being held in were clearly inhuman and degrading. The prison was built to hold 2000 prisoners but when I visited it held 6795. This population consisted of 6437 males, 200 females and 51 infants (held in a building attached to the male prison), 173

32 FC Directive on the Legal Jurisdiction Applicable to UNAMIR and Rwandan Authorities, 3 November 1994. [Thereafter Jurisdiction Directive].

33 The directive stated: Detainees are not to be handed to any other RPA authorities. A Prosecutor's Office is the only authorized Office for the processing and handing over of detainees in Rwanda.' Jurisdiction Directive, Annex D, Procedures for Handing Over Rwandan Nationals, para. 3.f.

minors (i.e. below the age of 16). On questioning the inmates, it was clear to me that most of them were held in custody because they were accused of genocide. This included all the minors I spoke with. All the inmates I spoke to said that they had received no judicial hearing to establish whether there was a prima facie case against them. My report recommended, among other things, that convicted criminals should be separated from those held in pre-trial custody; the living conditions be improved; minors be removed and kept in a separate facility from adults, and that pretrial hearing be held as a matter of urgency to ensure that there was a *prima facie* case against each prisoner. Needless to say, after my first visit to the prison I realised that most if not all the Rwandans that UNAMIR had handed to the Office of the Prosecutor were immediately imprisoned without a case being made against them.

7 Looking Back

When peacekeepers are dealing with an individual accused of committing serious crimes such as genocide, murder, rape or serious assaults the local authorities will expect that the individual will be handed to them to be dealt with in accordance with the applicable local law. A question that I have looked back on is how to deal with this expectation if there are substantial grounds for believing that the detainee will not receive fundamental due process rights, or the detainee will be ill-treated. Based on my experiences in Rwanda and other military operations where I have had to deal with detainees I addressed this issue in my PhD thesis.

The complexity in Rwanda was the tension between recognising that the Rwandan authorities had the right to deal with individuals who had committed serious crimes against their fellow citizens, and the obligation not to handover a detainee if there were substantial grounds for believing that the detainee would be in danger of being tortured, abused or ill-treated. The presumption against interfering in the 'domestic jurisdiction of any State', affirmed by article 2(7) of the Charter,[34] and several Security Council resolutions concerning

34 Article 2(7) of the *Charter of the United Nations*, above n 30, provides that:

> Nothing contained in the present *Charter* shall authorize the United Nations to intervene in matters which are essentially within the domestic jurisdiction of any state or shall require the Members to submit such matters to settlement under the present *Charter*; but this principle shall not prejudice the application of enforcement measures under Chapter VII.

UN peacekeeping operations[35] arguably severely restricts the legal authority of peacekeepers to hold detainees that are nationals of the host state in situations where the host state has consented to the peacekeeping operation. To argue otherwise would be to go against the 'logical manifestation of a world order of independent states … since the authorities of a state are responsible for the conduct of law and maintenance of good order within that state.'[36]

However, in circumstances where there is a substantial belief that a detainee may be tortured[37] by local authorities, it could be argued that pursuant to the *Convention against Torture and other Cruel, Inhuman or Degrading Treatment or Punishment* (CAT), peacekeepers are prohibited from handing the detainee over to those authorities.[38] In such cases the argument would be that sovereignty is irrelevant. But what of situations where the treatment does not amount to torture but does amount to cruel and inhuman treatment, which in my opinion existed in the Kigali goal at the time of my visit? Balancing the competing norms in such cases requires peacekeepers to place themselves in the difficult political and diplomatic position of assessing the host State's ability to deal with detainees. This was indeed the challenge facing Tousignant and UN New York. Furthermore, troop contributing States would most likely emphasise that, in accordance with general principles of international law, the obligation to comply with the CAT rests with the host State, particularly in situations where the consent of the host State is vital to the success of the operation. It is, therefore, the host State that must ensure it takes 'measures to prevent acts of torture in any territory under its jurisdiction.'[39] As Christopher

35 See for example, UNSC Resolution 1807 (2008) of 31 March 2008 S/RES/1807(2008), preamble, para 2; UNSC Resolution 2399 (2018) of 30 January 2018, S/RES/2399, (2018) preamble para 2; and UNSC Resolution 2459 (2019) of 15 March 2019, S/RES/2459 (2019), preamble para 2.

36 Malcolm Shaw, *International Law* (8th ed) (Cambridge, 2017), p. 489

37 The *Convention of Torture and other Cruel, Inhuman or Degrading Treatment or Punishment*, (entered into force 26 June 1987), art. 1(1) defines torture as: any act by which severe pain or suffering, whether physical or mental, is intentionally inflicted on a person for such purposes as obtaining from him or a third person information or a confession, punishing him for an act he or a third person has committed or is suspected of having committed, or intimidating or coercing him or a third person, or for any reason based on discrimination of any kind, when such pain or suffering is inflicted by or at the instigation of or with the consent or acquiescence of a public official or other person acting in an official capacity. It does not include pain or suffering arising only from, inherent in or incidental to lawful sanctions.

38 CAT art. 3(1) which provides: No State Party shall expel, return ("refouler") or extradite a person to another State where there are substantial grounds for believing that he would be in danger of being subjected to torture.

39 *Ibid.*, art 2(1).

Greenwood argues, it is difficult to see how a serious argument can be mounted that the principle of jurisdiction in article 2(1) of the CAT can apply in circumstances where the troop-contributing country is not 'exercising legislative, judicial or even administrative functions'.[40]

A further argument that limits the application of article 3 of the CAT is that allegations of torture and the decision to handover may in certain circumstances be matters of political, rather than judicial concern. The US Supreme Court in the case of *Munaf* took this position by finding that allegations that a person will be tortured if handed over to the host State's national authorities 'are of course a matter of serious concern, but in the present context [ie being handed over by US military forces in Iraq to the Iraqi authorities] that concern is to be addressed by the political branches, not the judiciary.'[41]

While not relevant specifically to peacekeepers at the point of detention, other concerns that arise in this context include the lifespan of the obligation to monitor, and the subsequent obligations for the peace operation to take custody again of the detainee, if the detainee is tortured.[42] Can the UN rely upon assurances from the host State that the State will not torture the detainee?[43] These matters are not dealt with by existing international instruments and remain unresolved as matters of law.

In practical terms peacekeepers are left with three choices when they have substantial grounds for believing that a detainee is likely to be abused or ill-treated by local authorities: keep the detainee, release the detainee, or handover the detainee. They could refrain from handing over the detainee. If this course of action is pursued the peace operation will need to set up its own detention facilities to ensure that detainees are provided with the appropriate conditions and oversight when detention is not temporary. UNAMIR was not resourced to set up its own detention facility and even if such resources were available, the Rwandan Government would never have supported such a step.

The other choice is to ensure that there is a memorandum of understanding (MOU) between the host state and the UN. Such an MOU should deal with

---

40 Christopher Greenwood, *International Law Framework for the Treatment of Persons Detained in Afghanistan by Canadian Forces: Report* (2007) para 47. This report was among the affidavits for the respondents examined by the Federal Court of Canada in *Amnesty International Canada v Canada (Minister of National Defence)* [2007] FC 1147. Cf Amnesty International, *Afghanistan – Detainees Transferred to Torture: ISAF Complicity?* (2007), 9–10.

41 *Munaf et al v Geren, Secretary of the Army et al*, 533 US 23 (2008).

42 For example, is there a legal obligation to track detainees after they have been sentenced?

43 See, for example, Human Rights Watch, *Still at Risk: Diplomatic Assurances No Safeguard against Torture* (2005).

expectations for minimum standards of treatment; the right of the UN to speak to the detainee and inspect the detention facility; and a framework for taking the detainee out of the custody of the host nation if the detainee is being tortured or ill-treated.

The approach of handing detainees to the Office of the Prosecutor in the presence of the ICRC was aimed at providing independent and objective scrutiny of the handover and to ensure that a record of the handover of the detainee exists, rendering the detainee traceable and maximising the prospect for subsequent treatment of the detainee to meet minimum international standards. This put a high burden on the ICRC and was arguably unfair to them.

The experience of dealing with detainees in Rwanda continued to plague me as a military officer and military lawyer after my UNAMIR deployment. I was however fortunate to have an opportunity to use some of the lessons from Rwanda to shape the detention regime implemented by INTERFET during its deployment in East Timor.[44] The experiences with East Timor further shaped my thinking when I was appointed the head of the Detainee Management Team in Iraq 2005. My operational experiences of dealing with detention matters in Rwanda, East Timor and Iraq shaped my contributions to drafting the UN interim standard operating procedures for detention,[45] and the Copenhagen Principles.[46]

8 Conclusion

Here are my 6 observations from my experiences in Rwanda:

1. If there is a likelihood that military personnel will have to deal with mass atrocities commanders must provide them with as much information as possible about what they will see and how to process that information.
2. Coordinate with stakeholders as to who will be responsible for investigating mass grave sites and the extent of military assistance. There must be

44 Bruce Oswald, 'The Interfet Detainee Management Unit in East Timor' 3 *Yearbook of International Humanitarian Law* (2000), pp. 347–361.

45 The draft Standard Operating Procedures for Detention were drafted in 200X. I understand that they remain applicable to all UN peacekeeping operations. They are classified and therefore not in the public domain.

46 See Bruce Oswald and Thomas Winkler, 'The Copenhagen Process: Principles and Guidelines on the Handling of Detainees in International Operations 128 *Nordic Journal of International Law* (2014) pp. 128–167.

clear guidelines for military personnel so that they know what they are expected to do when they come across a mass trauma site.

3. The justification of individual self-defence to a criminal charge is not an immunity from prosecution, and nor is a right (it cannot be interpreted as undermining commanders control of when and how force may be used). It is a claim that any soldier may make but it will be for the courts or the appropriate law enforcement authority to decide whether in the circumstances the claim is justified.
4. Commanders control the use of force and if they decide that force is not to be used in a circumstance their order is, *prima facie*, lawful.
5. Detainees will be taken on all operations. Consequently, plans must be made, training must be given, and resources must be devoted to ensuring that detainee operations are conducted effectively and efficiently, and that the fundamental rights of detainees are met.
6. Taking and handling detainees is a tactical, political and legal issue. At no stage should there be an assumption that holding detainees and/or transferring them will not have operational and strategic implications across the overlapping spheres of military operations, political concerns, and the application of law.

Acknowledgments

I owe Beth Wellington a great deal of gratitude for proof-reading and commenting on this paper. Beth has proof-read and commented on my written work for almost a decade and continues to support me notwithstanding her many other commitments. My thanks to Lizzie Saltnes for being with me for every step of my journey since my deployment to Rwanda. Lizzie is a veteran of the second MSF rotation to Rwanda. Major Richard Halford (UK ALS) provided me with very useful feedback on an earlier draft as did Major R. Scott Adams (USAF). Brigadier Pat McIntosh (Retired) and Lieutenant-General John Frewen added value to this chapter by providing me with comments. Finally, to those that served with me in Rwanda, it was my privilege to serve with each of you.

CHAPTER 7

Do Not Intervene: UNAMIR's Rules of Engagement from the Inside

Phillip Drew and *Major (ret'd) Brent Beardsley*

During the quarter of a century that has passed since Genocide gripped Rwanda, numerous articles have been written about the Rules of Engagement (ROE) for the United Nations Assistance Mission for Rwanda (UNAMIR). Understandably, many of those articles have focused on UNAMIR's failure to protect civilians, and how the force's limited mandate impacted the mission's ability (or lack thereof) to influence those genocide and events that surrounded it.

This article is about the Rules of Engagement that applied to personnel and contingents that were deployed to Rwanda under the UNAMIR banner between 1993 – 1996. Much of what has been written has been based on the limited information that the UN and Troop Contributing Nations (TCNs) have released over the past 25 years.[1] While a significant portion of the article relies on information that is now openly available, it also draws on the first hand knowledge, experiences and recollections of the authors, each of whom was employed in positions that required intimate knowledge of the use of force parameters for the mission. In this manner the article provides insight into the challenges that were met both in developing and implementing ROE for the mission, and the difficulties encountered by those who witnessed the unspeakable violence that was the Rwandan Genocide.

1 In spite of the fact that the UNAMIR mission formally ended in March 1996, a significant amount of the official documentation surrounding the development of ROE for the mission remains largely inaccessible. Indeed, had it not been for the public statements made by General Dallaire, and the incredible efforts highly talented investigative writers such as Linda Melvern, Andrew Wallis and a few select others, much of what is publicly known about UNAMIR would never have been revealed. It is to their credit that much of the story of the Rwandan genocide story can be told.

 | DOI:10.1163/9789004430129_009

1 Understanding Rules of Engagement

The North Atlantic Treaty Organization (NATO) defines ROE as, "directives to military forces (including individuals) that define the circumstances, conditions, degree, and manner in which force, or actions which might be construed as provocative, may be applied."[2] Although minor variations of the NATO definition are found in various ROE manuals, the common purpose of ROE is consistent across the board; they are a command and control mechanism that aims "to ensure that commanders and their subordinates do not use force or other measures beyond that authorized by higher command."[3]

As can be discerned from the above, the creation of ROE for a mission is not the task of the military commander of the mission. Rather, ROE are an integral part of the operational planning process and are always developed by a higher authority, such as a national headquarters or government ministry. Within the UN, it is the responsibility of the Department of Peacekeeping Operations (DPKO) to develop ROE for peacekeeping operations prior to the commencement of the mission. The authority to approve ROE rests solely with the Under-Secretary-General (USG) for Peacekeeping Operations.[4] It is only after the ROE are approved by the USG that they are issued to the relevant commander. Once issued, the ROE will apply in their entirety to all personnel who are deployed under the command of the Force Commander, such as headquarters staff, military observers and other persons who are not under the command of a national contingent.

While all forces that deploy on a mission will be subject to the limitations prescribed by the UN mission ROE, troop contributing nations may develop national ROE that differ from those applicable to those individuals employed directly under the command of the UN.[5] Importantly, the ROE of a TCN can never authorize any action that expands the amount of force that has been authorized by the UN. Rather, national ROE may only impose limits on use of force or other provocative activities that are more restrictive than those that apply to the over-all UN mission.[6] It is commonly accepted that there are four situations in which a TCN may issue national ROE that differ from those of the UN:

1. to ensure compliance with national law;
2. to ensure compliance with the State's differing interpretation of or obligations regarding international law;

2 *NATO Legal Desk Book* (2nd edn, 2010) 254.

3 *Use of Force for CFO perations* (Department of National Defence 2008) para 206.

4 'Guidelines for the Development of Rules of Engagement (ROE) for United Nations Peacekeeping Operations' para 7.

5 It is important to note that many countries do not have national ROE policies. In cases where TCN deploys forces without their own national ROE, the UN ROE applies to that force.

6 Camilla Guldahl Cooper, 'Rules of Engagement Demystified: A Study of the History, Development And' (2014) 53 Military Law and the Law of War Review 54, 93.

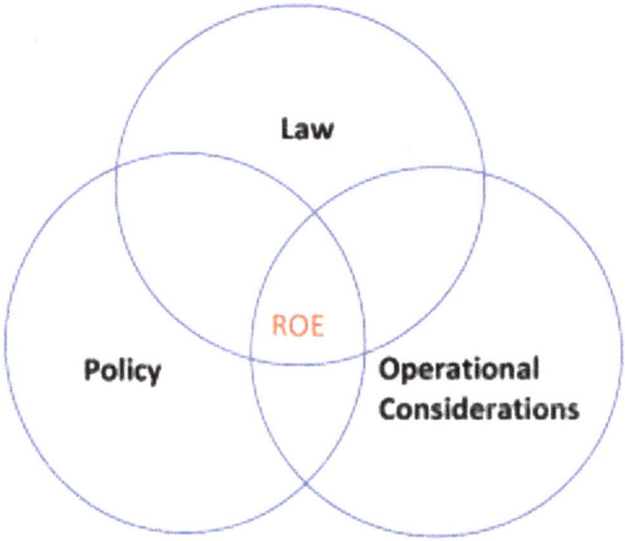

FIGURE 1 ROE factors

3. because the State interprets the [UN] mandate differently; or
4. to impose additional restrictions or limitations on the use of the State's forces, such as geographical limitations or prohibitions on using certain ammunitions…"[7]

As a result of the differences that may arise between national and UN ROE, the force commander may, in some cases, be faced with a scenario in which some national contingents may be prepared to use force or engage in tasks, while others might not. As will be discussed below, differing national interpretations, and the confusion that can arise therefrom, has the potential to undermine a force commander's ability to exercise command and control, sometimes with deadly consequences.

2 How ROE Are Developed

In order to understand the function of ROE, it is important to appreciate the procedures and factors involved in their design. Although they are a military command and control mechanism that regulates the circumstances under which force or other provocative measures can be used in the accomplishment

7 Fournier Sylvain, "NATO Military Interventions Abroad: How ROE Are Adopted and Jurisdictional Rights Negotiated' in Stefano Manacorda and Adan Nieto Martin (eds), *Criminal Law between War and Peace: Justice and Cooperation in Criminal Matters in International Military Interventions. Proceedings of the XVth International Congress on Social Defense* (Ediciones de la Universidad de Castilla-La Mancha 2009) 117.

of a mission, the development of ROE is very much a cooperative exercise that is undertaken at senior levels in headquarters. As depicted in the diagram above, the creation of ROE is driven by three major considerations: policy, law, and operational capacity.

3 Law

It goes without saying that ROE must comply with law. This requires not only that the ROE conform with all relevant national and international laws, but that the ROE respect and reflect the legal bases for the mission for which they are developed. In the United Nations, the legal bases for individual peacekeeping operations are found in the United Nations Security Council Resolution(s) (UNSCR) that establish and define the mandate for the mission. Under the construct of the UN Charter, peace operations are authorized either as measures to arrive at a peaceful settlement of disputes (Chapter VI), or as actions with respect to threats to the peace, breaches of the peace, and acts of aggression (Chapter VII).[8] The fundamental difference between the two types of peace operations is that while under Chapter VII missions, UN forces may be authorized to use all necessary force to restore international peace and security, under Chapter VI missions, the use of coercive force is not permitted and personnel may only use deadly force in self-defence.

Usually established under Chapter VI of the United Nations Charter, UN peacekeeping operations have traditionally been based on a model under which a peacekeeping force is deployed to support a peace agreement or monitor a ceasefire that is in place . The tasks assigned under the mandates for such missions typically involve the following: "observation, monitoring and reporting; supervision of cease-fire and support to verification mechanisms; and/or the interposition of forces as a buffer and confidence-building measure."[9] The theory under this model of peacekeeping is that "By monitoring and reporting on the parties' adherence to commitments regarding a cease-fire or demilitarized zone and by investigating complaints of violations, traditional peacekeeping operations enable each party to be reassured that the other party will not seek to exploit the cease-fire in order to gain military advantage."[10] In accordance with this framework, the policy for use of force in Chapter VI operations was that forces "engaged in the [peacekeeping] operation may

8 'United Nations Peacekeeping Operations: Principles and Guidelines' 13.

9 ibid 21.

10 ibid.

never take the initiative in the use of armed force, but are entitled to respond with force to an attack with arms, including attempts to use force to make them withdraw from positions which they occupy under orders from the Commander, acting under the authority of the Assembly and within the scope of its resolutions. The basic element involved is clearly the prohibition against any initiative in the use of armed force."[11]

As has been the case with the majority of UN peacekeeping operations conducted since the first deployment of armed UN peacekeepers in 1956, the mission in Rwanda was authorized under Chapter VI.[12] With a mandate to monitor the cease fire agreement[13] between the government of Rwanda and the Rwandan Patriotic Front (RPF),[14] UNAMIR was established with small, lightly armed contingents from Ghana, Tunisia, Bangladesh and Belgium, and unarmed military observers. The battalions that made up the peacekeeping force had no authority to use armed force other than in self-defence.

4 Self-Defence

The concept that a person may use as much force as is necessary to defend oneself against harm is enshrined in the domestic law of virtually all countries. While in some jurisdictions, self-defence is seen as an inherent right, in others it is considered to be a legal defence against criminal charges. No matter how it is seen, the exercise of self-defence is contingent on the actions of the defender being reasonable in the circumstances of the situation. In essence, in order to exercise the right, the defender must satisfy two requirements; he must possess a reasonable belief as to the existence of an assault or threat of death or grievous bodily harm, and the amount of force used to halt the assault must be reasonable, both in terms of necessity and proportionality.[15]

Because self-defence is enshrined in the domestic law of nations, there is no universal agreement as to the scope of the meaning of the term. Whereas in

11 'Summary Study of the Experience Derived from the Establishment and Operation of the Force: Report of the Secretary-General – Document A/3943' para 179.

12 'Security Council Resolution 872 – UNSCR' <http://unscr.com/en/resolutions/872> accessed 15 September 2019.

13 Peace Agreement Between the Government of the Republic of Rwanda and the Rwandese Patriotic Front 1993.

14 'Security Council Resolution 872 – UNSCR' (n 12) paras 2–3.

15 Department of Justice Government of Canada, 'Department of Justice – Bill C-26 (S.C. 2012 c. 9) Reforms to Self-Defence and Defence of Property: Technical Guide for Practitioners' (25 November 2016) <https://www.justice.gc.ca/eng/rp-pr/other-autre/rsddp-rlddp/p5.html> accessed 26 September 2019.

some jurisdictions, the right to self-defence is available only if the individual is protecting oneself, some domestic laws allow individuals to use force to defend other people, while others permit individuals to defend only themselves and those for whom they are legally responsible, such as family members.[16]

As a result of the differing interpretations of self-defence, soldiers from different countries will, unless directed otherwise, exercise self-defence in accordance with the understanding that is enshrined in the domestic law of their own states. Consequently, in multi-national operations, personnel may respond differently to a variety of circumstances, particularly when the defence of others is involved. As will be discussed below, in Rwanda the confusion caused by the dichotomy inherent in the various interpretations, and the inability of UN Headquarters to expound a clear policy on the scope of self-defence for the mission, was to prove deadly, both for those UNAMIR personnel who were unsure of their rights to defend themselves and others, as well as for those who they were tasked to protect.

5 Policy

Clausewitz informs us that the actions undertaken by armies "are nothing but expressions of policy itself"[17] and that "Policy is the guiding intelligence and war only the instrument, not vice versa."[18] To this end, the role of policy in the development of any ROE is subordinate only to law. In that respect, policy plays a fundamental role in the creation of ROE for any military mission.

The Rwanda mission befell the UN at a point in time in which the organization was experiencing unprecedented challenges. The conclusion of the Cold War at the beginning of the 1990s had upset the world order, resulting in the withdrawal of the influence of one of the two superpowers from many of the world's hot-spots. While many at the time had hailed the end of the Cold War as the beginning of a new era of peace, the reality was that the new world order heralded a period of political instability and chaos. By 1993, the UN's inability to rein in the violence in the former Yugoslav Republics, coupled with the disastrous mission in Somalia, had demonstrated that the peacekeeping model that had been employed effectively since 1956 was not suited to the contemporary

---

16 ibid.

17 Carl von Clausewitz, *On War* ((translated by M Howard & P Paret), Princeton University Press 1984) 607.

18 ibid.

reality of civil wars in which peace was either extremely precarious or non-existent.

As Marrack Goulding, the former Under-Secretary General for Peacekeeping noted in 1993, in the early 1990's the whole concept of peacekeeping was undergoing significant review and change. Prior to the 1990's there were three types of traditional peacekeeping operations: "unarmed military observer groups ...; armed infantry-based forces which are deployed in cases where the task is to control territory, as in Cyprus, Syria, southern Lebanon ... and Croatia; and operations, armed or unarmed, which are established as an adjunct of, or sequel to, a peace enforcement operation, as on the Iraq-Kuwait border."[19] As he was leaving his post in DPKO in 1993, Goulding noted that the changing security environment was giving rise to new types of missions that would pose challenges to the contemporary model of peacekeeping. Of note, he described the possibility that the following type of mission might be required in light of changing nature of conflict under which internal conflicts were becoming the preponderant form of warfare:

> A United Nations force would be deployed, after an agreement had been reached between the parties, with the authority and armament to use force against any party which violated the ceasefire or other agreed military arrangements. The mandate would be analogous to peacekeeping in that the parties would agree to the initial deployment of the force and the force would act impartially in enforcing the agreed arrangements. But it would differ from peacekeeping in that the force could open fire in situations other than self-defence, for example to silence guns that persisted in violating the ceasefire.[20]

Noting that such missions cross the threshold into peace-enforcement,[21] Goulding questioned whether the United Nations had the money or will to engage in these types of operations, and whether troop contributing nations would be prepared to contribute the resources (both in terms of personnel and equipment) necessary to ensure success. Although he had written his article before the creation of UNAMIR, Goulding described the situation in Rwanda to a tee; there was a peace agreement in place, but to Rwanda observers, there were many indicators that the peace was precarious. When the mission to

19 Marrack Goulding, 'The Evolution of United Nations Peacekeeping' (1993) 69 International Affairs 451, 457.

20 ibid 459.

21 ibid.

Rwanda was established, the answer to the questions that Goulding had posed with respect to the commitment of the UN and troop contributing nations was a resounding "no"; the UN was not prepared to pay for the type of force that was required to reinforce the peace process in Rwanda, and no countries were prepared to dedicate the personnel and equipment that would be necessary to defend the mission's mandate.

Given that UNAMIR had been authorized under Chapter VI, and that the UN was desperate to avoid yet another disaster like Somalia, there was understandably no appetite in New York for any type of mission that might involve the UN becoming embroiled in yet another civil war. In consideration of the constraints that were existent, both in terms of resources and political will, the mandate for the Rwanda mission did not permit the peacekeeping force to take any actions that might be seen as provocative. As outlined in UNSCR 872, the tasks for the mission were:

(a) To contribute to the security of the city of Kigali inter alia within a weapons-secure area established by the parties in and around the city;
(b) To monitor observance of the cease-fire agreement, which calls for the establishment of cantonment and assembly zones and the demarcation of the new demilitarized zone and other demilitarization procedures;
(c) To monitor the security situation during the final period of the transitional government's mandate, leading up to the elections;
(d) To assist with mine clearance, primarily through training programmes;
(e) To investigate at the request of the parties or on its own initiative instances of alleged non-compliance with the provisions of the Arusha Peace Agreement relating to the integration of the armed forces, and pursue any such instances with the parties responsible and report thereon as appropriate to the Secretary-General;
(f) To monitor the process of repatriation of Rwandese refugees and resettlement of displaced persons to verify that it is carried out in a safe and orderly manner;
(g) To assist in the coordination of humanitarian assistance activities in conjunction with relief operations;
(h) To investigate and report on incidents regarding the activities of the gendarmerie and police…[22]

While the mission was set up to support the implementation of the Arusha Accords, it was given no authority or capacity to maintain security or peace. In this manner, the mandate was short-sighted, particularly in light of the significant and specific warnings from UN investigative missions that had indicated

22 United Nations Security Council Resolution 872 (1993) 1993 para 3.

that Rwanda was gripped by a "climate of mistrust and terror,"[23] in which government officials were actively participating in the massacre of civilians, and engaging in other forms of politically and racially motivated violence.[24]

Arriving in New York for their initial pre-mission briefings in August 1993, Canadians, Major Brent Beardsley and UNAMIR Force Commander, Brigadier General Romeo Dallaire, found a headquarters that was still reeling from the experiences of Somalia, and focused primarily on the largely ineffective United Nations Protection Force (UNPROFOR) mission in the Former Yugoslav Republics. To make matters worse, at that point, the United States was far in arrears in paying its dues to the UN, with the result that resources were very limited. To put it mildly, the Department of Peacekeeping Operations was tapped out.

As Dallaire and Beardsley made their rounds in UN Headquarters it was made abundantly clear to them that the UN did not see Rwanda as a priority. Completely overwhelmed by other issues, New York was hoping that Rwanda would be a simple peacekeeping mission that could be accomplished quickly, inexpensively, and with little risk of casualties. Consequently, "UNAMIR was slow in being set up, and was beset by debilitating administrative difficulties,"[25] and it was terribly under-resourced.

Although the original reconnaissance report for the mission had determined that a contingent of 4260 personnel would be required,[26] the size of the force that the UN ultimately authorized was much smaller.[27] Dallaire was advised that the UN would not authorize a mission of more than 2500. After adjusting their estimate to reflect the reality that UNAMIR peacekeeping force would be much smaller than had been envisioned, Beardsley and Dallaire set about the process of acquiring ROE for the mission. While in normal circumstances, ROE are drafted by a headquarters and then discussed with the Force Commander before being approved,[28] such was not the case for UNAMIR. In

---

23 BW Ndiaye, 'Question of the Violation of Human Rights and Fundamental Freedoms in Any Part of the World, With Particular Reference to Colonial and Other Dependent Countries and Territories – Extrajudicial, Summary or Arbitrary Executions: Addendum – Report by Mr. B.W. Ndiaye, Special Rapporteur, on His Mission to Rwanda from 8 to 17 April 1993' (1993) Economic and Social Council E/CN.4/1994/7/Add.1 8.

24 ibid 10.

25 'Report of the Independent Inquiry into the Actions of the United Nations During the 1994 Genocide in Rwanda' (United Nations Security Council 1999) UN Secretary General S/1999/1257 30.

26 ibid 7.

27 ibid.

28 For an explanation on the process that is used to develop ROE, see: Phillip Drew and others, *The San Remo Handbook on Rules of Engagement* (International Institute for Humanitarian Law) 6.

spite of their efforts to coax mission ROE out of the DPKO, none were forthcoming. In response to the absolute lack of guidance from DPKO, Dallaire and Beardsley took it upon themselves to draft their own ROE for the mission. Looking for a model in which a peacekeeping force had been created under Chapter VI to uphold a peace agreement in a country that had experienced ethnic and political violence, they referred to the ROE that had been used by forces deployed with the UN Transitional Authority in Cambodia (UNTAC).[29] Included in paragraph 17 of the draft ROE was a provision that permitted peacekeepers to intervene to protect civilians:

> 17. There may also be ethnically or politically motivated acts committed during this mandate which will morally and legally require UNAMIR to use all available means to halt them. Examples are executions, attacks on displaced persons or refugees, ethnic riots, attacks on demobilized soldiers, etc. During such occasions, UNAMIR military personnel will follow the [ROE] outlined in this directive, in support of UNCIVPOL and local authorities or in their absence, UNAMIR will take the necessary action to prevent any crime against humanity.[30]

Paragraph 17 represented a departure from the passive form of self-defence that was common in UN missions. Indeed its very inclusion in the ROE demonstrated that it was not considered to be a component of self-defence, which had been defined at paragraph 7 as, "Action to protect oneself or one's unit, when faced with an instant and overwhelming need, leaving no choice of means and no time for deliberation."[31] Additionally, paragraph 11(a) broadened the scope for the use of the use of force by UNAMIR members, allowing them to, "defend themselves, other UN lives, or other persons under their protection, against direct attack."[32] Unfortunately there were several aspects of the ROE that made some TCN's question the authority of the document. The first involved the extension[33] of the right to use force to protect individuals who were neither members of the UN force nor otherwise employed by the UN. Given that protecting non-UN persons was not commonly considered to fall within the scope of a Chapter VI mandate, some questioned whether by doing so the

29 United Nations Security Council Resolution 745 1992.

30 'Operational Directive No. 02: Rules of Engagement (Interim)' para 17.

31 ibid 7.

32 ibid 11(a).

33 The fact that the protection of civilians was generally not considered to fall within the mandate of a peacekeeping force was reflected in the comments made by Iqbal Riza. See note 56.

force would be in breach of its requirement to remain impartial and neutral. The draft as written, also introduced some confusion as between paragraph 7 and 11, the former of which authorized the use of force in the face of hostile intent, and the latter of which authorized the use of force only in the case of hostile act.[34] For some states, this departure from the right to defend oneself from an imminent attack was an unlawful restriction. For others, it simply confused their understanding of the concept of self-defence.

In an to attempt to get their draft ROE approved, Dallaire and Beardsley began to walk the draft from desk to desk in the UN Headquarters. As the document circulated it was treated like a proverbial hot potato; nobody wanted anything to do with it, and all of those who briefly examined it encouraged the Canadian officers to take it to yet another UN official. Frustrated in their attempts to get their ROE Request authorized, they left New York with a draft ROE that had not been approved. Dallaire arrived in Rwanda on 22 October 1993. As one of his first tasks, he issued the ROE as an interim Directive, pending approval of an official version from UNHQ. Frustrated with the lack of action from New York, he resubmitted his draft ROE for approval on 19 November 1993.

As was the case when he and Beardsley had attempted to get the draft approved during their time in New York, Dallaire's ROE Request was never approved by UN Headquarters.[35] In light of DPKO's lack of urgency, Dallaire took the reasonable position that until the UN came back with a response, his draft would apply. The reality, however, was that as the country plummeted toward genocide, the peacekeeping force that the United Nations had deployed did not have valid rules of engagement.

Had Dallaire's proposed ROE been thoroughly and properly vetted by the staff at UN Headquarters, the internal inconsistencies would quite likely have been noted and corrected. The fact that they were not, meant that the discrepancies in the draft led to confusion within the force as to when and under what circumstances UNAMIR personnel could use their weapons. This lack of care at

34 For definitions of Hostile Act and Hostile Intent see: 'Guidelines for the Development of Rules of Engagement (ROE) for United Nations Peacekeeping Operations' (n 4).

35 Much criticism has been directed toward UNDPKO for their lack of action on the ROE file. While their inaction is inexcusable, it is apparent that there was a general lack of knowledge at the UN HQ level about ROE and how they work. At the time that the mission took place, formal rules of engagement were a relatively new item for ground forces, and were not in common use outside of the framework of a few western nations. Indeed, the "Guidelines for the Development of Rules of Engagement (ROE) for United Nations Peacekeeping Operations" were not published until 2002, and first multi-national ROE system, NATO MC362/1, was not created until 2003. See NATO *Legal Desk Book* (n 2) 254.

the UN headquarters level was partly responsible for the deaths of UNAMIR personnel as well as those who were ostensibly under their protection.[36]

As 1993 came to a close, Dallaire's numerous attempts to move the ROE file forward in UN headquarters proved as fruitless as had his efforts in September. An initial test of UNAMIR's powers presented itself in the second week of January 1994, when:

> Colonel Luc Marchal, the Belgian officer who was commander of UNAMIR's Kigali sector, … met in great secrecy with an informant referred to only as Jean-Pierre, apparently a senior member of the feared interahamwe militia. Jean-Pierre Twatsinze, as he was later known to be, told Marchal that he had no objection to war against the RPF, but that his "mission now was to prepare the killing of civilians and Tutsi people, to make lists of Tutsi people, where they lived, to be able at a certain code name to kill them. Kigali city, he said, was divided in a certain number of areas, and each area was manned by… 10 or maybe more people. Some were armed with firearms, some with machetes, and the mission of those persons was just to kill the Tutsi… Jean-Pierre gave… a very good and clear description about the interahamwe organization. He described the cells, the armaments, the training, and he told me that everybody was suspected….[The goal] was to kill a maximum of Tutsi… I felt it was a real killing machine because the objective was very clear for everybody – kill, kill, and kill…just Tutsi must be killed."[37]

After being briefed by Colonel Marchal, Dallaire consulted UN Headquarters, by sending what has become infamously known as the "Genocide Fax". In that facsimile he asked the DPKO for guidance on how to deal with what he considered to be a blatant violation of the Arusha Agreement and of the Kigali Weapons Secure Area. He requested permission to seize the weapons cache, and for authorization to provide protection to the informant. He also provided an ominous warning to UNHQ, advising them that once the violence commenced, "Belgian troops were to be provoked and if Belgians soldiers resorted to force a number of them were to be killed and thus guarantee Belgian withdrawal from Rwanda."[38]

---

36 'Report of the Independent Inquiry into the Actions of the United Nations During the 1994 Genocide in Rwanda' (n 25) 40–43.

37 Gerald Caplan, 'Rwanda: The Preventable Genocide – The Report of the International Panel of Eminent Personalities to Investigate the 1994 Genocide in Rwanda and the Surrounding Events' (Organization of African Unity 1998) para 13.26.

38 BGen Romeo Dallaire, Force Commander UNAMIR, 'Request For Protection of Informant' para 2.

Unlike in the cases where he had asked DPKO for his ROE to be approved, this time Dallaire received a swift and decisive response. Concerned that any provocative action would negatively affect the mission's neutrality, the leadership of DPKO instructed Dallaire not to conduct any operation to seize the weapons, stating that any such operation would be "beyond the mandate entrusted to UNAMIR under resolution 872 (1993)."[39] Instead, Dallaire and his civilian superior in UNAMIR, Jean-Jacques Booh-Booh, were instructed to brief President Habyarimana on the situation.

The instructions that Dallaire received in response to the Genocide Fax were as portentous as they were oblivious. The clear message from New York was "Do Not Intervene". Given that reports from Rwanda during the previous months had been describing increasing tension and episodes of government sponsored ethnic killings, a primary warning that the country was about to be engulfed in genocidal violence went virtually ignored. It was news that the UN did not want to hear. Although senior officials such as Iqbal Riza and Kofi Annan were aware of its existence, the fax was not disclosed to the Security Council.[40]

The UN's disinterest in, and indifference toward Rwanda was to have tragic consequences. As was noted in the report of the Independent Inquiry, so thorough was the neglect by the Directorate of Peacekeeping Operations in New York, that "by the time the genocide started, the mission was not functioning as a cohesive whole: in the real hours and days of deepest crisis [there was] a lack of political leadership, lack of military capacity, severe problems of command and control, and lack of coordination …."[41]

Some of the consequences of the UN's insouciant attitude toward the mission were borne out during the earliest hours of the commencement of the genocide. On the morning of 7 April, the residence of the Prime Minister, Mrs Agathe Uwilingiyimana, was invaded by members of the Rwandan Presidential Guard. Upon receiving news of this incident, Dallaire telephoned Assistant Secretary-General of the Department of Peacekeeping Operations, Iqbal Riza, to inform him that UNAMIR might have to use force to save the Prime Minister. Riza [stated] that UNAMIR was not to fire until fired upon.[42] This direction, which contradicts the right of an individual to protect oneself from imminent harm, placed the peacekeepers who had been sent to protect the Prime Minister in a very difficult situation. The killers could do their worst; so long as they

---

39 'Report of the Independent Inquiry into the Actions of the United Nations During the 1994 Genocide in Rwanda' (n 25) 11.

40 ibid 33.

41 ibid 30.

42 ibid 16.

did not directly attack Blue Helmets, they could get away with murder.[43] Having not been shot at, the peacekeepers did not use armed force to protect Uwilingiyimana. Instead, the five Ghanaians and ten Belgians surrendered their weapons to the Rwandan Government Forces, sealing the fate of the Prime Minister and the ten Belgians. As the UN soldiers stood by, the Prime Minister was murdered along with her husband. As had been foretold in the "Genocide Fax"[44] in January, the ten Belgian soldiers were subsequently[45] taken to an RGF compound where they were tortured and murdered.[46]

As UNAMIR struggled to survive through the next few days, the Belgian and Bangladeshi battalions abandoned the mission. As the peacekeepers fled, Rwandan civilians who had sought refuge with them were left to die at the hands of the Interahamwe. On 21 April, the Security Council issued UNAMIR a revised mandate.[47] Reduced to only a small headquarters staff, a few observers, and a small battalion of Ghanaian infantry soldiers, Dallaire's tiny force consolidated at the Amahoro Hotel and nearby stadium. Cut off from the rest of the world, they did their best to salvage what remained of the mission, and to protect as many people as they could, primarily those who had sought refuge in the Amahoro Stadium, the King Faizal Hospital, the Hotel Milles Collines and the Meridien Hotel.

After much vacillating, on 17 May 1994 the Security Council issued Resolution 918, authorizing an increase of the force structure for UNAMIR to 5500 troops, along with an expansion of its mandate as follows:

(a) To contribute to the security and protection of displaced persons, refugees and civilians at risk in Rwanda, including through the establishment and maintenance, where feasible, of secure humanitarian areas;

(b) To provide security and support for the distribution of relief supplies and humanitarian relief operations.[48]

Although the new mandate under UNSCR 918 called on UNAMIR to "contribute to the security and protection of displaced persons, refugees and civilians at risk in Rwanda,"[49] it did not change the parameters for the use of force. In this respect it is notable, that the ROE provisions found in paragraph 17 of Dallaire's ROE were not included in UNAMIR 2 ROE. The peacekeeping force was to

43 Caplan (n 37) para 15.4.

44 BGen Romeo Dallaire, Force Commander UNAMIR (n 38).

45 Caplan (n 37) para 15.9.

46 ibid.

47 United Nations Security Council Resolution 912 (1994).

48 United Nations Security Council Resolution 918 (1994) para 3. Of note, resolution 918 marked the beginning of what has become known colloquially as UNAMIR 2.

49 ibid.

continue its operations in accordance with Chapter VI, and force was to be used only in self-defence.[50]

Shortly after UNSCR 918 was issued, the Canadian, British and Australian contingents to UNAMIR 2 began their pre-deployment training. The first of the contingents to deploy were the Canadians, with most personnel drawn from the First Canadian Division Headquarters and Signal Regiment (1CDHSR) and 3 Commando (3Cdo) of the Canadian Airborne Regiment. For many deploying to Rwanda, particularly those from the Airborne, this was to be their second operational tour to Africa in as many years. With memories of Somalia fresh in their minds, the Canadians conducted their pre-deployment training in Petawawa, Ontario. Throughout that training it was impressed upon the troops that UNAMIR was Canada's first foray into Africa since the deeply embarrassing Somalia mission, and that the Canadians were to be on their very best behaviour during the Rwanda mission. Reminded that the eyes of the nation would be on them, it was made very clear to them that they were on a Chapter VI mission and that if any of them were to kill another person during the mission, they would be held to account for their actions in front of a court martial. It was under this cloud that the advance party for the contingent, consisting mainly of soldiers from 3 Commando, arrived at Kigali Airfield in mid July.

Phillip Drew was a member of the Canadian advance party. An Intelligence Officer by trade, he was officially deployed as the Canadian Contingent Operations Captain. Within hours of landing in Kigali he began to receive reports of civilians being killed in the streets of Kigali. In some cases it was apparent that the Rwandan Patriotic Army (RPA) was conducting summary executions of suspected genocidiares, while in other cases it was apparent that remnants of the Interahamwe were likely responsible. Faced with soldiers who were questioning what they were to do in cases where they saw civilians being killed, it was reiterated to them that force could be used only to protect themselves and other members of the mission. Otherwise, they were not to intervene.

The extent of the order to not intervene was illustrated in early September when Canadians were conducting a security patrol in the Kibungo prefecture. While driving along one of the roads in the area, one of the RPA vehicles that was accompanying the Canadians was ambushed by suspected Hutu insurgents, killing a number of soldiers. Reacting immediately, the Canadian Airborne soldiers followed their well-rehearsed drills and turned their armoured vehicles into the ambush. Whereas in most cases, the Canadian vehicles would have fired on the insurgents, the commander on the scene, who had recently completed a tour in Somalia, ordered his soldiers to hold fire unless and until

50 ibid 4.

the insurgents fired on them. The Canadians did not engage. The insurgents escaped into the jungle.

In late September, the UNAMIR contingents began to receive ROE cards, which outlined the circumstances under which their personnel could use force. The cards issued to Canadians spelled out the rules clearly; unless authorized by the force commander, they were not permitted to disarm paramilitaries or civilians, and they were not authorized to intervene to protect civilians.[51]

By the time the main body of the Canadian Contingent began to arrive in Kigali in early August, most killing in the city had ceased. Nonetheless, during the ensuing months, numerous Canadians were witness to persons being killed. Such killings were sometimes conducted by the RPA, who it seemed, had lists of people that they were hunting for. In some cases, convoys of UN vehicles returning refugees from neighbouring countries or Internally Displaced Persons (IDP) camps were stopped at RPA roadblocks and forced to unload their human cargoes. On several occasions, persons were selected from the groups that had been removed from the trucks, then taken into the jungle and shot.

Australian forces deployed during UNAMIR 2, experienced similar incidents. As with the Canadians, the Australians noted that by the end of 1994, their relationship with an increasingly belligerent RPA was becoming strained. For the Australians, one of the strongest tests of the ROE occurred in April 1995, in the IDP camp in Kibeho. The camp, which contained approximately 100,000 mainly Hutu refugees, was known to be harbouring former regime soldiers and militia members who had been involved in the genocide.[52] In an effort to return the IDPs to their home villages, and to disperse any groups that might be planning insurgency operations against the new government, the decision was made to empty the camp under a joint UNAMIR and RPA initiative called OP RETOUR. As is recalled in the Australian Military History Unit book on UNAMIR, "Initially the RPA appeared to be playing by the rules, channelling refugees into waiting trucks to take them to their home provinces. However, on closer inspection by the Australians it became apparent that the Rwandan soldiers were screening terrified Hutus and taking away anyone they didn't like the look of. Tutsi interrogators bashed, kicked and bayoneted those who were singled out. For young Aussie soldiers it was a nightmare scenario. They were entirely helpless to change the situation and had been explicitly ordered not to intervene."[53] It is estimated that approximately 4000 people were murdered in Kibeho.[54]

---

51 'Soldiers Guide – ROE for CF Members UNAMIR II' paras 4–5.

52 Kevin O'Halloran, *Rwanda: UNAMIR 1994/95* (Big Sky Publishing 2012) 108.

53 ibid 112.

54 Paul Jordan, 'Witness to Genocide: A Personal Account of the 1995 Kibeho Massacre' (2003) 1 Australian Army Journal 127.

6 Operational Considerations

While many commentators over the past 25 years have criticized UNAMIR for its inaction in the face of violence against civilians, such critics often overlook the fact that the peacekeepers were vastly outnumbered and out-gunned by the various factions that were operating in the country. As described earlier in this paper, the development of ROE must take into consideration three factors; law, policy and operational considerations. Chief amongst the operational considerations are the questions of whether a force is of sufficient size and combat power to be able to successfully engage in various scenarios, including self-defence. The corollary to that is that if a force does not have the capacity to perform a given task, then it is folly, and potentially dangerous, to provide it with ROE to do that thing.

The reconnaissance mission conducted during August of 1994 recommended that in order to achieve its mandate under UNSCR 872, UNAMIR would require a force of 4260 personnel. It must be recalled, that this estimate was based on a very optimistic assessment of the peace process, as well as the assumption that the parties would cooperate during the transition to a broad based government. For a variety of reasons (none of which were operationally based) Dallaire was informed that his force would be capped at 2450 personnel. Thus, even in the most positive circumstances, the force was too small and poorly equipped to accomplish its basic tasks.

While it is not uncommon for the UN to under-resource peacekeeping missions, the decision to deploy a reduced UNAMIR force, particularly in the face of credible warnings that the country could erupt into ethnic violence, was absurd. Geographically speaking, Rwanda is a land-locked country situated in the centre of Africa. It is accessible only by road from neighbouring countries, or by air. The major roads in the north and west of the country wind through mountain passes, while routes to the south and east are lined by jungle. In other words, UN forces in the country were completely isolated, with little hope that they could be readily reinforced or rescued in an emergency. This, added to the fact that there was no viable military force in the region that could deploy to Rwanda on short notice, meant that if the tiny UNAMIR force was to come under attack it would be quickly overwhelmed.

It is highly likely that Iqbal Riza's 7 April order to Dallaire to not permit his soldiers to fire unless fired upon,[55] was based on his own misinformed grasp of self-defence, rather than on a full understanding of the concept. Having stated

55 'Report of the Independent Inquiry into the Actions of the United Nations During the 1994 Genocide in Rwanda' (n 25) 16.

that, in retrospect it was fortuitous that the order to not fire unless fired upon was given. We witnessed the various parties engaged in their crazed killing frenzies, and there is little doubt in our minds that if they had been provoked, the RGF, the RPA and the various militias would have turned their rage on UNAMIR. Completely isolated, under-equipped, and lacking ammunition, the small peacekeeping force would have been overwhelmed and destroyed before any reinforcements could possibly have arrived, with the members likely facing the same fate as the Belgian paratroopers who were murdered and mutilated on 7 April 1994. As a consequence, it can be argued that the Riza's restriction on self-defence might well have spared the tiny UN force from annihilation.

7 Conclusion

It has often been stated by observers that had UNAMIR's rules of engagement been more robust, it may have been able to have stopped the genocide. This statement ignores the fact that even if UNAMIR had been authorized to intervene, there is no way that the small force could have influenced the outcome of the events of 1994. As it stands, UNAMIR was able to provide protection to approximately 30,000 people who took refuge in the Amahoro stadium and several other safe havens in the city, a task that was only accomplished by placing soldiers at the entrances to the facility so that anyone trying to enter would have had to use violence to get past them. During this period several UNAMIR soldiers demonstrated incredible bravery, particularly Tunisian Major Belgacem and Republic of the Congo Captain Mabiya, each of whom placed themselves in personal danger to prevent civilians from being killed.

When one considers the factors that affect the development of ROE, (i.e. law, policy and operational considerations) it is clear that even if UNAMIR had been a chapter VII mission with a clear mandate to protect civilians, the reality was that it was too small and too poorly equipped to have made any significant difference. It is a sad reflection on the UN that in the face of genocide, it deployed, and then refused to augment a force that was so weak and under-resourced that it could not possibly have defended itself, let alone civilians.

As the mission was being planned during the late summer of 1993, there were increasing signs that Rwanda was spiralling toward violence. In spite of the myriad of warnings that were received in the UN, the Security Council did not alter its assessment of what the mission required, or whether the mission was even viable. Instead, the Council ignored the realities on the ground, and deployed its force into a highly volatile environment. In what can be described as willful blindness, the Security Council sent UNAMIR soldiers into an impossible situation.

In an early attempt to deflect blame for the UN's negligence, Assistant Secretary-General Iqbal Riza, argued that UNAMIR's inability to protect civilians should not be viewed as a failure. After all, as he stated, the "mandate of UNAMIR had never been to protect all civilians, but rather to implement the Arusha agreement."[56] While Riza's statement is true, the fact that he made it demonstrates a callous disregard for Rwandans and the members of the UN force who were sent to the country to help them realize peace. The fact that early warnings pointed toward a resurgence of ethnic violence before UNAMIR was established should have sufficed for the UN to adjust the mandate and the force levels for the mission. Instead, even in the face of the Genocide Fax, no action was taken to provide any form of assistance to Dallaire's isolated force. Reflective of the UN's attitude toward Rwanda was DPKO's preference to draw down, rather than reinforce, the mission once the genocide started.

Those who believe that UNAMIR failed to protect civilians because of its ROE are wrong. UNAMIR was not destined to fail because of its ROE, but because of the willful neglect of the organization that created it. Without a doubt, it was the senior members of the Secretariat, the Security Council, and the international community as a whole, who failed the people of Rwanda. In the words of General Dallaire, "the international community has blood on its hands."[57]

---

56 Michael Barnett, 'The United Nations Security Council and Rwanda', *International Decision-Making in the Age of Genocide: Rwanda 1990–1994* (Holocaust Memorial Museum 2014) 5–6.

57 Caplan (n 37) para 15.40.

PART 2

The "G" Word

CHAPTER 8

Defining Genocide

Melanie O'Brien

1 Introduction

Genocide is an international crime, one that is sometimes referred to as 'the crime of crimes' because of its grave nature and the enormity of loss it effectuates. Genocide is not just the killing of multiple individuals, but rather destroying 'something more than or other than the sum of the individuals who belong to it… genocide is the killing or destruction of that "something more"'.[1] This article will explore aspects of the definition of genocide, from its creation as a word by Raphael Lemkin to the most recent case law emerging from international courts and tribunals.

When discussing the definition of genocide, the first place to turn is the Convention on the Prevention and Punishment of the Crime of Genocide (Genocide Convention).[2] In Article II, the Genocide Convention contains the definition agreed upon by states in 1948:

> [G]enocide means any of the following acts committed with intent to destroy, in whole or in part, a national, ethnical, racial or religious group, as such:
> (a) Killing members of the group;
> (b) Causing serious bodily or mental harm to members of the group;
> (c) Deliberately inflicting on the group conditions of life calculated to bring about its physical destruction in whole or in part;
> (d) Imposing measures intended to prevent births within the group;
> (e) Forcibly transferring children of the group to another group.

This definition remains the internationally accepted definition. This is the definition used in statutes of *ad hoc* international criminal courts and tribunals.[3] In 1998, the same definition was adopted into the Rome Statute of the

1 Christopher Powell, 'What do genocides kill? A relational concept of genocide' (2007) 9 Journal of Genocide Research 527, 528.

2 Convention on the Prevention and Punishment of the Crime of Genocide [1948] 78 UNTS 277, entered into force 12 January 1951.

3 ICTR, ICTY, ECCC Article 4.

 | DOI:10.1163/9789004430129_010

permanent International Criminal Court (ICC).[4] However, the definition in the Genocide Convention is lacking in detail, with no guidance as to the appropriate interpretation of each element of the crime. Thus, it has fallen to international courts and tribunals to assess the individual components of the definition of genocide. The case law emerging from these courts and tribunals, and a very few domestic courts, has provided significantly more detail of the parameters of the definition of genocide. Yet before we explore the case law on the parameters of genocide, it may be asked: from where did this word and its definition originate?

2 Lemkin's Definition

'Genocide' was a neologism created by Polish jurist Raphael Lemkin.[5] Lemkin grew up in the early 1900s in Poland, hearing of pogroms carried out against Jews in Eastern Europe, including very close to his home. In his mid to late teens, he began to think about the concept of 'destruction of groups'. This was particularly motivated by the Armenian massacres that took place in 1915, in which 1.2 million Armenians were killed by the Ottoman Empire, because of their religion and nationality.

Lemkin was motivated to study law, which he did in Krakow and Lwow; he eventually earned a doctorate in law in 1926. Lemkin's concern with destruction of groups was reawakened with the 1921 trial of Sohomon Tehlirian. This young Armenian had assassinated, in Germany, a former Ottoman leader part of the leadership circle responsible for the Armenian Genocide, Talaat Pasha. Tehlirian was found not guilty of murder. While Lemkin did not think that Tehlirian should have been able to act as judge and jury, he was more concerned

4 Rome Statute of the International Criminal Court [1998] 2187 UNTS 90, entered into force 1 July 2002.

5 For more on the life, studies and career of Lemkin, see Philippe Sands, *East West Street: On the Origins of Genocide and Crimes Against Humanity* (Weidenfeld & Nicolson 2016); Donna-Lee Frieze (ed), *Totally Unofficial: The Autobiography of Raphael Lemkin* (Yale University Press 2013); and the 2005 Vol. 7, Issue 4 of *Journal of Genocide Research*, special issue 'Raphael Lemkin: the "founder of the United Nation's Genocide Convention" as a historian of mass violence'.

Stiller remarks that Lemkin did not coin the word, but rather translated it into English from the German word '*Völkermord*', which was in use from at least 1831; Alexa Stiller, 'Semantics of Extermination: The Use of the New Term of Genocide in the Nuremberg Trials and the Genesis of a Master Narrative' in Kim C. Priemel and Alexa Stiller (eds), *Reassessing the Nuremberg Military Tribunals: Transitional Justice, Trial Narratives, and Historiography* (Berghahn Books 2012), 127 fn 16. However, Lemkin's hand-written notes of attempting to create the word do not indicate that he was seeking to translate this term; Sands, *East West Street: On the Origins of Genocide and Crimes Against Humanity*, 180.

that the perpetrators of the Armenian genocide were living unpunished. Lemkin was shocked to discover that there was no crime available to charge the Turks with killing millions.

Lemkin became a public prosecutor. He began to write, publishing pamphlets on the issue that moved him in international law. With the rise of Hitler in the 1930s, and the increasing persecution of Germany's Jews, Lemkin became more concerned that there was a need for rules prohibiting 'barbarity'. Lemkin went into private practice, but continued to publish books. Because of his connections, Lemkin was able to flee Nazi occupied Europe and arrived in Sweden in 1940. He began to collect Nazi laws, which he fortuitously believed would be proof of crimes committed. Through this, Lemkin first noticed what scholars now call the 'genocide process'- denationalisation, dehumanisation, cultural death, identification, seizure of property, forced labour, and death.[6] In 1941, Lemkin moved to the United States, which was to be his home for the remainder of his life until his death in 1959. He became an academic, and his campaign for the creation of a crime prohibiting the destruction of groups began in earnest.

In 1944 Lemkin coined the word 'genocide', in his book *Axis Rule in Occupied Europe*.[7] He formed the word from the Greek word 'genos' (family or offspring, used also as race, tribe, nation or kind) and the Latin word 'cide' (killing). This was a crime that concerned the extermination of nations and ethnic groups, through killing the intelligentsia, destruction of culture, transfer of wealth, depopulation of territory, and mass killing.

Lemkin was a one-man campaign, working across Europe and the US for the creation of a Genocide Convention. First, he was successful in having the word included in the charges at the International Military Tribunal which tried the leaders of the Nazi regime for their crimes committed in World War II and the Holocaust. While specific charges of genocide were not laid, the word was included as a characterisation of acts that would constitute war crimes.[8] Subsequently, Lemkin was part of a committee that drafted the text of what became the Genocide Convention.

---

6 E.g., Martin Shaw, *What is Genocide?* (Polity Press 2015); Sheri P. Rosenberg, 'Genocide Is a Process, Not an Event' (2012) 7 Genocide Studies and Prevention 16; Scott Straus, 'Contested meanings and conflicting imperatives: A conceptual analysis of genocide' (2001) 3 Journal of Genocide Research 349; Helen Fein, 'Accounting for genocide after 1945: Theories and some findings' (1993) 1 International Journal on Minority and Group Rights 79; Leo Kuper, *Genocide: Its Political Use in the Twentieth Century* (Yale University Press 1982).

7 Raphael Lemkin, *Axis Rule in Occupied Europe* (Carnegie Endowment for International Peace 1944).

8 Stiller, 'Semantics of Extermination: The Use of the New Term of Genocide in the Nuremberg Trials and the Genesis of a Master Narrative', 108–110.

Yet that definition was, as treaty content usually is, a result of significant compromise by states – and diminished from Lemkin's initial concept. Lemkin created the term genocide as a word to capture 'the destruction of essential foundations of the life of national groups', however he did not necessarily see killing as the crucial component of that destruction.[9] Instead, he saw the plan of destruction as encompassing 'the disintegration of political and social institutions, of culture, language, national feelings, religion, and the economic existence of national groups, and the destruction of the personal security, liberty, health, dignity, and even the lives of the individuals belonging to such groups'.[10] Lemkin clearly considered loss of life as part of genocide, but not the point around which the other crimes pivoted.[11] His focus was holistic, considering the social structure of the targeted communities, the removal of rights from that group, and 'the imposition of the national pattern of the oppressor' on the oppressed group.[12] Lemkin explicitly believed culture was an inherent need and factor of a group's existence, and thus the undermining of the culture of a group would result in disintegration of that group.[13] He presented multiple techniques of genocide: political, social, cultural, economic, biological, physical, religious and moral, which together, 'represent a concentrated and coordinated attack upon all elements of nationhood'.[14] Lemkin's comprehensive definition has, however, not been the one that has been adopted through the subsequent evolution in legal, scholarly and political discussion around the definition of genocide.

3 Case Law

Despite the nascent nature of the word itself, thanks to Lemkin's perseverance, some post-World War II (WWII) trials included genocide within charges of

9 Lemkin, *Axis Rule in Occupied Europe*, 79.

10 Ibid, 79; William A. Schabas, *Genocide in International Law* (2nd edn, Cambridge University Press 2009), 30.

11 Lemkin framed the social, cultural and economic aspects of genocide and the "biological aspect", which was "physical decline and even destruction of the population involved"; Lemkin, *Axis Rule in Occupied Europe*, 80. He also included religious and moral genocide techniques; ibid, 82–90.

12 Ibid, 79.

13 A. Dirk Moses, 'Raphael Lemkin, Culture, and the Concept of Genocide' in Donald Bloxham and A. Dirk Moses (eds), *The Oxford Handbook of Genocide Studies* (Oxford University Press 2010).

14 Lemkin, *Axis Rule in Occupied Europe*, 82–90.

crimes against humanity.[15] As such, genocide in these early cases was perceived as:

- An 'established governmental plan for the extermination of' Poles and Jews; a 'national program of racial persecution';[16]
- the 'wholesale extermination of the Jews and also of Poles' which had 'all the characteristics of genocide in the biological meaning of this term, and embraced in addition destruction of the cultural life of these nations';[17] and
- 'destruction of nations and ethnic groups within the German sphere of influence, in part by murderous extermination, and in part by elimination and suppression of national characteristics'.[18]

The commonality of these cases is a focus on 'extermination', but it is presented not solely as a concept of killing, but also including cultural life and the removal or dislocation of population. Note that these quotes come from cases from 1948 and 1949- at the time of, or after, the creation of the Genocide Convention- and yet still refer to the concepts of uprooting of a population and 'extermination and suppression of national characteristics'. As genocide was not a specific charge, there was no in-depth discussion or analysis in the judgements as to the definition of genocide, but rather a focus on the broader program of 'Germanisation' and the persecution of the Jews and some other groups.

In 1946, the UN General Assembly adopted a resolution in which it affirmed genocide as a crime under international law, and declared that

> [g]enocide is a denial of the right of existence of entire human groups... such denial... results in great losses to humanity in the form of cultural and other contributions represented by these human groups... Many instances of such crimes of genocide have occurred when racial, religious, political and other groups have been destroyed, entirely or in part.[19]

---

15 See Schabas, *Genocide in International Law*, 48–52 and Stiller, 'Semantics of Extermination: The Use of the New Term of Genocide in the Nuremberg Trials and the Genesis of a Master Narrative', 107–120, for further details of World War II cases in which genocide was charged or mentioned.

16 *United States of America v Altstoetter et al.* (*the Justices Case*), 3 TWC 3, 1128, 1156. Two of the defendants, Lautz and Rothaug, were convicted of genocide.

17 *Poland v Goeth*, (1946) 7 LRTWC 4 (Supreme National Tribunal of Poland).

18 *United States of America v Greifelt et al.* (*RuSHA* Case), (1948) 4 TWC 1, 609–10; and *United States v von Weizsaecker et al.* (*Ministries* Case), (1949) 14 TWC 308, 468.
RuSHA was the *Rasse- und Siedlungshauptamt der SS* (the SS Race and Settlement Main Office).

19 UNGA Res. 96(I) (1946).

This resolution also declared that genocide was committed 'whether the crime is committed on religious, racial, political or any other grounds'. It is clear, then, that the definition of genocide in this resolution was following Lemkin's broad concept of genocide, not only considering cultural destruction but also including political or 'any other' groups as potential victims of genocide. Interestingly, Resolution 96(I) was adopted unanimously and without debate, has been frequently cited in case law,[20] and is referred to in the preamble to the Genocide Convention. This provides a strong case for the content of Resolution 96(I) as codification of customary international law, although the revision of the contents through significant debates over the Genocide Convention and Rome Statute text creates a challenge to this customary status.

In 1961, the Israeli District Court presented genocide as a crime 'intended to exterminate the nation as a group', 'the extermination of members of a group as such', defining 'the crime against the Jewish People' with the same acts as genocide.[21]

Since the adoption of the Genocide Convention, there have been a number of international criminal courts and tribunals established, many of which have tried individuals for the crime of genocide. These courts and tribunals, along with International Court of Justice (ICJ) considerations of the cases based on the Genocide Convention, have contributed to a deeper development of the definition of genocide. Key definitional elements of genocide, emerging from modern case law, are discussed here.

3.1 *'Destroy'*

In the *RuSHA* Case (really the only 'genocide case' of the post-WWII trials), the Nuremberg Military Tribunal (NMT) held that the object of the program of genocide 'was to strengthen the German nation and the so-called "Aryan" race at the expense of such other nations and groups by imposing Nazi and German characteristics upon individuals selected therefrom…and by the extermination of "undesirable" racial elements'.[22] This was carried out through, inter alia, kidnapping children, preventing marriages, forced relocation, forced labour, destruction of property (cultural and other), persecution, and execution.[23] Thus, the NMT combined physical and cultural destruction into the definition of genocide.

---

20 See Schabas, *Genocide in International Law*, 56, fn. 207 for an extensive list of cases referring to the resolution.

21 *Attorney-General v Eichmann*, District Court of Jerusalem, Criminal Case No. 40/61, 1961, [38], [190]–[196].

22 *RuSHA* case, 610.

23 Ibid.

Yet, despite the post-WWII case law including cultural destruction in the concept of genocide, in the modern international courts and tribunals, focus has limited 'destruction' to physical or biological destruction of the group. That said, some findings have explored alternative aspects of the 'destruction' component of genocide. In the *Kayishama and Ruzindana* Trial Judgement, the International Criminal Tribunal for Rwanda (ICTR) Trial Chamber referred to the convictions in *Akayesu* for sexual violence and rape as genocide and noted that conduct that does not achieve complete annihilation (i.e. falls short of causing death) can be considered genocidal conduct.[24] In *Krstić*, the International Criminal Tribunal for the former Yugoslavia (ICTY) found that génocidaires 'identify entire human groups for extinction… [and] seek to deprive humanity of the manifold richness its nationalities, races, ethnicities and religions provide'.[25] In a German case, the Federal Constitutional Court held genocide to include 'the annihilation of a group as a social unit with its special qualities, uniqueness and its feeling of togetherness, not exclusively their physical-biological annihilation'. This definition was subsequently upheld by the European Court of Human Rights.[26]

However, aside from a few examples, courts and tribunals have remained adamant that the legal application of genocide remains confined to physical or biological destruction.[27] In *Karadžić*, the ICTY expressly stated that the 'Genocide Convention and customary international law prohibit only the physical and biological destruction of a group, not attacks on cultural or religious property or symbols of the group'.[28] In the most recent case on genocide, Case 002/02 at the Extraordinary Chambers in the Courts of Cambodia (ECCC), the Co-Prosecutors argued that destruction of a group could be other than physical or biological, arguing that 'dissolution of [the group's] unit and/or collective identity' was also part of genocide, leading to deprivation of existence 'through the destruction of [the group's] specific traits, or dispersal of its members'.[29] The Co-Prosecutors provided the example of forcible transfer of

24 *Prosecutor v Kayishema and Ruzindana*, Trial Judgement, ICTR-95-1-T, 21 May 1999 [97], citing *Akayesu*, Trial Judgement [731].

25 *Prosecutor v Radislav Krstić*, Appeal Judgement, IT-98-33-A, 19 April 2004 [36].

26 *Jorgić*, Bundesverfassungsgericht, 2 BvR 1290/99, 30 Aril 1999 reported in (1999) 3 StR 215/98, <https://www.bundesverfassungsgericht.de/entscheidungen/rk20001212_2bvr129099en.html> accessed 4 February 2020, [4]; and the European Court of Human Rights ruling: *Jorgić v Germany*, (No 74613/01) Judgment 12.7.2007 [104]–[105].

27 See e.g., *Prosecutor v Ratko Mladić*, Trial Judgement, IT-09-92-T, 22 November 2017, Vol. III of V [3435].

28 *Karadžić* [553].

29 Co-Prosecutors' Amended Closing Brief in Case 002/02, Case No. 002/19-09-2007-ECCC/TC, 2 October 2017, [102].

children and forcible conversion as genocide crimes that result in cessation of existence of a group.[30] This argument was rejected by the Court, ruling instead that the 'scope of the Genocide Convention was limited to the physical and biological destruction of the group to the exclusion of cultural genocide'.[31] The ECCC placed the definitional limitation that for the genocidal crimes which do not result in physical or biological destruction, these crimes must still be committed with the intent to achieve physical or biological destruction of the targeted group.[32]

3.2 *'In part'*

One of the specific challenges in the definition of genocide is determining what constitutes a 'part' of a group to satisfy crimes committed with an intent to destroy 'in part'. To qualify, the part 'must be a substantial part of that group… the part targeted must be significant enough to have an impact on the group as a whole'.[33] In *Sikirica*, the ICTY Trial Chamber determined that there must be 'intention to destroy a reasonably substantial number relative to the total population of the group'.[34] This is a quantitative assessment, where the 'number of individuals targeted should be evaluated not only in absolute terms, but also in relation to the overall size of the entire group'.[35]

However, if this quantitative requirement is not fulfilled, the Trial Chamber also allowed for considering 'if there is evidence that the destruction is related to a significant section of the group, such as its leadership'.[36] That is, the 'in part' may be determined as a substantial percentage of the population, or a significant section targeted for their prominent role in the group.[37]

---

30 Ibid., [102]–[107].The Co-Prosecutors in part relied on Judge Shahabuddeen's partly dissenting opinion in the *Krstić* Appeal, where the Judge found that destruction of a group through its characteristics would also be genocide; *Prosecutor v Radislav Krstić*, Appeal Judgement, Partial Dissenting Opinion of Judge Shahabuddeen, IT-98-33-A, 19 April 2004 [48]–[52].

31 *Prosecutor v Nuon Chea and Khieu Samphan,* Case 002/02, Trial Judgement, Case No. 002/19-09-2007/ECCC/TC, 16 November 2018 [800].

32 Ibid.

33 *Krstić*, Appeal Judgement, IT-98-33-A, 19 April 2004 [8]; Case 002/02 [802]. See also *Mladić* [3437]; *Karadžić*, [555]; *Prosecutor v Goran Jelisić*, Trial Judgement, IT-95-10-T, 14 December 1999 [82]; *Sikirica et al.*, Judgement on Defence Motions to Acquit, IT-95-8-T, 3 September 2001 [65]; *Kayishema and Ruzindana* [97].

34 *Sikirica* [65].

35 *Krstić*, Appeal Judgement [12]. See also *Karadžić* [555].

36 *Sikirica* [76]. See also *Kayishema and Ruzindana* [96].

37 *Mladić* [3437].

3.3 *'Groups'*

The groups listed in the definition of genocide are national, ethnical, racial and religious groups. The intention of the Genocide Convention drafters was to limit targeted groups to 'stable and permanent' groups; that is, groups whose membership was not voluntary.[38] The group 'must be a collection of people with a particular group identity… defined positively and have unique distinguishing characteristics'.[39]

The ICTY has determined that the status of a national, ethnical or racial group should be determined subjectively, from the perspective of the perpetrator group: 'It is the stigmatisation of a group as a distinct national, ethnical or racial unit by the community which allows it to be determined whether a targeted population constitutions a national, ethnical or racial group in the eyes of the alleged perpetrator.'[40] In other words, the definition of a protected group has to 'be assessed in the light of a particular political, social and cultural context'.[41] The ECCC has held that this approach 'accords with the object and purpose of the Genocide Convention'.[42]

The ICTR offers definitions of each group category, where a national group is a 'collection of people who are perceived to share a legal bond based on common citizenship, coupled with reciprocity of rights and duties';[43] an ethnic group is those who share a common language or culture; a racial group is a group with 'hereditary physical traits often identified with a geographical region, irrespective of linguistic, cultural, national or religious factors'; and a religious group shares the same religion, denomination or mode of worship.[44]

---

38 For this discussion, see, e.g., Sixty-Ninth Meeting of the Sixth Committee, 7 October 1948, UN Doc. A/C.6/SR.69. Of course, religion can be a choice, so this is a debatable allocation. See also *Akayesu*, Trial Judgement [511].

39 *Mladić* [3436]; Case 002/02 [793].

40 *Jelisić*, Trial Judgement [70]. See also *Prosecutor v Radislav Krstić*, Trial Judgement, IT-98-33-T, 2 August 2001 [557].

41 *Prosecutor v Rutaganda*, Trial Judgement and Sentence, ICTR-96-3-T, 6 December 1999 [56]; Case 002/02 [792]; *Krstić*, Trial Judgement [557].

42 Case 002/02 [792].

43 For further discussion on the parameters of 'national', see Marcelo Ferreira, 'Genocide, and its Definition as the "Partial Elimination of a National Group"' (2013) 8 Genocide Studies and Prevention 5.

44 *Akayesu*, Trial Judgement [512]–[515]. The definition of a national group is drawn from *Nottebohm (Liechtenstein v. Guatemala)*, ICJ, Judgment of 6 April 1955, 23.

3.4 *Specific Conduct*

Various cases have dealt with examples of the specific conduct that is included in the five listed crimes. Below is an overview of the definitions that have developed for each of the listed crimes, including specific conduct examples where relevant.

(a) *Killing members of the group* equates to the crime of murder, which occurs when death has been caused[45] due to an act or omission of the perpetrator which was intended to cause death or committed with reasonable knowledge that the act or omission would lead to death.[46] Killing does not have to be premeditated, although there is the underlying perception that all genocidal crimes are premeditated, given the broader intent of destruction of the group.[47]

(b) *Causing serious bodily or mental harm to members of the group.* This harm must be intentionally inflicted harm. There is conflicting jurisprudence with regards to one aspect of this genocidal crime. Some judgements, including from the ICJ, have held that said harm 'must be of such a serious nature as to contribute or tend to contribute to the [physical or biological] destruction of the group'.[48] However, in the 2016 *Karadžić* Trial Judgement, the ICTY determined that the judgements mentioning this qualification did not actually demonstrate that 'the harm was such as to threaten the group's destruction', and other judgements did not mention such an additional requirement at all. Consequently, the ICTY Trial Chamber was 'of the view that there is no additional requirement that the serious bodily or mental harm… be of such serious nature as to threaten the destruction of the group in whole or in part'.[49]

45 Elements of Crimes, ICC-ASP/1/3, Article 6(a)(1) footnote 2.

46 Case 002/02 [796]; *Mladić* [3049], [3434]; *Akayesu*, Trial Judgement [500].

47 *Akayesu*, Trial Judgement [501].

48 *Mladić* [3434], [3447]; *Prosecutor v Tolimir*, Trial Judgement, IT-05-88/2-T, 12 December 2012 [738]; *Prosecutor v Seromba*, Appeal Judgement, ICTR-2001-66-A, 12 March 2008 [46]; *Prosecutor v Krajišnik*, Trial Judgement, IT-00-39-T, 27 September 2006 [862]. The ICJ states that 'the ordinary meaning of "serious" is that the bodily or mental harm referred to in subparagraph (b) of that Article must be such as to contribute to *the physical or biological destruction* of the group, in whole or in part'; *Application of the Convention on the Prevention and Punishment of the Crime of Genocide* (*Croatia v Serbia*), ICJ, Judgment of 3 February 2015 [157], [160] (emphasis added).

49 *Karadžić* [544].

Beyond this debate, it is agreed that the serious bodily or mental harm does not necessarily have to be permanent or irremediable,[50] but it does have to 'go beyond temporary unhappiness, embarrassment or humiliation' and result 'in a grave and long-term disadvantage to a person's ability to lead a normal and constructive life',[51] amounting to 'more than minor or temporary impairment of mental faculties such as the infliction of strong fear or terror, intimidation or threat'.[52]

Examples of specific conduct include:

a. Torture;[53]
b. Cruel, inhumane or degrading treatment;[54]
c. Rape and other sexual violence;[55]
d. 'Non-fatal physical violence that causes disfigurement or serious injury to the external or internal organs';[56]
e. Enslavement;[57]
f. Starvation;[58]
g. Deportation/ forced displacement;[59]
h. Persecution;[60]
i. Detention in ghettos or camps;[61]
j. Death threats during interrogation;[62]

---

50 *Krstić*, Trial Judgement [513]; *Akayesu*, Trial Judgement [502].

51 *Karadžić*, [543]; *Krstić*, Trial Judgement [513].

52 *Seromba*, Appeal Judgement [46].

53 *Mladić* [3434]; *Akayesu*, Trial Judgement [504]; Elements of Crimes, Article 6(b)(1) footnote 3.

54 *Akayesu*, Trial Judgement [503]–[504]; *Eichmann* 1961; Elements of Crimes, Article 6(b)(1) footnote 3.

55 *Mladić* [3434]; *Karadžić*, [545]; *Case Concerning Application of the Convention on the Prevention and Punishment of the Crime of Genocide* (*Bosnia and Herzegovina v Serbia and Montenegro*), ICJ, Judgment of 26 February 2007 [300–303]; *Genocide Case* (*Croatia v Serbia*) [158]; *Prosecutor v Stakić*, Trial Judgement, IT-97-24-T, 31 July 2003 [319]; *Akayesu*, Trial Judgement [731]; *Kayishema and Ruzindana* [109]; Elements of Crimes, Article 6(b)(1) footnote 3.

56 *Mladić* [3434]; *Karadžić*, [545].

57 *Akayesu*, Trial Judgement [503]; *Attorney-General v Eichmann*, District Court of Jerusalem, Criminal Case No. 40/61 (1961).

58 *Akayesu*, Trial Judgement [503]; *Eichmann* 1961.

59 *Karadžić*, [545]; *Prosecutor v Blagojević*, Trial Judgement, IT-02-60-T, 17 January 2005 [647]; *Akayesu*, Trial Judgement [503]; *Eichmann* 1961.

60 *Akayesu*, Trial Judgement [503]; *Eichmann* 1961.

61 *Akayesu*, Trial Judgement [503]–[504]; *Eichmann* 1961.

62 *Karadžić*, [545]; *Akayesu*, Trial Judgement [711].

k. Beatings;[63]
l. Surviving genocidal massacres.[64]

(c) *Deliberately inflicting on the group conditions of life calculated to bring about its physical destruction in whole or in part.* These are 'methods of physical destruction, other than killing, whereby the perpetrator ultimately seeks the death of the members of the group',[65] however may include 'methods of destruction which do not immediately lead to the death of members of the group'.[66] It is not necessary to prove that 'the conditions actually led to death or serious bodily or mental harm of members' of the group.[67] Overall, this includes 'deliberate deprivation of resources indispensable for survival'.[68] Examples of specific conduct include:

a. Systematic expulsion from homes;[69]
b. Denial of medical services;[70]
c. 'Creation of circumstances that would lead to a slow death, such as lack of proper housing, clothing, and hygiene or excessive work or physical exertion';[71]
d. Deprivation of food;[72]
e. Forced displacement.[73]

---

63 *Karadžić*, [545]; *Akayesu*, Trial Judgement [711].

64 *Krstić*, Trial Judgement [635], which held 'the ordeal inflicted on the men who survived the [Srebrenica] massacres may appropriately be characterised as a genocidal act causing serious bodily and mental harm to members of the group pursuant to Article 4(2)(b). While the agreed objective of the joint criminal enterprise in which General Krstić participated was the actual killing of the military aged Bosnian Muslim men of Srebrenica, the terrible bodily and mental suffering of the few survivors clearly was a natural and foreseeable consequence of the enterprise.' See also *Blagojević*, [647].

65 *Genocide Case (Croatia v Serbia)* [161]; *Stakić*, [517]–[518]; *Akayesu*, Trial Judgement [505].

66 *Akayesu*, Trial Judgement [116].

67 *Karadžić*, [546].

68 Elements of Crimes, Article 6(c)(4) footnote 4.

69 *Mladić* [3434]; *Karadžić*, [546]; *Genocide Case (Croatia v Serbia)* [161]; *Akayesu*, Trial Judgement [506].

70 *Mladić* [3434]; *Karadžić*, [546]; *Genocide Case (Croatia v Serbia)* [161]; *Akayesu*, Trial Judgement [506]; *Akayesu*, Trial Judgement [115]; Elements of Crimes, Article 6(c)(4) footnote 4.

71 *Mladić* [3434]; *Karadžić*, [546]; *Genocide Case (Croatia v Serbia)* [161]; *Prosecutor v Brđanin*, Trial Judgement, IT-99-36-T, 1 September 2004 [691]; *Prosecutor v Stakić*, Trial Judgement, IT-97-24-T, 31 July 2003 [517]; *Akayesu*, Trial Judgement [115].

72 *Karadžić*, [546]; *Genocide Case (Croatia v Serbia)* [161]; *Akayesu*, Trial Judgement [506]; Elements of Crimes, Article 6(c)(4) footnote 4.

73 *Genocide Case (Croatia v Serbia)* [163]; Elements of Crimes, Article 6(c)(4) footnote 4.

(d) *Imposing measures intended to prevent births within the group.* The ICJ held that rape committed in this context must be specifically committed in order to prevent births.[74] In its 2007 judgment in the *Bosnia-Herzegovina v Serbia and Montenegro Genocide* Case, the ICJ rejected arguments that measures were imposed to prevent births because evidence was not presented that proved a reduction in birth rates or reproduction. Despite the phrasing of the Genocide Convention, proscribing the imposition of measures *intended* to prevent births, this ruling implies a requirement that the conduct actually *result* in prevention of births. If this requirement were intended, the provision would have been worded along the lines of: 'imposing measures resulting in prevention of births within the group'.

In its follow-up 2015 *Croatia v Serbia Genocide* Case judgement, the ICJ held that rape and other acts of sexual violence may constitute crimes under Article II(d), but again imposed the condition that said sexual violence must actually affect the capacity of members of the group to procreate. In another requirement not applied in the case to any of the other listed genocide crimes, the Court stated that rape and sexual violence committed under Article II(d) must be systematic.[75]

When considering genocide, the destruction of a group need not be completed for genocide to take place. Following this logic, it should not be interpreted that 'imposing measures intended to prevent births' requires the births to actually be prevented (i.e. that, for example, it be statistically proven that births have dropped). For example, it can be very clearly inferred that forced separation of men and women, which was one example of conduct argued to be genocide under Article II(d) in the *Bosnia-Herzegovina v Serbia and Montenegro Genocide* Case, is conduct intended to prevent births within the group, as it is an obvious outcome of said separation that reproduction can no longer occur. Given the lengthy history of the exclusion of rape and sexual violence from international humanitarian law and international criminal law,[76] it is indeed telling and concerning that, whilst there is no requirement that Article II(c) conduct actually leads to death (or harm), the Court nonetheless imposed

74 *Genocide Case (Croatia v Serbia)* [400].

75 *Genocide Case (Croatia v Serbia)* [166].

76 Melanie O'Brien, 'Sexual Exploitation and Beyond: Using the Rome Statute of the International Criminal Court to Prosecute UN Peacekeepers for Gender-based Crimes' (2011) 11 International Criminal Law Review 803.

the requirement that rape and sexual violence under Article II(d) must actually lead to prevention of births.

Examples of specific conduct include:
a. Rape and other acts of sexual violence;[77]
b. Sexual mutilation;[78]
c. Sterilisation;[79]
d. Forced birth control;[80]
e. Separation of the sexes;[81]
f. Prohibition of marriages.[82]

(e) *Forcibly transferring children of the group to another group*, includes circumstances where 'the objective is not only to sanction a direct act of forcible physical transfer, but also to sanction acts of threats or trauma which would lead to the forcible transfer of children from one group to another'.[83] The ICC Elements of Crimes provides for a broad interpretation of 'forcibly', including physical force but also threat of force or coercion, including 'that caused by fear of violence, duress, detention, psychological oppression or abuse of power', against the victim or a third person, or through 'taking advantage of a coercive environment'.[84]

3.5 *Intent*

The *dolus specialis*, or special intent, to commit genocide, is a unique part of the definition that differentiates genocide from any other crime- including other international crimes.[85] While the specific crimes of genocide require the standard *mens rea* of the underlying crime, that is, intent to commit that crime (e.g. murder), genocide also requires the special intent: the intent to destroy the group, in whole or in part. This intent is 'to destroy particular groups with particular identities', not merely to destroy individuals.[86] Individuals who are victims must belong to an identified group, and 'the alleged perpetrator must

---

77 *Genocide Case (Croatia v Serbia)* [166]; *Prosecutor v Akayesu*, Trial Judgement, ICTR-96-4-T, 2 September 1998 [507]–[508].
78 *Akayesu*, Trial Judgement [5–7].
79 *Akayesu*, Trial Judgement [5–7].
80 *Akayesu*, Trial Judgement [5–7].
81 *Akayesu*, Trial Judgement [5–7].
82 *Akayesu*, Trial Judgement [5–7].
83 *Akayesu*, Trial Judgement [509].
84 Elements of Crimes, Article 6(e)(1) footnote 5.
85 *Rutaganda*, Trial Judgement [451].
86 *Prosecutor v Stakić*, Appeal Judgement, IT-97-24-A, 22 March 20016 [20].

have committed his crimes as part of a wider plan to destroy the group as such'.[87]

Intent may be inferred, and does not have to be based on express statements.[88] Interestingly, while the courts and tribunals have rejected cultural or social aspects of the 'destruction' criterion, they have specifically allowed destruction of cultural property or symbols as evidence of intent to physically destroy the targeted group.[89]

4 Academic Debate

A divide exists in academic debate about the definition of genocide.[90] Legal scholars tend to apply the Genocide Convention definition strictly, employing case law interpretations, but not straying from the confines of the legal definition, in particular the listed targeted groups and the focus on physical destruction. Scholars in other disciplines, such as sociology, political science or anthropology, often take a broader perspective on genocide.[91] This broader perspective includes the crucial concept that genocide is a process, not an event,[92] and therefore includes conduct beyond killing. Behind this is the theory that the killing part of genocide cannot occur without the preparatory behaviour, including the dehumanisation of the targeted group.[93] For example, Fein presented genocide within the scope of the Holocaust with five stages: definition (of specific victims), stripping (of social roles, claims for respect, material goods and legal rights), segregation (enforced compulsory wearing of the yellow star creating stigma of Jews), isolation (requiring Jews to reside in

87 *Jelisić*, Trial Judgement [66]. See also *Karadžić*, [549]; *Akayesu*, Trial Judgement [498]–[499].

88 *Karadžić*, [550]; *Krstić*, Appeal Judgement [33]–[34].

89 *Karadžić* [553].

90 Only a brief discussion of this is possible here. For more discussion on differing scholars' views, as well as legal controversies, see Hannibal Travis, 'On the Original Understanding of the Crime of Genocide' (2012) 7 Genocide Studies and Prevention 30.

91 See Jones for a succinct summary of some key scholars' definitions of genocide; Adam Jones, *Genocide: A Comprehensive Introduction* (Routledge 2017), 23–27. Jones also provides a useful list of the other '-cides' that have been used to refer to atrocity crimes, such as politicide, ethnocide or gendercide; ibid, 34–37.

92 Rosenberg, 'Genocide Is a Process, Not an Event'.

93 See, e.g, Gregory Stanton, The Ten Stages of Genocide <http://genocidewatch.net/genocide-2/8-stages-of-genocide/> accessed 4 February 2020.

designated dwellings), and concentration (ghettoization).[94] These stages preceded the intensive mass killing of the Holocaust.

An example of broader definitions is found in Feierstein's work. He has referred to genocide as 'a specific technology of power for destroying and reorganizing social relations', noting that it 'is impossible to commit genocide without first building models of identity and Otherness'.[95] Card describes genocide as 'social death', distinct from killing large numbers of people through, for example, terrorism or war.[96] This is not to say, of course, that non-legal scholars ignore the physical or biological destruction aspect of genocide; as Snow notes, scholars 'often frame genocide in terms of biological death and body counts'.[97] Yet there is a greater propensity to acknowledge the significant role of culture as part of genocide.[98]

Scholars taking a non-legal approach believe that lawyers and jurists should take a broader approach to the interpretation of genocide, as it is a 'far more complex phenomena' then 'violent deaths and direct murder'.[99] The legal approach is certainly subject to significant conceptual constraints, but likewise so are other disciplines; with these constraints leading to exclusion of some mass atrocities by some scholars (or by courts) as 'genocide'.[100] For example,

94 Fein, 'Accounting for genocide after 1945: Theories and some findings', 60; Helen Fein, 'Genocide by Attrition 1939–1993: The Warsaw Ghetto, Cambodia, and Sudan: Links between Human Rights, Health, and Mass Death' (1997) 2 Health and Human Rights 10, 14.

95 Daniel Feierstein, *Genocide as social practice* (Rutgers University Press 2014), 205, 209.

96 Claudia Card, *Confronting Evils: Terrorism, Torture, Genocide* (Cambridge University Press 2010), Chapter 9 'Genocide is social death', 237–266.

97 James Snow, 'Claudia Card's Concept of Social Death: A New Way of Looking at Genocide' (2016) 47 Metaphilosophy 607, 608.

98 E.g., Uğur Ümit Üngör, 'Cultural Genocide: Destruction of material and non-material human culture' in Cathie Carmichael and Richard C. Maguire (eds), *The Routledge History of Genocide* (Taylor & Francis 2015).

99 Sheri P. Rosenberg and Everita Silina, 'Genocide by Attrition: Silent and efficient' in Joyce Apsel and Ernesto Verdeja (eds), *Genocide Matters: Ongoing issues and emerging perspectives* (Routledge 1999), 109.

100 David Moshman, 'Conceptual constraints on thinking about genocide' (2010) 3 Journal of Genocide Research 431. The political issues that apply to government use of the word may also be at play with regards to scholars' choice of definition, where they specifically do or do not want the term to apply to a particular situation; Jacques Sémelin, *Purify and destroy: The political uses of massacre and genocide* (Hurst and Co 2007).

An example of conduct that has faced challenges applying the term 'genocide' are indigenous/colonial genocides; see e.g., Colin Tatz, *Australia's Unthinkable Genocide* (XLibris 2017); Andrew Woolford, *This Benevolent Experiment: Indigenous Boarding Schools, Genocide, and Redress in Canada and the United States* (University of Manitoba Press 2015); A. Dirk Moses, 'An antipodean genocide? The origins of the genocidal moment in the colonization of Australia' (2010) 2 Journal of Genocide Research 89.

this challenge has been faced with regards to Cambodia, with scholars divided as to whether genocide was committed against the Khmer people, and the ECCC confirming that genocide was committed against minority groups, but no charges brought for genocide against the Khmer.[101]

5 The Weight of the 'G' Word

Genocide is sometimes called 'the crime of crimes'.[102] Competition arises between victim groups to have the atrocities committed against them termed 'genocide', because there is a perception that genocide is more serious than war crimes or crimes against humanity. This, of course, is far from the truth. All forms of atrocities are egregious and deserve attention through prevention, cessation and justice measures.

Yet one of the important issues with regards to labelling atrocities 'genocide' is that there is a Genocide Convention, but there is no 'war crimes' convention nor a convention dealing with crimes against humanity. War crimes are violations of international humanitarian law, which is found in a large number of treaties such as the Geneva Conventions of 1949, but there is no one treaty that collates war crimes specifically.[103] A project is underway to draft a crimes against humanity treaty.[104] While war crimes, crimes against humanity and genocide all exist in the Rome Statute of the International Criminal Court, this provides only for individual criminal responsibility. A general treaty would also ensure state action and responsibility.

---

101 Case 002/02 looked at genocide against the Vietnamese and Muslim Cham minorities, discussion at 1600–1782. Schabas (a legal scholar) has specifically rejected the term 'genocide' from applying to the crimes against the Khmer people; William A. Schabas, 'Cambodia: Was it Really Genocide?' (2001) 23 Human Rights Quarterly 470. Non-legal scholars such as Kiernan believe it was; Ben Kiernan, 'The Cambodian Genocide, 1975–1979' in Samuel Totten and William S. Parsons (eds), *Centuries of Genocide: Essays and Eyewitness Accounts* (Routledge 2012); Ben Kiernan, 'Genocidal Targeting: Two Groups of Victims in Pol Pot's Cambodia' in P. Timothy Bushnell (ed), *State Organized Terror: The Case of Violent Internal Repression* (Westview Press 1991). This author is a legal scholar but believes it was genocide, even within the legal definition, and a forthcoming monograph *From Discrimination to Death* will present the argument for this label.

102 This expression has been both approved and condemned by the ICTR, e.g. *Kayishema et al*, Appeal Judgment, ICTR-95-1-A, 1 June 2001 [367]; *Rutaganda*, Appeal Judgment, ICTR-96-3-A, 26 May 2003 [590] (criticism); and *Niyitegeka*, Appeal Judgement, ICTR-96-14-A, 9 July 2004 (approval).

103 For example, Geneva Convention relative to the Protection of Civilian Persons in Time of War [1949] 75 UNTS 287, entered into force 21 October 1950.

104 Crimes Against Humanity Initiative, http://sites.law.wustl.edu/WashULaw/crimesagainsthumanity/ accessed 4 February 2020.

One of the reasons that victims, particularly contemporaneously, want the atrocities against them to be termed genocide is because of the obligations that are triggered under the Genocide Convention. Under the Genocide Convention, state parties are obligated to prevent and punish genocide; therefore, if genocide is occurring, supposedly states should step in.[105] States can also be held accountable for violating their obligations under the Genocide Convention. Thus, whether atrocities are defined as genocide does have political and legal ramifications. While this author advocates for a broader definition of genocide, even from a legal perspective, it is not posited that the 'genocide' definition become so broad that it applies to all forms of atrocities. There are other categories of crimes better suited and more appropriate. Just because atrocities are being committed, this does not mean genocide is being committed; the term should not be used with abandon, but rather only when genocide is occurring or has occurred.

105 Although, as Glanville points out, this can have the opposite effect where states refuse to label a situation as genocide, with the specific aim of avoiding the triggering of Convention responsibilities; Luke Glanville, 'Is "genocide" sitll a powerful word?' (2009) 11 Journal of Genocide Research 467. See also Martin Mennecke, 'What's in a Name? Reflections on Using, Not Using, and Overusing the "G-Word"' (2007) 2 Genocide Studies and Prevention 57.

CHAPTER 9

Rwanda, the Holocaust, and the Predictable Path to Genocide

Phillip Drew

I was a member of the advance party for the Canadian contingent to the United Nations Assistance Mission in Rwanda (UNAMIR) when I arrived at Kigali airport in mid-July 1994. It is no exaggeration to say that when my colleagues (primarily members of 3 Commando, the Canadian Airborne Regiment) and I were unceremoniously dumped out of the back of a Canadian Airforce C-130 Hercules, we were greeted by a dead city. The Rwandan capital was in ruins; much of its infrastructure had been destroyed, there was no electricity or running water, feral dogs were running rampant, the streets were lined with corpses and the stench of death on the jungle air overwhelmed our senses.

As the Intelligence Officer for the Canadian contingent, one of my first tasks was to investigate the genocide, to find out why and how it had happened. Having studied and read extensively about the Holocaust while in university, and having visited several concentration camps in Europe, I was familiar with the concept of genocide and the mechanisms of its evolution. As I learned more about what had transpired in Rwanda, I noted that many of the events and characteristics of the Rwandan genocide bore an eerie resemblance to those of the Holocaust, which had occurred some 50 years earlier. Through subsequent study, particularly of materials that have been published as part of the incredible genocide scholarship that has emerged over the past two decades, I have learned that the patterns I had identified in 1994 were not mere similarities, but the key elements that make up the DNA of genocide.

As my knowledge on the subject of genocide increased, it became apparent that my task of determining why the genocide occurred was going to be more complex than I had originally anticipated, because genocides don't just happen; rather, they are the manifestation of planned and deliberate campaigns to bring about the destruction of an identifiable national, ethnical, racial or religious group. As in most cases of genocide, comprehending what, why and how the Rwandan Genocide happened would require an understanding of the history, culture and politics of the country (and the region).

 | DOI:10.1163/9789004430129_011

Although each genocide has its own unique characteristics, the creation of the conditions for genocide follows predictable patterns,[1] and requires that a number of common factors be in place.[2] In this manner, genocides are highly predictable; the corollary of which is that they are often preventable.[3]

This paper is a comparative study of the Rwandan Genocide and the Nazi Holocaust. In it, I examine the similarities and differences between the two genocides, with particular attention to the rise of the genocidal culture in the respective countries. Referring to the model set out in Stanton's Ten Stages of Genocide, I focus on the ways that the governments of Germany and Rwanda exploited racism, education and propaganda to create intolerance and inspire extremism in their populations.

1 Building the Foundations of Genocide

In his opening statement to the Nuremberg trials, prosecutor Robert H. Jackson famously stated, "the idea that a state, any more than a corporation, commits crimes, is a fiction. Crimes always are committed only by persons."[4] While at its core Jackson's statement is correct, it holds equally true that no person or group can carry out a genocide without controlling the mechanisms of state; "genocides ...are never accidental, nor are they acts of individuals. The key is that they are carried out at the explicit or tacit direction of state authorities, or those who claim state authority."[5]

By virtue of its legal definition, the crime of genocide applies only in cases in which "a national, ethnical, racial or religious group"[6] is specifically targeted for destruction.[7] As outlined below, in both Germany and Rwanda, state governments identified target groups (Jews and Tutsis) and created the conditions

1 Robert Payne, *Massacre: The Tragedy at Bangladesh and the Phenomenon of Mass Slaughter Throughout History* (The MacMillan Company 1973) 76.

2 See, Barbara Harff and Ted Robert Gurr, 'Systematic Early Warning of Humanitarian Emergencies' (1998) 35 Journal of Peace Research 551.

3 Thomas Cushman, 'Is Genocide Preventable? Some Theoretical Considerations' (2003) 5 Journal of Genocide Research 523, 541.

4 'Opening Statement before the International Military Tribunal' (*Robert H Jackson Center*) <https://www.roberthjackson.org/speech-and-writing/opening-statement-before-the-international-military-tribunal/, https://www.roberthjackson.org/speech-and-writing/opening-statement-before-the-international-military-tribunal/> accessed 18 July 2019.

5 Barbara Harff, 'No Lessons Learned from the Holocaust? Assessing Risks of Genocide and Political Mass Murder since 1955' (2003) 97 The American Political Science Review 57, 58.

6 Convention on the Prevention and Punishment of the Crime of Genocide 1948 s 2.

7 Rudolph J Rummel, 'The Holocaust in Comparative and Historical Perspective' (1998) 3 IDEA <http://www.ideajournal.com/articles.php?id=17.> accessed 23 July 2019.

necessary for genocide. The goals of creating genocidal societies were achieved through the development of a combination of exclusionist policies and ideologies, racial laws, relentless propaganda, and the capacity of the respective governments to monopolize violence.

Writing shortly after the Rwandan genocide, Rudolph Rummel stated that "the extent to which a regime controls absolutely all social, economic, and cultural groups and institutions, the degree to which its elite can rule arbitrarily, largely accounts for the magnitude and intensity of genocide and mass murder…In other words, power kills, and absolute power kills absolutely."[8] Analysis of data collected from twentieth century genocides shows that the existence of a totalitarian state is a virtual prerequisite for the occurrence of genocide or mass murder of groups within a society.[9] That is not to say, however, that all dictatorships will ultimately engage in mass violence against their populations. As Barbara Harff notes, "A regime's power is a permissive condition, not a root cause of mass violence."[10] Rather, the creation of a genocide depends on the coexistence of a number of factors, the first of which is a government that has "the intent to destroy a group"[11] as part of its core ideological imperative.[12] It is with this understanding that I will begin the comparisons of the two genocides.

2 Racism as a Core Ideology

Racism was the core ideology of the German National Socialist Party (Nazis). Early evidence of Nazism's racist philosophy was made abundantly clear in Hitler's Mein Kampf, wherein he expounded upon the myth of 'Aryanism' and advocated for "conformity with the eternal Will that dominates the universe, to postulate the victory of the better and stronger and the subordination of the inferior and weaker."[13] Describing the Jewish people as "a moral pestilence… who stood out as a different people from the other citizens…,"[14] in their early writings, Hitler and his colleagues, Rosenberg, Eckhart and Feder, promoted the

8 Rudolph J Rummel, 'Democracy, Power, Genocide, and Mass Murder' (1995) 39 Journal of Conflict Resolution 3, 25.

9 ibid.

10 Barbara Harff, 'The Comparative Analysis of Mass Atrocities and Genocide' in Nils Petter Gleditsch (ed), *R.J. Rummel: An Assessment of His Many Contributions*, vol 37 (Springer International Publishing 2017) 118 <http://link.springer.com/10.1007/978-3-319-54463-2_12> accessed 24 July 2019.

11 Convention on the Prevention and Punishment of the Crime of Genocide 1948 art. 2.

12 Harff (n 10) 118.

13 Adolf Hitler, *Mein Kampf (Translated by James Murphy)* (Free Thought Library 2014) 308.

14 ibid 42.

idea that "Jews and other 'non-Germans' [should be] excluded from the rights of citizenship and expelled from all public offices at every level of government."[15] As the Nazi party grew in influence between its inception in 1920 and its ascendance to ultimate power in 1933, its racist rhetoric grew increasingly vehement, leaving German voters with little doubt as to the party's core doctrine of anti-Semitism. In spite of this, post-War discontent, fear of Communism and the ultimate collapse of the economy during the great depression, left the people of Germany in search of a solution to their woes. They found their answer in a new party which had not been associated with any of the failed policies that had characterized German politics during the period of the Weimar Republic.

By 1930 Nazi Party had become a "unique phenomenon in German electoral politics, a catchall party of protest whose constituents, while drawn primarily from the middle-class electorate, were united above and beyond all by a profound contempt for the political and economic system."[16] As a result of a strong showing in the elections of 1931, the Nazis became the largest political party in Germany. After having engaged in a campaign of political skirmishing and deceit Hitler was appointed as Chancellor of the country on 30 January 1933. He immediately set about using his control over the Reichstag to reform German laws and to ultimately dissolve democracy.[17] Following the death of President von Hindenberg in 1934, Hitler became the undisputed leader and dictator of Germany. From that point on, he was free to enact whatever policies he wished and to use the might of the state to crush any opposition.

Rwanda's road to genocide was somewhat longer than that of Germany, with blatant anti-Tutsi racism forming much of government policy in the period between the country's colonial independence from Belgium (1962) and the commencement of the 1994 genocide.[18] While anti-Tutsi sentiment simmered throughout the country's colonial period (1884–1962), the creation of the extremist Hutu Emancipation Movement Party (Parmehutu) in 1959, under the leadership of Grégoire Kayibanda, exacerbated tensions between the majority Hutu population (approximately 85%) and the minority Tutsi (14%). Proliferating the myth of two separate races (a concept that had been largely introduced by the colonial powers) to differentiate the traditional ruling elite (Tutsis) from the remainder of the population (Hutus), Hutu nationalism and

15 Thomas Childers, *The Nazi Voter: The Social Foundations of Fascism in Germany, 1919 – 1933* (Nachdr, Univ of North Carolina Press 1990) 45.

16 ibid 268.

17 William L Shirer and Ron Rosenbaum, *The Rise and Fall of the Third Reich: A History of Nazi Germany* (Simon & Schuster 2011) 150–187.

18 Linda Melvern, *A People Betrayed: The Role of the West in Rwanda's Genocide* (New updated ed, Zed Books 2009) 16–26.

Hutu unity were the central doctrines of the virulently anti-Tutsi Parmehutu party.[19] In creating its doctrine, Parmehutu played upon the discontent of the majority Hutu population, most of whom were poor farmers, by blaming their troubles on their historic exploitation by the elitist Tutsi. In 1959, while the country was still under Belgian rule, Parmehutu was at the vanguard of Rwanda's first anti-Tutsi pogrom. Over several weeks of violence, several thousand Tutsis were murdered and tens of thousands were exiled. Much of the violence that was meted out in 1959 was carried out by peasant farmers who were urged on by extremist elements, and the perpetrators of the violence were generally not held to account. Although the violence in 1959 was relatively limited, Hutu extremists learned two critical lessons; Tutsi could be killed with impunity, and farmers could be counted upon to kill their Tutsi neighbours.

In 1962, Kayibanda's party was elected in the country's first, and only, democratic election. In shoring up its power, the Kayibanda regime "practiced capricious violence against Tutsi who challenged the new political order."[20] As a result of Kayibanda's racist rhetoric "violence against ethnic Tutsi became commonplace."[21] During subsequent pogroms in 1963 and 1973, the regime was responsible for the deaths of tens of thousands of Tutsi, and the displacement of hundreds of thousands more, with many of the refugees settling in Uganda.[22]

In 1973, Kayibanda was overthrown in a coup led by his defence Minister, Juvenal Habyarimana.[23] Habyarimana's ascendance to power brought a reprieve from government sponsored violence against the Tutsi. While his newly formed National Republican Movement for Democracy and Development (MRND), maintained its racist ideology, the relative economic and social stability that persisted between 1973 and 1990 meant that Tutsis were not regularly subjected to government sponsored violence. By the late 1980's however, storm clouds had begun to build on the horizon. Torn by internal strife caused by regional and inter-familial power struggles, rampant corruption, a faltering economy and a re-surgent Rwandan Patriotic Front (RPF) that had fallen out of favour with its Ugandan hosts, the relative peacefulness of the Rwandan regime was beginning to falter. As Uganda pressured the Rwandan government to facilitate the return of Tutsi refugees, and concern grew over the potential return of power-hungry Tutsis, significant rifts developed within the MRND. Within a short period of time, anti-Tutsi sentiment was renewed.

19 ibid 16–18.

20 Susan Thomson, *Rwanda: From Genocide to Precarious Peace* (Yale University Press 2018) 46.

21 ibid 47.

22 Gérard Prunier, *The Rwanda Crisis: History of a Genocide* (7. impression, Hurst 2010) 41–92.

23 Kayibanda was ultimately starved to death in a Rwandan prison.

The commencement of a civil war which was initiated by an RPF attack from Uganda into northern Rwanda on 1 October 1990, had the dual effect of bolstering anti-Tutsi resentment amongst many of the ruling elite, and providing the government with a scapegoat for its economic woes. Following the invasion, "Rwanda endured three and a half years of violent anti-Tutsi incidents, each of which in retrospect can easily be interpreted as a deliberate step in a vast conspiracy culminating in … the genocide."[24]

As it became clear that the RPF was not going to be easily driven from its newfound foothold in the north of the country, the possibility of a power-sharing arrangement began to take hold. In June 1992, delegations from the RPF and the Rwandan Government began negotiations toward establishing a peace treaty and power-sharing agreement. The resulting Arusha Accords sought to end Hutu political hegemony in the country, democratize the Rwandan government and re-integrate tens of thousands of Tutsi exiles back into Rwandan society. With the signing of the Arusha Accords, opposition toward Habyarimana from within his own party increased, and plans for the final eradication of Tutsis in Rwanda were commenced. The fate of the Arusha Accords was sealed when Habyarimana was assassinated as part of a military coup on the evening of 6 April 1994, when members of his own Presidential Guard shot down his airplane as it approached Kigali airport.[25]

3 The Perversion of Law

A primary indicator of a racist regime's ultimate intentions can often be found in discriminatory laws aimed at the target minority(s). Widely seen as a crucial first step toward the isolation of a group that is being targeted for genocide, racist laws are designed to "anathematize whole classes of citizens"[26] under laws that appeal to the majority, and to 'normalize' racism through wrapping it in the cloak of law. It is with this in mind that the Nazis went to great lengths to make their assault on the Jews appear legal. Under the cover of the 'rule of law' the Nazis 'legally' forbade Jews from marrying non-Jews, deprived Jews of

24 Gerald Caplan, 'Rwanda: The Preventable Genocide – The Report of the International Panel of Eminent Personalities to Investigate the 1994 Genocide in Rwanda and the Surrounding Events' (Organization of African Unity 1998) para 7.4.

25 This conclusion is based on insight that the author gained through a number of interviews that he conducted in Kigali in July 1994. All persons interviewed were first hand eyewitnesses to the shooting down of the President's airplane.

26 Adam Jones, *Genocide: A Comprehensive Introduction* (3rd edition, Routledge, Taylor & Francis Group 2017) 324.

the right to work and earn a living, expropriated their property, denied them education and went so far as to make it illegal to buy milk from a cow owned by a Jew.[27] During the period of its twelve year reign the Third Reich enacted nearly 2000 laws that were aimed at dehumanizing and discriminating against Jews.

During its early years in power, the Nazi regime "was still rather shaky and the Nazis feared opposition from within and resistance from without, they did nothing drastic, and the first measures appeared, in relative terms, to be rather mild."[28] The first of the anti-Jewish laws, *The Law for the Restoration of the Professional Civil Service,*[29] which was passed in April 1933, employed measured language that did not specifically target any group, made provision for the continuing service by those who had served in the First World War, as well as those who had a father or son killed in action during the war. Benign by its title, the purpose of the act was to exclude officials of non-Aryan descent (i.e. Jews) from serving in the civil service.[30]

As Hitler had hoped, the passage of the law garnered little attention and was met with only minimal opposition in the Reichstag.[31]

By 1935, the Nazis had solidified their hold on power and announced their intention to re-arm Germany. Buoyed by its successes, both internally and internationally, in September 1935 the government passed "The Law for the Protection of German Blood and German Honour,"[32] and the "Reich Citizenship Law." Also known as the 'Nuremberg Racial Laws' the legislation deprived Jews of their German citizenship, prohibited Jewish households from employing German maids under the age of 45, prohibited any non-Jewish German from marrying a Jew and outlawed sexual relations between Jews and Germans.[33] With the first of its targeted racial laws having been accepted with little reprobation, "the number of anti-Jewish laws and measures increased rapidly, and

27 'Anti-Jewish Decrees' (*The British Library*) <https://www.bl.uk/learning/histcitizen/voices/info/decrees/decrees.html> accessed 1 August 2019.

28 'The Nuremberg Laws' (*The United States National Archives*, 15 August 2016) <https://www.archives.gov/publications/prologue/2010/winter/nuremberg.html> accessed 29 July 2019.

29 Gesetz zur Wiederherstellung des Berufsbeamtentums 1933 (Reichsgesetzblatt Berlin: Reichsverlagsamt, 1933).

30 ibid 3.

31 Michael Stolleis, *The Law under the Swastika: Studies on Legal History in Nazi Germany* (University of Chicago Press 1998) ix.

32 Gesetz zum Schutze des deutschen Blutes und der deutschen Ehre 1935 (Berlin: Reichsverlagsamt, 1935).

33 Reichsburgergesetz 1935 (Berlin: Reichsverlagsamt, 1935).

discrimination and persecution became more blatant."[34] Perhaps the most sinister of the anti-Semitic measures was the incorporation of the requirement for Jewish people to carry identification cards and to wear the yellow Star of David[35] whenever they were in public. These two measures were designed to isolate and separate Jews from the remainder of society, and most importantly, were used to identify Jewish people so that they could be targeted by government officials and all others who wished to discriminate against them.

Rwanda's racial laws, while not as systematic as those of Germany, were equally discriminatory. The promulgation of anti-Tutsi laws began in the very early days of the establishment of the Parmehutu regime in the immediate post-colonial period. As was the case with the Weimar Republic, the decolonization process in Rwanda imposed democracy into a society that had traditionally been ruled by monarchies and selected elites. Similar in many respects to the Nazi treatment of the Jews, the Kayibanda government actively deflected any criticism against it by blaming the country's woes on the Tutsis and restricting their rights and privileges. Through legislation and other administrative measures, people were reminded that Tutsis were not only different but potential enemies within [the country], resulting in a pool of scapegoats that could be targeted in times of [social] unrest.[36] That social unrest began in the nascent days of the Rwandan Republic, with ethnic violence forcing the first of several mass emigrations of Tutsis to surrounding countries beginning in 1959. Tutsi who remained in the country under Kayibanda's regime were subjected to quotas; they were prohibited from serving as officers in the military, no more than ten percent of the civil service could be Tutsi, and Tutsis were allotted no more than ten percent of the spaces in schools and other educational institutions.[37] Furthermore, early calls to abolish racial identity cards that had been introduced under Belgian rule were dismissed.

While the progress of anti-Semitic laws in Germany was virtually continuous from 1935 onward, the evolution of racial laws in Rwanda between 1959–94 was intermittent, with anti-Tutsi measures generally being introduced in response to attacks from Tutsi refugee organizations that were based in Uganda and Burundi.[38] After each such major incursion, the "Rwandan government

34 Stolleis (n 31) ix.

35 Police Regulation for the Labelling of Jews 1941 (Reichsgesetzblatt).

36 Kenneth R White, 'Scourge of Racism: Genocide in Rwanda' (2009) 39 Journal of Black Studies 471, 475.

37 Alain Destexhe, *Rwanda and Genocide in the Twentieth Century* (1995) 36–47.

38 Alan J Kuperman, 'Provoking Genocide: A Revised History of the Rwandan Patriotic Front' (2004) 6 Journal of Genocide Research 61, 63.

retaliated by escalating oppression of, and attacks against, Tutsi within the country."[39]

While there was reprieve from organized violence against Tutsis during the first part of Habyarimana's regime, racial laws remained in place and Tutsis continued to face discrimination on a daily basis. The relative tranquility that had accompanied Habyarimana's early years in power began to unravel in the late-1980's when Rwanda was hit by a drought that coincided with the collapse of world coffee prices. With its economy in turmoil, the Habyarimana regime began to face serious challenges from within its own ranks. The attack by the RPF into northern Rwanda in October 1990 provided the government with the scapegoat it needed to deflect attention away from its own corruption and ineptness. "'The carefully inculcated fears about Tutsi conspiracies – fears about alleged plots to regain control of the republic and launch merciless attacks on all Hutu – that had been dormant for so many years were deliberately revived. The nation was reminded that the Tutsi from Uganada were, "all alien invaders [and that] all Tutsi were accomplices of the invaders."[40]

Other than the adoption of racist laws, one of the hallmarks of the failure of the rule of law is impunity for those who engage in violence against targeted groups, and the creation of government-sponsored para-military organizations whose thuggery is directed toward the targeted racial groups. While racist laws were fundamental aspects of the Nazi and Hutu regimes, neither initially condoned or authorized wide scale indiscriminate violence against the victim groups.

In the case of Germany, the Sturmabteilung (SA), known informally as the "Brownshirts", initially acted as early Nazi bodyguards and aggressors. A group of thugs consisting mainly of former convicts and disgruntled ex-soldiers, they harassed, assaulted, and murdered communists, social democrats, and any others who opposed the Nazi party. Shortly after the elections of 1933, they turned their sights on the country's Jewish population, blocking access of regular Germans into Jewish business establishments, vandalizing Jewish property, and beating up Jews on the streets.[41] Somewhat taken aback by the initial violence, and concerned that continuing violence might undermine support for the Nazi party, both at home and internationally, Hitler reined in the SA, and killed off its leadership on the 'Night of the Long Knives", 30 June 1934. The decapitation of the SA marked the beginning of an interlude from official

39 ibid.

40 Gerald Caplan, 'Rwanda: The Preventable Genocide – The Report of the International Panel of Eminent Personalities to Investigate the 1994 Genocide in Rwanda and the Surrounding Events' (Organization of African Unity 1998) 36.

41 Richard J Evans, *The Third Reich in Power, 1933–1939* (Penguin Press 2005) 13–17.

violence that was to continue until after the completion of the Berlin Olympics in 1936. In the aftermath of the games however, the discontent with the Nazis was growing amongst the German population, due partially to an economic slowdown. Recognizing an opportunity to shift focus to 'enemies of the Reich', the Nazis ramped up anti-Semitic propaganda and resumed boycotts and harassment against Jews.

The policy of harassment against Jews entered a new phase in November 1938, when a young Jewish man entered the German embassy in Paris and assassinated a German diplomat. The Nazis used the incident as a pretext to launch antisemitic attacks on the night of 9–10 November 1938; 'Kristallnacht'. "The extreme violence and deliberate, demeaning humiliation meted out to the Jews [that night] was familiar from the behaviour of the Brownshirts,"[42] but on Kristallnacht it was much worse. Across the country approximately 7,500 of 9,000 Jewish businesses were destroyed or seriously damaged, as many as 1,000 synagogues were torched, and upwards of 30,000 Jewish men were arrested and sent to various concentration camps around the country.[43] The Kristallnacht pogrom signalled a re-start to the rabid anti-Semitism that had characterized the early behaviour of the Nazis, except that the emphasis changed from mere anti-Semitic rhetoric to the eradication of Jewish people from German Society. As racist laws increased and became progressively more extreme, many Jews chose to leave Germany. Jewish persons who remained in Germany after 1938 were subjected to random violence; those who engaged in violence against Jews did so with virtual impunity.

As was the case with Nazi Germany's treatment of Jews and other opponents, the early years of Parmehutu were marked by violence against the Tutsi, followed by a lull, and then a final resurgence of violence. The first instance of major violence against the Tutsi population occurred in November 1959, when a group of Tutsi militants attacked the Parmehutu leader. The incident sparked wide-spread violence that forced tens of thousands of Tutsis to flee to neighbouring countries. The violence reached a crescendo in 1963, following an attack by Tutsi rebels who were based in Burundi. Coming to within 25 kilometres of Kigali, the attack alarmed the government which, in turn, urged regular Rwandans to hunt down and kill every Tutsi they could find. Within four weeks as many as 14,000 people had been killed, and many of the surviving Tutsis fled to Burundi, the Congo and Uganda.[44] Although there was sporadic violence aimed at Tutsis throughout remainder of the period of Hutu rule, cases of

42 ibid 536.
43 ibid 580–610.
44 Melvern (n 18) 15–21.

organized violence were rare. This changed abruptly in October 1990 when the RPF invaded from Uganda. Much as the murder of Ernst vom Rath had been the catalyst for renewed violence against Jews in 1938, the 1990 invasion inflamed anti-Tutsi sentiments in the country and spurred a new era of racist terror against the Tutsi population. Under the guidance of Hutu extremists within the government, Rwanda's Presidential Guard, assisted by the Gendarmerie, was the main perpetrator of violence against the Tutsis in the early 1990s. Acting with impunity, they "test[ed] various killing techniques"[45] as part of a dress rehearsal for genocide.

4 The Role of Hate Propaganda

"Genocide does not start with the murder of masses of people, it starts in peoples' minds."[46] While racist laws set the groundwork for the impunity that is required to conduct genocide, the laws, in and of themselves, are not sufficient to incite hatred that is strong enough to turn a society genocidal. Ultimately genocide will only come to fruition when fertilized by concerted and long-term propaganda campaigns that dehumanize the target group and advocate for their annihilation.

"Propaganda is a deliberate and systematic attempt to shape perceptions, manipulate cognitions, and direct behavior to achieve a response that furthers the desired intent of the propagandist."[47] Because propaganda is a deliberate process, it follows a plan that requires the propagandist to continuously review and modify the message.[48] When designing a campaign to instigate violence, two distinct types of propaganda are employed; integration propaganda, and instigation propaganda.[49] Of the two, integration propaganda is the more sophisticated and methodical. In order to be successful it must appeal to the wider population and "reshape thoughts and behavior in terms of the permanent social setting."[50] It is through the deliberate process of integration propaganda that "unconscious actions of members of a society [are transformed]

45 ibid 70.

46 Hege Løvdal Gulseth, 'The Use of Propaganda in the Rwandan Genocide: A Study of Radio-Télévision Libre Des Mille Collines (RTLM)' (University of Oslo 2004) 9.

47 Garth Jowett and Victoria O'Donnell, *Propaganda & Persuasion* (Sixth edition, SAGE 2015) 6.

48 ibid 280.

49 Jacques Ellul, Propaganda: The Formation of Men's Attitudes (Vintage Books 1973) 70–75.

50 ibid 75.

into consciously desired activity that is visible, laudable, and justified,"[51] and that a group can be persuaded to hate another.[52] It is only when that goal has been reached that an instigation propaganda campaign can be successfully employed to initiate mass violence.

In the case of hate propaganda, the primary goal of the integration propagandist is to frame and define the opposed group as different, with an emphasis on exploiting ingrained myths and fears based on the confabulation of the 'foreign invader', with the intent of creating hatred or indifference toward the group. The essence of the role of hate propaganda in genocide was outlined in the Nuremberg trial of Otto Dietrich, the Press Chief of the Third Reich. In its judgement the Tribunal held:

> The only reason for [the propaganda] campaign was to blunt the sensibilities of the people regarding the campaign of persecution and murder which was being carried out. These press and periodical directives were not mere political polemics, they were not aimless expression of anti-Semitism, … [The directives'] clear and expressed purpose was to enrage Germans against the Jews, to justify the measures taken and to be taken against them, and to subdue any doubts which may arise as to the justice of measures of racial persecution to which Jews were being subjected.[53]

The propagandists in Nazi Germany and Rwanda shared the benefit of having identifiable 'foreign' groups toward whom their vitriol could be targeted. In Germany the task of creating hatred, or at least indifference, toward the Jewish population was helped by the long history of pan-European anti-Semitism and the stereotypical depiction of Jews as greedy, miserly anti-Christian money lenders whose over-all goal was world domination.[54] Categorized as foreign elements who threatened the German way of life, and the very existence of the German people, the Jews were an easily discernable target for propaganda. In similar fashion, Hutu extremists in Rwanda were able to build upon the

51 ibid.

52 A classic example of an integration propaganda failure occurred in 1940 with the anti-Jewish propaganda film, 'Der Ewige Jude "The Eternal Jew". The vile depiction of Jews in the film was too much for the regular German population to bear. "The horror scenes disgusted viewers and the documentary aspect was considered nerve racking." 'Der Ewige Jude "The Eternal Jew"' (Holocaust Research Project) <http://www.holocaustresearchproject.org/holoprelude/derewigejude.html> accessed 9 August 2019.

53 *Trials of War Criminals Before the Nuernberg Military Tribunals Under Control Council Law No 10 'The Ministries Case'* (1949) XIV (Nuremberg Tribunals) 575–76.

54 Jeffrey Herf, *The Jewish Enemy: Nazi Propaganda during World War II and the Holocaust* (The Belknap Press of Harvard University Press 2006) 6–8.

characterization of the Tutsies as foreign invaders, a narrative that was rooted in European-inspired theories as to the origin of the different social classes that colonizers found when they first arrived in Rwanda. Basing much of their propaganda on the Hamitic myth that described the Tutsi as originating in Ethiopia, Hutu extremists characterized the Tutsi as being foreign elites who had come to Rwanda to oppress and dispossess the traditional owners of the land – the Hutus.[55] In each case, the propaganda depicted the majority as being the victims of the foreign invaders.

The evolution of propaganda in each of the countries followed similar paths. In both situations, early propaganda focussed on differentiating the targeted group from the majority, with the aim of enshrining the attitude of "us versus them". As noted above, depicting the target group as 'foreign' was the first crucial step in the respective propaganda plans. Once the concept of "us versus them" was firmly established, the focus of the propaganda campaign switched, with emphasis being placed on dehumanizing the 'enemy of the people' by depicting them as vermin, parasites or other similarly repugnant creatures.

The Nazi and Hutu propagandists used the mass media to great effect in their campaigns. While the messages built upon historic bias and racism that had been reinforced in virtually all sectors of society, including educational institutions, it was governmental domination of the press that ensured that only approved messages could be disseminated to all corners of the respective countries. In Germany, the two primary methods of promulgation were the printed press and film. There, magazines such as Der Stürmer printed cartoons that depicted Jews as spiders or other pests that were intent on sucking the lifeblood from Germany, whereas in Rwanda the magazine Kangura portrayed Tutsis as Inyenzi (cockroaches) and rats, and government owned Radio Rwanda provided a continuous stream of similar messaging.

5 The Extermination

The final stage of the lead-up to genocide commences when the decision is made to eradicate the targeted group. In the case of Germany, a number of incidents and opportunities led to the decision to embark on the Final Solution.[56] While Hitler's early writings had advocated the destruction of Judaism in Europe, the Reich did not begin to engage in the mass murder of Jews until after the invasion of the Soviet Union commenced in June 1941. As part of the

---

55 Prunier (n 22) 5–16.

56 Saul Friedländer, *Nazi Germany and the Jews* (1st ed, HarperCollins 1997) 350.

invasion, Einsatzgruppen death squads and Order Police battalions were tasked with rounding up and killing (usually by shooting) the Jewish populations of various regions and cities. "By the end of 1941, about 600,000 Jews had been murdered in the conquered eastern regions."[57] At this point, as well, "the vilest of anti-Jewish invectives and threats"[58] were made in Hitler's public statements and distributed in Propaganda. From this point onward, much of the Nazi propaganda was aimed at encouraging Germans to participate in the pogrom.

With a vastly increased number of Jews under their control, senior Nazis met in Berlin in December 1941, at which time the decision was likely made to eliminate all Jews from Europe.[59] Shortly thereafter, in January 1942, the architects of the Final Solution, meeting in Wannsee, developed the plan to move all remaining European Jews to Poland, where they would eventually be killed.[60]

One of the early obstacles that the Germans had to overcome before they could activate the Final Solution was that of finding an efficient way to kill millions of people. Experience in the latter half of 1941 had taught German officials that mass executions by firing squads was not particularly efficient nor effective. The solution to the problem came with the discovery in the autumn of 1941 that the rat poison Zyclon B could be employed with great effect against humans in confined spaces. Used first against Russian prisoners in Auschwitz,[61] it became the weapon of choice for the mass extermination of the Jews.[62] By the spring of 1942, the death camps at Chelmno, Belszec, Sobibor, and Treblinka were in full operation, each with the capacity to kill 15,000 people per day.[63]

In a similar fashion, it is difficult to determine the exact point at which the decision to exterminate the Tutsi was made in Rwanda, however, it is apparent that the decision was made at some point between the RPF invasion in October 1990 and the publication of the Hutu Ten Commandments in the Kangura

57 ibid 208–209.

58 ibid 272.

59 Lorraine Boissoneault, 'The First Moments of Hitler's Final Solution' (*Smithsonian*) <https://www.smithsonianmag.com/history/first-moments-hitlers-final-solution-180961387/> accessed 9 August 2019.

60 Friedländer (n 56) 330–335.

61 Rudolf Höess, *Commandant of Auschwitz: The Autobiography of Rudolf Hoess* (Phoenix Press 2000) 185–86.

62 'At the Killing Centers' <https://encyclopedia.ushmm.org/content/en/article/at-the-killing-centers> accessed 9 August 2019.

63 Herf (n 54) 139.

magazine in December 1990.[64] The Ten Commandments were a call to action, inciting all Hutu to unite …against the common enemy – the Tutsi.[65] As is clearly evident in other articles from the same edition of Kangura, by late 1990 the tone of propaganda had undergone a transition from integration toward instigation. Similarly, in December 1990 the tone of Radio Rwanda changed when its moderate director was replaced by an extremist intellectual, Ferdinand Nahimana, "who used the radio to shamelessly manipulate public opinion, experimenting with techniques that were to become part of the Interahamwe arsenal during the 1994 genocide."[66] From that point onward, the anti-Tutsi propaganda become increasingly vile, and calls for Hutus to cleanse the country of cockroaches intensified. The incorporation of Radio Télévision Libre des Mille Collines (RTLM) in April 1993 was an additional tool for the regime's propaganda campaign. Broadcasting a continuous stream of violent rhetoric (including death threats), its message reached all corners of the country. As the genocide neared, the programming became increasingly vicious. Once the genocide commenced, it was employed to guide the population in its "work" of eradicating the Inyenzi.

In December 1991, Habyarimana met with approximately 100 government and army personnel to discuss how best to defeat the Tutsi. From that meeting, Theoneste Bagosora, one of the architects of the genocide,[67] was tasked to determine the best way to eradicate the threat. That the Wannsee meeting in 1942, and the Habyarimana meeting of 1991 represented turning points in the respective genocides is unquestionable. From those points onward, extermination plans were drawn up, methods of killing were tested and rehearsed, and preparations for the ultimate annihilation of the target groups were made. "It was the organization of extremist militias, however, that marked the organizational turn toward genocide. In 1992, the *Interahamwe,* the militia of the ruling MRND party, was created. It was soon followed by the *Impuzamugambi,* the militia of the Coalition pour la Défense de la République (CDR), an extreme Hutu Power party organized by the *Akazu* elite."[68]

---

64 'Appel a La Conscience Des Bahutu' *Kangura* (Kigali, December 1990) 6 6–8.

65 Andrew Wallis, *Stepp'd in Blood: Akazu and the Architects of the Rwandan Genocide against the Tutsi* (2019) 261.

66 William A Schabas, 'Hate Speech in Rwanda: The Road to Genocide' (2000) 46 McGill Law Journal 141, 146.

67 Judge Theodor Meron and others, Théoneste BAGOSORA and Anatole NSENGIYUMVA v. The Prosecutor 2011 [Case No. ICTR-98-41-A] 292.

68 Gregory Stanton, 'The Rwandan Genocide: Why Early Warning Failed' (2009) 1 Journal of African Conflicts and Peace Studies 6, 10.

Just as the Einsatzgruppen had done in Soviet territories fifty years earlier, the regime began to experiment with mass killing. Starting in the region of Bugesara in March 1991, the army carried out a series of planned massacres throughout the country. In these dress rehearsals, the army incited regular civilians to participate.[69] Unlike the Nazis, who had industrialized their killing machine and located its death camps in places that were out of sight and out of mind to the average German, the Rwandans had determined that the most efficient way to kill large numbers of people was through fully incorporating the population in the slaughter of their neighbours. By the end of 1993, the preparation and planning for genocide had been completed. Weapons were stockpiled, and local paramilitaries were primed and ready. All that was required was a spark. As history tells us, the fuse for Rwanda's genocide was lit when Habyarimana was assassinated in a military coup.

6 Denial and Escape

According to Stanton's, "The Ten Stages of Genocide", the last stage in every genocide is denial. During this phase, which begins while the genocide is still occurring, the perpetrators and their supporters commence a disinformation campaign in which they "deny that they committed any crimes, and often blame what happened on the victims."[70] Just as holocaust deniers have questioned the existence and extent of the Nazi genocide, genocide deniers have been conducting a well orchestrated campaign of disinformation and denial about Rwanda's genocide since 1994.

The Denial campaign was kick-started in the Security Council on 16 May 1994. In what former New Zealand Ambassador, Colin Keating, described as "a shameful distortion of the truth,"[71] the Rwandan former Minister of Foreign Affairs, Jerome Bicamumpaka, accused the RPF of "systematically massacring people, particularly Hutus."[72] In the time since Bicamumpaka's prevarications were made in the UN, a new generation of Ernst Zündels has emerged, all of whom have attempted to change the narrative of the genocide by spouting what have become commonly referred to in the contemporary political climate as 'alternative facts'.

69 Wallis (n 65) 307–312.

70 Gregory H Stanton, 'The Ten Stages of Genocide' (*Genocide Watch*, 2013) <http://www.genocidewatch.org/genocide/tenstagesofgenocide.html>. Accessed 19 August 2019.

71 'United Nations Security Council: 3377th Meeting Report' (United Nations Security Council 1994) Provisional S/PV.3377 11.

72 ibid 5.

One of the most notable early attempts to shift the blame for the genocide occurred in August 1994. At that time, I was tasked by the UNAMIR force commander to investigate reports that the RPF was conducting mass killings in a variety of locations throughout the country. The reports originated from the United Nations High Commission for Refugees (UNHCR), and were apparently based on eye-witness accounts contained in an unspecified study that had been conducted in the country.[73] My task was straight-forward; go to the specified locations and verify whether the RPF was conducting mass killings.

Within a short time, a multi-national team was assembled. In the team were intelligence personnel, criminal investigators with forensic training, and a translator. Because we were expecting to encounter hostile elements from the RPF who would not want us to enter areas in which they were conducting killings, we also included a security detail from 3 Commando of the Canadian Airborne Regiment. As it turned out, there was no requirement for the additional security. The RPF was not present in any significant strength in any of the places we visited.

After compiling a list of massacre sites in which the RPF was allegedly killing people, the team set about creating a plan. Commencing in the south-east, we worked our way counter-clockwise from the area of the Tanzania/Burundi border through the Kibungo Prefecture, to Nyarabuye, Rwamagana, north to Byumba, and finally to the Ruhengari and Gisenyi Prefectures. As had been stated in the reports that the Force Commander had received, in most of the places we investigated, we found bodies, in some cases many hundreds of them. In a few places we were unable to find any evidence that mass killings had occurred; no bodies, no mass graves, no victims shoved into wells or latrines.

A significant amount of evidence was gathered during the investigations, including eye-witness statements, diaries, forensics and the ubiquitous identification cards found amongst the bodies. Through an examination of the evidence that we had gathered, we were able to conclude that the massacres identified in the reports had occurred early in the genocide (i.e. not during the time that the RPF had been in control of the respective areas), and that the overwhelming majority of the victims were Tutsi. We were also able to determine that the Interahamwe was responsible for the vast majority of the killings. As a result, we reported that the allegations made against the RPF in the UNHCR reports were not supported by evidence.

73 The source of the information has been widely reported as the Gersony Report. In spite of numerous requests, I have never been provided with a copy of the Gersony Report.

In spite of the overwhelming evidence to the contrary, there are some, who for a variety of reasons, remain motivated to obscure the fact that the genocide in Rwanda was well planned and carried out by the Habyarimana regime. They continue to write books, publish papers and otherwise advocate their cases to sympathetic audiences. Amongst those of us who were witness to the events of 1994, and those who have studied the events closely, however, there are very few who give any credence to the Denial movement. As Gerald Caplan so aptly noted in his report to the Secretary General of the African Union:

> In the end, however, we harbour no illusions that universal agreement will be found on this visceral issue. After all, there are still Holocaust deniers who refuse to acknowledge Hitler's crimes, Khmer Rouge leaders who have never admitted to their own genocidal actions and, we regret to say, Rwandans who refuse to acknowledge the genocide of 1994.[74]

That there remains a core group who know the truth of who was responsible for the planning and the conduct of the genocide is undeniable. In similar fashion to the exodus of the Nazi leadership at the end of the Second World War, many of those responsible for the genocide fled to France, Belgium, Canada and several African countries. While some were captured and prosecuted by the International Criminal Tribunal for Rwanda, others have found refuge in safe havens, evading justice and continuing their attempts to undermine the current Rwandan government. All of them continue to deny their complicity in one of the most vicious events of the twentieth century, while pointing their fingers at the victims.

7 Conclusion

When one considers Stanton's Ten Stages of Genocide, it is abundantly clear that post-1959 Rwanda was a society that was well primed for genocide; all of the Hallmarks of a pending genocide were present. In spite of the many warning signs, particularly following the RPF invasion of 1990, the United Nations and the rest of the world did precious little to prevent the descent toward mass slaughter. Once the genocide commenced, the UN cowered, failing to adequately support its own personnel or stop the genocidal violence.

While reviewing and comparing the paths to genocide in Nazi Germany and pre-1994 Rwanda cannot change history, an exercise in comparative genocide

---

74 Caplan (n 24) 7.

can potentially help to identify societies in which there is a substantial risk that genocidal violence may occur. Additionally, such studies can and should be seen for their value in demonstrating how a society can be conditioned to engage in ethnic violence.

Government policies that single out ethnic or religious groups for special treatment, create groups designed to carry-out ethnic violence, issue racial identity cards, or create an atmosphere of 'us versus them' within countries, are warning signs that a society is at risk of descending toward genocide. As Gerald Caplan noted in his report to the African Union, "There were a thousand early warnings that something appalling was about to occur in Rwanda."[75] Intervention by the international community at a number of points right up until April 1994 could have prevented the genocide. There is also little doubt that had the world reacted with military force in April 1994, the genocide could have been stopped in its tracks. The fact that we stood by and did nothing is "An unforgivable tragedy."[76]

75 ibid 62.
76 ibid.

CHAPTER 10

Moral Equivalence

The Story of Genocide Denial in Rwanda

Linda Melvern

From the moment when the leadership of Hutu Power seized control of the government of Rwanda on the evening of 6 April 1994, it had determined to distort the reality of events surrounding the genocide to the outside world. The United Nations was central to these plans. In a sad irony the General Assembly had elected Rwanda to one of the 10 non-permanent seats in the Security Council, and so when the genocide of the Tutsi was getting underway in April 1994, the genocidaires had an ideal forum to promote the denial of their crime and spread fake news and disinformation in the meetings, hallways and lounges of the United Nations' New York headquarters.

The foundation stone upon which the campaign of genocide denial had depended was that, far from being organised, the widespread killing throughout the country had resulted from a "spontaneous" uprising. In the wake of the resumed civil war with the Rwanda Patriot Front (RPF), the population attacked neighbours in fear and in anger. According to this narrative, there was no planning; the massacres were a failure of the human condition and followed centuries-long hatreds and in this "inter-ethnic" killing, both sides were to blame.

The notion of moral equivalence in the circumstances of the 1994 genocide of the Tutsi persists to this day. The idea of two genocides, the first nearly wiping out the Tutsi minority, and the second secretly committed by the Tutsi-dominated RPF against Hutu, would have been a sensational news story, if true. In July after the RPF achieved military victory there was a proliferation of rumours about human rights abuses committed by these troops. A US journalist, Mark Fritz, spent nearly a month looking for evidence but found nothing. A British journalist reporting from Rwanda for the BBC, Mark Doyle, wrote a dispatch to London explaining no convincing evidence existed of the RPF massacring civilians. Doyle warned the BBC news desk not to broadcast claims about RPF abuses until some convincing evidence emerged. 'I used to take regular calls from BBC editors in London asking me to make sure I put the other side', Doyle wrote later. Doyle told them this was not a balanced picture, and there was no moral equivalence. Another experienced UK journalist, Mark Huband of the Observer noted only 'second-hand reports' about RPF killing

 | DOI:10.1163/9789004430129_012

coming from the UN High Commission for Refugees (UNHCR), and the vast newly created refugee camps on Rwanda's borders.

The over-flowing refugee camps in neighbouring countries in the aftermath of the genocide of the Tutsi were the result of one of the more calculated strategies devised by the Hutu Power leadership. In inciting the population to flee, a stream of fake news in bulletins on radio RTLM called on the 'Hutu nation' to immediately leave the country. In response whole communities took to the roads. The resulting exodus, during which an estimated two million people fled from Rwanda, broke world records and was unprecedented in speed and size. In Tanzania, an estimated 500,000 people settled at a camp called Benaco. Two hundred thousand refugees fled to Burundi. An estimated 1 million people passed into Zaire at Goma, and 200,000 more into Bukavu.[1]

These people were not, as some journalists and aid agencies later supposed, fleeing the genocide; they included the Interahamwe militia and the authorities who planned and perpetrated the crime of genocide. The camps were beyond the reach of international justice and in these murderous and terrible places the Hutu Power authorities kept control. The same administrative structures that existed in Rwanda were swiftly re-created – the *préfectures, communes, secteurs* and *cellules*.[2] The *bourgmestres*, were the same men who had issued the orders to kill Tutsi. Soon a web of Hutu Power committees, neighbourhood security units and associations embraced almost all segments of refugee society.[3] The threat from the militia prevented international agencies from registering the refugee population, and as a result of the exodus, the region risked destabilisation. Rwanda, in the words of one US diplomat, was surrounded by a "constrictive belt of insecurity". The Hutu Power forces launched attacks into Rwanda from these camps, one of which (Mugunga) contained the defeated Rwandan government army of 33,000 troops along with weapons that had been supplied from French military stocks.

In late July and early August, a trickle of refugees returned home but the movement soon slowed. While the return and resettlement of refugees was considered essential to Rwanda's future long-term stability, aid agency staff in the camps watched a determined campaign to prevent people from returning. The refugees were told that any Hutu who went back to Rwanda would be

---

1 Larry Minear and Philippe Guillot, *Soldiers to the Rescue: Humanitarian Lessons from Rwanda*, Development Centre of the Organization for Economic Cooperation and Development, Paris, 1996, 63.

2 *The International Response to Conflict and Genocide*, Volume 3, 96.

3 Fiona Terry, *Condemned to Repeat? The Paradox of Humanitarian Action*, Ithaca: Cornell University Press, 2002.

massacred immediately by the RPA.[4] There were anonymous pamphlets distributed claiming that no one who had returned tp Rwanda from the camps had survived.[5]

One practical attempt to counteract this Hutu Power propaganda in the camps came from a UN headquarters staff member, a Canadian officer, Phillip Drew who served in the UN Assistance Mission for Rwanda (UNAMIR II). Drew designed leaflets to be dropped into the camps from UN helicopters visually portraying Rwanda as a lush and fertile place of safety showing security, fresh water and food. The plan backfired when at the last minute the UN guarantee of safe passage to returning refugees was put on hold when the UN discovered that possession of one of these leaflets by refugees in the camps was tantamount to an automatic death sentence.

In September the repatriation policy that UNAMIR II tried to foster was thrown into disarray. A panicked phone call to UN secretary-general, Boutros Boutros-Ghali in New York from the UN High Commissioner for Refugees (UNHCR), Sadako Ogata, in Geneva had some disturbing news. Ogata told Boutros-Ghali that information received by her office showed the RPF troops had slaughtered 30,000 Hutu civilians in systematic and preordained massacres as they took control of the country. The information had come from an experienced consultant Robert Gersony, a US national contracted for sixty days by the UNHCR to organise a voluntary repatriation programme for refugees. Only later did it transpire that Gersony had secretly briefed US officials on his findings, the information reaching Brian Atwood, appointed by President Bill Clinton's special envoy to Rwanda. Information in declassified US state department documents reveals a briefing on September 20 when Gersony provided US officials with graphic descriptions of how RPF troops hunted Hutu from house to house and their weapons hoes, axes, machetes and fire. The burial of bodies was a problem. As the team travelled towards the southeast, they found the stench of recently dead bodies was overpowering.

Gersony told US officials that the voluntary repatriation of the refugees currently promoted by the UNHCR could under no circumstances be justified. A return home for Hutu refugees was too dangerous. According to US cables Gersony dismissed reports of Hutu Power intimidation in the camps. From his recent interviews in the camps there was little evidencc of forcing refugees to stay put. Gersony had apparently over a five-week period met privately with

4 Laurence Binet, 'Genocide of the Rwandan Tutsis', MSF Speaking Out, September 2003.

5 Rwanda and Burundi, *The Return Home: Rumours and Realities*, Amnesty International, January 1996, Cited in Fiona Terry.

200 refugees on a random basis, and his team of three experts had visited 41 of Rwanda's 45 communes.[6]

The information from Gersony ran counter to all the intelligence received in the US State Department that confirmed that the RPF had killed Hutu in battle, and while the RPF had admitted to targeting extremist Hutu whom it believed to be responsible for the massacre of Tutsi, generally the RPF protected Hutu within the territory it controlled. A partly declassified memorandum from Toby T. Gati to George Moose, the assistant secretary of state for African Affairs, on 16 May 1994, informed him of the killing of Tutsi behind government lines with systematic executions by government-supported militias. Unlike these government forces, the RPF did not appear to have committed what was called in the cable "Geneva Convention–defined genocidal atrocities".

The Gersony story was meet with consternation in the ranks of UNAMIR. That revenge killing by RPF soldiers took place was not in dispute; what was shocking was the claim of massacres of Hutu civilians in a systematic and targeted way. There were no reports of such killings in any UNAMIR reports. Additionally the RPF policy of conducting courts martial and punishment of soldiers for revenge killings suggested there was no such RPF campaign. Irrespective, the unverified information from the UNHCR consultant spread like wildfire.[7]

'It was a major crisis on our doorstep', recalled the recently appointed UN Special Representative for Rwanda, Ambassador Shaharyar M. Khan, a former foreign minister of Pakistan, who arrived in Kigali on 4 July 1994. The Gersony figures challenged the credibility of the UN and cast doubt on the competence of the new Force Commander of UNAMIR II, Canadian general Guy Tousignant, who arrived on 16 August 1994.[8] He was keen to explain how the UN was fostering a climate of trust and confidence to prepare for refugee return.

In UN headquarters, secretary-general Boutros-Ghali determined to brief the security council on this dramatic turn of events and the under-secretary-general Kofi Annan, then head of the Department of Peacekeeping Operations (DPKO) was dispatched immediately to Rwanda. Annan met with Gersony in Kigali and was given an oral briefing from notes Gersony kept in his pocket. Gersony described to Annan how the RPF conducted their massacres used 'subtlety and finesse, covering their tracks with greater dexterity than the militia' when they carried out their killings. Gersony believed that between 25,000

---

6 The Gersony team of three people with anonymous Rwandan interpreters claimed to have visited nine UNHCR refugee camps and ninety-one locations in Rwanda with more than 200 individuals interviewed. There were 145 communes in Rwanda.

7 African Rights, 'Death, Despair, Defiance', August 1995, 1084–5.

8 UNAMIR became UNAMIR II on 17 May 1994 under Security Council resolution 918.

and 45,000 people had been killed by the RPF including 5,000 people in August. Listening to these accounts with disbelief was the UN special representative for Rwanda Ambassador Khan, who was aware that UN Military Observers and aid agencies staff were present in the areas Gersony talked about. Khan wondered how it was be possible to massacre 30,000 people without attracting attention. In any case, the RPF did not travel with hoes and machetes. When briefing members of the new Rwandan government the following day, Gersony told them there had been 'a mass genocide by the RPA'.[9]

At a later meeting at UNAMIR headquarters in Kigali, the deputy Force Commander, Brigadier-General Henry Anyidoho, and Colonel Isoa Tikoca, head of the UN Military Observers (MILOBS) decided to verify the information Gersony provided. They dispatched experience military observers to those places Gersony mentioned in his briefings. Afterwards these officers were convinced that Gersony and his colleagues were the subject of planted and dramatized evidence. Charles Petrie, deputy director of the UN Rwanda Emergency Office (UNREO), who also heard rumours about RPF massacres, carried out a careful investigation with the aid agencies in the region, and he rejected the idea of preordained massacres. UNAMIR information officers investigated three out of seven cases of alleged RPF abuses, and all three were inaccurate, if not outright fabrications.[10]

Annan and Khan personally visited some of the sites mentioned by Gersony and asked peacekeepers, doctors and engineers working at the grassroots level in the communes about the treatment of returning Hutu to the region. They were told Hutu who left in panic were returning, but there were pockets of territory still under the control of Hutu Power. Khan recalled that the descriptions given to Gersony were generally accurate, but the identity of the perpetrators and victims transposed. Khan visited a team of US and Canadian doctors in a region Gersony identified as 'the massacre belt', and none of the medical staff confirmed the claims. The US also wanted to put the Gersony claims to the test. In Kigali, the US military attaché Tom Odom believed that 10–15,000 secret killings a month inside a UN-monitored area as small as Rwanda was a startling figure.

At the direction of the Force Commander, Canadian intelligence officer Phillip Drew was tasked with the establishment of a team to investigate. The team assembled was multi-national; a group of intelligence officers of different

9 UN Document, Outgoing Code-cable, The Gersoni Report, Rwanda, To Annan, Goulding, From Shaharyar Khan, UNAMIR Kigali, 14 October 1994.

10 US State Department, Rwanda/Burundi Situation Report, 23 September 1994, Declassified in full.

nationalities recruited to work with criminal investigators from several UN contingents and non-troop contributing nations. With the protection of members of the Canadian contingent the team left Kigali headed first to the village of Zaza. The team included a forensic entomologist who was able to determine the approximate date of death of the human remains. The first massacre site was in the south-west, near Kibungo, where Gersony said many Hutu had been slaughtered in the school a few weeks earlier. Drew recalled how arriving at the school they found partially decomposed bodies everywhere, including in cisterns, wells and latrines. Many of the human remains in the classrooms and outdoor compounds had skeletonized, and identity cards found on some of the bodies showed victims were Tutsi. Drew recalled finding a diary. "There was an entry describing how the Interahamwe beheaded its victims. The diary stopped on April 14, the most likely date of this massacre", he remembered.

A forensic examination of the bodies by the entomologist established the killing had taken place from mid to late April, when Hutu Power was in control of the area as the genocide of the Tutsi progressed countrywide. In the days to follow the intelligence team visited each site Gersony mentioned and failed to corroborate any of his claims. Many places had seen large numbers of killings, but of Tutsi. Drew never forgot these terrible days as the team visited successive massacre sites. After they finished their work they concluded that Gersony and his colleagues had been duped by people in the refugee camps in Zaire. The génocidaires were trying to pin the blame on the RPF while hiding from justice in the camps, knowing exactly where in Rwanda dead bodies were located. Some speculated that Gersony never set foot in Rwanda and that he relied entirely on information gleaned in the camps. The individual reports written by the intelligence officers in this unique investigative mission remain hidden in government archives.[11] Odom never did believe the RPF was systematically killing Hutu in Rwanda.[12] 'We found old massacre sites but nothing new', he wrote later. Odom believed there were killings, but they were probably isolated acts of revenge. Meanwhile, Odom reported, Hutu Power was rearming in the camps.[13]

Declassified documents from the US State Department reveal that the French were also dismissive of the Gersony claims. In Kigali a French diplomat, Jacques Courbin, told a US counterpart that the UNHCR had bungled the

11 Interviews with Dr. Phillip Drew, Associate Professor, Australian National University, College of law, 2019.

12 US State Department, Country Director's evaluation of post reporting for Rwanda, From Ste to Kigali, State 307914, 16 November 1994.

13 Thomas P Odom, *Journey into Darkness: Genocide in Rwanda*, College Station, TX: Texas A&M University Press, 2005.

Gersony report. There had been serious lapses and the collection of inaccurate data. 'In some cases, they had charged the RPF with site-specific atrocities on dates when the sites were not yet in RPF hands', Courbin reported. 'The non-report was flawed, and he doubted that the RPF had engaged in pre-planned systematic killing as it advanced', a US diplomat reported to Washington.[14]

As a result of the numerous investigations conducted by various teams and officials, the senior UN officials on the ground, Major General Tousignant and the UN Special Representative, Shaharyar Khan, along with the US ambassador David Rawson and others, eventually dismissed the Gersony allegations. Gersony was invited to take part in a joint investigation team established with four Rwandan ministers and four UN representatives, but declined. No Gersony report emerged and his claims ran counter to a tide of overwhelmingly contrary evidence. This did not matter to the media. Three days after Robert Gersony met Kofi Annan in Kigali, when Annan assured him there would be an investigation into his claims, the Gersony figures appeared in the *New York Times*, reporting 'an unmistakable pattern of killings and persecution' by soldiers of the RPF and 'aimed at Hutu populations'. Gersony achieved his wish and in a reversal of UN policy the peacekeepers of UNAMIR II stopped further efforts to encourage refugee return.

On 11 October 1994 Gersony briefed the members of the Commission of Experts, established by the UN Security Council to investigate the 1994 genocide of the Tutsi. He spoke of systematic and sustained killing and persecution of the civilian Hutu populations by the RPF between April and July 1994. He claimed large-scale indiscriminate killings of men, women and children, including the sick and elderly, had been consistently reported. The only written account of the Gersony claims is a precis of what he told this meeting.

In 1999, the Gersony figures were published in a Human Rights Watch report book by Alison Des Forges after a personal briefing.[15] She described the figures as the 'first convincing evidence' of widespread, systematic killings by the RPF and claimed that the UN suppressed 'the Gersony report' by claiming it did not exist.[16] Des Forges described how Gersony had spoken to a wider number and variety of witnesses than any other foreigners working in Rwanda during this period. She somehow forgot the UNMILOBS and the peacekeepers of UNAMIR, present in Rwanda in some cases since October 1993 and some of whom had

14 US State Department, Kigali 02142, '11/10 Tour d'Horizon with French chargé', From Kigali to Secretary of State, Washington, 10 November 1994.

15 Interview, Oxford, 2013.

16 Human Rights Watch/Federation Internationale des Ligues des Droits de l'Homme, *Leave None to Tell the Story: Genocide in Rwanda*, 1999.

thoroughly investigated the Gersony claims and dismissed them as just not credible.

In the years that followed, there were dramatic increases in the death toll of these supposed RPF killings. In February 1996, *Libération* published an investigation by journalist Stephen Smith. The investigation examined claims of Hutu people allegedly killed by the post-genocide regime and estimated that there were more than 100,000 victims during the RPF's first year in power. *Libération* published an eyewitness account of a Rwandan nurse who described sites, one near Kigali, where prisoners were put to death (their skulls were crushed), and another in a game reserve, the Akagera National Park, where scores of Hutus were cremated.

It did not end there. In a sensationalist book published in 2018 called *In Praise of Blood* a Canadian journalist, Judi Rever, claimed a second genocide of the Hutu took place and that the methods used resembled those of the Nazis. According to her account, the RPF had established death camps that included cremation pits. Rever claimed an estimated death toll in hundreds of thousands killed, burned or dissolved in acid, their ashes dispersed with bulldozers. Rever further alleged that the Hutu genocide was carried out in total secrecy; the mass murder leaving barely a trace, and that the western allies lent a hand in the cover—up. She also made the noxious claim that during the genocide RPF commandos infiltrated Hutu militia and '"assisted directly in killing Tutsi at roadblocks"'.

The UNHCR held a small internal enquiry about the events of 1994 which recognised the difficulties with a refugee leadership implicated in genocide and a wide-spread intimidation and abuse in the camps. It acknowledged that in the exodus of people from Rwanda into eastern Zaire, the political, social and security structure of Hutu Power had survived intact, thanks to the support of the international community.

Despite the UNHCR's long involvement in the countries of origin, there had existed a lack of understanding of the social, cultural and political background of the refugees. A stronger protection presence in the field, combined with a better understanding of the refugees' background, would have yielded beneficial effects, notwithstanding the extreme complexity of the problems involved. The UNHCR should have been able to rapidly develop a coherent policy to deal with the various disruptive forces active in the camps, many of whom may have been subject to the exclusion clause due to their involvement in the genocide. In future, a roster of anthropologists and other regional experts needed to be developed with specialist knowledge to provide briefings on the cultural and political backgrounds of refugees.

The pernicious influence of Hutu Power lives on in rumour, stereotype, lies and racist propaganda. The movement's campaign of genocide denial has confused many, recruited some and shielded others. Its intent is to deceive, and its purpose the destruction of truth and memory.[17]

17 Lessons Learned from the Rwanda and Burundi Emergencies EVAL/04/96/Rev.1 By Inspection and Evaluation Service 1 December 1996.

CHAPTER 11

Gendering Rwanda

Genocide and Post-Genocide

Adam Jones

1 Introduction

In my first essay about the Rwandan genocide, focusing on its gender component, I asserted that "The aspect of gender in the Rwandan genocide is perhaps more extraordinarily intricate and multifaceted than in any genocide in history."[1] I pointed to several themes that I will touch upon in this chapter, including the *génocidaires*' exploitation of gendered anxieties among Rwandan Hutus of both sexes; the gendercidal targeting of Tutsi men and boys by the Hutu Power regime (and Hutu males by the forces of the Tutsi-dominated Rwandan Patriotic Front [RPF]); the rampant sexual violence against Tutsi women; the unusually prominent role of female Hutu perpetrators in the genocide of Tutsis; and the skewed gender ratios of the immediate post-genocide period.

From a present-day perspective, the claim of an "extraordinarily intricate and multifaceted" gender component might also be seen to characterize the nearly two decades that have elapsed since that earlier writing. The RPF's gendered strategies of persecution and killing of opponents, especially younger Hutu males, extended well into the post-genocide period, and have also featured in the genocidal crimes perpetrated by the Rwandan army and its Banyamulenge (Congolese Tutsi) militias in The Democratic Republic of the Congo. At the same time, the RPF regime under President Paul Kagame has sought to deflect criticism of its political dictatorship and dismal human-rights record by 'performing' a mode of gender-inclusive governance that, in at least one respect, is without equal: no other country can claim such a high representation of women (fully two-thirds) in its national parliament. Finally, the model of international justice-seeking for the genocide, the International Criminal Tribunal for Rwanda (ICTR), was notably influenced by feminist critiques of sexual and gender violence, crafting an understanding of 'genocidal rape' that has commanded interest around the world.

I hope to address these wide-ranging subjects here, and place them within a comparative-genocide framework. In doing so, I will deploy Joshua Goldstein's

1 Adam Jones, "Gender and Genocide in Rwanda" (2002) 4(1) 65.

 | DOI:10.1163/9789004430129_013

definition of "gender," which encompasses both cultural understandings of masculinities and femininities, and recognition of the sexed bodies upon which these cultural 'scripts' are written, often to devastatingly destructive effect. Goldstein "use[s] 'gender' to cover masculine and feminine roles and bodies alike, in all their aspects, including the (biological and cultural) structures, dynamics, roles, and scripts associated with each gender group."[2] The 'gendering' of a given genocide therefore encompasses the cultural configurations that influence the mobilization of perpetrators and the targeting of victims, as well as the sexed bodies that are damaged or destroyed in genocidal campaigns.

2 Origins and Mobilization

To mobilize individuals for a task as extreme as genocide, a panoply of positive and negative inducements must be applied, generally by state authorities. This is particularly the case when the designated agents of the genocide extend beyond 'violence specialists' – such as military men and women, police and security forces, and paramilitary formations.[3] Such specialists took the lead in the genocide of Tutsis, as they typically do in instances of orchestrated mass violence. But the 1994 holocaust that consumed Rwanda was distinctive in the comparatively high level of involvement among ordinary Rwandan Hutus. They had to be encouraged, coerced, lured, and manipulated to participate even in the killing of neighbours with whom they had long coexisted peacefully. In this, appeals to gendered ambitions and anxieties were strikingly prominent.

The foundational document of Hutu Power, the 'Hutu Ten Commandments,' is the clearest roadmap to the mobilization of Rwanda's ethnic majority for the destruction of the Tutsi minority. Published in *Kangura* magazine in December 1990, it emphasized the need for Hutus to be "vigilant against their common enemy: the Tutsi" and to "constantly counter Tutsi propaganda" (article 9); it called for "strategic positions such as politics, administration, economics, the military and security [to] be restricted to the Hutu," who should also predominate in the educational system (articles 5–6). These formulaic injunctions, however, were accompanied by a veritable rant at the outset of the declaration (articles 1–3), in which the gendered anxieties of Hutu men and women alike were exhibited and exploited:

---

2 Joshua S. Goldstein, *War and Gender: How Gender Shapes the War System and Vice Versa* (CUP 2001) 2.

3 See, e.g., Charles Tilly, *The Politics of Collective Violence* (Cambridge University Press 2003).

1. Every Hutu must know that the Tutsi woman, wherever she may be, is working for the Tutsi ethnic cause. In consequence, any Hutu is a traitor who:
   - Acquires a Tutsi wife;
   - Acquires a Tutsi concubine;
   - Acquires a Tutsi secretary or protégée.
2. Every Hutu must know that our Hutu daughters are more worthy and more conscientious as women, as wives and as mothers. Aren't they lovely, excellent secretaries, and more honest!
3. Hutu women, be vigilant and make sure that your husbands, brothers and sons see reason.[4]

The appeal to ethnic and sexual purity, and to conventional gender roles, is standard in genocidal campaigns. Nazi constructions of militarized masculinity and domestically-focused femininity are only the best-known case. Equally common is the sense of gendered *disruption* and *humiliation*, bordering on *social death*,[5] that underpins calls to "reclaim" an essential – and essentially gendered – identity. For the Nazis, that disruption and humiliation was the result of the cataclysm of World War One and the subsequent slide into economic depression. German men were first humiliated by military defeat and then by unemployment and an inability to fulfill 'provider' expectations. German women not only witnessed the shame and incapacity of husbands, fathers, and sons, but had their own 'provider' status undermined by household scarcity.

A similar dynamic was evident in Rwanda as the Hutu Power movement surged at the outset of the 1990s. The economy, never robust, entered a drastic tailspin as coffee prices collapsed and sources of foreign aid began to dry up with the end of the Cold War. Other sources of gendered anxiety arose with the Tutsi-dominated RPF's invasion of northern Rwanda in 1990, and subsequent internationally-mediated attempts to resolve the crisis and civil war. The Rwandan military crumbled in the face of the RPF advance, and had to be rescued by troops sent by its main foreign sponsor, France. Hutu men in the security forces, moreover, confronted the prospect of a peace agreement with dread, since it would inevitably mean the demobilization (read: unemployment) of thousands of Hutu soldiers, and their replacement by Tutsi/RPF ones. The emasculation and existential crisis of Hutu men in this period perhaps

4 Quoted in Randall Fegley, *A History of Rwandan Identity and Trauma: The Mythmakers' Victims* (Lexington Books 2016) 41.
5 Claudia Card, "Genocide and Social Death" (2003) *Hypatia* 18(1) 63–79.

spurred the sexualized atrocities, notably castration, inflicted on Tutsi male victims (including young boys) during the 1994 genocide.

And yet, the first three of the 'Hutu Ten Commandments' do not represent a call to Hutu men's action and empowerment – rather, they are fundamentally preoccupied with the roles and duties of Hutu and Tutsi women. Here is a striking element of the Rwandan genocide's gendering. Just as Tutsi men (whether resident in Rwanda or invading from without) constituted a humbling military and economic elite in the eyes of Hutu Power, so did Tutsi women pose a threat to the self-esteem of Hutu women – in part because of their 'trophy' appeal to the narrow elite of Hutu males. So a litmus test of commitment to the Hutu cause was forswearing marriage or sexual liaisons with Tutsi women; there is an almost pathetic plaintiveness to the second commandment, with its plea to recognize Hutu women as "more worthy and … conscientious" than Tutsi women, no less "lovely," and "more honest." Hutu Power visual propaganda, meanwhile, demonized Tutsi women as spies, subversives, and sexual sirens, corrupting both Hutu men and the foreign forces being introduced (again humiliatingly for Hutus) to police the ceasefire, following the Arusha peace accords of August 1993.

The horrific levels of sexual violence, including protracted enslavement and mutilation, inflicted upon Tutsi women likewise seemed spurred by these manipulations of gendered anxieties. And we begin to understand better why Hutu women, while still constituting only a few percent of the killers in 1994, were nonetheless more prominent as genocidal agents than in any other genocide in the historical record. "It is far from clear whether these genocidal women directed the majority of their atrocities against Tutsi women [as opposed to men]," I wrote in 2002; "but to the extent that they did, there appears to have been a kind of gendered jubilation at the 'comeuppance' of Tutsi females, who had for so long been depicted in Hutu propaganda as Rwanda's sexual elite."[6]

Might some generalizations be ventured here with regard to prevention of, and intervention in, future genocides?

First, I believe there is a need to recognize the devastating impact of economic crisis and accompanying 'austerity' measures, often imposed externally and coercively, and to acknowledge their profoundly gendered aspects. Women, with their stereotypical household/caregiving burdens and disproportionate lack of economic resources, may be even more dramatically and negatively affected than men in such situations. But given that men are overwhelmingly more likely to be recruited for genocidal tasks, we need to understand the particular explosiveness of undermining their economic livelihoods and piling on

6 Jones (n 1) 84.

gendered humiliations. Rapid demobilizations of military and security forces may be important to stabilize conflict situations. But if little consideration is given to where the demobilized will go and what substitute forms of subsistence will be available, the policy may create fresh problems in seeking to solve existing ones.

Second, the role of gendered propaganda before and during genocidal outbreaks should be recognized as an especially intimate and potentially toxic element. Out-group women may be the targets of demonization strategies that pave the way for their systematic murder and rape, while in-group women (as in the 'Hutu Ten Commandments') may be lured by gender-specific appeals to play crucial supporting roles, sometimes overtly genocidal ones. Out-group men, meanwhile, will typically be the focus of such propaganda efforts, since they are viewed as the pre-eminent threat to the designs of the *génocidaires*. And in-group men are standardly targeted for recruitment via gendered appeals by genocidal organizers and agents. Where such strategies are evident and increasing, they may suggest that a genocidal situation is nearing a boiling point, or spiralling out of control.

Finally, the Rwandan case suggests that in-group women need to be understood not simply as bystanders or cheerleaders in genocidal processes, but as active agents and, indeed, potential killers. As I wrote in "Gender and Genocide in Rwanda," the "Rwanda test" suggests that

> If women anywhere can participate in genocide on such a scale, and with such evident enthusiasm and savagery, then it seems a valid *prima facie* assumption that they are capable of such participation everywhere. The search then becomes one not for some essential 'difference' in women's approach to war and peace, but for the range of cultural and policy mechanisms that either allow or, more frequently, inhibit the expression of women's aggressive and genocidal tendencies.[7]

Women's status worldwide has advanced in leaps and bounds in recent decades; and "As women's freedoms increase, so will their violence," as Caron Gentry and Laura Sjoberg pithily phrased it.[8] Understanding how women, along with men, mobilize and are mobilized to violent ends will thus be an ever more urgent task as the genocides of the future unfold.

---

7 Jones (n 1) 88.

8 Caron E. Gentry and Laura Sjoberg, *Mothers, Monsters, Whores: Women's Violence in Global Politics* (Zed Books 2007) 4.

3 Gender Dimensions of Sexual Violence and Mass Killing

In 1985, the US scholar Mary Anne Warren coined the term 'gendercide' to connote gender-selective mass killing: that is, "the deliberate extermination of persons of a particular sex (or gender)." While acknowledging that terms "such as 'gynocide' and 'femicide'" had been proposed for the gender-selective killing of women and girls, Warren argued for "a sex-neutral term, in that the victims [of gendercide] may be either male or female. There is a need for such a sex-neutral term, since sexually discriminatory killing is just as wrong when the victims happen to be male."[9]

In applying Warren's concept to genocides throughout history and around the contemporary world, I argued that strategies of gendered killing were extraordinarily significant in understanding both a genocide's dynamics and its underlying ideological and cultural assumptions. In doing so, I challenged the standard feminist narrative in which 'gender' was equated with women/femininity alone, and males were drawn into the analysis overwhelmingly as perpetrators of violence against females. I suggested that genocides could be divided into two broad types – *gendercide* and *root-and-branch genocide*, distinguished by the different operations of the gender variable in each. In numerous, perhaps most, instances of genocidal killing, the selective targeting of males, especially men of a "battle age" (roughly 15–55 years old), substantially bounded and delineated the murderous dimension. Killing a community's males, while expelling, enslaving, and/or sexually predating upon its females, was a typical pattern. In virtually no case on the historical record was the opposite trend manifested, i.e., the selective murder of women while men were preserved alive.

In many other cases, an *initial* targeting of men and adolescent boys served as a harbinger and enabling element of "root-and-branch" genocide: the extension of mass killing to females, and to all age groups. Whether or not *génocidaires* consciously planned it for this purpose, the elimination of the menfolk removed the element of the target group's population that was best equipped and culturally conditioned to resist the perpetrators' designs, leaving the remainder of the population largely defenceless. I showed that in the twentieth century, this phase-model was evident in the two most widely studied cases of genocide: the Armenian holocaust during World War One, and the Nazi holocaust of Jews during World War Two.

9 Mary Anne Warren, *Gendercide: The Implications of Sex Selection* (Rowman and Allanheld 1985) 22.

Rwanda conforms in part to this model, but with important qualifications grounded in the fact that from the outset of full-blown genocide in April 1994, vast root-and-branch massacres against all demographic sectors of the Tutsi population racked the country. One of them, on 20 April at Karama parish in Butare prefecture, may stand as the most epic ground-level slaughter of the century, with 35,000 to 43,000 people murdered "in less than six hours."[10] Here, as in even larger (though longer) massacres such as the multi-week extermination of Tutsis at Bisesero, a survivor's recollection – that the killers "shot and shot and shot. There was no distinction. Everyone died – adult men and women, young men and women and children" – attests to the relentlessly indiscriminate character of the genocidal rampage. "And yet," I wrote in 2002, "the general thrust of the human rights reportage suggests that, on balance, males were overwhelmingly targeted in the genocide's earliest and most virulent stages."[11] In its gigantic early compendium of the crimes, African Rights was categorical in stating:

> The primary target of the hunt [for survivors of the opening massacres] were Tutsi men, particularly what extremist propaganda portrayed as the "ultimate" enemy – rich men, men between their twenties and forties, especially if they were well-educated professionals or students. Most hated of all were well-educated Tutsi men who had studied in Uganda (and to a lesser extent Tanzania and Kenya) who were immediately suspected of being members or supporters of the RPF. Within days, entire communities were without their men; tens of thousands of women were widowed, tens of thousands of children were orphaned.[12]

The account hints at a common co-factor of the killing of a community's males: the phenomenon of *eliticide*, whereby men's social power and prominence makes them especially attractive targets for *génocidaires*. It would be erroneous, therefore, to depict the selective killing of men and boys as governed solely by feelings of hostility and fear. Decimating the male members of a target community is therefore an effective way of undermining or destroying outright the social power of the group as a whole.

The gendercidal slaughter of Tutsi men was reflected in the widely-noted gender disparity that afflicted Rwanda in the wake of the 1994 genocide, with

10 African Rights, *Rwanda: Death, Despair and Defiance* (African Rights 1995) 26. Human Rights Watch gives the death total as 40,000: see Human Rights Watch, *Leave None to Tell the Story: Genocide in Rwanda* (Human Rights Watch 1999) 448.

11 Jones (n 1) 71.

12 African Rights (n 10) 597–98.

estimates (apparently exaggerated) of females constituting up to 70 percent of the surviving population. To the extent that women and girls were more likely to survive, however, this was almost universally at the cost of savage sexual assault and exploitation. Indeed, the Rwandan genocide is established as one of the quintessential twentieth-century examples of mass sexual violence against women in war and genocide. As such, it takes its place alongside the Ottoman depredations against Armenian (and other Christian) women, the Japanese 'Rape of Nanjing,' the Soviet mass rape of German (and Manchurian Chinese) women in the late stages of World War Two and its aftermath, and the West Pakistani atrocities against Bengali women in 1971. The earliest systematic treatment of sexual violence against Tutsi women – the Human Rights Watch report, *Shattered Lives* – cited the testimony of Perpetué, a resident of Gitarama prefecture, which must stand here for tens of thousands of similar cases:

> I was in the church building when the Interahamwe [genocidal militia] came there on May 15 and told us that it was our turn to be burnt. They took a lot of people outside to kill them. One Interahamwe chose me, but told me that he would protect me so that I would not be burnt to death. He took me to another building near the church and raped me there. Before he raped me, he said that he wanted to check if Tutsi women were like other women before he took me back to the church to be burnt. There were other women being raped there at the same time, maybe ten women and seven young girls. The next day, two Interahamwe watched over us while the others went to kill. The two were complaining they were feeling tired from all the killing. Then, one of them sharpened the end of the stick of a hoe. They held open my legs and pushed the stick into me. I was screaming. They did it three times until I was bleeding everywhere. Then they told me to leave. I tried to stand up, but I kept falling down. Finally I crawled outside. I was naked[,] crawling on the ground[,] covered in blood. I tried to ask someone on the road for help, but they thought I was a madwoman and just ignored me. I finally found a house where they gave me some medicine to apply to the area between my legs. They also gave me some clothes, but because I was bleeding so much the skirt became soaked with blood.[13]

The account attests to core features of many of the Hutu-male sexual attacks against Tutsi women. There is the targeting of "young girls" as well as adult

13 Human Rights Watch, *Shattered Lives: Sexual Violence during the Rwanda Genocide and Its Aftermath* (Human Rights Watch 1996) 26.

women; the reprieve (usually temporary) granted to enable protracted sexual enslavement; the element of sexual humiliation mixed with fetishization ("he wanted to check if Tutsi women were like other women"); and, perhaps most viscerally repugnant, the infliction of "life force atrocities,"[14] here taking the form of the sharpened stick thrust in the victim's vagina.

The horror and generalized character of the sexual violence wreaked upon Rwandan Tutsi women blended with the growing prominence of a gender perspective in international law to influence the operations of the ICTR's Arusha tribunal, most notably in its deliberations surrounding the case of Jean-Paul Akayesu, a burgomaster (mayor) from the Taba commune in Gitarama prefecture. As few readers will need reminding, Akayesu was found guilty in 1998 of, among other crimes, supervising rapes committed *as a strategy of genocide*: such acts "constitute genocide in the same way as any other act as long as they were committed with the specific intent to destroy, in whole or in part, a particular group, targeted as such."[15] The tribunal's deliberations imbued Article 2(b) of the Genocide Convention – which outlaws "causing serious bodily or mental harm to members of the group" – with an explicit gender dimension, perhaps for the first time. They were also instrumental in redefining rape under international law, as "a physical invasion of a sexual nature, committed on a person under circumstances which are coercive" – a definition that "represented a significant departure from a traditional, or mechanical, description which identified the crime in terms of the victim's non-consent to sexual intercourse and in terms of parts of the body of the perpetrator and the victim."[16]

While there is a general acceptance that the ICTR's reconfiguration of "rape" in the Akayesu verdict is a watershed, greater controversy attaches to whether the trial, and the ICTR's deliberations more generally, have fundamentally bolstered the place of anti-female sexual violence in the international law surrounding genocide. In the two decades since the decision was rendered, no other accused perpetrator has been charged with rape-as-genocide, either by the International Criminal Court or by one of the ad-hoc tribunals. In my view, this reflects not only the conceptual and legal complexities of rape-as-genocide, but also (and relatedly) the growing preference for prosecution under crimes against humanity legislation, rather than the Genocide Convention. The Rome

14 Elisa von Joeden-Forgey, "The Devil in the Details: 'Life Force Atrocities' and the Assault on the Family in Times of Conflict" (2010) *Genocide Studies and Prevention* 5(1) 1–19.

15 Suzanne Chenault, "And Since Akayesu? The Development of ICTR Jurisprudence on Gender Crimes: A Comparison of Akayesu and Muhimana" (2008) *New England Journal of International and Comparative Law* 14 221–37.

16 Chenault (n 15) 224.

Statute of the International Criminal Court includes sexual violence in its framing of crimes against humanity, a concept that may have less rhetorical punch, but which is not subordinate to genocide in international law.[17] The evidentiary bar for such crimes is lower than in the case of genocide: instead of demonstrating the intentional targeting of victims on the basis of a collective identity ("national, ethnical, racial, and religious groups" in the language of the Genocide Convention, adopted verbatim for the ICC charter), prosecutors need only show that the victims were civilians and were targeted with the knowledge that the crimes were part of a "widespread or systematic" campaign. If they can so demonstrate to the satisfaction of the judges, the sentence meted out to the perpetrator is likely to be all but indistinguishable from that for genocide. Accordingly, prosecutions for genocide as such have become increasingly focused on the mass killing element, and this is unlikely to change in the foreseeable future.

4 The Rwandan Patriotic Front: Crimes and Post-Genocide Governance

In the aftermath of the 1994 holocaust, the Tutsi-dominated Rwandan Patriotic Front (RPF – I include here its armed wing, the Rwandan Patriotic Army [RPA]) was generally viewed as the "good guys," a perception that has largely endured ever since. Depicted in the standard narrative as seeking only a pact that would allow Tutsi refugees to claim their right of return to Rwanda, the RPF was also credited with having brought the genocide to an end. Thereafter, it broadly forswore revenge against the Hutu majority, seeking a 'post-ethnic' model of governance in the interest of all Rwandans, and promoting development initiatives that promised to turn the tiny country into 'the Singapore of Africa.'

Key elements of this depiction were challenged early on. Within two years of the genocide, the RPF was embroiled in a war in neighboring eastern DR Congo (then Zaïre), and a number of journalists and scholars – including Howard French, René Lemarchand, and Filip Reyntjens – unsparingly catalogued the genocidal crimes perpetrated against Hutu refugees by the Rwandan military and its allied Banyamulenge militias. In her report for Human Rights Watch, *Leave None to Tell the Story*, Alison Des Forges devoted over 40 pages to RPF massacres of civilians during 1994. In successive editions of my *Genocide*

17 See Adam Jones, *Crimes Against Humanity: A Beginner's Guide* (Oneworld Publications 2008).

textbook,[18] I drew on the work of these critical voices to highlight RPF atrocities during the 1994 events and thereafter, in part to question the rosy image that the Paul Kagame dictatorship had courted during its (so far) quarter-century in power.

However, due recognition of RPF crimes, including genocide, was impeded by a number of factors: the ICTR's abjuring of investigations into those crimes, as part of a deal cut with the post-genocide Rwandan government; the UN's cynical suppression of the 1994 "Gersony Report" that "provided credible eyewitness accounts of numerous RPA crimes, including between fifteen and thirty thousand execution-style deaths in just four communes within its survey area"[19] (although note that Des Forges was able to access the report to underpin her account in *Leave None to Tell the Story*); the outside world's overwhelmingly favorable evaluation of the RPF, anchored in its hunger for a "good-news" story, that influenced most media coverage and foreign-aid policies; and the fact that the loudest voices raised against the RPF tended to belong to former members of the Hutu Power regime, or their allies and legal representatives. Only in recent years has a more critical stance toward Kagame's regime emerged, with, for example, denunciations of RPF warmongering in Congo by the UK and others, accompanied by threats to restrict aid; and with highly critical studies of the RPF during the genocide and throughout its years of rule. Two of the most potent recent contributions are Judi Rever's *In Praise of Blood: The Crimes of the Rwandan Patriotic Front*[20] and Susan Thomson's *Rwanda: From Genocide to Precarious Peace*.[21]

What do these varied sources tell us about the gendering of RPF mass violence, and its governing strategies once it seized nationwide power in Rwanda?

In "Gender and Genocide in Rwanda," I summarized evidence indicating "the pronounced gendercidal character of reprisals during and after the genocide by RPF forces and their allies and agents," which had "apparently also contribut[ed] to the gender disproportion" widely noted in post-genocide Rwanda.[22] These were also accompanied by largescale root-and-branch killings of Hutu civilians, though there is evidence that at least in the most notorious and closely-investigated case – the RPF's genocidal massacre of thousands of Hutus held captive at the Byumba Stadium in April 1994 – the killing

18 E.g. Adam Jones, *Genocide: A Comprehensive Introduction* (Routledge 2017) ch 9.
19 Susan Thomson, *Rwanda: From Genocide to Precarious Peace* (Yale University Press 2018).
20 Judi Rever, *In Praise of Blood: The Crimes of the Rwandan Patriotic Front* (Random House Canada 2018).
21 Thomson (n 19).
22 Jones (n 1) 65.

followed the phase-model (gendercide to root-and-branch) discussed earlier. According to Rever, "Military Police and members of Kagame's High Command unit began picking out the strongest males from the families on the pitch and in the bleachers, leading hundreds of them over to the stadium's dugout"; she cites eyewitness testimony that the RPF "wanted to massacre the strongest quickly."[23] On another occasion along the Nyabugogo River early in May 1994, an informant

> witnessed RPF soldiers surround a few thousand Hutu refugees, then separate the women from the group. The women were escorted to a camp of Tutsi survivors in nearby Rutare. The refugees who remained were young and old men, boys and male babies. The soldiers directed the refugees to take off their shirts and made the strongest Hutus tie the arms of the others behind their backs using their own clothing. The Hutu men were then ordered to hack them to death with hoes. Then they themselves were killed.[24]

When RPF/RPA killing became more targeted and selective within Rwanda, during the early years of its rule, "the gendercidal component, if anything, seems to have become more prominent." The very first snippet from media coverage of post-genocide Rwanda that I cited quoted the former RPF Minister of the Interior, Seth Sendashonga, describing a pattern that will be familiar to students of mass repression and genocide: "In many cases the Army came for men, ages 18 to 55, and took them away by night, never to be seen again. Their families search for them in vain, in the prisons of Rwanda, but they all died at the hands of the Rwandan Patriotic Army."[25] Susan Thomson likewise reports that during the two or three years following the 1994 genocide, the RPF's campaign of killing and systematic repression targeted principally Hutu men, who were deemed "guilty of acts of genocide regardless of what they may have done or not done" in 1994.[26]

According to sources such as the long-suppressed UN Mapping Report (finally released in 2010), similar strategies – of gendercidal and root-and-branch strategies combined – appear to have prevailed in what I have called "the

---

23 Rever (n 20) 74.

24 Elsewhere, Rever (2019) refers to extensive post-genocide "killing [of] Hutu males" by the RPF as "acts of androcide." Judi Rever, "Why We Must Listen to Those Who Have Fled Kagame's Rwanda" (2019) OpenCanada.org <https://www.opencanada.org/features/why-we-must-listen-those-who-have-fled-kagames-rwanda> accessed 20 June 2019.

25 Adam Jones, "Gendercide and Genocide" (2000) *Journal of Genocide Research* 2(2) [86].

26 Thomson (n 19) 63.

genocide of the camps," in which the attack on Hutu-populated refugee camps in eastern DR Congo/Zaire assumed an exterminatory character. However, in the Congolese case, a large proportion of those killed were clearly targeted *indirectly* and *structurally* – that is, by "deliberately inflicting on the group conditions of life calculated to bring about its physical destruction in whole or in part" (to cite Article 2(c) of the Genocide Convention), through starvation, disease, and denial of medical care. Statistical investigations by Thomas Plümper and Eric Neumayer have contended that the consequences of this indirect killing – perpetrated by many actors beyond the RPF and its allies – were heavily skewed against Congolese women and girls.[27]

The RPF's multifarious crimes, and their gendering, have been only sketchily acknowledged in foreign media coverage and academic analyses. (They are, of course, taboo and dangerous subjects in Rwanda itself.) Instead, a very different 'gendering' has been applied to the RPF and its strategies of governance – self-servingly promoted by the Kagame regime. Rwandan authorities have positioned the country as a development model for Africa and a progressive paragon, and a key component of this self-image has been the emphasis on women's rights, education, and political representation. As a highly laudatory account in *Marie Claire* magazine summarized it:

> On paper, Rwanda is the world's gender equality champion. The country boasts the highest percentage of women in parliament – 67.5 percent – and, according to the World Economic Forum, ranks sixth for its effort to reduce the gender gap (preceded only by four Scandinavian countries and Nicaragua). More than two decades after the 1994 genocide, Rwanda's top-down policies actively enforce women's empowerment at all levels. … The new "gender paradigm" sought parity in enrollment for both sexes in both primary and secondary education, while the new constitution of 2003 introduced aggressive quotas to scale up female representation in all government positions. Five years later, the tiny East African country of almost 12 million made headlines for being the first in history to achieve a female majority parliament, with 56 percent. In 2013, that figure grew to a striking 64 percent. Women became the face of the "new" Rwanda …[28]

27 For details and references for the sources and claims noted in this paragraph, see Adam Jones, "Masculinities and Vulnerabilities in the Rwandan and Congolese Genocides" in Amy E. Randall (ed) *Genocide and Gender in the Twentieth Century: A Comparative Survey* (Bloomsbury 2015) 62–79.

28 Caterina Clerici and Eléonore Hamelin, "Rwanda's Future is Female" (*Marie Claire*, 1 February 2019) <https://www.marieclaire.com/politics/a26078762/rwanda-women-equality/> accessed 22 June 2019.

Few observers of Rwanda would deny the Kagame regime's impressive accomplishments, which include Africa's first universal healthcare system. But trenchant criticisms have also been raised, questioning the depth and significance of some of the proclaimed transformations. The representation of women, for example, is of limited import when the country is run as a dictatorship, in which parliament serves as a rubber stamp for Kagame and his ruling clique. In an interview with *Deutsche Welle*, Rwandan journalist Fred Muvunyi dismissed the world-beating number of women in parliament as "for publicity .... When you look into deeper issues and what we should be expecting from these women, you don't see the results." Muvunyi also noted the regime's harsh treatment of women in opposition, such as Diane Rwigara, who sought to challenge Kagame for the presidency in the 2017 elections, and was subjected to dirty tricks and criminal charges as a consequence. "If you claim that you are empowering women and at the same time you put in prison those ones who feel empowered and ready to run for the highest office, what kind of empowerment are you talking about?"[29]

5 Conclusion

I have sought, in this chapter, to provide a sense of the significance of gender to both the Rwandan genocide of 1994 and patterns of political repression and representation since those terrible events. As with most genocides throughout history, gender played an overriding role in who was recruited and mobilized to do the killing; who was targeted for mass murder and other forms of violence, notably sexual atrocities; and the dynamics and phases of the genocide's unfolding. Rwanda is no exception; indeed, the genocide of Tutsis displays an extraordinarily complex and multifaceted tapestry of gendered influences and outcomes. These continued in the post-1994 period, as reflected in strategies of political and genocidal violence pursued in both Rwanda and DR Congo, and in strategies of domestic governance and foreign relations under Paul Kagame's RPF regime. Approaching the subject inclusively – that is, with attention to men and masculinities alongside women and femininities – is vital to understanding the workings of the gender variable. Such an understanding, in turn, is essential to understanding Rwanda's historical experience and its present sociopolitical trajectory. It may also point to useful avenues of study and investigation in the years ahead.

29 Muvunyi quoted in Deutsche Welle, "Rwanda – Real Equality or Gender-Washing?" (DW.com, 7 March 2019) <https://www.dw.com/en/rwanda-real-equality-or-gender-washing/a-47804771> accessed 22 June 2019.

PART 3

Prosecuting Genocide

CHAPTER 12

The ICTR and Its Contribution to the Revivification of International Criminal Law

Emily Crawford

1 Introduction

In the aftermath of the Second World War, the international community of the time, embodied as it was in the newly-formed international organisation of the United Nations, undertook an ambitious project. This project involved codifying established and emergent international laws for the protection and enforcement of human rights and humanitarian norms in both peace and wartime, and establishing mechanisms to enforce those laws. To that end, in the five years following the end of hostilities in 1945, a number of noteworthy treaties and documents were adopted, and new institutions established, including *inter alia*, the military tribunals in Nuremburg[1] and Tokyo,[2] the Universal Declaration of Human Rights,[3] the Geneva Conventions,[4] and the Genocide Convention.[5]

Additional to the work in the UN proper, the International Law Commission undertook a program of work with the dual objective of outlining a category of serious crimes to be known as 'Offences Against the Peace and Security of Mankind',[6] and of exploring the 'desirability and possibility of establishing an

1 Charter of the International Military Tribunal – Annex to the Agreement for the Prosecution and Punishment of the Major War Criminals of the European Axis, 8 August 1945 ('Charter of the IMT').
2 Charter of the International Military Tribunal for the Far East, 19 January 1946 ('Charter of the IMTFE').
3 UNGAR 217A, UN Doc. A/RES/3/217A, 10 December 1948.
4 Comprising Geneva Convention for the Amelioration of the Condition of the Wounded and Sick in Armed Forces in the Field, 12 August 1949 (hereinafter Geneva Convention I or GCI) 75 UNTS 31; Geneva Convention for the Amelioration of the Condition of Wounded, Sick and Shipwrecked Members of Armed Forces at Sea, 12 August 1949 (hereinafter Geneva Convention II or GCII) 75 UNTS 85; Geneva Convention Relative to the Treatment of Prisoners of War, 12 August 1949 (hereinafter Geneva Convention III, GCIII or the POW Convention) 75 UNTS 135; and Geneva Convention Relative to the Protection of Civilian Persons in Time of War, 12 August 1949 (hereinafter Geneva Convention IV, GCIV, or the Civilians Convention) 75 UNTS 287.
5 Convention on the Prevention and Punishment of the Crime of Genocide, 9 December 1948, 78 UNTS 277.
6 UNGAR 177 (II), UN Doc. A/CN.4/4, 21 November 1947, 9.

 | DOI:10.1163/9789004430129_014

international judicial organ for the trial of persons charged with genocide or other crimes over which jurisdiction will be conferred upon that organ by international conventions',[7] with the aim of possibly 'establishing a Criminal Chamber of the International Court of Justice'.[8]

The work collectively being undertaken towards protecting international human rights and enforcing international criminal law was ground-breaking. However, the optimism of that period – specifically, that there could be permanent international criminal court (ICC) – would soon, if not evaporate entirely, then at least stall, as the ILC, over the course of the following years and decades, would debate the prospects of an international criminal court, but seemingly make no progress.[9] Indeed, it was not until the early 1990s that the possibility of a permanent court became reality, with the ILC finally adopting, in 1994, the draft statute for the ICC,[10] which would itself become the Rome Statute of the ICC in 1998.[11]

That the International Criminal Court came into being when it did was due, in no small part, to the establishment of two institutions – the International Criminal Tribunal for the Former Yugoslavia, and the International Criminal Tribunal for Rwanda. Together, these two ad hoc tribunals effectively revived international criminal law from its dormant state, and were integral to building the groundswell of support for a permanent institution, in the form of the ICC. Beyond just their mere existence, the case law of the tribunals, the ICTR in particular, were pivotal in progressively developing the international law of genocide, and the law of non-international armed conflict.

With this background in mind, this article will explore how and why the ICTR was pivotal to reviving international criminal law after Nuremburg and Tokyo, looking at how international criminal law came to stagnate after the Nuremburg and Tokyo tribunals, and how the Statute of the Tribunal, and its case law, explained, expanded, and developed international criminal law during its lifetime.[12]

---

7 UNGAR 260 B (III), UN Doc. A/RES/3/260, 9 December 1948.

8 Ibid. See further M. Cherif Bassiouni, 'The History of the Draft Code of Crimes against the Peace and Security of Mankind', 27 *Israel Law Review* 247 (1993).

9 Discussed in more detail below, but see also M. Cherif Bassiouni, 'The History of the Draft Code of Crimes against the Peace and Security of Mankind', 27 *Israel Law Review* 247 (1993).

10 Draft Statute for an International Criminal Court, text adopted by the International Law Commission at its forty-sixth session, in 1994, and submitted to the General Assembly as a part of the Commission's report covering the work of that session, reprinted in *Yearbook of the International Law Commission*, 1994, vol. II, Part Two.

11 Rome Statute of the International Criminal Court, 17 July 1998, 2187 UNTS 90.

12 Note that more detailed analyses of the ICTR's Statute case law on inter alia, genocide, can be found in this volume.

2 International Criminal Law before Rwanda

It is conventional in the literature on the history of international criminal law to date its modern incarnation as having begun at the Nuremburg Tribunal;[13] that in the wake of the atrocities of the Second World War, the international community was compelled to prosecute those most responsible for the horrors of the conflict, namely the Axis leaders responsible for orchestrating and ordering the egregious violence against civilians and prisoners of war in occupied Europe and Asia. This is partly true – statements made at the Tribunal for Nuremburg did indeed advance a notion that the crimes for which the defendants were being prosecuted were of such gravity and magnitude that all nations had an interest in punishing perpetrators.[14]

However, this central idea of international criminal law – that all nations must seek out and punish certain categories of offender for crimes that are an offence against all humankind – had earlier antecedents.[15] Indeed, a nascent form of international criminal law found expression in international laws designed to prevent, repress, and punish persons engaged in the practice of piracy and the slave trade, law first codified in the 1500s.[16] By the latter-1800s, the idea that persons who violate certain international treaties should be held accountable in an international criminal court was being advocated for by scholars and practitioners such as Gustave Moynier, who, in 1872, in his capacity as President of the International Committee of the Red Cross, suggested that persons who violated the 1864 Geneva Convention for the Amelioration of the Wounded in Armies in the Field should be brought before an international criminal court.[17]

---

13 See, for example, Claus Kress, 'International Criminal Law', Max Planck Encyclopedia of International Law.

14 See, for example, the comments made by Robert Jackson in his opening statement before the Nuremburg Tribunal: 'The wrongs which we seek to condemn and punish have been so calculated, so malignant, and so devastating, that civilization cannot tolerate their being ignored, because it cannot survive their being repeated.' ('Second Day, Wednesday, 11/21/1945, Part 04', in *Trial of the Major War Criminals before the International Military Tribunal. Volume II. Proceedings: 11/14/1945-11/30/1945* (IMT 1947), 98–102.

15 See generally Timothy McCormack, 'From Sun Tzu to the Sixth Committee: The Evolution of an International Criminal Law Regime', in Timothy McCormack and Gerry Simpson (eds), *The Law of War Crimes: National and International Approaches* (Kluwer 1997).

16 Roger S Clark, 'The Development of International Criminal Law', in Chile Eboe-Osuji (ed), *Protecting Humanity: Essays in International Law and Policy in Honour of Navanetham Pillay* (Brill 2010), 371–372.

17 Gustave Moynier, 'Note sur la création d'une institution judiciaire internationale propre à prévenir et à réprimer les infractions à la Convention de Genève', *Bulletin international des Sociétés de secours aux militaires blessés*, Comité international, No. 11, Avril 1872, 122.

Moynier's suggestion for a permanent criminal court failed to gain traction, even as an increasing number of treaties regarding permissible and impermissible means and methods of warfare were adopted (treaties that banned certain weapons, and certain tactics of war, but which made no provision for criminal accountability for violations of, for example, the prohibition of the use of expanding or explosive bullets).[18] However, the mass slaughter of the Armenian population in 1915,[19] and the atrocities of the First World War[20] prompted certain members of the international community to again call for some form of mechanism to hold individuals accountable for crimes against international law.[21] Indeed, the Versailles Peace Treaty of 1919 had originally intended for Kaiser Wilhelm II to be prosecuted by the Allied and Associated Powers in a joint tribunal for 'a supreme offence against international morality and the sanctity of treaties.'[22]

The creation of the League of Nations further spurred calls for the creation of a permanent international criminal court; indeed, the notion of creating an

---

18 For example, the Declaration Renouncing the Use, in Time of War, of Explosive Projectiles Under 400 Grammes Weight, Saint Petersburg, 29 November/11 December 1868, reprinted in Dietrich Schindler and Jiri Toman, *The Laws of Armed Conflict: A Collection of Conventions, Resolutions and Other Documents* (Martinus Nijhoff 1988), 102 (hereafter St Petersburg Declaration); see also Convention with Respect to the Laws and Customs of War by Land and its Annex: Regulations Respecting the Laws and Customs of War on Land, 29 July 1899, (1898–99) 187 CTS 429; and Convention concerning the Laws and Customs of War on Land and its Annex: Regulations Respecting the Laws and Customs of War on Land (signed 18 October 1907), (1907) 205 CTS 277.

19 For a history of the Armenian genocide, see generally Fatma Müge, Göçek Suny, and Norman M. Naimark (eds), *A Question of Genocide: Armenians and Turks at the End of the Ottoman Empire*, (Oxford University Press 2011). For an investigation into the Armenian genocide at the time of the genocide, see James Bryce and Arnold J. Toynbee, *The Treatment of Armenians in the Ottoman Empire, 1915–1916: Documents Presented to Viscount Grey of Fallodon by Viscount Bryce* (Hodder and Stoughton 1916).

20 For an account of the violations of international law that took place during the First World War, see generally Isabel V. Hull, *A Scrap of Paper: Breaking and Making International Law during the First World War* (Cornell University Press 2014).

21 In the form of the fifteen-member commission established by the victorious States in the aftermath of the First World War (the 1919 Commission on the Responsibility, who issued a report calling for the establishment of an international tribunal to prosecute German officials, including the Kaiser – see the *Report of the Commission to the Preliminary Peace Conference*, reprinted in 14 *AJIL* 95 (1920). See generally M. Cherif Bassiouni, 'From Versailles to Rwanda in Seventy-Five Years: The Need to Establish a Permanent International Criminal Court', 10 *Harvard Human Rights Journal* 11 (1997).

22 Under Article 227(1); the Versailles Treaty also intended for prosecutions against those 'responsible for criminal acts against the nationals of more than one of the Allied and Associated Powers' (Article 229(2)).

ICC was debated at length in the League of Nations.[23] However, the collapse of the League, and the outbreak of the Second World War, meant that such debates were suspended. That being said, this suspension of debate was only temporary. As early as 1941, the Allies, aware of the widespread violations of the 1907 Hague Regulations and 1929 Geneva Conventions occurring in Axis-held territories, began making plans for holding the architects of the conflict accountable under international law. The first significant step towards this goal came in January 1942, when representatives from the governments of occupied Belgium, Czechoslovakia, France, Greece, the Netherlands, Luxembourg, Norway, Poland, and Yugoslavia issued a joint declaration proclaiming German atrocities in occupied Europe were a violation of the laws and customs of war, and that an object of the war effort was to ensure 'the punishment, through the channel of organised justice, of those guilty of or responsible for these crimes, whether they have ordered them, perpetrated them, or participated in them'.[24] This was followed in 1943 with the Declaration of German Atrocities,[25] where Stalin, Roosevelt and Churchill jointly declared that 'those German officers and men and members of the Nazi party who have been responsible for or have taken a consenting part in the above atrocities, massacres, and executions, will be punished by the joint decision of the Governments of the Allies.'[26] Following the German surrender in May 1945, plans for the international tribunal began to solidify, and by June 1945, the basic agreement for International Military Tribunal of Nuremburg was drafted, later adopted in August 1945 as the Agreement for the Prosecution and Punishment of Major War Criminals of the European Axis, and Establishing the Charter of the International Military Tribunal.[27]

While significant focus was directed towards prosecuting Nazi war criminals, some Allied States were equally of the opinion that Japanese war atrocities

---

23 The League of Nations debated the creation of an international criminal court in relation to the 1937 Convention for the Prevention and Punishment of Terrorism (see LoN Final Act of Conf, Geneva, 16 Nov 1937, LoN Doc C.548.M385.1937.V; (1938) 19 LoN OJ 23, reprinted in Yonah Alexander, Marjorie Browne, and Allan Nanes (eds), *Control of Terrorism: International Documents* (Crane Russak 1979), 19). See further Ben Saul, 'The Legal Response of the League of Nations to Terrorism', 4 *Journal of International Criminal Justice* 78 (2006).

24 See also the Draft Convention for the Establishment of a United Nations War Crimes Court, UN War Crimes Commission, UN Doc. C.50(1), 30 September 1944.

25 The so-called 'Moscow Declaration' – reprinted in *A Decade of American Foreign Policy: Basic Documents, 1941–49* (Washington, DC, Government Printing Office, 1950).

26 Ibid.

27 Charter of the International Military Tribunal, between the US, USSR, UK and France, and later joined by Australia, Belgium, Czechoslovakia, Denmark, Ethiopia, Greece, Haiti, Honduras, India, Luxembourg, the Netherlands, New Zealand, Norway, Panama, Paraguay, Poland, Uruguay, Venezuela, and Yugoslavia.

should not go unpunished. The July 1945 Potsdam Declaration, adopted by the US, UK, and China (and later USSR) called for a full Japanese surrender and announced the intention to prosecute Japanese war criminals.[28] However, the Potsdam Declaration did not explicitly state an intention to create an international military tribunal; rather, in the Japanese Unconditional Surrender of September 1945, the Japanese signatories agreed to 'take whatever action may be required by any … designated representative of the Allied Powers for the purpose of given effect to [the Potsdam declaration]'.[29] By January 1946, the International Military Tribunal for the Far East was established, with the jurisdiction to try 'those persons charged individually or as members of organisations … with offences which include crimes against the peace'.[30]

3 The Aftermath of the Nuremburg and Tokyo Tribunals: the Plan for an International Criminal Court

Both the Nuremburg and Tokyo trials were successful endeavours, demonstrating the workability of international criminal law in practice, with 24 indictments at Nuremburg,[31] and 39 in Tokyo.[32] With the success of the Tribunals in mind, the logical next step seemed to be further developing international criminal law, with the ultimate aim of establishing a permanent international criminal court. The first move towards this goal occurred on 11 December 1946, when the United Nations General Assembly affirmed the principles of international law recognized by the Charter of the Nuremberg Tribunal, and recognised the importance of codifying international criminal law.[33] This was followed in 1948, with the adoption of the Genocide Convention; similar progress regarding codifying and progressively developing the law on war crimes came with the adoption in 1949 of the four Geneva Conventions, relating to the protection of civilians, prisoners of war, and the wounded and sick in armies and wounded sick and shipwrecked naval forces.

28 Reprinted on the Japanese government website 'Birth of the Constitution of Japan', available at http://www.ndl.go.jp/constitution/e/etc/c06.html.
29 Japanese Instrument of Unconditional Surrender, 2 September 1945, available at the US National Archives website, https://catalog.archives.gov/id/1752336.
30 International Military Tribunal for The Far East, Special Proclamation by the Supreme Commander for the Allied Powers at Tokyo, 19 January 1946, Article 1.
31 See *Nuremburg Military Tribunals: Indictments* (Office of Military Government for Germany (US), Nuremberg 1946).
32 See Robert Cryer and Neil Boister (eds), *Documents on the Tokyo International Military Tribunal: Charter, Indictment, and Judgments* (Oxford University Press 2008).
33 In UNGAR 95 [I], UN Doc. A/RES/1/95, 11 December 1946.

Alongside work being undertaken in the UN and by States to codify the law, the International Law Commission also undertook a program of work to codify the law enunciated at Nuremburg. In 1949, the ILC started work on the 'Formulation of the Nuremberg Principles and Preparation of a Draft Code of Offenses Against the Peace and Security of Mankind' (Draft Code), with the intention of formulating 'the principles of international law recognised in the Charter of the Nuremburg Tribunal and in the Judgment of the Tribunal'.[34] In 1950, the special rapporteur, Jean Spiropoulos, submitted his First Report,[35] in which he expressed his hope that the report would give the International Law Commission 'a working paper which will help the Commission in accomplishing its task'[36] of developing a Code of Offences.

Nevertheless, standard-setting alone would be insignificant if there was no enforcement mechanism.[37] Thus, the second part of the international community's move to develop international criminal law came with work examining the possibility of creating a permanent international criminal tribunal. To that end, the ILC was tasked with creating a draft statute of a permanent international criminal court, with special rapporteur Ricardo Alfaro submitting his first report to the ILC in March 1950.[38]

However, neither the Draft Code, nor the Draft Statute for the Establishment of an International Criminal Court (Draft Statute), progressed any further than the ILC. In relation to the Draft Code, there was an inability to come to agreement on, *inter alia*, a definition of aggression.[39] In relation to the international criminal court, support among States for such an institution was mixed, with the UK, the USSR, and the US, supportive of the *concept* of a permanent international court, but reluctant to make such a concept reality.[40]

---

34 UNGAR Res 177(II), UN Doc. A/CN.4/4, (1947), 9.

35 2 *Yearbook of the International Law Commission* 253 (1950), UN Doc A/CN.4/25.

36 2 *Yearbook of the International Law Commission* 253 (1950), UN Doc A/CN.4/25, 255.

37 See comments by ILC Special Rapporteur Ricardo Alfaro: 'If the rule of law is to govern the community of States and protect it against violations of the international public order, it can only be satisfactorily established by the promulgation of an international penal code and by the permanent functioning of an international criminal jurisdiction.' (Report on the Question of International Criminal Jurisdiction by Ricardo J. Alfaro, Special Rapporteur, A/CN.4/15 and Corr.1, 2 *Yearbook of the International Law Commission* 1 (1950), 17.

38 Report on the Question of International Criminal Jurisdiction by Ricardo J. Alfaro, Special Rapporteur, UN Doc. A/CN.4/15 and Corr.1, 2 *Yearbook of the International Law Commission* 1 (1950).

39 For an explanation and analysis of the Draft Code of Crimes against Mankind, see further M Cherif Bassiouni, 'The History of the Draft Code of Crimes Against the Peace and Security of Mankind', 27 *Israel Law Review* 247 (1993).

40 See for example the *Report of the Sixth Committee to the General Assembly*, UN Doc. A/1639 (1950), reprinted in Benjamin B. Ferencz, *An International Criminal Court, A Step Toward World Peace: A Documentary History and Analysis* (Oceana Publications 1980), 306–311.

Both the Draft Code and the Draft Statute languished in the ILC (and General Assembly) for several decades.

International criminal law was thus in a unique situation for the majority of the latter part of the 20th century: the international community had made remarkable progress in setting standards, through the adoption of the Genocide Convention, the Geneva Conventions, and, in 1977, the Protocols Additional to the Geneva Conventions.[41] However, while violations of these treaties were justiciable in domestic courts,[42] there was no permanent international mechanism for holding individuals accountable for their violations of these standards.

Indeed, international criminal law (at least as practiced on the international plane) might well have continued to remain only an essentially theoretical field were it not for a few key events in the early 1990s. The first major event that set the stage for the revival of international criminal law was the dissolution of the former Soviet Union and the end of the Cold War.[43] This seismic shift in international relations resulted in a temporary diminution of stalemates in the UN Security Council,[44] which itself provided the political "breathing room" for a revisiting of the dormant Draft Code and Draft Statute.[45]

---

41 Protocol Additional to the Geneva Conventions of 12 August 1949, and relating to the Protection of Victims of International Armed Conflicts, 8 June 1977, 1125 UNTS 3 (hereinafter Protocol I or API) and Protocol Additional to the Geneva Conventions of 12 August 1949, and relating to the Protection of Victims of Non-International Armed Conflicts, 8 June 1977, 1125 UNTS 609 (hereinafter Protocol II or APII).

42 The Geneva Conventions provide that States parties must enact domestic legislation in order to criminalise grave breaches of the Conventions; Article 129 of Geneva Convention III provides that the 'High Contracting Parties undertake to enact any legislation necessary to provide effective penal sanctions for persons committing, or ordering to be committed, any of the grave breaches of the present Convention defined in the following Article.'

43 There is copious literature on the end of the Cold War – for a starting point, see generally Nick Bisley, *The End of the Cold War and the Causes of Soviet Collapse* (Palgrave Macmillan 2004), and Matthew Evangelista, *Unarmed Forces: The Transnational Movement to End the Cold War* (Cornell 1999).

44 See generally Adam Roberts and Dominik Zaum, *Selective Security: War and the United Nations Security Council since 1945* (Taylor and Francis 2009), specifically Chapters 2 and 4.

45 See Roger S Clark, 'The Development of International Criminal Law', in Chile Eboe-Osuji (ed), *Protecting Humanity: Essays in International Law and Policy in Honour of Navanetham Pillay* (Brill 2010), 378; see also M. Cherif Bassiouni, 'From Versailles to Rwanda in Seventy-Five Years: The Need to Establish a Permanent International Criminal Court', 10 *Harvard Human Rights Journal* 11 (1997), 38–40; and more generally David Forsythe, '"Political Trials"? The UN Security Council and the Development of International Criminal Law' in William Schabas, Yvonne McDermott, and Niamh Hayes (eds), *The Ashgate Research Companion to International Criminal Law: Critical Perspectives* (Routledge 2013).

However, moves towards adopting the Draft Code (and Draft Statute) would likely not have been any more successful in the early nineties were it not for the outbreak of two cataclysmic armed conflicts. The first of these was the conflict that erupted in Yugoslavia in 1991.[46] The scale of the hostilities and reported atrocities taking place prompted the Security Council to request the Secretary-General establish a Commission of Experts to investigate whether violations of international humanitarian law were occurring in that conflict;[47] the Commission would eventually recommend the establishment of a Tribunal, that would become the International Criminal Tribunal for the Former Yugoslavia.[48] The second armed conflict was that which broke out in Rwanda in 1994.[49] The scope of the atrocities that took place during the genocide in Rwanda also prompted a call for the Security Council to establish an international tribunal to prosecute the perpetrators.[50] This call would ultimately lead to the creation of the International Criminal Tribunal for Rwanda.[51]

4 The ICTR's Contribution to Reviving and Developing International Criminal Law

Together, the ICTY and ICTR essentially revived international criminal law as a discipline, and as Matheson and Scheffer note, 'in a political and legal sense, the creation of the Yugoslav and Rwanda Tribunals triggered a massive revival

46 For a background to the conflict and the history of the conflict itself, see further Laura Silber and Alan Little, *The Death of Yugoslavia* (Harmondsworth 1996).

47 UN Security Council Resolution 780, UN Doc. S/RES/780, 6 October 1992. See also Interim Report of the Commission of Experts Established Pursuant to Security Council Resolution 780 (1992), UN Doc. S/25274, 10 February 1993, and UN Security Council Resolution 808, UN Doc. S/RES/808, 22 February 1993, in which the Security Council agreed on the creation of the Tribunal.

48 For an account of the creation of the ICTY, see generally Michael Matheson and David Scheffer, 'The Creation of the Tribunals', 110 *AJIL* 173 (2016); Mohamed Shahabuddeen, 'The International Criminal Tribunal for the Former Yugoslavia: The Third Wang Tieya Lecture', 11 *Chinese Journal of International Law* 13 (2012); and William A. Schabas, *The UN International Criminal Tribunals: the former Yugoslavia, Rwanda and Sierra Leone* (Cambridge 2006), specifically Chapter 1.

49 See further the chapters within this volume that detail on the history of the conflict in Rwanda and the events that took place during the genocide.

50 UN Security Council Resolution 935, UN Doc. S/RES/935, 1 July 1994; see also the Preliminary Report of the Independent Commission of Experts Established in Accordance with Security Council Resolution 935, UN Doc S/1994/879, 26 July 1994; and see further David Scheffer, *All the Missing Souls: A Personal History of the War Crimes Tribunals* (Princeton 2012), 69–70.

51 See further within this volume for a more detailed account of the creation of the ICTR.

of the prospects for international prosecution of international crimes.'[52] Indeed, as Goran Sluiter notes, 'one can hardly overestimate the importance of the United Nations ad hoc tribunals for the development and operationalisation of international criminal law'.[53]

It might be tempting to diminish or downplay the significant of the ICTR, as the *second* of the modern international criminal tribunals (thus lacking the "pioneering" aspect of the ICTY as the first international criminal tribunal since Nuremburg and Tokyo). However, it is arguable that the ICTR, as the second of the tribunals, played more of a role in reviving international criminal law in the early 1990s was made possible by the ICTR, perhaps more so than the ICTY. As an ad hoc body, the ICTY could have been seen as a "one-off" response to the conflict in the former Yugoslavia, rather than as a template for a more permanent institution. The international community could have 'stalled' with the creation of a post-ICTY permanent court, in the same way that, for decades, there was little movement on the creation of a post-Nuremburg permanent court. However, the atrocities committed in Rwanda, coming so soon after the creation of the ICTY, logically raised the question that, if the conflict in the former Yugoslavia was deserving of a tribunal, why not the conflict in Rwanda? Given that two tribunals were created so close to one another, it seemed logical to consider perhaps creating a more permanent body to deal with violations of international criminal law. Indeed, as Matheson and Scheffer note:

> the creation of the Yugoslav and Rwanda Tribunal revived international criminal prosecution as a means for dealing with serious atrocities, providing justice, contributing to the resolution of conflicts, and deterring future crimes … the creation of the Tribunals served as the essential legal and political basis for the modern international criminal system … [and while this] may seem obvious and inevitable today, it was not so at the time that the international community was trying to decide what to do about the atrocities sweeping through the former Yugoslavia. No such international tribunal has been created for decades and only in the context of a world war. But in the immediate wake of the Yugoslav conflict and the creation of the Yugoslav Tribunal, the genocide in Rwanda compelled the Security Council to create a second such tribunal. The die was cast for a significant transformation in the international legal order.[54]

52 Michael Matheson and David Scheffer, 'The Creation of the Tribunals', 110 *AJIL* 173 (2016), 177.

53 Goran Sluiter, 'Ad Hoc International Criminal Tribunals (Yugoslavia, Rwanda, Sierra Leone)', in William Schabas (ed), *The Cambridge Companion to International Criminal Law* (Cambridge 2016), 117.

54 Michael Matheson and David Scheffer, 'The Creation of the Tribunals', 110 *AJIL* 173 (2016), 190. See also Sara Kendall and Sarah Nouwen, 'Speaking of Legacy: Towards and Ethos of Modesty at the International Criminal Tribunal for Rwanda' 110 *AJIL* 212 (2016), 217–222.

Thus, it was the ICTR, in conjunction with the ICTY, that created the modern international criminal law paradigm that exists today.

However, the ICTR has contributed to the development of international criminal law beyond just its mere existence. Additional to the important work done to better define and develop the crime of genocide,[55] the ICTR also saw ground-breaking work undertaken on sexual violence.[56] Moreover, as a tribunal that dealt entirely with a non-international armed conflict, the ICTR's Statute and case law did much to contribute to the law of war crimes and crimes against humanity in non-international armed conflict. In a number of judgments,[57] the ICTR better clarified the scope of the notion of 'attack' for the purposes of a crime against humanity,[58] and firmly established that crimes against humanity, unlike war crimes, do not require a nexus to an existing armed conflict in order to have been committed.[59]

In relation to war crimes, the ICTR Statute was also the first document to criminalise violations of both Common Article 3 and Additional Protocol II,[60] a pivotal development that was crucial to the later inclusion in the ICC Statute of serious violations of both Common Article 3 and Protocol II in non-international armed conflicts.[61] Prior to the adoption of the ICTR Statute, violations of Common Article 3 and Protocol II were not considered as coming within the purview of the international law of war crimes.[62] By the time the Rome Statute of the ICC came to be negotiated, the majority of States at the

55 The ICTR's work on the definition of genocide is discussed in more detail in this volume. But see also Larissa van den Herik, *The Contribution of the Rwanda Tribunal to the Development of International Law* (Martinus Nijhoff 2005), Chapter 3.

56 See infra this volume for the chapter on sexual violence and the ICTR; see also Alexandra Adams, 'The Legacy of the International Criminal Tribunals for the Former Yugoslavia and Rwanda and their Contribution to the Crime of Rape', 29 *EJIL* 749 (2018); and Larissa van den Herik, *The Contribution of the Rwanda Tribunal to the Development of International Law* (Martinus Nijhoff 2005), 141–144, 161–174, 191–196.

57 Including *Nahimana et al* (Case No. ICTR-99-52-A), para. 918, and *Kayishema and Ruzindana* (Case No. ICTR-95-1-T), para. 122.

58 Article 3 of the ICTR Statute provides: 'The International Tribunal for Rwanda shall have the power to prosecute persons responsible for the following crimes when committed as part of a widespread or systematic attack against any civilian population on national, political, ethnic, racial or religious grounds…'.

59 *Théoneste Bagosora and Anatole Nsengiyumva* (Case No. ICTR-98-41-A), para. 415.

60 In Article 4, ICTR Statute. See further the Secretary-General Report pursuant to para. 5 of SC Res 955, UN Doc. S/1995/134, 13 February 1995, para. 11.

61 See generally Justice Hassan Bubacar Jallow, 'The ICTR's Elaboration of the Core International Crimes of Genocide, Crimes Against Humanity and War Crimes and Modes of Liability', in Anne-Marie Brouwer and Alette Smeulers (eds), *The Elgar Companion to the International Criminal Tribunal for Rwanda* (Elgar 2016), and Eve de la Haye, *War Crimes in Internal Armed Conflicts* (Cambridge 2008), Chapters 4 and 6.

62 See further the Secretary-General Report pursuant to para. 5 of SC Res 955, UN Doc S/1995/134, 13 February 1995, para. 12.

Diplomatic Conference were of the opinion that violations of Common Article 3 and Protocol II should be included in the war crimes regime,[63] and made explicit reference to the ICTR Statute as evidence of the crystallising custom.[64] In terms of the ICTR's case law, the Tribunal also contributed to clarifying the concept of command responsibility,[65] including that command responsibility encompasses both civilian and political superiors, as well as military superiors.[66]

5 Conclusions

The International Criminal Tribunal for Rwanda officially closed on 31 December 2015. In its twenty years of operation, it issued a number of landmark cases, and was the first international institution to deliver verdicts against persons responsible for committing genocide, recognising that rape should be considered as a mean of perpetrating genocide.[67] While the record of the ICTR was not without its problems,[68] it nevertheless was an important institution, both for its own program of work, as well as for its contribution to re-establishing international criminal law as a distinct and permanent part of the international legal landscape.

---

63 See the 1995 Ad Hoc Committee Report on the Establishment of an International Criminal Court, UN Doc. A/50/22 (1995), para. 74, and the 1996 Preparatory Committee Report on the Establishment of an International Criminal Court, UN Doc. A/51/22 (1996), para. 78 (reprinted in *The Statute of the International Court: A Documentary History* (M. Cherif Bassiouni ed, Transnational Publishing 1998).

64 UN Doc. A/51/22 (1996) para. 78. See further Eve de la Haye, *War Crimes in Internal Armed Conflicts* (Cambridge 2008), 136–144.

65 *Bagilishema*, Case No. ICTR -95-1-A-A, (3 July 2002), paras. 33–37.

66 *Kayishema*, Case No. ICTR-95-1-T (21 May 1999), para. 208.

67 ICTR website, http://unictr.irmct.org/en/tribunal.

68 For an introduction to critical evaluations of the ICTR and its legacy, see further Shane Darcy and Joseph Powderly (eds), *Judicial Creativity at the International Criminal Tribunals* (Oxford University Press 2010); Kirsten Keith, 'Justice at the International Criminal Tribunal for Rwanda: Are Criticisms Just?', 27 *Law in Context* 78 (2009); and Nobuo Hayashi and Cecilia Bailliet (eds), *The Legitimacy of International Criminal Tribunals* (Cambridge University Press 2017).

CHAPTER 13

Post-Genocide Justice in Rwanda

M.A. Drumbl

1 Introduction[1]

Between April and July 1994, approximately 500,000 to 800,000 people were massacred in genocidal pogroms in Rwanda. This is a staggering amount of death in a country with a total population at the time of around 8 million. Many of the killings were unspeakably brutal. They were in no way depersonalized through technology: a study conducted by the Rwandan government concluded that nearly 38% of victims were murdered by machete, 16.8% by club, and 14.8% by firearm; other means of murder included grenades, swords, knives, drowning, sticks, rock, and barehanded assault.[2]

The perpetrators of the violence were members of the majority Hutu ethnic group, many of whom were ordinary citizens radicalized by an extremist government. The overwhelming majority of victims were members of the minority Tutsi group. The Hutu comprised approximately 85% of Rwanda's population, the Tutsi 14%. The genocide was quelled when a Tutsi army (the RPA), based in neighboring Uganda, ousted the genocidal Hutu government and seized power in July 1994. The RPA's General, Paul Kagame, currently serves as Rwanda's Head of State.

William Schabas notes that in the many years that have ensued Rwanda "insisted upon holding perpetrators accountable […] while many other post-conflict societies have delayed, postponed and even prevaricated."[3] As a result of this commitment, Rwanda instituted national trials within chambers specially established within the regular court system and, subsequently, proceedings within neo-traditional venues called *gacaca* for genocide. The international

1 Parts of this chapter draw from, condense, and update the author's prior publications *Atrocity, Punishment, and International Law* (Cambridge University Press, 2007) (specifically pages 71–96) and "Justice Outside of Criminal Courtrooms and Jailhouses", in *Arcs of Global Justice* (eds. deGuzman and Amann, Oxford University Press, 2018).

2 *Dénombrement Des Victims Du Genocide: Rapport Final*, Ministère de l'Administration locale, de l'Information, et des Affaires sociales 26 (2002).

3 W A Schabas, 'Post-Genocide Justice in Rwanda: A Spectrum of Options' in P Clark and Z D Kaufman (eds), *After Genocide: Transitional Justice, Post-Conflict Reconstruction and Reconciliation in Rwanda and Beyond* (CUP 2009) 207.

 | DOI:10.1163/9789004430129_015

community, for its part, formally prosecuted higher-ranked offenders at the International Criminal Tribunal for Rwanda (ICTR), sited in Arusha (Tanzania). A handful of states foreign to Rwanda also conducted national proceedings, at times based on principles of universal jurisdiction, against Rwandan nationals who generally shared some connection to those states.

In short, the Rwandan genocide has triggered a vast number of criminal and quasi-criminal prosecutions. While redress for Holocaust-era crimes of the 1940's continues to be an ongoing pursuit, including against defendants aged in their nineties, accountability in the sense of penal proceedings for Rwanda's genocide has largely wrapped up. The little country of Rwanda, then, represents a robust and rapid implementation of criminal accountability for atrocity. Rwanda, moreover, departed from other countries, such as South Africa, by eschewing a truth and reconciliation process as part of a transitional justice process.

This chapter unpacks three levels of judicialization that promoted criminal responsibility for atrocity in Rwanda. To recap, these three layers are: the ICTR, specialized chambers of national courts, and *gacaca* proceedings. The ICTR indicted roughly 90 individuals, the national courts convicted in the area of 10,000 defendants (with some proceedings remaining ongoing), while roughly one million individuals proceeded through *gacaca*. The ICTR and *gacaca* proceedings have been concluded for several years already. This chapter will not discuss a fourth level, namely, the handful of proceedings conducted extraterritorially – for example, in Canada, Belgium, France, and Germany.[4]

Rwanda's domestic pursuit of extensive criminal prosecutions in the aftermath of genocide is all the more remarkable in light of the absolute destruction that the genocide wrought to the country's legal system and legal profession. Schabas was among the first foreign experts to arrive in Rwanda in the wake of the genocide. He recalls:

> In September 1994, Rwanda's then-Minister of Justice, Alphonse-Marie Nkubito, working from an office whose windows had been knocked out, and whose walls were decorated only by gunshots, appealed to the international community for assistance in rebuilding the country's devastated justice system. [...] There were only around 20 lawyers with genuine legal education in the country when I visited Rwanda in November 1994 as part of the international response to Minister Nkubito's appeal.[5]

4 Discussion can be found at Helen L. Trouille, "France, Universal Jurisdiction and Rwandan *génocidaires*: The *Simbikangwa* Trial", 14:1 *Journal of International Criminal Justice* (2016) pp. 195–217; Leila Sadat, "Transjudicial Dialogue and the Rwandan Genocide: Aspects of Antagonism and Complementarity", 22:3 *Leiden Journal of International Law* (2009), pp. 543–562.

5 Schabas, supra note 3, at 212.

I worked as a public defender in Kigali, Rwanda's capital, in 1998. At the time, nearly 130,000 detainees accused of genocide-related crimes were crammed into prisons with the capacity to hold about 15,000. I worked in a prison that housed approximately 9,000 suspects. At the time, here's how I described the setting:

> They [the prisoners] stand, sit and sleep in one courtyard. Overcrowding is so pronounced that one had to step over and on bodies in order to cross to the other side of the courtyard. Bunkbeds layered on top of each other finger the sky, hooked together with clothes lines from which the prisoners' pink correctional uniforms hang. Between the beds narrow pathways wind through the congestion.[6]

The massive nature of the genocide, and the staggering number of genocide suspects, did more than, to draw from Hannah Arendt, "explode the limits of law",[7] they also exploded the capacity of whatever infrastructure that remained.

Schabas was a catalyst in developing the domestic Organic Law that ultimately would form the basis for prosecutions for genocide and crimes against humanity in the specialized chambers of the national court system.[8] To be sure, the many proceedings conducted thereunder oozed with due process concerns; their contribution to reconciliation, moreover, is unclear. Notwithstanding these limitations, Rwanda's attempts to thwart impunity, develop an historical record, and promote accountability in the wake of a genocide that implicated broad swaths of the population as perpetrators represents for Schabas "one of the most principled manifestations of the commitment of international human rights law and policy".[9] While Schabas' endorsement may tend towards the optimistic, and contrasts with others who take a dimmer view,[10] the fact remains that Rwanda took post-conflict justice very seriously. This Chapter unpacks these modalities of post-conflict genocide justice in Rwanda.

6 Mark A. Drumbl, "Rule of Law Amid Lawlessness: Counseling the Accused in Rwanda's Domestic Genocide Trials", 29 *Columbia Human Rights Law Review*, 545, 572 (1998).

7 Hannah Arendt and Karl Jaspers, *Correspondence 1926–1969*, New York, HBJ, 1992, p. 54.

8 In Rwanda, the term "Organic Law" refers to laws that rank higher in normativity to ordinary laws, and are secondary only to the Constitution.

9 Schabas, supra note 3, at 207.

10 *See, e.g.* Lars Waldorf and Scott Strauss (eds), *Remaking Rwanda: State Building and Human Rights After Mass Violence* (University of Wisconsin Press 2011).

2 The ICTR

The United Nations Security Council established the International Criminal Tribunal for Rwanda (ICTR) through Resolution 955 in November 1994. The Security Council elected to site the ICTR in Arusha (Tanzania). Rwanda, then a member of the Security Council, did not support the ICTR in part because of its location outside Rwanda and because it could not award the death penalty as a sentence.

The ICTR has primacy over national institutions. It has jurisdiction over genocide, crimes against humanity, and war crimes.[11] The ICTR has sentenced 59 of its 90 indictees. Seventeen of these are life sentences. In *Nchamihigo*, an ICTR Trial Chamber held that:

> [A] sentence of life imprisonment is generally reserved for those who planned or ordered atrocities and those who participated in the crimes with especial zeal or sadism. Offenders receiving the most severe sentences also tend to be senior authorities.[12]

The ICTR Appeals Chamber in *Nchamihigo* (a defendant who had been a deputy prosecutor, so not a senior authority within the government) ultimately reversed some of the convictions and substituted a term sentence of 40 years. Life sentences however, have been routinely imposed against senior government authorities, along with persons who did not hold government positions. Examples include a tea factory director, and a high-level official in the *Interahamwe* militia – a group of zealots who supported the genocidal cause with avidity and committed many horrendous massacres.

Among the ICTR's 42 determinate sentences, the median sentence is 25 years and the mean sentence is 24.67 years.[13] The shortest determinate sentence issued by the ICTR is 6 years, while the maximum is 47 years. In addition, at the ICTR, 14

---

11 Articles 2, 3, and 4 of the Statute of the International Criminal Tribunal for the Prosecution of Persons Responsible for Genocide and Other Serious Violations of International Humanitarian Law Committed in the Territory of Rwanda and Rwandan Citizens Responsible for Genocide and Other Such Violations Committed in the Territory of Neighbouring States, Between Jan. 1, 1994 and Dec. 31, 1994. S.C. Res. 955, Annex, U.N. Doc. S/RES/955 (1994).

12 The Prosecutor v. Siméon Nchamihigo ICTR-01-63-T (Judgment, 12 November 2008), para. 388.

13 All of the ICTR data are compiled and analyzed by Professor Barbora Holá (Free University of Amsterdam) and shared with the author on January 7, 2017 (results on file with the author).

individuals have been acquitted, 5 referred to national jurisdictions for trial, 2 deceased prior to or during trial, and 2 indictments withdrawn before trial.

Article 23(1) of the ICTR Statute, which limits penalty to imprisonment, stipulates that, in determining the terms of imprisonment, the ICTR shall have recourse to the general practice regarding prison sentences in the courts of Rwanda. The ICTR has concluded that although it has an obligation to consider such practice, this provision does not imply an obligation to conform thereto.[14] No obligation arises to take into account the sentencing practice of national jurisdictions other than Rwanda.[15] Although sentences in similar cases adjudicated at the ICTR are instructive, these antecedents are not binding as benchmarks.[16] When it comes to determining sentence, ICTR judges took into account "the gravity of the offence and the individual circumstances of the convicted person."[17] A convict may be incarcerated for a term up to life. Since there is no mandatory minimum sentence, ICTR judges therefore have the power to impose any sentence ranging from one-day imprisonment to life imprisonment for any crime within their jurisdiction. In the initial years of its work, the ICTR sentenced somewhat erratically. Greater consistency emerged over time,[18] at least in the case of the identification of principles to guide gravity and individualization of sentence. D'Ascoli concludes that among the most influential factors in the quantum of sentence are the type of crime, the victimization, superior position of the convict, and abuse of authority.[19]

ICTR trials have raised international awareness of what happened in Rwanda in 1994 and have developed an historical record. Far more muddied is the evidence that ICTR trials have contributed to reconciliation in the country. ICTR jurisprudence certainly has advanced and clarified numerous aspects of international criminal law. This jurisprudential contributon is significant. For example, the *Akayesu* decision provided a sophisticated definition of

---

14 The Prosecutor v. Semanza ICTR-97-20-A (Judgement, 20 May 2005), paras. 345, 347, 377; Bikindi v. The Prosecutor ICTR-01-72-A (Judgement, 18 March 2010), para. 148.

15 Bikindi v. The Prosecutor ICTR-01-72-A (Judgement, 18 March 2010), para. 154.

16 Prosecutor v. Nyiramasuhuko et al. ICTR-98-42-T (Trial Judgement and Sentence, 24 June 2011), para. 6190.

17 Statute of the ICTR, *supra* note 11, article 23(2).

18 Silvia D'Ascoli, *Sentencing in International Criminal Law* (Hart 2011); Barbora Holá, Catrien Bijleveld and Alette Smeulers, 'Consistency of International Sentencing: ICTY and ICTR Case Study' (2012) 9 *European Journal of Criminology* 539–52; Kai Ambos, *Treatise on International Criminal Law – Volume II* (Oxford University Press 2014) 268; Barbora Holá, Alette Smeulers and Catrien Bijleveld, 'International Sentencing Fact and Figures: Sentencing Practice at the ICTY and ICTR' (2011) 9 *Journal of International Criminal Justice* 411–39.

19 D'Ascoli, *supra* note 18, at 259–60.

ethnicity (for the purposes of proving genocide) and also advanced a progressive understanding of sexual violence in which rape was constructed as a tool of genocide.[20] The *Musema* decision extended command responsibility outside of the military context and into a private corporate environment.[21] In *Barayagwiza*, the ICTR issued the first verdict ever to media leaders for inciting genocide and differentiated statements of ethnic pride (protected by virtue of freedom of expression) from incitement to hate (not protected by freedom of expression).[22] The *Nyiramasuhuko* case involved one of the first convictions of a woman for genocide and crimes against humanity, including on charged of ordering mass rape.[23]

The ICTR has wound down its activities. The International Residual Mechanism for Criminal Tribunals (UNMICT), a separately created entity, picks up the outstanding work, including criminal proceedings. The UNMICT assumed responsibility for the supervision of all sentences pronounced by the ICTR as of 1 July 2012, including the process of early release of convicts. The ICTR delivered its last trial judgment on 20 December 2012, in the *Ngirabatware* case.[24] Its last Appeals Judgement was delivered in December 2015 in the *Nyiramasuhuko* case. ICTR and UNMICT sentences are enforced in States that have signed cooperation agreements and in accordance with international standards of detention and the applicable law of the enforcing State. ICTR convicts have for example been incarcerated in Mali, Bénin, Italy, and Sweden (nearly all in Mali and Bénin, however).

3 Chambres Specialisées

3.1 *Criminal Charges*

The 1996 Organic Law, which generated the legal basis for prosecutions in the national and military courts of Rwanda for genocide and crimes against

---

20 Prosecutor v. Akayesu, Case No. ICTR-96-4 (ICTR Appeals Chamber, 2001, affirming judgment of ICTR Trial Chamber).

21 Prosecutor v. Musema, Case No. ICTR-96-13-T (ICTR Appeals Chamber, Nov. 16, 2001).

22 Prosecutor v. Nahimana, Barayagwiza, and Ngeze, Case No. ICTR-99-52-T (ICTR Trial Chamber, Dec. 3, 2003).

23 Prosecutor v. Nyiramasuhuko et al. ICTR-98-42-A (ICTR Appeals Chamber, December 14, 2015).

24 The Prosecutor v. Ngirabatware ICTR-99-54-T (Judgement and Sentence, 20 December 2012).

humanity, initially created four categories of culpability.[25] These were: (a) Category 1 (planners, organizers, those in positions of authority, notorious murders (with zeal or excessive malice), sexual torturers and rapists); (b) Category 2 (perpetrators of intentional homicide or serious bodily assault causing death); (c) Category 3 (perpetrators of other serious assaults); and (d) Category 4 (perpetrators of property offenses). War crimes were excluded from the jurisdiction of the Organic Law.

Article 14 of the initial Organic Law dealt with punishment. It linked the severity of punishment, as well as its form, to the gravity of the offense as represented ordinally by the category of culpability. Category 1 offenses, initially sanctioned by death, became punished by life imprisonment after Rwanda's abrogation of the death penalty in 2007. Part of this involved a dance between the ICTR, whose judges refused to refer cases to the courts of Rwanda through the transfer mechanism (having the death penalty on the books in Rwanda barred transfer), and national authorities in Rwanda.[26] The Organic Law encouraged defendants to confess their guilt through a detailed guilty plea schematic.

Article 17 of the Organic Law permitted additional sanction by stripping the convict of certain civic rights. This could be permanent (*dégradation civique perpétuelle et totale* (sometimes referred to as *défintive*) or limited either in scope or temporal duration (*dégradation civique limitée*). Examples of those civic rights or privileges stripped through *dégradation civique* include: the right to vote; other political rights (such as to be a candidate); an inability to serve as an expert or witness in trials or to be deposed judicially other than for the giving of simple facts (although it has been held that proceedings from previous trials may be admissible);[27] the right to carry arms; to serve in the armed forces; to be police; and to teach or to be employed in any educational institution as professor, monitor, teacher, or supervisor.[28]

25 Organic Law No. 8/96 on the organization of prosecutions for offenses constituting the crime of genocide or crimes against humanity committed since 1 October 1990 (Journal Officiel No. 17 du Sept 1, 1996) (establishing categories of offenders, punishments, a trial and appellate structure, and limiting jurisdiction to events occurring from October 1, 1990, to December 31, 1994).

26 The referral of cases to Rwanda was contemplated by Rule 11*bis* of the ICTR Rules of Procedure and Evidence.

27 Ministère Public v. Nteziryayo (Emmanuel) et al. (November 30, 2001, 1ière instance, Butare), RMP 44223/S8/KA, RP 84/2/2001, p. 21.

28 Ministère Public v. Kabirigi et al. (Dec 10, 1998, 1ière instance, Kibuye), RMP 51.498/S4/C.M./KBY/97, RP Ch. Sp.005/01/97, pp 29–30. Article 66 of the Rwandan Code of Criminal Procedure defines *dégradation civique* and this definition is incorporated by the 1996 Organic Law.

In a December 2002 report, Amnesty International compiled statistics regarding a total of 7,181 persons that had been ajudged in Rwanda since 1997.[29] Amnesty International found that 9.5% of defendants were sentenced to capital punishment, 27.1% to life imprisonment, 40.5% to fixed prison terms, and that 19.1% were acquitted. Longitudinally, the Amnesty International study demonstrates the following trends: decline in capital punishment sentences from 30% of perpetrators in 1997 to 3.4% in 2002 – with steady annual declines; decline in life imprisonment 32.4% in 1997 to 20.5% in 2002, and increase in fixed prison terms from 27.7% in 1997 to 47.2% in 2002.[30] These trends arise from a number of factors, including that the initial trials focused on the more notorious killers and that with the passage of time increased recourse was made of guilty pleas.

I conducted a qualitative review of the published judgments (in French) of the Rwandan genocide courts.[31] The database of judgments I reviewed was compiled and maintained by Avocats sans frontières (ASF) and were published in bound volumes and posted on line on their website.[32] These judgments comprise a large, representative sample from across Rwanda. In the cases I reviewed, when aggregated, defendants received the following sentences (largely consonant with the Amnesty International findings): 15% death, 30% life imprisonment, 55% fixed terms. Among the fixed terms, I calculated the median term to be 11 years, and the mean term 15.25 years.

The domestic Rwandan courts identified factors to consider in quantifying sentence in individual cases. Aggravating factors often are assumed from the grisly nature of the conduct. What is more, in the Rwandan context aggravating factors already are implied in the severity of sanction insofar as the factors that go to identifying liability for a Category 1 offense (such as senior position, zeal, organizing, notoriousness, and particular brutality (*méchanceté excessive*)) correspond to those factors that judges pursuing retributive goals could be expected to turn to in order to fix sentence within an entirely discretionary sentencing structure. My review of the early case-law reveals recourse to the following as mitigating factors: (a) partial, incomplete, tardy, or irregular guilty pleas; (b) minor status; (c) *contrainte* (coercion); and (d) individual characteristics, such as that the defendant sheltered Tutsi during the genocide,[33] lack of

29 Amnesty International, GACACA: A QUESTION OF JUSTICE 17 (December 2002) (AI Index: AFR 47/007/2002) (referencing Liprodhor statistics).

30 Id.

31 See Mark A Drumbl, *Atrocity, Punishment, and International Law* 77–80 (2007).

32 http://www.asf.be/FR/Frameset.htm.

33 Ministère Public v. Munyangabo et al. (June 10, 1998, 1ière instance, Gikongoro), RMP 98809/S2/MP/97 R.P. 0017/1/GIRO ("habituellement elle est d'un esprit compatissant comme en témoigne le fait d'avoir caché trois enfants Tutsis jusqu'à l'arrêt de la guerre.").

education,[34] the defendant's weak physical health,[35] and that the defendant did not organize the attacks.[36]

3.2 *Civil Sanctions*

In the case of virtually all convicted defendants, specialized chambers of national courts also issued orders for restitution/compensation based on collateral private lawsuits (*parties civiles*) filed by the victims and/or surviving family members. No civil damage awards could be issued if the accused had been acquitted on all charges: the awards remain contingent on a criminal conviction. In theory, *partie civile* claims pushed in a restorative and compensatory direction. In light of the impecuniousness of the defendants, however, the awards ended up largely serving only expressive or symbolic purposes.

In one judgment, a Rwandan national court adopted a complex grid of damages,[37] in Rwandan francs, to attach to the kinds of losses and injuries documented:

Moral damages:	10 million Rwanda francs for the loss of a mother or a father 8 million for a child 5 million for a sibling 3 million for another close relative (e.g. uncle, aunt, nephew, niece)
Material damages:	300,000 for a cow, 20,000 for a goat, 2,000 for a chicken, 1,000 for a rabbit 2 million for a house built out of wood and thatch 5 million for a house built out of bricks with metal doors 5 million for household articles 1 million for the harvest

34 Ministère Public v. Siborugirwa et al, (Oct. 22, 1999, 1ière instance, Gitarama); Ministère Public v. Sibomana et al. (Dec. 3, 1998, ch. sp. 1ière instance Rushashi), RMP 110 502/NK.A/J.T., RP 017/S1/98.

35 Ministère Public v. Siborugirwa et al, (Oct. 22, 1999, 1ière instance, Gitarama) at pp. 14, 16.

36 Ministère Public v. Munyangabo et al. (June 10, 1998, 1ière instance, Gikongoro), RMP 98809/S2/MP/97 R.P. 0017/1/GIRO p. 13 ("[il] n'a pas fait parti des personnes qui ont preparé l'attaque"); Ministère Public v. Rukeribuga et al. (Dec. 17, 2001, 1ière instance, Kibuye), RMP 51336/S4/G.M./NSE/97, RP Ch.Sp. 19/01/00 ("diminution de peine car responsibilité moindre par rapport a ses coauteurs at qualité de délinquant primaire.").

37 Ministère Public v Nteziryayo (Emmanuel) et al. RMP 44223/S8/KA, RP 84/2/2001 (30 November 2001) 1 ière instance, Butare.

While moral damages refer to harms and pain arising from the loss of certain relatives, material damages refer to goods and property that have been pillaged, stolen, or destroyed. In the mid 2000's the exchange rate for the Rwandan franc to the US dollar was about 1 to 575. Hence an award of one million Rwandan francs amounted to approximately US $1,700 – a sum larger than the then *per capita* annual GDP in Rwanda.

The *partie civile* claims conveyed considerable narrative value. The text of the Rwandan civil judgments reads very differently than the text of the criminal judgments. The civil judgments foreground the victims rather than the defendant. The storytelling is much more about the victims, the details of their suffering, and exactly what they lost.

4 Gacaca

Historically, *gacaca* was a form of local dispute resolution that percolated throughout Rwanda. *Gacaca* means "justice on the grass" in Kinyarwanda.[38] *Gacaca* was traditionally deployed to referee property disputes, regulate small-scale violence, and redress conflict among neighbors. With its prisons bulging with suspects in the wake of the genocide, Rwanda's government was hard pressed to assess how exactly to process such a large volume of individuals. Beginning in earnest in the mid-2000s, the government turned to *gacaca* to this end.

Traditionally *gacaca* was informal, local, and somewhat organic. It was also starkly patriarchal. The Rwandan government, however, formalized and modernized *gacaca* through national legislative enactments (an Organic Law, routinely amended), mandated the election of lay judges, required the participation of women, and established a detailed organizational structure. This transformation yielded many benefits; along the way however it also morphed *gacaca* from a restorative system to more of a retributive system. In the end, "*gacaca* for genocide" materially departed from traditional *gacaca*.

The Organic Law on Gacaca Jurisdictions, first enacted in 2001 and subsequently amended (including important amendments in 2004 and 2007), created the *gacaca* tribunals and, like the 1996 Organic Law for the specialized chambers, limited the jurisdiction of *gacaca* tribunals to charges of genocide and crimes against humanity committed between October 1, 1990

38 *See* Adrien Katherine Wing & Mark Richard Johnson, *The Promise of a Post-Genocide Constitution: Healing Rwandan Spirit Injuries*, 7 MICH. J. RACE & L. 247, 280 n.321 (2002).

and December 31, 1994.[39] These laws created categories of offenders and linked punishments to the specific category. In this regard, the approach was once again similar that of the 1996 Organic Law for the specialized chambers of national courts (discussed in the previous section and to which some *gacaca* indictees are referred). Article 51 of the 2004 *gacaca* legislation created three categories of offenders. Category 1 offenders were excluded from the *gacaca* courts.[40] It specified prison sentences and determined their length through a detailed sentencing grid. The *gacaca* legislation, however, also diversified sanction by introducing the possibility of community service, which was made available for certain defendants who admitted to their crimes.[41] So, for example, a convict could serve part of the sentence in jail, part in community service, and part released, albeit in suspended sentence. A very detailed schematic was set out in this regard. For example, Article 14 of the 2007 amendments to the Organic Law provided as follows:

> Defendants falling within the second category referred to in the first, second and third paragraph of article 11 of this organic law,[42] who:
> 1° refused to confess, plead guilty, repent and apologise, or whose confessions, guilt plea, repentance and apologies have been rejected, incur a prison sentence of thirty (30) years or life imprisonment

39 Organic Law establishing the organization, competence and functioning of Gacaca Courts charged with prosecuting and trying the perpetrators of the crime of genocide and other crimes against humanity, committed between October 1st, 1990 and December 31, 1994, Nos. 40/2000 (January 26, 2001) and 33/2001 (June 22, 2001). For amendments, *see e.g.* Organic Law No 10/2007 of 01/03/2007 modifying and complementing Organic law No 16/2004 of 19/6/2004 establishing the organization, competence and functioning of Gacaca Courts charged with prosecuting and trying the perpetrators of the crime of genocide and other crimes against humanity, committed between October 1st, 1990 and December 31, 1994 as modified and complemented to date. /2001 (June 22, 2001).

40 Organic Law establishing the organization, competence and functioning of Gacaca Courts charged with prosecuting and trying the perpetrators of the crime of genocide and other crimes against humanity, committed between October 1st, 1990 and December 31, 1994, No. 16/2004 (June 19, 2004), art. 2(2).

41 *Dégradation civique* also was contemplated as an adjunct sentence (article 15 of the 2007 amendments to the Organic Law).

42 The three subcategories of the second category referred to are as follows:
1° the well known murderer who distinguished himself or herself in the area where he or she lived or wherever he or she passed, because of the zeal which characterized him or her in the killings or excessive wickedness with which they were carried out, together with his or her accomplices
2° the person who committed acts of torture against others, even though they did not result into death, together with his or her accomplices;
3° the person who committed dehumanising acts on the dead body, together with his or her accomplices.

2° confessed, pleaded guilty, repented and apologised after being included on the list of the accused and whose confession, guilt plea, repentance and apologises have been accepted, incur a prison sentence ranging from twenty- five (25) to twenty-nine (29) years, but:
a) they serve a third (1/3) of the sentence in custody;
b) a sixth (1/6) of the sentence is suspended;
c) half (1/2) of the sentence is commuted into community service.
3° confessed, pleaded guilty, repented and apologised before being included on the list of the accused, incur a prison sentence ranging from twenty (20) to twenty-four (24) years, but:
a) they serve a sixth (1/6) of the sentence in custody;
b) a third (1/3) of the sentence is suspended;
c) half (1/2) of the sentence is commuted into community service

The 'list' is a list of individuals drawn up by the prosecutor for indictment. Clearly the intent is for persons to come forward and confess before being investigated or targeted by the prosecutor.

Community service was initially conceptualized as a way to promote reconciliation and managerial ends while ensuring that a huge chunk of the workforce was not idling away in prison but, rather, was put to use to motor the country's post-conflict transition and also learn some practical skills. Community service was thereby presented as a sentencing option that was less onerous than imprisonment, and therefore served as an inducement to confess. Sanctions were established in the event of a convict's failure to perform community service.[43]

In principle, community service could involve the convict going directly to the victims and offering labor or donating produce as recompense for the harms that had been inflicted – in other words, working to rebuild destroyed homes and farms, to till the land, and to ameliorate public services in the region. In practice, however, this would be mightily complex, entail significant

43 Article 17 of the 2007 amendments provided penalties in case of default by the convicted person to properly carry out community service:

In case of default by the convicted person to properly carry out community service, the concerned person is taken back to prison to serve the remaining sentence in custody.

In that case, the Community Service Committee in the area where the convicted person is carrying out community service shall prepare an ad hoc report and submit it to the Gacaca Court of the Sector where community service is perlodged which will fill in the form to return the defaulting person to prison.

In case this is not possible, that report shall be submitted to the Gacaca Court that tried the person serving his or her community service.

A Presidential Order shall establish and determine modalities for carrying out community service.

monitoring costs, and trigger poignant emotional reactions. Some survivors would not want the perpetrator around; service relationships would be difficult to supervise, control, and manage. So, in practice, the government instead began to favor broad community service projects – *travaux d'intérêt général* (TIG) – and the use of labor camps. These projects involved agricultural work and building roads, houses, and infrastructure. The work was not specifically undertaken with specific connection to the place where the convicts had committed their crimes. It involved the convicts (also known as *tigistes*) working in groups.

Gacaca involved the local community sitting in judgment of persons accused of having committed mass atrocity within the same community. *Gacaca* judges were elders and "people of integrity" (*Inyangamugayo*) elected from local communities throughout Rwanda. They were laypersons who received some limited legal training. One hundred and seventy thousand judges sat in approximately 10,000 panels *in toto*. These were composed at the lowest level (that of the *cellule*) of 9 judges with 5 deputies. There also were two higher levels of panels at the *secteur* and appellate levels (each of these two levels had about 1,500 panels). Suspects were to be brought to the villages where they were alleged to have committed their crimes. Practically speaking, the decentralized nature of the *gacaca* process facilitated access to justice by reducing transportation costs (and language barriers) for witnesses and victims. At the proceedings, the public could raise issues – discursively – that exceeded the microscopic truths that would arise at trials. They could ask questions of suspects, to which the suspects are permitted to reply. However, the judges were empowered to control the discussion, the flow of evidence, and maintain order at the proceedings. In the end, although the judges primarily adjudicated, they also acted as mediators to help the gathered community attain both legal and *extra*-legal goals. Defense lawyers were excluded, purportedly to ensure the open, participatory nature of the proceedings.

The Rwandan government created *gacaca* tribunals for several reasons. One was managerial, namely, to accommodate the sheer number of suspects. A second reason was to diversify the legal response to genocide by invoking mechanisms more steeped in reconciliation, reconstitution, and reintegration. This diversification, in theory at least, would depart from repression and retribution, a development which was deemed particularly appropriate for lower level offenders. Consequently, the Rwandan government touted both retribution and reconciliation as goals of *gacaca* adjudications; and the *gacaca* framework noted the importance of penalties that permit convicts to "amend themselves" and reintegrate into Rwandan society.[44] A third reason was simply to "disclose the truth," although the *gacaca* process, whether traditional or in modified form for the genocide, is not a truth and reconciliation commission.[45] A fourth reason pertained to sovereignty, namely the Rwandan government's perception that Rwanda needs to develop "by itself" solutions to the genocide and its consequences.[46] A fifth reason was participatory – to open up a local democratic space for discussion and decision-making on issues that relate to the suspect, but also on a broader array of legal and non-legal matters that radiate from the genocide. In this sense, *gacaca* could promote what some have called "African-style democracy," which envisions a "democracy built on such practices as consensus building and populist input [... which] begin at the village level."[47] In sum, *gacaca*'s purposes were broad, touching on the legal, the social, and the political. This meant that the sharp due process critiques that many outsiders (in particular liberal legalists concerned with fair trial rights, provision of defense lawyers, and criteria of evidentiary admissibility) delivered against *gacaca* could be contextualized. Phil Clark puts it well:

> [T]he dominant [international] discourse on gacaca is severely flawed for two main reasons: first, because it mistakenly views gacaca exclusively as a legal institution, which can be analysed solely through the legal statutes that underpin it; and second, because it interprets formal, deterrent justice as the only objective of gacaca, while neglecting more crucial aims, particularly reconciliation, and more negotiated processes during hearings. -In short, the dominant discourse fails to account for the hybrid nature of gacaca and the hybrid methods and objectives it embodies. We therefore require a more nuanced interpretation of gacaca and its objectives if we are to offer more appropriate suggestions as to how gacaca may be reformed to aid its effectiveness as a tool of post-genocide reconstruction.[48]

44 2004 Organic Law, *supra* note 40, pmbl ("Considérant qu'il importe de prévoir des peines permettant aux condamnés de s'amender et de favoriser leur réinsération dans la société rwandaise sans entrave à la vie normale de la population"). *See also Tribunaux gacaca et travail d'intérêt general*, 13–14 REFORME PÉNALE ET PÉNITENTIAIRE EN AFRIQUE 1–2 (mai 2001) (on file with author).

45 2004 Organic Law, *supra* note 40, pmbl.

46 Ibid.

47 Matthew Todd Bradley, *"The Other": Precursory African Conceptions of Democracy*, 7 INT'L STUD. REV. 407, 413 (2005).

48 Phil Clark, *Hybridity, Holism and "Traditional" Justice: The Case of the Gacaca Courts in Post-Genocide Rwanda*, GEORGE WASHINGTON INTERNATIONAL LAW REVIEW, December 2007.

The *gacaca* trials ended in 2012. Estimates vary wildly, but it is commonly noted that approximately one million people went through the system.

5 Conclusion

Three layers of penal jurisdiction filled Rwandan post-conflict spaces. These were: the ICTR, the national courts, and the neo-traditional gacaca. This chapter has discussed each separately. But it is important to note that the three layers did not operate in parallel, but intersected in a variety of ways. In her 2015 book, *Courts in Conflict: Interpreting the Layers of Justice in Post-Genocide Rwanda*, Nicola Palmer demonstrates how these different layers each were animated by the pursuit of different goals.[49] For example, Palmer finds that ICTR judges and lawyers were motored by the consolidation and development of the jurisprudence of international criminal case-law. The national courts, she determines, were spirited by advancing judicial competence, credibility, independence, and domestic reform. And, finally, the many *gacaca* tribunals were animated by the goal of establishing local narratives of who did what to whom and why.

Insofar as manufacture of case-law serves as the primary ambition of the ICTR, Palmer's research intimates that the ICTR may have strayed from its initial retributive, deterrent, and reconciliatory aspirations. While certainly incapacitating the genocidal leadership, however, the ICTR over time came to curry more of a bureaucratic function, to wit, creating a clarified body of law. The ICTR's legacy is not life in Rwanda, as Palmer notes, but the life of international law, the development of precedent, and the construction of persuasive authority. The lack of congruence between the objectives of the ICTR, on the one hand, and the two domestic systems (which themselves are incongruent) is a very valuable insight. Whether the intense turn to criminal law in the aftermath of the Rwandan genocide – regardless of the layer at which this occurred – attained retributive, deterrent or expressive goals remains debated. The same could certainly be said of the turn to penal law in the aftermath of any episode of massive human rights abuses.

49 Nicola Palmer, *Courts in Conflict: Interpreting the Layers of Justice in Post-Genocide Rwanda* (OUP, 2015).

PART 4

Rwanda's Legacy

CHAPTER 14

Rwanda: Lessons Observed. Lessons Learned?

Jane Boulden

1 Article

Rwanda. In the context of the United Nations peace operations system one need only say the word to evoke a sense of failure and devastation. The extent and nature of that failure and devastation, across various levels of the UN system, as well as within its member states, is well documented in this volume. While the explanation of what happened is multi-faceted and multi-layered, the fact that a peacekeeping operation was present in Rwanda while the genocide unfolded around it remains a poignant and complex symbol of the inherent constraints in the peacekeeping model. The purpose of this special issue is to examine whether and in what way the Rwandan genocide has been a catalyst for political and legal reform at the international level. The purpose of this article is to discuss whether the Rwandan genocide was a catalyst for change in peacekeeping.[1]

Has peacekeeping changed since Rwanda? No. Not fundamentally. Not in the sense that it is still an exercise based on its founding principles of consent, impartiality, and minimum use of force. Of course, a number of changes can be identified in peacekeeping broadly conceived since the end of the Cold War. These include, *inter alia*, the creation of more complex, multi-dimensional mandates, the inclusion of the protection of civilians as a standard mandate task, an increased reliance on regional actors as partners and leaders in peace operations, the more regular authorization of the use of force for specific purposes beyond self defence, and the UN's willingness to engage in operations associated with tenuous peace agreements. Nonetheless, even in the context of these types of changes, peacekeeping continues to be based on its three founding principles, and in that sense it has not changed since Rwanda.

1 Peacekeeping as a term is now often used to refer to a specific type of "traditional" peacekeeping common during the Cold War. The United Nations now uses the term peace operations in order to encompass the wide range of types of operations they now use as conflict management tools. Nonetheless, the term peacekeeping persists and is often used interchangeably with the phrase peace operations. For ease of reference, the term peacekeeping is used here.

 | DOI:10.1163/9789004430129_016

The nature of this exercise prompts the question as to why one would expect such a change. The United Nations Assistance Mission in Rwanda (UNAMIR),[2] the operation in place when the genocide began, was underequipped, poorly supported politically, had a limited mandate, and was reduced in size at a key moment in the crisis. On this basis one could argue that peacekeeping was not itself at issue. Rather, it was the political decision-making around it that was problematic, and where change was needed and could be expected. Similarly, there has been much discussion of the idea that peacekeeping was and is a completely unsuitable tool for dealing with genocide, and in that respect, it is unfair to characterize the Rwandan experience as a failure of UN peacekeeping. What practical impact could a small-scale peacekeeping operation with a limited mandate have on a planned genocide the scale of Rwanda?

Nonetheless, peacekeeping remains at the centre of the soul searching, discussions, reports, and changes that came after Rwanda. And, looking back over the past 25 years of peace operations one can, indeed, identify changes associated with the lessons learned from the Rwanda experience. Foremost among these are: the extent to which the protection of civilians has become a mainstay in peacekeeping mandates, the development of international legal accountability at the individual level for war crimes, and an increased focus on the humanitarian effects of conflicts. It is a starting assumption of this analysis that Rwanda was a catalyst for these normative changes. Each of those changes are covered in separate articles in this journal, which is itself a testament to their importance.

Catalyst is a key word here. Even with these normative changes it is difficult to attribute direct cause and effect to the Rwandan experience since each change could be seen as a product of the UN's early post-Cold War experience as a whole. One of the analytical challenges inherent in studying peacekeeping is that it is difficult to isolate a given operation from the operations that precede it or are ongoing at the time of its authorization. For example, the UN's decisions about a response in Rwanda must take into account the ongoing events in difficult operations in Somalia and Bosnia, which the Secretariat and Council members were dealing with on a daily basis at the time of UNAMIR's creation.[3] And an analysis of the operations in Somalia and Bosnia requires a sense of the context established by the more successful preceding operations

2 On occasion analysts speak of UNAMIR I and UNAMIR II. UNAMIR II refers to the re-expanded operation authorized in May 1994. The United Nations uses UNAMIR to refer to the entire operational period. That practice is adopted here.

3 The Lessons Learned report points out that the infamous Blackhawk Down incident in Somalia occurred two days prior to UNAMIR's authorization. *Lessons Learned*, p. 21. Also, *Independent Inquiry*, p. 41 section with title "The shadow Somalia". OAU *Report*, 13.11.

in Namibia and Central America, and even the enforcement operation in the Persian Gulf. Equally, any given peace operation must also be understood in the context of the political environment of the Security Council at the time in which the mandates of operations are authorized or adjusted, which can be affected by any number of factors, including some that extend well beyond the politics of peacekeeping.

2 How to Evaluate whether Peacekeeping Has Changed?

How, then, to determine whether peacekeeping has changed as a result of a given set of events? One way to determine the impact of the Rwandan experience on peacekeeping as a whole is to look at the way and extent to which the United Nations has continued to use peacekeeping as a tool since the UNAMIR operation concluded. The Rwandan experience had such a significant impact at the UN that at the time there were predictions that it would lead to a pause in the authorization of new peacekeeping operations. This was not the case. The Security Council continued to authorize new operations while UNAMIR was ongoing, and after its completion. The rate of authorization of new operations slows somewhat after 2000 but does not decline significantly.[4] A late 1990s dip in the number of peacekeepers on the ground is evident between 1996 and 2000.[5] But, from 2000 onwards, the number of peacekeepers rises steadily with the current total at just under 90,000.[6] On this basis, therefore, there seems little sign of change in the willingness of the UN to use peacekeeping as a conflict management tool.

The Council's authorization of operations that address intra-state conflict also continues after Rwanda. The use of peacekeeping operations in intra-state conflict is largely, though not exclusively,[7] a post-Cold War trend reflecting the

4 United Nations, 'List of Peacekeeping Operations 1948-2018' <https://peacekeeping.un.org/sites/default/files/180413_unpeacekeeping-operationlist_2.pdf> accessed 7 June 2019. Also, Alex J. Bellamy and Paul D. Williams, "Trends in Peace Operations, 1947–2013," in Joachim A. Koops, Norrie MacQueen, Thierry Tardy, and Paul D. Williams (eds), *The Oxford Handbook of United Nations Peacekeeping Operations*, (Oxford University Press 2015).

5 International Peace Institute, "Total peacekeepers deployed by type, November 1990-October 2018. <https://s3.amazonaws.com/providing-for-peacekeeping-docs/summaries/Monthly+Deployments.png> accessed 7 June 2019. Chris Perry, Adam C. Smith, Trends in Uniformed Contributions to UN Peacekeeping: A New Dataset, 1991-2012, International Peace Institute, Providing for Peacekeeping no. 3, 2012.

6 https://peacekeeping.un.org/sites/default/files/msrs_march_2019.pdf.

7 The Cold War peacekeeping operation in the Congo from 1960–1964 (ONUC) is a clear exception, for example.

increase in conflict of this type,[8] especially after the end of the Cold War. The Council's willingness to see these types of conflicts as fitting their international peace and security mandate is a linked and parallel trend that remains constant after Rwanda. Here again there is little change. With the exception of the UN operation in response to the conflict between Ethiopia and Eritrea, the conflicts addressed by the Security Council with peace operations are intrastate in nature after Rwanda.

One possibility is to track peacekeeping mandates and Security Council debates about peacekeeping mandates over the 25 years since the Rwandan operation in order to look for signs of change that can be traced back to that start point. Mandates have become more detailed and fine-tuned in that period and a research project of that kind might generate some interesting results. But such a study is well beyond the scope of this work.

We have the benefit, however, of a number of formal institutional reports based on extensive consultation and research that can act as markers for thinking about peacekeeping in the immediate aftermath of the Rwandan operation. The approach in this article, therefore, is to look at those reports to determine what was said about peacekeeping at that moment in time. What did the international community, in the form of decision-makers and analysts tasked specifically with this task, think about the way ahead for peacekeeping after Rwanda? How did they think peacekeeping could or should change?

The Rwandan conflict and genocide along with the international response to it is one of the most studied sequences of events in the post-Cold War international environment. In the aftermath of the genocide, the international community expended considerable effort in examining what happened with a view to drawing out lessons that would ensure such a sequence of events would be avoided in future.

A fully inclusive sweep of such reports, especially if one includes national studies, generates a long list. In focusing specifically on the United Nations peacekeeping aspect of the story, this article examines five such reports in order to generate an understanding of the lessons specific to peacekeeping that the United Nations had in hand as a result of the experience. This "study of the studies" has little corollary in the vast literature on peacekeeping and Rwanda. This is in part because it tells us little about what has happened on the ground,

8 Uppsala Conflict Data Program, "Armed Conflict by Type, 1946–2018" <https://www.pcr.uu.se/research/ucdp/charts-graphs-and-maps/> accessed 7 June 2019.

which is where most peacekeeping research focuses.[9] It does, however, provide insight into thinking about peacekeeping at a particular point of time.

International thinking about the specific lessons for peacekeeping come from three Rwanda-specific reports. The first document is an internal report put together by the then newly established Lessons Learned Unit of the Department of Peacekeeping Operations.[10] This report, which is internal to the Organization, examines the UNAMIR operation and is focused on how the peacekeeping operation was created and carried out. It is a product of a series of consultations with decision-makers who were involved in UNAMIR within UN Headquarters and in the field, as well as outside experts. The second document is the report of an independent commission established by Secretary-General Kofi Annan to look into United Nations actions at the time of the Rwandan genocide.[11] The commission comprised a high-level three-person panel of international experts. In contrast to the internal lessons learned process the commission was focused more broadly on the UN's response to the genocide, of which the peacekeeping operation was one aspect. They were asked to establish the facts of the UN response to the genocide and to make recommendations on that basis.

The third analysis is one undertaken by the Organization of African Unity (OAU). The OAU was deeply involved in the negotiations that led to the Arusha Accords, as well as the decision-making that followed inside and outside the Security Council. The OAU inquiry had a much broader mandate to examine the events leading to the genocide as well as the genocide itself and the international response. The resulting report[12] is lengthy and wide ranging. It also reflects the views of an international institutional actor other than the UN that was itself part of the events in question and thus provides a semi-outsider perspective.

---

9 There are some particularly strong studies of the peacekeeping experience in the secondary literature. These include: Michael Barnett, *Eyewitness to a Genocide, The United Nations and Rwanda* (Cornell University Press, 2002) and Bruce D. Jones, *Peacemaking in Rwanda: The Dynamics of Failure*, (Lynne Rienner, 2001).

10 United Nations, Lessons Learned Unit, Department of Peacekeeping Operations, *Comprehensive Report on Lessons Learned from United Nations Assistance Mission for Rwanda (UNAMIR) October 1993-April 1996*, 1996. Hereafter, *Lessons Learned.*

11 *Report of the Independent Inquiry into the actions of the United Nations during the 1994 Genocide in Rwanda*, 15 December 1999. Available as United Nations document S/1999/1257, 16 December 1999. Hereafter, *Independent Inquiry.*

12 *International Panel of Eminent Personalities to Investigate the 1994 Genocide in Rwanda and Surrounding Events. Special Report*, 7 July 2000. Hereafter, *OAU Report.* The full report can be difficult to track down. It can be found in *International Legal Materials*, vol. 40, 2001, pp. 141–235.

The reports were issued between 1996 and 2000. They differ in their purview and tone, but each are a product of a formal institutional effort to step back and assess peacekeeping, its role and the role of the United Nations. Taken together they provide an overview of the thinking of the international community about how and even whether peacekeeping should change after Rwanda. This analysis will inevitably be a poor cousin to these three Rwanda-specific reports. Each, in their own way, provide a window into the interaction of the horrific events on the ground and the decision-making about a UN response. They are compelling narratives and need no augmentation. They paint a clear, grim picture of dysfunction, missed opportunities, and failure at almost every turn. The intention here is not to recapitulate that story in full. Rather, the goal is to use the reports as a baseline for establishing what kinds of lessons institutional actors drew from the Rwanda experience in the first few years after it was over.

Assessments of peacekeeping in a more general sense come from two reports, 15 years apart, generated by panels of experts commissioned by the Secretary-General. The Brahimi Report[13] was the product of a commission led by the former Foreign Minister of Algeria, Lakhdar Brahimi. Its goal was a review of UN "peace and security activities" with a view to providing recommendations for how the United Nations might conduct "such activities better in the future."[14] Although the Brahimi Report is not a direct outcome of the failures of peacekeeping in Rwanda it is the first report after the Rwandan experience to provide recommendations about the future of peacekeeping broadly defined. In 2014, Secretary-General Ban Ki-moon commissioned a similar process. The resulting report known as the HIPPO Report was published in 2015. The distance in time between the two reports gives us an imperfect but still usable comparison. What the HIPPO Report says about the state of peacekeeping and what needs to be improved will help us understand what has changed since the Brahimi Report and what has remained constant.

---

13 Report of the Panel on United Nations Peace Operations, A/55/305, S/2000/809, 21 August 2000. Hereafter, *Brahimi Report*.

14 Identical letters dated 21 August 2000 from the Secretary-General to the President of the General Assembly and the President of the Security Council, A/55/305, S/2000/809, 21 August 2000.

3 Lessons Observed: What Was Said about Peacekeeping after Rwanda

The nature of the mandate of the UNAMIR operation, and the way in which the Security Council altered the mandate in response to the changing situation on the ground are at the heart of much of the discussion across all of the reports. Three inter-related themes are constants: the UN's misreading of the solidity of the peace agreement and then later the nature of the conflict, the creation and evolution of the mandate as a function of the interests of member states rather than as a function of what needed to be done, and, the inability or unwillingness of the UN to change its focus on the peace agreement even once the genocide began. Each of these themes are rooted in the UN's conscious and unconscious adherence to the peacekeeping approach to the conflict.

UNAMIR's mandate was based on the Arusha Peace Accords and a joint request from the Rwandan government and the Rwandese Patriotic Front (RPF) for a UN peacekeeping operation to support the implementation of the agreement. As the Lessons Learned report indicated, "Rwanda seemed to be a textbook case for a successful peacekeeping operation."[15] But, as the report goes on to demonstrate, the creation of UNAMIR was founded on a vision of the situation that was, from the onset, based on a very limited understanding within the Secretariat and the Council of the political dynamics on the ground. That limited understanding derived from the lack of any institutional depth of knowledge or political analysis within the Secretariat. That was equally the situation within the Security Council with the exception of some member states who had access to more information but did not share it with other Council members or personnel in the Secretariat.[16]

This problem was compounded by the silo effect across departments within the UN that meant that crucial information readily to hand in one section of the Organization, in this case the Special Rapporteur on extrajudicial, summary or arbitrary executions in the Commission on Human Rights, was not shared with nor sought by other decision-makers.[17] The nature of the situation can be attributed, at least in part, to the fact that these were the early days of the post-Cold War period. At that point, the UN's experience with operations based on tenuous peace agreements was limited, as was their experience in dealing with a number of such operations simultaneously, as they were doing when UNAMIR began. Nonetheless, the combined effect of an approach that

15 *Lessons Learned*, p. 21.

16 *Independent Inquiry*, p. 47, *OAU Report*, para. 13.5.

17 *Independent Inquiry*, p. 31.

did not move beyond the assumption that the peace agreement was solid provided a shaky start. As the Independent Inquiry stated, "The mission's mandate was based on an analysis of the peace process which proved erroneous, and which was never corrected despite the significant warning signs that the original mandate had become inadequate."[18]

When the situation deteriorated after the shooting down of the President's aircraft on 6 April 1994, the lack of information in some quarters, accompanied by the unwillingness to take on board its implications, or share it in others, underpinned the tendency within both the Secretariat and the Security Council to stay focused on the need to negotiate a ceasefire and shore up the Arusha Accords. Arguing that the Secretariat needs to do more to ensure the Council is "fully briefed" in these situations, the Lessons Learned report notes that the "Council only dimly perceived the steady deterioration of the situation in Rwanda and, even then, saw it only as a delay in the implementation of the Arusha process, not a prelude to a genocide."[19] The Independent Inquiry and the OAU report are more forthright in their assessments. The Independent Inquiry calls the "continued emphasis on a cease-fire" disturbing,[20] and a "costly error of judgement."[21] The OAU calls that perspective "too generous" and spoke of the UN response as "a clear-cut case of rote diplomacy."[22]

The focus on a ceasefire and the peace agreement is a well-established part of the peacekeeping approach. An effort to bring the situation back to that foundation point is understandable as a standard response to a flare up in a standard conflict. But, as these reports and many analyses beyond them have indicated, using a conflict management approach in a situation of genocide is at the very best an ill-fated ineffectual exercise. At worst, it provides a diversion and delay that allows the genocide to continue unabated.

The UN's reflexive conflict management response was a product of past practice, undertaken in a fast-moving situation at a time of significant crisis in two other complex operations. It is difficult to decouple that tendency from a determined effort to turn the other way in the face of genocide. The resistance on the part of key members of the Security Council to using the genocide label is well known and was an outcome of and contributed to the focus on the use of peacekeeping as a conflict management tool. Both the Independent Inquiry and the OAU report note and criticize this fact. The OAU states that "Until the day the genocide ended with the RPF's military victory in the civil war, the UN,

18 *Independent Inquiry*, p. 30.
19 *Lessons Learned*, p. 24.
20 *Independent Inquiry*, p. 41.
21 Ibid., p. 42.
22 *OAU Report*, para. 10.5 and 10.6.

the governments of the US, France, and Belgium, African governments and the OAU, all failed to define the massacres as a full-blown genocide."[23] The Independent Inquiry states that "the United Nations had an obligation to act which transcended traditional principles of peacekeeping."[24] And, that "the delay in identifying the events in Rwanda as a genocide was a failure by the Security Council. The reluctance by some States to use the term genocide was motivated by a lack of will to act, which is deplorable."[25]

This deliberate and determined effort to avoid using the genocide label, and thus avoid any requirement to respond to the genocide links to an unwillingness to support Rwanda and UNAMIR that predates the beginning of the genocide. The Independent Inquiry establishes that even before the proposal for UNAMIR went to the Council, in anticipation of what the Council might accept the Secretariat reduced the number of troops required that had been suggested by the reconnaissance team. And, once the proposal went to the Council, member states such as the US worked to limit the scope of the mandate. This meant that the authorized operation was significantly different than what had been envisaged in the negotiations leading to the Arusha Accords, and in the accords themselves.[26] The OAU report states that "the significance of the Security Council's action should not be underestimated: Its refusal to sanction a serious mission made the genocide more likely."[27] Once the genocide began it took time for the Council to consider options for change. Infamously, it ultimately decided to reduce the mission numbers, and gave serious consideration to complete withdrawal.[28] The Independent Inquiry found the very fact of the consideration of these options "difficult to justify."[29]

The lack of political will to support the mission continued even after the genocide was over. The Secretariat struggled to find troop contributors to meet the now expanded troop requirements.[30] Leaving aside the unwillingness to recognize the genocide, the reports point to the linked but different problem that no state had a strategic interest in Rwanda or the region generally.[31] This meant that there was already a predisposition in place to resist support, a predisposition that was only further entrenched by the almost simultaneous

---

23 *OAU Report*, para. E.S. 42, para. 13.44.
24 *Independent Inquiry*, p. 50.
25 Ibid., p. 38. See also, *OAU Report*, para. 15.13.
26 Independent Inquiry, p. 32. *OAU Report*, E.S. 35.
27 *OAU Report*, E.S. 36.
28 *Lessons Learned*, p. 32.
29 *Independent Inquiry*, p. 37.
30 Ibid., pp. 43–44.
31 Ibid., p. 44. IPEP, E.S. 33.

events in Somalia that led to a distinct pulling back on the part of the United States, not just from Somalia but from peacekeeping generally.

This unwillingness extended to the Security Council's resistance to authorizing the use of force beyond self defence. In the many debates after Rwanda there was considerable discussion about the idea that a larger force, perhaps of 5,000 troops[32] could have done much more to protect Rwandan citizens and may even have been able to stop the genocide. One of the alternative scenarios is that the existing peacekeeping force, then numbering roughly 2,500 could itself have done more if it had been properly equipped and been given a mandate to use force.[33]

All of this is part of a larger discussion around the idea that the mission on the ground could have done more than they did by pushing the limits of the rules of engagement (ROE)[34] and/or that they should have been given a Chapter VII authorization that would have allowed them to use force offensively. However, even if the operation had been willing to stretch the limits of the ROE or had a Chapter VII authorization to use force beyond self defence, there is universal agreement amongst the reports that they simply did not have the means to do so.

Indeed, the extent to which the operation was under-resourced is legendary. The Lessons Learned report gives a brief insight into the scale of the problem:

> The Mission had neither the appropriate mandate nor the means to take any effective action. Senior military officials are in agreement that the force level of 2,545 was too small for any military action to protection victims of the slaughter, even in self-defence, ... With an extremely weak logistics base, UNAMIR was also rapidly running out of food and medical supplies, even sandbags to protect its accommodation. It had no ambulances and mainly soft-skin vehicles for the transportation of troops.[35]

All of this speaks to the extent to which members of the Council were acting in pursuit of their own national interests rather than that of the Organization.[36] The Security Council was designed to act as a collective entity on behalf of the Organization as a whole. It was envisaged to be an entity greater than the sum of its parts that would pursue international peace and security on behalf of all member states. There was little evidence of that kind of attitude here. An effort

32 For example, *OAU Report*, para. 10.8, 10.9.

33 *Independent Inquiry*, p. 30, 35.

34 *Lessons Learned*, p. 23.

35 Ibid.

36 *Lessons Learned*, p. 20.

to avoid such outcomes in future was the impetus behind the development of the doctrine of a responsibility to protect. This is covered in detail in Stacey Henderson's article "Humanitarian Intervention and R2P." The idea behind R2P was, in part, to establish that the lack of strategic interest in a given situation was not an excuse for inaction. The international community had a responsibility to respond.

In July 1995, a year after the genocide in Rwanda, the massacre at Srebrenica was carried out by Serbian troops. The very fact of this event only a year after the genocide suggests that even if UN personnel and Security Council member states had, at that point, developed lessons learned from the Rwandan experience, they were not yet implementing them. This is most evident on the question of impartiality, one of the core principles of peacekeeping. Secretary-General Kofi Annan, who was Assistant Secretary-General for Peacekeeping at the time of the massacre, issued a report on the events in Srebrenica in November 1999.[37] As with Rwanda, lack of resources and perceptions about what the Security Council would accept in terms of the mission's mandate affected the options the Secretariat put to the Council for consideration. And, as in the Rwandan case, in retrospect, one of the lessons for the UN is the complete inutility of impartiality when faced with actors intent on ethnic cleansing and genocide. In discussing this aspect in his report, Secretary-General Annan spoke of errors of judgement within the United Nations "rooted in a philosophy of impartiality and non-violence wholly unsuited to the conflict."[38]

In the Rwanda case the same reluctance to shift from peacekeeping, and thus impartiality, is present.[39] That reluctance is linked to factors already discussed such as the reluctance to label what was going on as genocide, and the determination to stay focused on the peace agreement. In each case, to do otherwise would have marked an end to impartiality. Both the OAU report and the Independent Inquiry argue that the UN had an obligation to push past an impartial posture. The Independent Inquiry stated that "the United Nations had an obligation to act which transcended traditional principles of peacekeeping. In effect, there can be no neutrality in the face of genocide, no impartiality in the face of a campaign to exterminate part of a population."[40]

Of the three core principles of peacekeeping, impartiality is the one that is most difficult to define. This is in part because it exists in the realm of perception. It is difficult to separate the question of whether a mandate is impartial

---

37 The report had been requested by the UN General Assembly.
38 A/54/549, 15 November 1999, para. 499.
39 *Independent Inquiry*, p. 32.
40 *Independent Inquiry*, p. 50.

from whether its implementation is impartial.[41] And, in the end, what matters most is not an objective determination of impartiality but the perceptions of those on the ground. In any peace operation the maintenance of impartiality is a delicate balance. In Rwanda, that balance was upended by the lack of a serious response to the genocide, and then further undermined by two sets of actions that laid bare a fundamental double standard on the part of other states. The speed and strength of support for first, the efforts of some states to evacuate their citizens and personnel, and then second the French-led Operation Turquoise, was a sharp contrast to the unwillingness of states to respond similarly to the needs of the Rwandan people. As the Independent Inquiry said, it is "unfortunate that the resources committed by France and other countries to Operation Turquoise could not instead have been put at the disposal of UNAMIR II."[42]

The only time UNAMIR received instructions from UN Headquarters that allowed for acting beyond their peacekeeping mandate was with respect to the evacuation of nationals. The instructions to UNAMIR are so telling they are replicated in each of the reports. "You should make every effort not to compromise your impartiality or to act beyond your mandate but may exercise your discretion to do [so] should this be essential for the evacuation of foreign nationals."[43] As the OAU report points out "no such latitude was ever authorized for the protection of Rwandan nationals."[44]

4 From Brahimi to HIPPO

As indicated in the introduction to this piece, the Brahimi Report provides a general review of the UN's peace and security activities and is thus not specific to Rwanda. Nonetheless, the Rwandan experience was a major element in its deliberations, and it provides a useful benchmark for international and institutional thinking about UN peace operations in the late 1990s. The report was provided to the Secretary-General in August 2000. The HIPPO report was issued 15 years later in June 2015. The mandate for the HIPPO panel was to

41 Jane Boulden, "Mandates Matter, An Exploration of Impartiality in UN Operations," *Global Governance*, vol. 11, no.2, 2005, pp. 147–160; Emily Paddon Rhoads, *Taking Sides in Peacekeeping, Impartiality and the Future of the United Nations* (Oxford University Press, 2016).

42 *Independent Inquiry*, p. 49. Also see *OAU Report* para. 15.31 on the unwillingness of states to assist in getting an Ethiopian contingent to Rwanda in contrast to their willingness to respond immediately to evacuate their own nationals.

43 As quoted in the *OAU Report*, para. 15.6.

44 Ibid., para. 15.7.

provide a "thorough overview"[45] of peace operations and it thus provides a useful marker 15 years after the Brahimi Report that allows us to make a determination as to whether changes in peace operations have occurred. For analytical consistency, the themes relating to peacekeeping that were developed in the analysis of the three Rwanda-specific reports are used as the baseline in these two peacekeeping-oriented reports to determine what kinds of changes may have occurred.

While the reports derive from different contexts and emphasize different aspects of the broader peace and security agenda, with respect to the issues under discussion here – the issues arising in the Rwanda-specific reports – Brahimi and HIPPO overlap considerably in the points they raise and the recommendations they provide. This demonstrates that not very much may have changed in 15 years. The HIPPO Report's statement that "chronic challenges remain"[46] for peacekeeping gives support to that idea.

The assertion that little has changed sounds akin to criticism. There is certainly lots of room for the argument that required changes in peacekeeping, said to be absolutely necessary after Rwanda, remain out of reach. On the other hand, the fact that there were significant normative changes that emerged in the aftermath of Rwanda needs to be reiterated.

4.1 *Impartiality*

The centrality and desirability of the three core principles of peacekeeping are affirmed in both the Brahimi and HIPPO reports.[47] Both, however, also identify ways in which those principles can be manipulated or stretched thereby creating problems for the mission. This is particularly the case in their treatment of impartiality. Brahimi echoes the Rwanda reports' concerns that in some circumstances adherence to impartiality can have devastating consequences. "No failure did more to damage the standing and credibility of United Nations peacekeeping in the 1990s than its reluctance to distinguish victim from aggressor."[48] This sentiment is echoed in the HIPPO Report, which states that the peacekeeping principles should "never be used as an excuse for failure to protect civilians or defend the mission proactively,"[49] and argues that the current volatile conflict environment faced by the UN "calls for a flexible and progressive interpretation"[50] of the peacekeeping principles.

45 A/70/95-S/2015/446, 17 June 2015. Hereafter, *HIPPO Report*.
46 *HIPPO Report*, p. 9.
47 *Brahimi Report*, p. ix, HIPPO Report, para. 122.
48 *Brahimi Report*, p. ix.
49 *HIPPO Report*, para. 125.
50 Ibid.

4.2 *Use of Force*

A more flexible and progressive interpretation of the use of force principle has been in play for some time. On this issue we find a clearer transition between the two reports. The Brahimi Report argues that the recent examples of "worst-case behaviour" on the part of local actors means that "mandates should specify an operation's authority to use force." It means the UN should deploy forces "able to pose a credible deterrent threat, in contrast to the symbolic and non-threatening presence that characterizes traditional peacekeeping. According to the Brahimi Report, United Nations forces for complex operations should be sized and configured so as to leave no doubt in the minds of would-be spoilers as to which of the two approaches the Organization has adopted."[51] In the time since Brahimi, the specific authorization of the use of force beyond self defence in peace operations mandates has become a regular, almost ordinary occurrence. The HIPPO Report reflects this shift as a given and focuses on the need for clarity about the way in which force is used. It also echoes the Brahimi Report's assertion that troops must be deployed in a way that provides them with a range of options. "Different threats must be met with the appropriate use of military force, ranging from containment, via deterrence and coercion to direct confrontation, particularly when civilians or peacekeepers are at risk."[52]

4.3 *The Tradition of Undersupport*

But the expansion of the willingness to authorize the use of force in peace operations has not been matched by the linked requirement that UN troops be sized and configured accordingly. The Brahimi Report puts considerable emphasis on the importance of peacekeepers being able to carry out their mandate. "In the past, the United Nations has often found itself unable to respond effectively" to the challenges of complex conflicts. "It is a fundamental premise of the present report, however, that it must be able to do so."[53] The report makes a very specific recommendation that Security Council resolutions authorizing the creation of a peacekeeping mission should be held in draft form until firm commitments of troops are in place. This idea has not been taken up. Indeed had it been, the rate of peacekeeping authorization since Rwanda is likely to have been far lower.

---

51 *Brahimi Report*, para. 51.

52 *HIPPO Report*, para. 128.

53 *Brahimi Report*, para. 49.

Reflecting that reality, the HIPPO Report reiterates the need to ensure adequate support for missions and provides a range of recommendations on this issue that extend from ways to develop a better force generation process to the need to strengthen the Secretariat's capacity to gather and assess information, and plan operations.[54] With respect to force generation in particular, the HIPPO Report suggests that Security Council members, especially permanent members should do more to contribute to peace operations because of their ability to offer specialized and highly capable troops and equipment, but also because this would send a signal of political commitment to the peace process.[55] This last point echoes one of the more painful aspects of the Rwanda experience, which was the extent to which all states, including permanent members of the Security Council, turned the other way rather than respond to the genocide.

4.4 *A Collective Approach*

This last point brings us back to the issue that lies at the heart of the Rwandan experience from the perspective of the United Nations: the degree to which states rejected their collective obligations under the Charter and approached the issue from a national interest only perspective. The Brahimi Report asserts that most peacekeeping failures occurred because the Council and member states "crafted and supported ambiguous, inconsistent and under-funded mandates and then stood back and watched as they failed, sometimes even adding critical public commentary as the credibility of the United Nations underwent its severest tests."[56] The HIPPO Report reads very much along those lines. The call for genuine collective action, a sense of collective responsibility, and a "partnership within" the Organization runs throughout the report. One of its concluding statements calls for a recommitment to strengthening peace operations "as a tool for all, in support of common purposes....To succeed, commitment must be explicit and action sustained."[57] Such collective commitment and action were precisely what was absent in Rwanda.

---

54 *HIPPO Report*, especially Chapter Three, Empowering the Field.
55 *HIPPO Report*, para. 210 and 216 (c).
56 *Brahimi Report*, para. 266.
57 *HIPPO Report*, para. 350.

5 Conclusion: Lessons Learned?

Could it happen again? Could genocide occur while a peacekeeping operation was in place? One would hope that the answer is no. The commitment to the protection of civilians, the existence of the responsibility to protect doctrine, the ongoing willingness of the United Nations to use peace operations as a conflict management tool, and its accompanying willingness to authorize the use of force on a regular basis, all suggest that new mechanisms are in place to ensure that kind of sequence of events is not repeated.

The existence of such mechanisms, however, does not guarantee their use. And all of the elements that made possible obfuscation and non-responsiveness are still available to international actors. Those elements include peacekeeping as an approach to conflict that is based on the three core principles of consent, impartiality and minimal use of force. This review of international institutional reports on Rwanda and peacekeeping demonstrates that it was not the fact of peacekeeping or its core principles that were at issue in Rwanda but the decision-making that surrounded them that was the problem. The dramatic and chronic undersupport of the operation, the dogged adherence to impartiality and a return to the peace agreement, the unwillingness to stray from the use of force only in self defence, were all a reflection of the lack of a collective will to see and address what was happening. They were not a reflection of an inherent problem in peacekeeping. In that sense, the fact that peacekeeping has not varied from its core principles since Rwanda is not surprising. But it also means that the possibility for repetition remains.

CHAPTER 15

Some Rules of Engagement Legacies of the 1999 *Report of the Independent Inquiry into the Actions of the United Nations during the 1994 Genocide in Rwanda*

Rob McLaughlin

The international community did not prevent the genocide, nor did it stop the killing once the genocide had begun. This failure has left deep wounds within Rwandan society, and in the relationship between Rwanda and the international community, in particular the United Nations. These are wounds which need to be healed, for the sake of the people of Rwanda and for the sake of the United Nations. Establishing the truth is necessary for Rwanda, for the United Nations and also for all those, wherever they may live, who are at risk of becoming victims of genocide in the future.[1]

1 Introduction

As a point of fracture in the – at that time – orthodox approach to UN peace operations, 'Rwanda was to prove a turning point in United Nations peacekeeping, and came to symbolise a lack of will to commit to peacekeeping, and above all, to take risks in the field'.[2] Or, as Trevor Findlay cuttingly but correctly assessed, UNAMIR 'was a nil return in the ledger of the use of force by UN missions, since it declined to use force.'[3] He then concluded that, 'Quite apart from the shortcomings of the peacekeeping model itself, the Rwanda tragedy illustrated once more the continuing lacuna in UN peace operations doctrine regarding the use of force for the protection of innocent civilians from organised

1 *Report of the Independent Inquiry into the actions of the United Nations during the 1994 genocide in Rwanda* (S/1999/1257) dated 15 December 1999, p3 (hereinafter 'the 1999 Independent Inquiry Report').
2 Ibid, p39.
3 Trevor Findlay, *The Use of Force in UN Peace Operations*, SIPRI, Solna / OUP, Oxford, 2002, p276.

 DOI:10.1163/9789004430129_017

violence and genocide…'.[4] Similarly, as Michael O'Donnell concisely argued in 2003: 'If the mere presence of a sizable UNAMIR had failed to deter the genocidaires, the UN could (and should) have invoked its Chapter VII powers and used force to stop the massacre.'[5] The litany of, and literature on, the failures of the traditional UN peace operations model in the first half of the 1990s is extensive and distressing; for any scholar or practitioner of use of force in UN peace operations, reading – for example – Shawcross on UN operations in the 1990s,[6] Ashdown and Simms on Bosnia,[7] and Dallaire on Rwanda[8] – is a sobering and distressing experience. Within this context, the UN's formal 1999 Rwanda and Srebrenica Reports – although, each from the other, quite differently structured and narrated – are milestones in the recent history of UN peace operations. One reason for this is the degree to which each of these reports identified the consequences of mismatched, conflicting, and unclear mandates, use of force doctrine, and rules of engagement (RoE).

The purpose of this chapter is to describe, analyse, and assess the context and legacy of the 1999 *Independent Inquiry Report* into the 1994 Rwanda genocide through the lens of UN doctrine on matching use of force and RoE. However, it is important to note upfront that I will not provide a detailed outline of the UNAMIR Interim RoE in force at the time – this is a task undertaken most eloquently in other chapters, particularly by Drew and Beardsley. To that end, the chapter is structured in three parts. Part I consists of a recounting of the background to the 1999 *Independent Inquiry Report*. Part II comprises an analysis and assessment of the explicit and implicit RoE related comments, findings, and recommendations to be drawn from the 1999 *Independent Inquiry Report*. Part III then provides a critical, chronological assessment of the extent to which the problems and solutions identified in the 1999 *Independent Inquiry Report* have influenced or been manifested in the admittedly halting and hesitant progress of UN peace operations doctrine since the tragedy of Rwanda in 1994, and in particular since the Report itself in 1999.

---

4 Ibid, p284.

5 Michael O'Donnell, 'Genocide, the United Nations, and the Death of Absolute Rights' (2003) 23:2 *Boston College Third World Law Journal* 299, at p410.

6 William Shawcross, *Deliver Us from Evil: Peacekeepers, Warlords and a World of Endless Conflict*, Simon and Schuster, NY, 2001.

7 Paddy Ashdown, *Swords and Ploughshares: Bringing Peace to the 21st Century*, Weidenfeld and Nicolson, London, 2007; Brendan Simms, *Unfinest Hour: How Britain Helped to Destroy Bosnia*, Penguin Press, London, 2001.

8 Romeo Dallaire, Shake Hands with the Devil: The Failure of Humanity in Rwanda, Random House, Toronto, 2003.

2 The Background to the 1999 *Independent Inquiry Report*

2.1 *What Went Before*

The first major inquiry into the UN and the Rwandan genocide was the 1994 Commission appointed pursuant to UNSCR 935 (01 July 1994).[9] Its chairman was Mr Atsu-Koffi Amega, 'a former President of the Supreme Court and former Foreign Minister of Togo'; the other members were Mrs Habi Dieng, 'Attorney-General of Guinea', and Mr Salifou Fomba, 'Professor of International Law from Mali and a Member of the United Nations International Law Commission'.[10] Their mandate to act as 'an impartial Commission of Experts to examine and analyse information submitted pursuant to that resolution, with a view to providing the Secretary-General with its conclusions on the evidence of grave violations of international humanitarian law committed in the territory of Rwanda, including the evidence of possible acts of genocide.'[11] The Commission ultimately concluded that:

> 181. The Commission of Experts concludes on the basis of ample evidence that individuals from both sides to the armed conflict in Rwanda during the period from 6 April 1994 to 15 July 1994 perpetrated serious breaches of international humanitarian law, in particular of obligations set forth in article 3 common to the four Geneva Conventions of 12 August 1949 and in Protocol II additional to the Geneva Conventions and relating to the protection of victims of non-international armed conflicts of 8 June 1977.
>
> 182. The Commission of Experts concludes also that ample evidence indicates that individuals from both sides to the armed conflict perpetrated crimes against humanity in Rwanda in the period mentioned above.
>
> 183. After careful deliberation, the Commission of Experts has concluded that there exists overwhelming evidence to prove that acts of genocide against the Tutsi group were perpetrated by Hutu elements in a concerted, planned, systematic and methodical way.

---

9 *Final Report of the Commission of Experts established pursuant to Security Council resolution 935 (1994)*, 9 December 1994 (S/1994/1405), at http://www.legal-tools.org/doc/361096/pdf/.

10 https://peacekeeping.un.org/en/mission/past/unamirFT.htm.

11 1994 *Commission of Experts Report*, para 1.

> 184. Abundant evidence shows that these mass exterminations perpetrated by Hutu elements against the Tutsi group as such, during the period mentioned above, constitute genocide within the meaning of article II of the Convention on the Prevention and Punishment of the Crime of Genocide, adopted on 9 December 1948.[12]

A further International Commission of Inquiry (ICOI) – called for in UNSCR 1011 (16 August 1995) – was then authorised to conduct an investigation into allegations of arms flows and training provided to former Rwandan government forces in the Great Lakes region.[13] This inquiry, however, was narrowly related to the arms embargo introduced by UNSCR 918 (1994) subsequent to the commencement of the genocide.

This still left, consequently, the deeper analysis of the operational 'how and why' of 1993–1994 yet to be done. The first attempt to distil such broader lessons learned from the UNAMIR experience was an internal DPKO report – the 1996 *Comprehensive Report on Lessons Learned from United Nations Assistance Mission for Rwanda (UNAMIR)*.[14] However, as Findlay and others have observed, this report – which delivered a number of sensible and justified recommendations, but none of which 'related to the use of force, even in self-defence'[15] – was dismissive of many of those factors the latter 1999 Independent Inquiry would find to be fundamental to the tragedy of UNAMIR.

2.2 *The Origins of the 1999 Report*

On 18 March 1999, the UN Secretary-General informed the Security Council that he would commission an independent inquiry into the conduct and performance of the UN, including UNAMIR and the Secretariat, in relation to the

---

12 Ibid, paras 181–184.

13 UNSCR 1011 (16 August 1995), OP 2; https://peacekeeping.un.org/en/mission/past/unamirFT.htm. UNSCR 1013 (7 September 1995), OP 1, then requested the Secretary-General to establish this commission to investigate apparent violations of the arms embargo as a matter of urgency. This followed an earlier report by Mr Aldo Ajello on arms flows in the region (*Report of the Secretary-General on the Implementation of Paragraph 6 of Security Council Resolution 997 (1995) of 9 June 1995*, 9 July 1995 (S/1995/552). The ICOI was chaired by Ambassador Mahmoud Kassem of Egypt, with its final report (save an amendment in 1998) submitted on 24 December 1997 (S/1997/1010), at https://undocs.org/S/1997/1010.

14 DPKO, Comprehensive Report on Lessons Learned from United Nations Assistance Mission for Rwanda (UNAMIR), December 1996. For a comprehensive collection of UN documents relating to Rwanda 1993–1996 (but not including this particular report) see: *The United Nations and Rwanda, 1993–1996*, United Nations Blue Book Series, Vol x, 1996, at https://documents-dds-ny.un.org/doc/UNDOC/GEN/NL9/600/08/PDF/NL960008.pdf?OpenElement.

15 Findlay, *The Use of Force in UN Peace Operations*, p322.

1994 genocide in Rwanda.[16] This Independent Inquiry comprised Ingvar Carlsson (former Prime Minister of Sweden), Professor Han Sung-Joo (former Foreign Minister of the Republic of Korea), and retired Lieutenant-General Rufus Kupolati (Nigeria). The mandate of the inquiry related to

> ...the actions of the United Nations as a whole. The task of the Inquiry thus included studying the actions of UNAMIR, the Secretary-General and the Secretariat, as well as the Member States of the organisation and the political organs in which they are represented.[17]

However, the inquiry addressed member state actions only in respect of 'positions taken which affected the response of the United nations to the tragedy in Rwanda', noting – and representing obvious constraints that it would be 'the task of other bodies to analyse the broader issues raised by individual countries positions on the Rwandan issue'.[18] Belgium and France conducted their own reviews and assessments of the Rwanda operation,[19] and other States have examined the Rwanda genocide from more targeted perspectives such as human rights,[20] or more tangentially as a contextual factor in issues such as veteran's health.[21]

2.3 *Main Aspects of the Report*

The backbone of the 1999 *Independent Inquiry Report* is a narrative and chronological timeline to the Rwanda genocide, which supports a series of nuanced

16 *Letter from Secretary-General to President of the Security Council*, 18 March 1999 (S/1999/339).

17 1999 *Independent Inquiry Report*, p4.

18 Ibid.

19 Belgium Senate, *Parliamentary Commission of Inquiry regarding the events in Rwanda*, 6 December 1997, at http://www.senate.be/english/rwanda.html; for an assessment of the Belgium Senate Commission Report, see, Koenraad Van Brabant, 'Security and protection in peacekeeping: A critical reading of the Belgian inquiry into events in Rwanda in 1994' (1999) 6:1 *International Peacekeeping* 143; France, Assemblee Nationale, *Par la Mission D'information de la Commission de la Défense Nationale et des Forces Armées et de la Commission des Affaires Étrangères, sur les opérations militaires menées par la France, d'autres pays et l'ONU au Rwanda entre 1990 et 1994*, 15 December 1998, at http://www.assemblee-nationale.fr/dossiers/rwanda/r1271.asp.

20 For example, *US Department of State Country Report on Human Rights Practices 1994 – Rwanda*, 30 January 1995, at https://www.refworld.org/country,,USDOS,,RWA,,3ae6aa4a0,0.html.

21 For example, Catherine Runge et al, *Rwanda Deployment Health Study Report*, University of Queensland Centre for Australian Military and Veterans' Health, Brisbane, 2014.

conclusions and recommendations, which amply demonstrate, and cohere to, the three broad purposes envisioned by its authors:

'In seeking to establish the truth about the role of the United Nations during the genocide, the Independent Inquiry hopes to [1] contribute to building renewed trust between Rwanda and the United Nations, [2] to help efforts of reconciliation among the people of Rwanda, and [3] to contribute to preventing similar tragedies from occurring ever again.'[22]

The coherence of the Report is built around a golden thread – the distillation of a single 'fundamental'[23] or 'overriding'[24] (indeed paradigmatic) failure. This failure is identified by three key manifestations of that failure, and this methodology in turn grounds the identification and assessment of a series of consequential, cascading, and deeply interlinked sub-failures and outcomes (both systemic and discrete) that stemmed from these three manifestations of the key fundamental failure. The fundamental failure was 'the lack of resources and political commitment devoted to developments in Rwanda and to the United Nations presence there.'[25] The three cascading systemic failures were: (1) 'a persistent lack of political will by Member States to act, or to act with enough assertiveness'; (2) 'the response by the Secretariat and decision-making by the Security Council' and to a lesser extent, the inability to secure 'the necessary troops [from TCNs] for the United Nations Assistance Mission for Rwanda (UNAMIR)'; and (3) despite the 'chronic lack of resources and political priority' which dogged UNAMIR, it was inescapable that 'serious mistakes were made with those resources which were at the disposal of the United Nations.'[26] The main body of the Report then identifies, analyses, and links 17 separate issues to the fundamental failure and its three primary manifestations.[27] These issues range from thematic (failure to respond to genocide,[28] and inadequacy of the mandate[29]), to indicative (confusion over the Rules of Engagement,[30] and focus on achieving a ceasefire as the genocide commenced[31]), to systemic (lack of analytical capacity in the Secretariat,[32] and how to manage a crisis when the territorial state is a member of the UNSC[33]), through to discrete

22 1999 *Independent Inquiry Report*, p3 (my numbering).
23 Ibid, p3.
24 Ibid, p30.
25 Ibid, p3.
26 Ibid.
27 Ibid, pp20–52.
28 Ibid, issue 5, pp35–39.
29 Ibid, issue 2, pp31–32.
30 Ibid, issue 4, p35.
31 Ibid, issue 8, pp41–42.
32 Ibid, issue 9, pp42–43.
33 Ibid, issue 18, p50.

and specific (failure to protect political leaders who were assured of UNAMIR protection,[34] and the co-existence of a short notice Chapter VII third state nationals evacuation operation – Operation Turquoise – in the same battlespace[35]).

That states and the UN failed to head the early warning signs is now well accepted,[36] and the 'final observation' of the Report is that 'The United Nations failed the people of Rwanda during the genocide in 1994.'[37] What is not expressly stated as a final observation, but is nevertheless clearly implicit, is that the UN also failed UNAMIR, its peacekeepers, and itself. This assessment is clearly evident in the 14 recommendations, and observations regarding UN responses to the experience of Rwanda between 1994–1999, that comprise the rest of the main body of the Report. It is to one of these recommendations that this chapter now turns in order to assess one specific doctrinal legacy of the *1999 Independent Inquiry Report*.

2.4 *'Recommendation Two' from the Report*

As had been identified even before UNAMIR was deployed, three significant mission indicators of success or failure were evident at the outset: As the 1996 *The International Response to Conflict and Genocide: Lessons from the Rwanda Experience: Study 2 – Early Warning and Conflict Management* recounted, these were 'the timeliness of deployment, the size of the force, and the precise mandate as well as rules of engagement for the force.'[38] However, as the 1996 *Study 2* went on to note:

> The issue of UNAMIR's mandate prior to April has been exaggerated. *Far more important were the rules of engagement and the narrow strictures within which the force was ordered to operate.* Nevertheless, the dichotomy between Chapter VI and VII operations sows confusion because it conceals a range of actions that are neither pure peacekeeping (VI) nor classical enforcement against an aggressor (VII). Colloquially identified as Chapter six-and-a half actions, these include a variety of circumstances and responses that need to be specified separately. Doctrine needs to be developed for their utilization instead of relying on ad hoc innovation.[39]

34 Ibid, issue 11, pp44–45.

35 Ibid, issue 17, pp49–50.

36 See, inter alia, Gregory Stanton, 'Could the Rwandan genocide have been prevented?' (2004) 6:2 *Journal of Genocide Research* 211.

37 1999 *Independent Inquiry Report*, p51.

38 Howard Adelman and Astri Suhrke, *The International Response to Conflict and Genocide: Lessons from the Rwanda Experience: Study 2 – Early Warning and Conflict Management*, p34, at https://www.oecd.org/derec/unitedstates/50189764.pdf.

39 Ibid, p81 (my italics).

Recommendation Two from the 1999 *Independent Inquiry Report* echoes this finding; it is as follows:

> Renewed efforts should be made to improve the capacity of the UN in the field of peacekeeping, including the availability of resources... In each peacekeeping operation it should be clear which Rules of Engagement apply.[40]

The Report then assessed any preliminary progress the UN had made in relation to this recommendation between 1994–1999 and identified ten further 'tasks' or outcomes necessary to achieve the recommendation.[41] Two of these are as follows:

> Ensuring that Lessons Learned from previous missions are integrated into the planning of new peacekeeping operations...
> There should never be any doubt as to which Rules of Engagement apply during the conduct of a peacekeeping mission. Rules of Engagement must be given formal approval by Headquarters.[42]

The remainder of this chapter will now turn to an examination of the evolution and consequences of these two these sub-recommendations in the context of RoE.

3 An Assessment and Analysis of the 1999 *Independent Inquiry Report* in Relation to Rules of Engagement

3.1 *Introduction*

Alan Kuperman has argued that 'more troops with the proper equipment, a broad mandate, and robust rules of engagement could have deterred the outbreak of killing or at least snuffed it out early.'[43] But we must also not hesitate to acknowledge the operational cusp within which UNAMIR took place, represented by the evolving concept of peace enforcement, which deeply challenged the traditional attitudinal approach to use of force in peacekeeping

40 1999 *Independent Inquiry Report*, p53.
41 Ibid, pp54–56.
42 Ibid, p56.
43 Alan Kuperman, 'Rwanda in Retrospect' (2000) 79:1 *Foreign Affairs* 94, at p116.

operations. As Marrak Goulding observed in 1993 (just after his tenure in DPKO had concluded), this attitude was as follows:

> ...since 1973 self-defence had been deemed to include situations in which peacekeepers were being prevented by armed persons from fulfilling their mandate. This was a wide definition of 'self-defence'. In practice commanders in the field had only very rarely taken advantage of the authority to open fire on, for instance, soldiers at a roadblock who were denying passage to a United Nations convoy. This reluctance was based on sound calculations related to impartiality, to their reliance on the continued cooperation of the parties and to the fact that their force's level of armament was based on the assumption that the parties would comply with their commitments. The peacekeepers could perhaps win the firefight at that first roadblock. But, in lands of the vendetta, might they not find themselves out-gunned in the third or fourth encounter?[44]

This attitudinal disconnect was highlighted by the 1999 *Independent Inquiry Report*, which identified a series of RoE issues that were both contributory to and representative of the challenges posed and created by the Rwanda mission. Some are explicit, some are implicit, but three are indicative of the general malaise: Mandate-RoE matching and currency; inconsistency in application and interpretation; and RoE processes. However, it must also be recalled that some elements of UNAMIR nevertheless found ways to employ the RoE 'to protect tens of thousands of foreign and Rwandan civilians who sought protection in hotels, hospitals, and the Amahoro stadium'.[45] Nevertheless, as Findlay continues, 'While some UN troops risked their lives and acted bravely in seeking to protect Rwandans, others turned a blind eye to the massacres taking place in front of them', and this was in part due to 'serious misconceptions about the ROE, making them unnecessarily passive'.[46]

3.2 *Mandate-RoE Matching and Currency*

The first broad-based set of critiques made in the Report related to the need to match RoE to the mandate, and to adjust this RoE in parallel with both anticipated and unanticipated contextual changes within the area of operations. First, in relation to the initial UNAMIR mandate, UNSCR 872 (1993) – establishing

44 Marrak Goulding, 'The Evolution of United nations Peacekeeping' (1993) 69:3 *International Affairs* 451 at p455.

45 Findlay, *The Use of Force in UN Peace Operations*, p278.

46 Ibid, p279.

the force – provided for a more limited mandate than initially proposed. The mandate ultimately delivered by the UNSC was:

> (a) To contribute to the security of the city of Kigali inter alia within a weapons-secure area established by the parties in and around the city;
> (b) To monitor observance of the cease-fire agreement, which calls for the establishment of cantonment and assembly zones and the demarcation of the new demilitarized zone and other demilitarization procedures;
> (c) To monitor the security situation during the final period of the transitional government's mandate, leading up to the elections;
> (d) To assist with mine clearance, primarily through training programmes;
> (e) To investigate at the request of the parties or on its own initiative instances of alleged non-compliance with the provisions of the Arusha Peace Agreement relating to the integration of the armed forces, and pursue any such instances with the parties responsible and report thereon as appropriate to the Secretary-General;
> (f) To monitor the process of repatriation of Rwandese refugees and resettlement of displaced persons to verify that it is carried out in a safe and orderly manner;
> (g) To assist in the coordination of humanitarian assistance activities in conjunction with relief operations;
> (h) To investigate and report on incidents regarding the activities of the gendarmerie and police…[47]

The Independent Inquiry concluded that 'UNAMIR's mandate was cautious in its conception; it was to become equally so in its application on the ground.'[48] This view was echoed in the Belgian Senate Commission Report:

> The [Belgian Senate] commission notes the following lapses with regard to the performance of the United Nations secretariat and the DPKO during the mission:
> …an overly centralised approach by the DPKO; the DPKO interpreted the mandate and the rules of engagement (ROE's) in an overly restrictive manner, including the provisions that clearly covered the responsibility of men on the ground; the force commander, General Dallaire, consequently adopted an overly reserved attitude, which was reflected when

47 UNSCR 872 (5 October 1993), OP 2–3.

48 1999 *Independent Inquiry Report*, p32.

an arms cachet was discovered: the DPKO rejected the authorisation to dismantle them.[49]

Captured by the doctrinal principle of neutrality – as opposed to impartiality – the implementing approach to both the mandate and its derivative RoE was neither assertive, preventive,[50] nor situationally flexible.[51] But this is not the full context, for the tragic mandate and RoE timidity displayed is also partly explicable by the fact that the Secretariat – and some states[52] – were also captured by 'the shadow of Somalia' and the exhortation of the UN Commission of Inquiry Report into some incidents in Somalia to the effect that 'the UN should refrain from undertaking further peace enforcement actions within the internal conflicts of States'.[53]

Of single significance in the ultimately approved mandate was the absence of a disarmament authority – a point the Independent Inquiry determined to be of notable importance to subsequent events, including UNAMIR's paralysis in the face of the Secretariat's failure to react appropriately to credible evidence of the existence of militia arms caches and distribution activities just prior to the genocide, and plans (inter alia) to kill UNAMIR force members, and to assassinate political leaders.[54] And although Dallaire and others believed that the UNAMIR mandate permitted raids on such arms caches, the Secretariat did not.[55] This was primarily a function of the mandate limitation to assisting the parties to establish a weapons-free zone in Kigali,[56] and in this respect the Secretariat's view was actually endorsed by the Independent Inquiry (which also speaks to the formalised mismatch between mandate, resources, and RoE). Indeed, as Crystal Faggart has observed, it was recognised even at the initial planning stages of the operation that 'arms recovery' would be critical to

49 1997 *Belgium Senate Commission Report*, ch 4, section 4.

50 In particular, as the 1999 *Independent Inquiry Report* pointed out (p34), in relation to taking early preventive action – after being explicitly warned about arms caches and weapons distribution plans – to seize these caches before they were distributed to militias and rebel forces.

51 For example, to facilitate interdicting the establishment of militia and Rwandan army roadblocks immediately after the aircraft crash, which subsequently and severely limited UNAMIR response options and timelines: 1999 *Independent Inquiry Report*, p35.

52 Sharwcross on US.

53 *Report of the Commission of Inquiry established pursuant to Security Council resolution 885 (1993) to investigate armed attacks on UNSOM II*, 1 June 1994 (S/1994/653), para 270; 1999 *Independent Inquiry Report*, p41; Findlay, *The Use of Force in UN Peace Operations*, p277.

54 1999 *Independent Inquiry Report*, p8.

55 It should be noted that some analysts, such as Alan Kuperman, doubt that the seizure of the arms caches in Kigali would ultimately have prevented the genocide: Kuperman, 'Rwanda in Retrospect', p114.

56 Findlay, *The Use of Force in UN Peace Operations*, p279.

success; 'Yet, the mandate proscribed that the parties were to provide a weapons free area within which the UN would work, rather than the UN assisting in the efforts.'[57] Nevertheless, the Report did find that the Secretariat failed to give sufficient credence to the 11 January 1994 cable from Dallaire to General Baril (Military Adviser to the Secretary-General, and CDS Canada),[58] and analysts have also observed that this narrow interpretation was to some extent enabled by the excessively cautious approach of the Secretariat to the mandate.[59] That is, whilst the mandate and hence the available interpretation of the RoE in relation to disarmament authorisations were very narrow, given the intelligence available and the evolving operational situation they should not have been.

This brings us to the second general point about the failure to match mandate, resources and RoE: The failure to ensure RoE evolved in tandem with transitions in the overall operational context. This issue is well expressed in the Belgian Senate report, and is worth quoting at length:

> At no time did the United Nations authorities or military authorities on site apply article 17 of the ROE'S, which stipulates:
>
> *'Ethnically motivated criminal acts may also be perpetrated during this mandate and will morally and legally require that UNAMIR use all means available to terminate the same. Examples: execution, attacks against displaced people or refugees, ethnic riots, attacks against demobilised soldiers, etc. When this happens, UNAMIR military personnel shall follow this directive's ROE'S, in support of UNCIVPOL and the local authorities, or in their absence, UNAMIR shall take the necessary action to prevent any crime against humanity.'*
>
> Although it appears that the situation on the ground justified the application of this article 17 and that international law permitted, or indeed required, a military action to prevent the massacres, it is necessary to assess the balance of power on the ground. Although it appeared, on many occasions, that UNAMIR, in particular its Belgian component, was in difficulty on the ground, the pooling of all of [the] West's military forces available in Kigali or in neighbouring countries would have made it possible to avoid the scopc of the genocide.[60]

57 Crystal Faggart, 'UN Peacekeeping After Rwanda: Lessons Learned or Mistakes Forgotten?' (2008) 27:2 *Penn State International Law Review* 495, at pp506–507.

58 1999 *Independent Inquiry Report*, pp32–34.

59 See, inter alia, Findlay, *The Use of Force in UN Peace Operations*, p279.

60 *Belgium Senate Commission Report*, ch 4, section 13.

In relation to this critique, the *Independent Inquiry Report* specifically notes the issue of an enduring mismatch between the operational and humanitarian imperative identified in the Secretary-General's letter of 29 April 1994[61] – that is, to halt the genocide – and the extant mandate in UNSCR 912, which still emphasised the centrality of neutral mediation and facilitating the (by now non-existent) political negotiations between the Rwandan parties.[62] The UNSC responded with a Presidential Statement,[63] which indicated but did not manifest 'a shift in emphasis'.[64] This is despite the fact that UNAMIR Force Commander Dallaire advised in a cable to UNHQ on 5 May 1994 that 'UNAMIR, under its current structure and mandate, is not capable of countering the civil defence militia actions. UNAMIR cannot take forceful actions that are overtly confrontational in nature as the current self-protection capabilities of the Force cannot meet all the essential requirements'.[65] As Scott Feil observed in 1998, 'Intervening forces require strategic direction, giving the commander the latitude to increase or decrease the use of force to contain the violence. Rules of engagement must be flexible and understood to permit the intervening force to respond instantly to or pre-empt violent acts… Rather than really using deadly force, the most important point is to be able to do it.'[66] Similarly, Hikaru Yamashita records how 'as the scope of the genocide was becoming clearer, the Security Council "in light of the current situation in Rwanda" decided in mid-April 1994 to lower the scale of the operation (from 2,539 troops to 270 troops) and to reduce the

61 *Letter from the Secretary-General to the President of the Security Council*, 29 April 1994 (S/1994/518): 'In particular, it has become clear that that mandate does not give UNAMIR the power to take effective action to halt the continuing massacres. At best it can provide limited protection to small groups of threatened persons in the city of Kigali and it would be unable to save them if a new wave of massacres were to start. According to some estimates, as many as 200,000 people may have died during the last three weeks. This humanitarian catastrophe is rightly a matter of growing anguish in Africa and the rest of the world and demands urgent action by the international community.'

62 UNSCR 912 (21 April 1994), OP 7–8: for example 8(a) – 'Decides, in the light of the current situation in Rwanda, to adjust the mandate of UNAMIR as follows: (a) To act as an intermediary between the parties in an attempt to secure their agreement to a cease-fire…'.

63 *Security Council Presidential Statement*, 30 April 1994 (S/PRST/1994/21).

64 1999 *Independent Inquiry Report*, pp22–24.

65 Cable, *Proposed Future Force Structure and Mandate of UNAMIR*, Dallaire to Baril and Annan, 05 May 1994, para 7, at https://www.documentcloud.org/documents/1392934-footnote-140-mir-907.html.

66 Scott Feil, 'Preventing Genocide: How the early use of force might have succeeded in Rwanda', *Carnegie Commission on Preventing Deadly Conflict*, April 1998, p21, at https://www.carnegie.org/media/filer_public/02/45/0245add3-b6aa-4a08-b9fc-6eb91f4e2975/ccny_report_1998_genocide.pdf.

mandate to an intermediary role to secure a ceasefire agreement'.[67] That is, more robust mandate interpretation and RoE employment was both warranted and permissible, but was not initially implemented.

Ultimately, the first steps towards a more robust UNAMIR response were delayed until 17 May 1994 (UNSCR 918, including an explicit authorisation to use force in 'self-defence' of civilians, as amplified in UNSCR 925[68]) – by which time 'several hundreds of thousands had been killed'.[69] And whilst the proposed tasks and roles of the expanded UNAMIR specifically included what is now known as a protection of civilians mandate,[70] contributions to the

---

67 Hikaru Yamashita, 'Re-examining Peacekeeping: The "Brahimi Report" and Onward' (2006) 7 *NDIS Security Reports* 41 at p54.

68 UNSCR 918 (17 May 1994), OP 3–4: '3. Decides to expand UNAMIR's mandate under resolution 912 (1994) to include the following additional responsibilities within the limits of the resources available to it:

(a) To contribute to the security and protection of displaced persons, refugees and civilians at risk in Rwanda, including through the establishment and maintenance, where feasible, of secure humanitarian areas;

(b) To provide security and support for the distribution of relief supplies and humanitarian relief operations;

4. Recognizes that UNAMIR may be required to take action in self-defence against persons or groups who threaten protected sites and populations, United Nations and other humanitarian personnel or the means of delivery and distribution of humanitarian relief…';

UNSCR 925 (08 June 1994), OP 4–5: '4. Reaffirms that UNAMIR, in addition to continuing to act as an intermediary between the parties in an attempt to secure their agreement to a cease-fire, will:

(a) Contribute to the security and protection of displaced persons, refugees and civilians at risk in Rwanda, including through the establishment and maintenance, where feasible, of secure humanitarian areas; and

(b) Provide security and support for the distribution of relief supplies and humanitarian relief operations…'.

69 1999 *Independent Inquiry Report*, p25; *Report of High Commissioner for Human Rights* (Jose Ayala Lasso), 21 July 1994 (S/1994/867). The official DPKO record states: 'After having visited Rwanda in May 1994, the High Commissioner for Human Rights urged that a Special Rapporteur on Rwanda be appointed to examine all human rights aspects of the situation, including root causes and responsibilities for the atrocities. The Commission subsequently designated Mr. René Dégni-Ségui as Special Rapporteur for Rwanda…' – https://peacekeeping.un.org/en/mission/past/unamirFT.htm.

70 *Report of the Secretary-General to the Security Council on the Protection of Civilians in Armed Conflict*, 08 September 1999 (S/1999/957), for example at para 31: 'In resolution 955 (1994), of 8 November 1994, on Rwanda, the Council indicated that genocide and other systematic widespread and flagrant violations of international humanitarian law constituted a threat to international peace and security.' This was also Recommendation 5 in the 1999 *Independent Inquiry Report* (pp53, 57): 'Efforts need to be made to improve the protection of civilians in conflict situations…'.

mission were very slow to materialise. Ultimately the RoE were revised and 'expanded UNAMIR's mandate to enable it to contribute to the security and protection of refugees and civilians at risk, through means including the establishment and maintenance of secure humanitarian areas, and the provision of security for relief operations to the degree possible.'[71] But the mandate was still a Chapter VI mandate – with the exception of the arms embargo component, which was authorised under Chapter VII.[72] However, the parallel willingness of some states – and a more circumspect willingness amongst the UNSC[73] – to sanction a parallel Chapter VII force (Operation Turquoise) via UNSCR 929[74] – clearly indicates that states and the UNSC knew what sort of RoE was necessary; but politics, doctrine, history, and bureaucracy prevented this clear understanding from being implemented for UNAMIR. As the UN's own record of the operation recounts:

> On 22 June 1994, acting under Chapter VII of the Charter, the Council, by its resolution 929 (1994), authorized Member States to conduct the operation using all necessary means to achieve their humanitarian objectives. The operation would be limited to two months, unless UNAMIR was able to carry out its mandate before then. Costs of implementing the operation would be borne by the Member States concerned. The French initiative, named Operation Turquoise, was launched on 23 June 1994. On 2 July, France announced that Operation Turquoise would establish a 'humanitarian protected zone' in the Cyangugu-Kibuye-Gikongoro triangle in south-western Rwanda, covering about one fifth of Rwandese territory.[75]

Indeed, the Report records how the Independent Inquiry team found it 'unfortunate that the resources committed by France and other countries to Operation Turquoise could not instead have been put at the disposal of UNAMIR II', and that having 'two operations present in the same conflict area with the authorisation of the Security Council but with such diverging powers was

71 https://peacekeeping.un.org/en/mission/past/unamirFT.htm.

72 See, for example, Findlay, *The Use of Force in UN Peace Operations*, p281.

73 See 1999 *Independent Inquiry Report*, p28.

74 UNSCR 929 (22 June 1994), OP 3: '3. Acting under Chapter VII of the Charter of the United Nations, authorizes the Member States cooperating with the Secretary-General to conduct the operation referred to in paragraph 2 above using all necessary means to achieve the humanitarian objectives set out in subparagraphs 4 (a) and (b) of resolution 925 (1994)…'. That is, the UNSC endowed this independent mission with Chapter VII powers to carry out a component of UNAMIR's mandate, whilst not giving UNAMIR a similar Chapter VII authorization.

75 https://peacekeeping.un.org/en/mission/past/unamirFT.htm.

problematic'.[76] This said, however, it is not unusual for the UNSC to recognise when high-end enforcement and even warfighting RoE are required (as with, for example, INTERFET, ISAF, and the Haiti and Iraq MNFS) and to then subcontract those mandates to standing or bespoke coalitions and alliances. However, the recent MONUSCO Force Intervention Brigade experiment was a relatively successful (but not unproblematic) departure from this norm,[77] and a welcome response to reality, and adoption of responsibility, by the UNSC.

3.3 *Inconsistency in RoE Interpretation and Application*

Closely related to, but ultimately separate from, this first set of critiques is the second general critique related to RoE identified by the Independent Inquiry – the question of inconsistency in RoE application and interpretation. This critique is multifaceted; however, three indicia will illustrate the general concern.

The first indicia is whether UNAMIR adopted a sufficiently robust interpretation of its extant RoE as the crisis escalated after the shoot down of President Habyarimana's aircraft, the killing of Rwandan officials and Belgian UNAMIR peacekeepers, and the start of the genocide.[78] A case in point here is the Report's assessment of the conundrum UNAMIR faced: If a 'Kigali defensive concentration' was maintained – as the RoE, some argued, effectively required through its focus on force protection and self-defence rather than mandate implementation – the security situation would quickly deteriorate.[79] Indeed, this fundamentally defensive interpretation – to the extent of passivity in the face of manifest illegality and atrocity – of the RoE ensured that the UNAMIR force element sent to the crash site of President Habyarimana's aircraft, soon after it was reported, was 'disarmed and held at the airport'.[80]

This interpretation of the RoE – do not fire unless fired upon, and even suffer disarmament (in the hope of de-escalation) rather than use force to resist disarmament – also played a role in several other incidents immediately following the crash, not least the disarming and subsequent execution of Belgian

76 1999 *Independent inquiry Report*, p49.

77 See, inter alia: Scott Sheeran and Stephanie Case, *The Intervention Brigade: Legal Issues for the UN in the Democratic Republic of the Congo*, International Peace Institute, 2014, at https://www.ipinst.org/wp-content/uploads/publications/ipi_e_pub_legal_issues_drc_brigade.pdf; Bruce Oswald, 'The Security Council and the Intervention Brigade: Some Legal Issues' (06 June 2013) 17:15 *ASIL Insights*, at https://www.asil.org/insights/volume/17/issue/15/security-council-and-intervention-brigade-some-legal-issues.

78 See 1999 *Independent Inquiry Report*, pp15–19.

79 Ibid, p13.

80 Ibid, p16.

UNAMIR force members (see below).[81] Indeed, the advice of the then Chef de Cabinet in the Executive Office of the Secretary-General, when informed that UNAMIR may need to use force to protect the Rwandan PM who had escaped into the UN Volunteer / UNDP compound, was that the RoE required UNAMIR to hold fire unless fired upon. This did not stop UNAMIR despatching an escort force to the compound to find and protect the PM, but it was to no avail: Before they could arrive, Rwandan soldiers entered the compound with impunity, found the PM, and executed her.[82]

The common thread in these incidents was that officials and commanders held sometimes starkly different interpretations of what the RoE permitted. As a result, as Alan Kuperman has noted, 'Rules of engagement were somewhat ambiguous but were generally interpreted to bar the use of force except in self-defense or in joint operations with Rwandan national police.'[83] The key obstacle – the assertion that a UN Force of the nature of UNAMIR could not fire back unless and until fired upon – was historically inaccurate, tactically nonsensical (in that self-defence does not require one to take the first hit), and legally incorrect (in that imminent threat of serious harm or death is a valid threshold, given that failure to act first might effectively negate any right to self-defence through death or injury sustained). But this mantra had taken on the veneer of scripture when in fact it was actually more a tenet of dogma. As the Belgian Senate Commission Report found:

> Moreover, the military attitude that it adopted prior to 7 April 1994 played an important role. Among other things, this attitude meant that UNAMIR became less and less credible in the eyes of the Rwandans (for example, by refraining from liquidating arms cachets, by not reacting to numerous provocations, etc.), which consequently gave the impression that they could impede UNAMIR'S work with impunity. For UNAMIR'S men, this passive attitude, combined with the 'fear of mistakes', produced a state of psychological disarmament. Moreover, the restricted interpretation of the ROE'S made some of the men lose their normal instincts regarding legitimate defence.[84]

The second indicia relates to whether UNAMIR undertook to provide protective services, and signalled use of force intentions to that effect, when

81 Ibid, pp16–17.

82 Ibid.

83 Kuperman, 'Rwanda in Retrospect', p104.

84 *Belgium Senate Commission Report*, ch 4, section 11.

(depending upon interpretation) the force was not entitled, under the RoE, to furnish this protection. The case in point was the promise of protection for senior local officials, including 'a number of politicians who were of key importance to the implementation of the Arusha Agreement',[85] as a component of 'self-defence'.[86] In the broad, the Independent Inquiry assessed that, 'the Rules of Engagement which governed the mission permitted the use of force in self-defence, as well as action to prevent crimes against humanity.'[87] The 1999 *Independent Inquiry Report* thus described the resultant conundrum as follows:

> The mission was under rules of engagement not to use force except in self-defence. It had taken upon itself to protect politicians, but then in certain circumstances did not do so in the face of threats by the militia. Civilians were drawn to UNAMIR posts but the mission proved incapable of sustaining protection for them.[88]

As the Report goes on to note, this incapacity was not simply one of RoE interpretive gridlock, but was also a functional own goal by the UN itself in that it had not managed the redeployment by some states of their force elements from UNAMIR to third state national evacuation operations (including France, Belgium, Italy, US); nor had it acted upon evidence that other states had instructed their contingents to cease responding to Force Commander orders (Bangladesh). This deprived the Force Commander of capability and placed UNAMIR in a position where it could not realistically even defend itself let alone implement its already limited (and by now effectively irrelevant) monitor and assist mandate.[89] Nevertheless, the consequence was that 'There is a pattern to these events which shows a failure by UNAMIR troops to guarantee the protection to these political personalities that had been assured and expected'.[90]

At core, however, is the fact that UNAMIR's monitor and assist mandate was understood (fairly, I think) by the Special Representative (Ambassador Booh

85 1999 *Independent Inquiry Report*, p44.
86 Ibid, p35.
87 Ibid, p45.
88 Ibid, pp35–36.
89 Ibid, pp36–37; it should also be noted that the Independent Inquiry recognized that 'the extremist forces had had time to observe the strength of UNAMIR guard posts and overwhelm them with larger force' (p45), although the extent to which a more robust response by better trained and disciplined UNAMIR force elements may have deterred the militia and rebel elements of the Rwandan army will remain unknown.
90 Ibid, pp44–45.

Booh of Cameroon), the Force Commander (Dallaire), and others to include authority for protection of local officials (to whom the task of negotiating and implementing the Arusha Peace Agreement had devolved)[91] such that UNAMIR force elements were assigned to provide (as became evident, effectively toothless) security at officials' homes. However, as the crisis deepened, resistance to armed militia and Rwandan soldiers arriving at family homes to detain or kill government leaders, including the Prime Minister, folded. As the Report concluded, this failure is attributable to a range of factors, including the conduct of 'the peacekeepers themselves, who by not resisting the threat to the persons they were protecting [in some enumerated cases]…as would have been covered by their Rules of Engagement, showed a lack of resolve to fulfil their mission'.[92] As Astri Surkhe has observed of the record set out in the Belgian 'Kigali Battalion' (KIBAT) Operations Log,

> At times, the dilemma appeared to be one of saving themselves versus saving others. At other times the choice was between protecting expatriates or Rwandans. At critical points the choice was made for them. During the few days after 6 April when the battalion remained in Kigali, its resources were tied up by orders to help evacuate expatriates. About the same time, the Belgian government gave priority to saving the Belgian peacekeepers by unilaterally deciding to withdraw the battalion (announced on 12 April).[93]

91 Ibid, pp6–7.

92 Ibid, p45.

93 Astri Surkhe, 'Dilemmas of Protection: The Log of the Kigali Battalion' (1998) 5:2 *International Peacekeeping* 1, at p2. Surkhe reports that the Log described how 'In the kit given each soldier was a one-page summary of the Rules of Engagement, condensed into six points from the complicated and detailed original rules issued (in English) by the UN Department of Peacekeeping Operations. The six points were clear. Force was to be used only in self-defense, or when specifically authorized by higher echelons. If incidents arose, the soldiers were instructed to demonstrate non-aggressive and cooperative behavior: Try first to defuse the situation verbally, the rules proclaimed, then enlist the help of the Rwandan gendarmerie, which was UNAMIR's designated local partner. If that does not work, do not use force unless authorized. Before firing a single shot from a non-automatic weapon, obtain authorization from the battalion commander…'. Surkhe also reports how 'an incident in March 1994 – only a month before the genocide – served more than anything else to bring home the central message that force was not to be used. At that time, a battalion unit had reacted to a nasty crowd situation by shooting without obtaining prior authorization. Although nobody was hurt, the unit involved was sternly reprimanded and sent home early as part of a rotation roster. The whole battalion was lectured on the peaceful nature of the operation.'

A third indicia of this interpretive inconsistency was confusion as to what the RoE actually required or authorised. One example of this radically limited view of the RoE was that UNAMIR APCs attempting to get through roadblocks to the UNV / UNDP compound where the Prime Minister had sought refuge, believed that they 'were unable, under the RoE, to fight through the roadblocks'.[94] However, the case in point here is the disarming of Belgian peacekeepers, described in detail by Surkhe in terms of a combination of, inter alia, task incapacity (inability to actually protect the Prime Minister), tactical confusion (were the Rwandan soldiers really going to use force?), lingering passivity in terms of seeking to deescalate at all costs, and RoE timidity.[95]

This tragedy of misunderstood or inappropriately limited use of force rules to prevent disarmament of UN force elements contributed directly to the deaths of ten Belgian soldiers.[96] This killing of the Belgian peacekeepers was a planned Interahamwe strategy, reported in Dallaire's 11 January 1994 cable, which set out the details of militia plans he had received from an informant. The essence of this component of the strategy, as the Report recorded, was that the militia would 'provoke the killing of Belgian soldiers and the Belgian battalion's withdrawal… Belgian troops were to be provoked. If the Belgian soldiers used force, a number of them would be killed, which was to guarantee the withdrawal of the Belgian contingent from Rwanda.'[97] Of course, this is precisely what occurred; the Belgium Senate Report noted that

> The government took a unilateral decision to withdraw the Belgian component of UNAMIR as a result of its analysis, ie that the United Nations did not want to modify the mandate, the Belgian government believed that the Belgian troops were in danger and had become useless and that Belgium could not act alone. Prime Minister Jean-Luc Dehaene told the commission that if the situation were to repeat itself, he would take the same decision.[98]

Nevertheless, as the Senate concluded, 'In any case, the commission cannot understand the Belgian diplomatic offensive which, in parallel to the decision to withdraw, was intended to terminate the entire UNAMIR operation, mainly

94 Findlay, *The Use of Force in UN Peace Operations*, p280.

95 Astri Suhrke, 'Facing Genocide: The Record of the Belgian Battalion in Rwanda' (1998) 29:1 *Security Dialogue* p37, at pp39–43.

96 See: *Belgium Senate Commission Report*, ch3, section 5.2.

97 1999 *Independent Inquiry Report*, p10.

98 *Belgium Senate Commission Report*, ch 4, section 13.

for psychological reasons.'[99] The Belgian patrol sent to secure Prime Minister Agathe Uwilingiyimana's home and escort her to the radio station soon after the aircraft crash has been confronted by 'about 20 Rwandan soldiers armed with guns and grenades' who, in league with the Presidential guard, told the Belgians to disarm. The Belgian battalion commander had initially told the on scene Belgian officer he should not disarm; however, after an almost two hour stand-off during which four Belgian soldiers had already been disarmed, the on-scene officer was authorised to lay down arms if it became necessary. As the Belgian Senate Report recounts, this commander 'continued to believe that the Rwandan armed forces and gendarmes were acting in good faith and wished to co-operate, even though, early in the morning of 7 April 1994, it turns out that this trust was unfounded and the men were in serious danger.'[100] The Belgians were disarmed, and were then moved to Camp Kigali by Rwandan soldiers, and there executed.[101] Within five days, Belgium had called for the withdrawal of UNAMIR and, failing that, reported that the Belgian contingent was to be withdrawn from UNAMIR.[102] In 1996, the senior Belgian officer in UNAMIR at the time, Colonel Luc Marchal (Commander Kigali Sector) was acquitted in a Belgian military court on charges relating to the accidental / negligent homicide ('homicide by lack of foresight and precaution') of the ten Belgian soldiers.[103]

---

99 Ibid.

100 Ibid, ch 4, section 11.

101 1999 *Independent Inquiry Report*, pp16–20; *Belgium Senate Commission Report*, ch 4. The Rwandan commander responsible was latter apprehended, prosecuted, and convicted in Belgium: Julien Ponthus, 'Rwandan convicted of killing Belgian peacekeepers', *Reuters*, 5 July 2007, at https://www.reuters.com/article/us-rwanda-genocide-belgium/rwandan-convicted-of-killing-belgian-peacekeepers-idUSL0469900520070704; he applied for asylum in Belgium after his release from prison in 2018: Daniel Boffey, 'Fury over asylum application by Rwandan who killed 10 Belgians', *The Guardian*, 10 August 2018, at https://www.theguardian.com/world/2018/aug/09/bernard-ntuyahaga-jailed-over-deaths-of-10-belgian-soldiers-seeks-asylum-in-belgium.

102 1999 *Independent Inquiry Report*, p19; The political context surrounding Claes' statement and Belgium's decision is representative of the tragic disconnect between politics, will, information, legal interpretation, resources, and operational reality that confounded UNAMIR – see, for example, Human Rights Watch, *Ignoring Genocide*, 1999, at https://www.hrw.org/reports/1999/rwanda/Geno15-8-01.htm.

103 'Colonel blamed for the death of his men', *The Independent*, 30 December 1995, at https://www.independent.co.uk/news/world/colonel-blamed-for-death-of-his-men-1527761.html; 'Colonel cleared in Rwanda trial', *The Irish Times*, 5 July 1996, at https://www.irishtimes.com/news/colonel-cleared-in-rwanda-trial-1.64438.

3.4 *The Deleterious Consequences of the Lack of Formal RoE Processes*

The third broad-based critique made in the Report relates to process, and centres upon the official inaction surrounding the RoE request sent by the Force Commander to UNHQ, which was never actioned or responded to:

> On 23 November 1993, Dallaire sent Headquarters a draft set of Rules of Engagement (ROE) for UNAMIR, asking for the approval of the Secretariat. The draft included in paragraph 17 a rule specifically allowing the mission to act, and even to use force, in response to crimes against humanity and other abuses [including 'executions, attack on displaced persons or refugees']...Headquarters never responded formally to the force Commander's request for approval.[104]

Dallaire's 'Operational Directive No.2 Rules of Engagement (Interim)' dated 19 November 1993[105] contains several paragraphs that relate directly to use of force in self-defence and in mission accomplishment, ranging from: Devolved authorisations (Battalion Commander through to NCO on the scene) for use of 'personal weapons for single shot fire' in defence;[106] four situations where use of defensive force was permitted (including self-defence and defence of others, and to respond to forceful attempts to prevent discharge of mandate duties);[107] and an authority 'to take the necessary action to prevent any crime against humanity'.[108] Indeed, as the Report went on to point out, UNHQ 'did not have a procedure in place for the formal approval of draft Rules of Engagement'.[109] The uncertainty thus created was more than merely bureaucratic – whilst the Force Commander assumed the draft RoE applied unless and until told otherwise, another senior commander within the force 'told the Inquiry' that the draft RoE 'did not conform to reality and he ignored them'.[110] This 'disturbing...lack of clarity' as to 'which rules were in force'[111] – and the consequential freedom to ignore them as claimed by some – thus bears some responsibility for the parlous state of RoE interpretation,

104 1999 *Independent Inquiry Report*, p9.
105 Romeo Dallaire, *Operational Directive No.2 Rules of Engagement (Interim)*, dated 19 November 1993, at https://assets.documentcloud.org/documents/1392396/footnote-105-op-dir-02-roe.pdf.
106 1999 *Independent Inquiry Report*, para 8c.
107 Ibid, para 11.
108 Ibid, para 17.
109 Ibid, p35.
110 Ibid.
111 Ibid.

compliance, and implementation at precisely the time of crisis when the need for a unity of mission and RoE application was most critical. Ultimately, the Report concluded that 'There should never be any doubt as to which Rules of Engagement apply during the conduct of a peacekeeping mission. Rules of Engagement must be given formal approval by Headquarters.'[112]

4 Rules of Engagement and the Subsequent Development of UN Peace Operations Doctrine

4.1 *Introduction*

A key recommendation from the 1999 *Independent Inquiry Report* was that the UN must ensure 'that Lessons Learned from previous missions are integrated into the planning of new peacekeeping operations'.[113] That this was a key finding is not surprising, and discussion and analysis of the RoE failure had commenced almost immediately – for example, a November 1994 Canadian study of the failures in Rwanda specifically identified the lack of UN RoE doctrine and processes as a contributing factor, and as a matter requiring urgent resolution: 'Canada should encourage the holding of working meeting of UN troop contributing nations, humanitarian agencies, and human rights agencies (UN and NGO), to create standard operating procedures and model Rules of Engagement for UN peacekeeping and humanitarian missions.'[114]

The issues identified in 1999 *Independent Inquiry Report* in Part II above were grouped broadly under three headings: Mandate – RoE mismatch; inconsistency in interpretation; and RoE processes. These three issues will provide the general lens through which the post-1999 doctrinal legacy of the *Independent Inquiry Report's* assessment of RoE is described. There are two thematic trends which this exploration discloses. The first trend is that since 1999 there have in effect been two competing doctrinal approaches at play: A progressive, mission-tailored, robust RoE approach (now championed by the UNSC and Secretariat); and an approach centred on maintaining the traditional, doctrinally

112 Ibid, p56; see also, *Belgium Senate Commission Report*, ch 3, section 4, including in relation to Belgium's advocacy for more robust RoE.

113 1999 *Independent Inquiry Report*, p56: This was a component of Recommendation 2, at p53, concerning improved UN capacities in relation to peacekeeping.

114 Paul Larose-Edwards, *The Rwandan Crisis of April 1994: The Lessons Learned*, 30 November 1994, p22 (a report for Regional Security and Peacekeeping Division (IDC) International Security, Arms Control, and CSCE Affairs Bureau Department of Foreign Affairs and International Trade Ottawa, Canada), at https://repositories.lib.utexas.edu/bitstream/handle/2152/5102/2414.pdf?sequence=1.

orthodox, emphasis upon limited and caveated peacekeeping (now championed by the UNGA Special Committee). The second thematic trend is that the 'one step forward, two steps back' course of doctrinal development since 1999 is in many ways the inevitable result of the UN's current inability to achieve an effective doctrinal reconciliation of these two approaches. However, as the following analysis tentatively concludes, it is the progressive approach that is now arguably on the ascendency, as the success of the MONUSCO FIB experiment and the 2017 Use of Force Guidelines tend to evidence.

4.2 *Initial post-April 1994 Developments in Peace Operations Doctrine and RoE*

Immediately following Rwanda, and Srebrenica, there was a series of reviews and doctrinal advances in relation to UN peace operations, the application on the ground of which never achieved sufficient momentum to engineer enduring doctrinal and operational change. The first such attempt was the 1995 *Supplement to An Agenda for Peace*, which represented a sobering and significant change in tack for UN peace operations. Mats Berdal describes the context thus: 'Taking stock in early 1995, Boutros Ghali issued a *Supplement to An Agenda for Peace*; a document markedly different in tone from the optimism of three years earlier and, more significantly, gloomy in its conclusions regarding the prospects for the use of force in peacekeeping operations.'[115] This was a post-Somalia, post-Rwanda, and post-Srebrenica 'retreat' from the 1992 *Agenda for Peace*,[116] but was itself merely a waypoint on the long and continuing road towards a UN peace operations doctrine that recognises and reflects the diversity of actual UN peace operations, missions, and tasks. However – as is representative of the complex and conflicted path through UN Doctrine of recognition of the need for context and mission-appropriate RoE – in that same year, the *General Guidelines for Peacekeeping Operations* (although focussed upon peacekeeping rather than enforcement) nevertheless once again, post-Rwanda, reiterated the hesitancy and discomfort of the Secretariat towards robust use of force RoE in what DPKO still labelled as a peacekeeping context:

> The international community has responded with a new kind of operation to escort or conduct humanitarian relief activities and to be able to

115 Mats Berdal, 'What Are the Limits to the Use of Force in UN Peacekeeping?', in de Coning and Peter (eds), *United Nations Peace Operations in a Changing Global Order*, Plagrave Macmillan, Cham, 2019, p113, at p117.

116 Findlay, *The Use of Force in UN Peace Operations*, p318.

> protect them in self-defence if attacked. In such situations of sustained hostility, even the restrained use of force by UN troops has led, perhaps inevitably, to their being drawn into confrontations and conflict, demonstrating the limits of peace-keeping operations confronted with a determination of one side or the other to continue war.[117]

The ongoing hesitancy and confusion as to the future of UN peace operations – illustrated by the gloom underpinning the *Supplement*, and the caution expressed in the *General Guidelines* – has continued to dog both operations and doctrine, prompting Mats Berdal to observe that,

> As the spate of new operations since 1999 has shown, the apparent determination to ensure that the horrors of Rwanda and former Yugoslavia would never again be repeated on the UN's watch has emphatically not resolved the deeper tension between ends and means highlighted by the Supplement, tensions which, if anything, have become more acute.[118]

However, this 1994–1999 period of doctrinal churn also resulted in an interesting twist in the evolution of doctrinal treatments of RoE issues from 1999 onwards in that the stuttering conversion of the Secretariat (and to some extent the UNSC) towards doctrinal recognition of the place and need for more robust RoE postures and profiles really commenced at this point. But this shift in Secretariat and UNSC views also prompted a delayed reaction in the form of, inter alia, the Special Committee (of which, more below). What is inescapable, however, as Berdal goes on to note, is that the progressive approach has 'influence[d] the mandate and change[d] the operational focus of UN peacekeepers, with important implications for the question of the use of force. The single most important manifestation of this change is the growing centrality of the 'Protection of Civilians' (POC) as a task formally entrusted to UN peacekeepers.'[119] And the most significant – indeed arguably the first and most fundamental post-1999 – step in this direction was the *Brahimi Report*.

4.3 *The Progressive Approach gains Traction: the 2000 Brahimi Report*

The most significant step in doctrinal evolution – subsequent to the excoriation of both the Rwanda and Srebrenica Reports – was the August 2000 *Report on the Panel on United Nations Peace Operations* – better known as 'the Brahimi

117 DPKO, *General Guidelines for Peace-keeping Operations*, October 1995, p12.
118 Berdal, 'What Are the Limits to the Use of Force in UN Peacekeeping?', p117.
119 Berdal, 'What Are the Limits to the Use of Force in UN Peacekeeping?', pp117–118.

Report'.[120] In relation to the nexus between RoE and the lessons from UNAMIR – as identified in the 1999 *Independent Inquiry Report* – the Brahimi Report stated as a 'key recommendation on peacekeeping doctrine and strategy' that 'once deployed, United Nations peacekeepers must be able to carry out their mandates professionally and successfully and be capable of defending themselves, other mission components and the mission's mandate, with robust rules of engagement, against those who renege on their commitments to a peace accord or otherwise seek to undermine it by violence.'[121] 'Indeed', the *Brahimi Report* continued,

> ...peacekeepers — troops or police — who witness violence against civilians should be presumed to be authorized to stop it, within their means, in support of basic United Nations principles and, as stated in the report of the Independent Inquiry on Rwanda, consistent with 'the perception and the expectation of protection created by [an operation's] very presence'.[122]

In terms of UN use of force and RoE (noting that the UN was also engaged in attempting to produce UN RoE Guidance at this time – see below), the *Brahimi Report* indicates two significant outcomes. The first, which Ronald Hatto assessed to be both an outcome and a challenge, was that the *Brahimi Report*

> ...maintained that UN forces should be able to use force to prevent atrocities against civilian populations. While that recommendation in the Brahimi Report enabled a response to be made to the criticisms of the PKOs since the massacres in Rwanda and Bosnia, it nonetheless ran up against two major obstacles: the fears of the developing countries...with regard to interference in their internal affairs, and the lack of willingness among most of the troop-contributing countries to risk the lives of their soldiers deployed in UN operations.[123]

---

120 *Report on the Panel on United Nations Peace Operations*, 17 August 2000 (A/55/305; S/2000/809) ('Brahimi Report').

121 Brahimi Report, para 55, and Annex III, para 3.

122 Brahimi Report, para 62.

123 Ronald Hatto, 'From peacekeeping to peacebuilding: the evolution of the role of the United Nations in peace operations' (2013) 95:891/892 *International Review of the Red Cross* 495, at p513; See, for example, *Brahimi Report*, para 50 ('Such impartiality is not the same as neutrality or equal treatment of all parties in all cases for all time, which can amount to a policy of appeasement. In some cases, local parties consist not of moral equals but of obvious aggressors and victims, and peacekeepers may not only be operationally justified in using force but morally compelled to do so. Genocide in Rwanda went as far as it did in part because the international community failed to use or to reinforce the operation then on the ground in that country to oppose obvious evil.');

Consequently, as the Report forcefully put it,

> Rules of engagement should not limit contingents to stroke-for-stroke responses but should allow ripostes sufficient to silence a source of deadly fire that is directed at United Nations troops or at the people they are charged to protect and, in particularly dangerous situations, should not force United Nations contingents to cede the initiative to their attackers.[124]

The second significant RoE related set of outcomes from the *Brahimi Report* addressed the interpretive consistency and procedural aspects of the problems identified in the 1999 *Independent Inquiry Report* in that TCNs, their PKF contingents, and the UN itself often 'lack common operating procedures and have differing interpretations of key elements of command and control and of the mission's rules of engagement, and may have differing expectations about mission requirements for the use of force.'[125] The solution, the Brahimi Panel proposed, was that 'Troop contributors must ensure that the troops they provide fully understand the importance of an integrated chain of command, the operational control of the Secretary-General and the standard operating procedures and rules of engagement of the mission.'[126] Noting the ongoing conceptual debate that – to this day – still inhibits discussion about the robustness of RoE, it is in some respects arguable that this second, more procedural recommendation – for formalised RoE procedures as part of a more formalised doctrinal appreciation of UN peacekeeping control and responsibilities arrangements, one of the key concerns identified in the 1999 *Independent Inquiry Report* –is actually the most enduring RoE legacy of the *Brahimi Report*. That there is some link between this recommendation and the UN Secretary-General's determination to semi-formalise the draft RoE Guidelines and Master List in 2001, against some vocal member state opposition, is perhaps unstated but none the less clear.

4.3.1 Reception of the *Brahimi Report*

The UN encouraged TCNs to adopt the *Brahimi Report* recommendations.[127] However, as a Stimson Centre report observed, a number of member state groupings and committees 'avoided endorsing the Report's call for "robust"

124 Brahimi Report, para 49.

125 Brahimi Report, para 108.

126 Brahimi Report, para 267.

127 A/C.4/55/6, 4 December 2000, para. 8.

forces and rules of engagement (ROE) and bridled at revising UN peacekeeping "doctrine".'[128] By contrast,

> The Security Council, on the other hand, urged DPKO to come up with new doctrine as quickly as possible and recognized the 'critical importance of a credible deterrent capability' and 'the possibility that some parties may seek to undermine peace through violence'. As TCCs, then, states appear worried that they could be asked to undertake robust operations; as decision makers (Council members) they appear worried that no one would answer the call.[129]

This summation lays bare the political imperatives behind the now evident and obvious hardening of lines between the Secretariat and UNSC preferred progressive approach to robust peace operations RoE, and the defence of traditional doctrinal calls for RoE caution and limitation now being mounted by a vocal group of member states.

4.3.2 The *No Exit without Strategy Report*

Quickly upon the heels of the *Brahimi Report* came the Secretary-General's report on *No exit without strategy: Security Council decision-making and the closure or transition of United Nations peacekeeping operations*.[130] This report did not engage directly with the issue of RoE; however, in relation to the lessons of Rwanda identified in the 1999 *Independent Inquiry Report*, the *No exit without strategy Report* did attempt to 'quantify' (in comparative dollar terms) the cost of the UN and state failure to 'radically reduce, rather than reinforce, the capacities of UNAMIR'. As the report observed,

> when the international community belatedly accepted responsibility for addressing the humanitarian crisis in the Great Lakes region, the consequent costs of refugee assistance vastly exceeded the largest estimates of the costs of a reinforced UNAMIR. For example, in financial terms, the actual cost of UNAMIR was $4.37 million; the annual cost of the additional 5,000 soldiers the Force Commander, General Romeo Dallaire, thought were needed to prevent or stop the genocide has been estimated at $500 million; the cost of humanitarian assistance to Rwanda and the region consequent on the genocide was in excess of $4.5 billion.[131]

128 William Durch et al, *The Brahimi Report and the Future ofUNPeace Operations*, Henry L Stimson Centre, NY, 2003, pp22–23.

129 Ibid.

130 *No exit without strategy: Security Council decision-making and the closure or transition of United Nations peacekeeping operations*, 20 April 2001 (S/2001/394).

131 *No exit without strategy*, para 28.

4.4 *A Concrete Step forward for UN Mission RoE: The 2002 UN Guidelines and Master List of Rules of Engagement*

Findlay has described how, 'Sadly emblematic of the tortuous process of reform of UN peace operations and its "one step forward, two steps back" quality was the fate of the model ROE which the Secretariat had been trying for three years to draft.'[132] Despite extensive consultations and reviews, the Special Committee and the Secretariat could not agree; in late 2001 the Secretary-General opted to short-circuit the impasse and announced that DPKO would use the *Guidelines and Master List*.[133] As Chesterman observes,

> Further consultation in 2001 — after the Rwanda and Srebrenica reports, and the Brahimi Report had been published — saw an evolution in thinking, but little consensus. In December 2001, the Secretary-General simply announced that the document, now known as the Guidelines for the Development of Rules of Engagement (ROE) for United Nations Peacekeeping Operations, would remain a 'work in progress', but in the meantime was being used by military planning staff to prepare mission-specific rules of engagement and would soon be used for training purposes in troop contributing countries.[134]

In reality, however, DPKO and UN missions were already using the *RoE Guidelines and Master List*, and formalisation was consciously in train even before the Secretary-General made this statement. A case study is the INTERFET RoE (which were approved by the UN) and the follow-on UNAET RoE (which were formal UN RoE, staffed by DPKO and approved by the Secretary-General).[135] The UNTAET RoE – which was signed by the Under-Secretary-General for Peacekeeping Operations, not by the Force Commander – has since been

132 Findlay, *The Use of Force in UN Peace Operations*, p347.

133 *Guidelines for the development of Rules of Engagement (ROE) for United Nations Peacekeeping Operations*, 15 May 2002 (MD/FGS/0220.0001)

134 Simon Chesterman, *External Study for DPKO: The Use of Force in UN Peace Operations*, August 2004, pp19–20; Findlay, *The Use of Force in UN Peace Operations*, pp347–350.

135 On INTERFET RoE see, inter alia: Michael Kelly et al, 'Legal aspects of Australia's involvement in the International Force for East Timor' (2001) 841 *International Review of the Red Cross* 101, at pp128–130; On UNTAET RoE, see inter alia: Centre on International Cooperation, *Annual Review of Global Peace Operations, 2006*, Lynne Rienner, London, 2006, Section 3.5, at pp62–63, at https://peaceoperationsreview.org/wp-content/uploads/2015/04/2006_annual_review.pdf; Dale Stephens, 'The lawful use of force by peacekeeping forces: the tactical imperative' (2005) 12:2 *International Peacekeeping* 157; Dale Stephens, 'Military involvement in law enforcement' (2010) 92:878 *International Review of the Red Cross* 453, at pp457–463.

publicly disclosed and analysed.[136] Thus despite these chequered origins, there is no doubt that the publication and employment of the more formalised RoE doctrine, format, and processes set out in the *UN ROE Guidelines and Master List* has promoted the responsiveness of UNHQ and DPKO to RoE development and alteration requests.

4.4.1 Reception of the *UN RoE Guidelines*

Whilst the *UN ROE Guidelines* were broadly welcomed, and usefully employed, concerns remained as to mandate-RoE matching. One trend in this concern is evidenced in a 2003 Stimson Centre report, for example, which predicted that 'Civilian protection will remain a dilemma for any future operation that faces outbreaks of conflict with too little force to protect itself and the rest of the international community and the population at large. TCCs, moreover, may insist on rules of engagement that exclude such responsibility.'[137] Similarly, in 2004, John Borton and John Eriksson assessed that

> ...it would appear that Security Council Members remain generally reluctant to provide the mandates and rules of engagement necessary to enable UN Peacekeeping Forces to respond effectively to all the potential threats to them and civilians in their area of operation and troop contributing states do not always provide forces equipped sufficiently to enable them to engage in more forceful ways than self- defense.[138]

Chesterman also ultimately returned to the 1999 *Independent Inquiry Report* conclusion that 'whether or not an obligation to protect civilians is explicit in the mandate of such a force, the United Nations and other actors must be prepared to respond to the expectation of protection created by their very presence.'[139] The second area of concern was the still simmering tension between the progressives and the traditionalists, in that the latter continued to object to the signalling implicit in the adoption in practice of the *UN RoE Guidelines*. In 2006, for example, Bernadette Boss – discussing one thread of

136 *Rules of Engagement for the Military Component of the United Nations Mission in East Timor* (*UNTAET*) (MPS/3633), dated 38 April 2000, in Australian Defence Force Military Law Centre / Asia Pacific Centre for Military Law, *Law and Military Operations in East Timor* (*UNTAET*) *Feb 2000 – May 2002*, Annexure X.

137 Durch et al, *The Brahimi Report and the Future of UN Peace Operations*, pp24–25.

138 John Borton and John Eriksson, *Assessment of the Impact and Influence of Joint Evaluation of Emergency Assistance to Rwanda*, Danish Ministry of Foreign Affairs, December 2004, p60.

139 Chesterman, *External Study for DPKO: The Use of Force in UN Peace Operations*, p22.

this concern – noted the 'implied requirement for UN forces equipped with robust rules of engagement to be involved in what [some scholars] argue are effectively counterinsurgency actions. [These scholars] put forward the argument that such operations involve a level of information protection that cannot be achieved in a multinational command. Also, such operations impeach the impartiality of UN forces.'[140] For all their doctrinal and practical utility, the *UN RoE Guidelines* still could not bridge or resolve the debilitating tension between these two interpretive camps.

4.5 *A Step Sideways: Traditional Peacekeeping Redux in the 2008 Capstone Doctrine*

Writing in 2004, Simon Chesterman argued that

> The United Nations has generally been reluctant to allow military units under its command to use force. The three peace operations in which troops under UN command engaged in the use of force on a significant scale — Congo from 1960–1963, Somalia in 1993, and Bosnia and Herzegovina from 1994–1995 — were traumatic experiences for the organization; the controversies to which they gave rise were surpassed only by two occasions on which force was not used at all, in Rwanda and Srebrenica. Such reluctance is consistent with the traditional conception of peacekeeping as an impartial activity undertaken with the consent of all parties, in which force is used only in self-defence. Over the years, however, all three characteristics of traditional peacekeeping (consent, impartiality, minimum use of force) have been brought into question.[141]

The 2008 *Capstone Doctrine* in some ways represents a response to this observation in that it clearly hearkens back to the traditional pillars of peacekeeping, and thus appears to endorse a turn away from the progressive approach to robust RoE and a return to more narrow conceptions of the purpose and functions of RoE in UN peace operations. The *Capstone Doctrine* observes of RoE that:

> The mission-wide ROE for the military and DUF for the police components of a United Nations peacekeeping operation will clarify the different

140 Bernadette Boss, *Law and Peace: A Legal Framework for United Nations Peacekeeping*, PhD Thesis, University of Sydney, 2006, pp111–112, at https://ses.library.usyd.edu.au/bitstream/2123/1204/2/02whole.pdf.

141 Chesterman, *External Study for DPKO: The Use of Force in UN Peace Operations*, p6.

> levels of force that can be used in various circumstances, how each level of force should be used, and any authorizations that must be obtained by commanders. In the volatile and potentially dangerous environments into which contemporary peacekeeping operations are often deployed, these ROE and DUF should be sufficiently robust to ensure that a United Nations peacekeeping operation retains its credibility and freedom of action to implement its mandate. The mission leadership should ensure that these ROE and DUF are well understood by all relevant personnel in the mission and are being applied uniformly.[142]

However, this seeming retreat from the progressive approach to RoE in the *Capstone Doctrine* is actually more limited than it first appears. This is because the 2008 doctrine also recognises the shadow of Rwanda and the experience of UNAMIR by restricting its purview to traditional peacekeeping. The *Capstone Doctrine* achieves this by clearly differentiating between 'robust peacekeeping', and Chapter VII peace enforcement. This distinction (which is doctrinal rather than operational or practical, in my view) is then employed to hedge, and limit, discussion within the doctrine to the core principle on 'non-use of force except in self-defence and defence of the mandate'. In this respect, the *Capstone Doctrine* genuflected to ongoing TCN concerns in relation to inappropriate or counter-productive 'robustness' in peacekeeping use of force and RoE:

> A United Nations peacekeeping operation should only use force as a measure of last resort, when other methods of persuasion have been exhausted, and an operation must always exercise restraint when doing so. The ultimate aim of the use of force is to influence and deter spoilers working against the peace process or seeking to harm civilians; and not to seek their military defeat. The use of force by a United Nations peacekeeping operation should always be calibrated in a precise, proportional and appropriate manner, within the principle of the minimum force necessary to achieve the desired effect, while sustaining consent for the mission and its mandate. In its use of force, a United Nations peacekeeping operation should always be mindful of the need for an early de-escalation of violence and a return to non-violent means of persuasion.
>
> The use of force by a United Nations peacekeeping operation always has political implications and can often give rise to unforeseen circumstances. Judgments concerning its use will need to be made at the appro-

142 DPKO / DFS, *United Nations Peacekeeping Operations Principles and Guidelines* ('Capstone Doctrine'), 2008, p35.

> priate level within a mission, based on a combination of factors including mission capability; public perceptions; humanitarian impact; force protection; safety and security of personnel; and, most importantly, the effect that such action will have on national and local consent for the mission.[143]

However, in doing so, the *Capstone Doctrine* also created a doctrinal space for progressive approach advocacy of more robust RoE solutions by indicating that doctrine is itself contextual rather than universal, and by – once again – reaffirming that not every UN peace operation should or could be governed by the traditional three pillars of peacekeeping and the approach to RoE limitation that historically informed that doctrine.

4.6 *Charting a Possible Reconciliation: the 2009 New Horizon Initiative*

In one sense, the 2009 *New Horizon Initiative* arose out of this ongoing inability of the Secretariat to reconcile, in doctrinal terms, the two competing threads of doctrinal development that continued to animate discussion: On one hand, the recognised post-1999 imprimatur for progressive doctrinal development, recognition of cross-mission enduring mandates in areas such as protection of civilians, and the formalisation of more robust RoE; on the other, the enduring attraction of the pre-1990 orthodoxy of cautious mission restraint, the doctrinal centrality of the three pillars of traditional peacekeeping, and an (increasingly irrelevant?) adherence to impractical doctrinal distinctions between peacekeeping and peace enforcement, and unwillingness to adopt the spectrum approach to use of force and RoE. The approach taken by the *New Horizon Initiative* in seeking to sponsor engagement between the views was a dialogue regarding capability gaps. To this end, the *New Horizon Initiative* concluded that 'This process [of addressing capability gaps] must include a dialogue with Member States to ensure that troop and police contributors deploying to missions with robust concepts of operation are consulted and understand and accept assigned tasks and rules of engagement, and that they deploy assets with a minimum of caveats.'[144] However, despite this noble objective, hesitancy and concern at the concept of 'a robust approach to peacekeeping' – and thus to robust RoE – has lingered: As Progress Report No.1 on the implementation of the *New Horizons Initiative* observed:

143 Ibid, p35.

144 Department of Peacekeeping Operations and Department of Field Support, *A New Partnership Agenda: Charting a New Horizon forUNPeacekeeping*, July 2009, p22.

> In comparison with the membership's supportive conclusions on peacebuilding roles of peacekeepers and the protection of civilians, the General Assembly gave a more nuanced response to early conceptual thinking on the robust approach to peacekeeping. The membership requested continued dialogue on requirements for enhancing the effectiveness of peacekeeping, including by addressing requirements for peacekeepers to be able to deter through their posture and actions threats to mandate implementation, the safety and security of personnel, and the overall peace process. This dialogue is ongoing and will continue on a regional basis in the months ahead…[145]

This was a valiant attempt to reframe the issue by re-opening dialogue between the progressives and the traditionalists; but it did not really succeed. Indeed, the traditional approach went in search of, and found, a new collective outlet for its advocacy. In February 1965 the UNGA had created the Special Committee on Peacekeeping Operations ('C34').[146] Although more traditionally focussed upon financing and related issues, some of the more recent *Reports of the Special Committee on Peacekeeping Operations* tend to reflect and reiterate caveats and cautions in relation to 'robust peacekeeping' similar to those evident in the 2008 *Capstone Doctrine*. In its 2014 *Report*,[147] for example, the Special Committee indicated that it was 'of the view that, whenever the mandate of a mission is changed or amended, the views of the troop- and police-contributing countries should be fully taken into account, and that the Secretariat should ensure that they are reflected in the operational documents (including concept of operations and rules of engagement).'[148] This tentativeness on the part of TCNs, and the Special Committee is tenacious; the same caveats were still being expressed in the 2018 *Report of the Special Committee on Peacekeeping Operations*: 'The Special Committee requests that any significant adjustments in or changes to the original concept of operations, rules of engagement or force requirements should be made in close consultation with,

145 DPKO / DFS, *New Horizon Initiative Progress Report 01*, October 2010, p15; these doubts continued to dog progress with respect to this initiative – DPKO / DFS, *New Horizon Initiative Progress Report 02*, December 2011, p12.

146 *Comprehensive review of the whole question of peace-keeping operations in all their aspects*, UNGA Resolution 2006 (XIX), 18 February 1965.

147 *Report of the Special Committee on Peacekeeping Operations*, 01 April 2014 (A/68/19).

148 Ibid, para 77; the same hesitancy from the perspective of TCNs was also evident at paras 51, 228, 232.

and with the consent of, the troop-contributing and police-contributing countries.'[149]

4.7 A Further Attempt at Reconciliation: the 2015 *HIPPO Report*

The most recent review of UN peacekeeping and issues of, inter alia, use of force and RoE, is the 'HIPPO' – the *High-level Independent Panel on Peace Operations*.[150] This report says two important things about RoE. First, the *HIPPO* makes the following assertion:

> The Panel believes that the following considerations will be important to enabling a United Nations peacekeeping operation to operate with even limited success in [conflict management] settings:...
> (g) They must operate on the assumption that the use of force may be necessary from the outset to protect civilians and to defend the mission and its mandate... Contingents must deploy with the necessary equipment and training and a clear understanding of the mission rules of engagement.[151]

Second, the *HIPPO* then proceeds to crystallise one of the key debates around use of force that has (for quite some time) debilitated any possibility of a rapprochement of – or perhaps, more accurately, recognition of possible co-existence between – the progressive and traditional approaches to RoE:

> 'Self-defence' is a well-recognized concept and is thoroughly defined in United Nations rules of engagement. However, the concept of 'defence of

149 *Report of the Special Committee on Peacekeeping Operations*, 15 March 2018 (A/72/19), para 58, echoed at paras 51, 116, 323, 337; however, the 2018 Report also clearly recognised the importance of appropriate RoE to protection of civilians at, for example, para 295: 'The Special Committee stresses that the protection of civilians in peacekeeping operations may comprise, in accordance with the mission's mandate and taking into account the primacy of political resolution of conflicts, activities by all the components of a mission in order to prevent or respond to acts of violence against civilians, including the use of force as a last resort when required, according to the mandate and the rules of engagement, to provide security to civilians under threat of physical violence within areas of operations, without prejudice to the primary responsibility of the host government to protect its civilians...'; para 303: 'The Special Committee notes that the authorization to use force in peacekeeping operations in order to respond to threats of physical violence against civilians must be implemented in accordance with applicable legal obligations and in compliance with the mandate established by the Security Council and the mission-specific rules of engagement.'

150 *Report of the High-level Independent Panel on Peace Operations on uniting our strengths for peace: politics, partnership and people*, 06 June 2015 (A/70/95, S/2015/446).

151 Ibid, para 116.

> the mandate' requires clarity as to which tasks within the mandate may require the use of force. It should always include the responsibility to protect civilians and missions should be proactive in doing so. Different threats must be met with the appropriate use of military force, ranging from containment via deterrence and coercion to direct confrontation, particularly when civilians or peacekeepers are at risk. The actual use of force may not be necessary if the potential attackers perceive and know United Nations troops have the determination and capabilities to respond forcefully in case of attack.[152]

Then – significantly, relevantly, and in a departure from *Capstone Doctrine* – the *HIPPO* concluded that 'The Panel notes, however, that ultimately the clarity of what is required for any particular mission is not found in doctrine, but contained in clear and mission-specific statements of unit requirements, guidelines for troop- and police-contributing countries and rules of engagement.[153]

This is, in my view, the singularly most important statement about RoE made in any UN mandated review or report since the *Brahimi Report* in 2000. That is, one might say, the real lesson from Rwanda (and since) is that if RoE is hostage to doctrine – and in particular the increasingly artificial distinction between (rather than spectrum approach to) peacekeeping and peace enforcement – the chances of failure are exacerbated. When RoE is derived from mandate, resources, and operational context, the chances of success can be increased, although not assured. As one analysis of the implementation challenges facing the *HIPPO* report observes, 'In their submissions to HIPPO, Brazil called for greater efforts to remove the "illusion of sequencing" between peacekeeping and peacebuilding, and Luxembourg and Thailand considered peacebuilding and peacekeeping complimentary and closely linked.'[154]

---

152 Ibid, para 128.

153 Ibid, para 129.

154 Alexander Ilitchev, 'Implementing the HIPPO Report: Sustaining Peace as a New Imperative?', *International Forum for the Challenges of Peace Operations*, December 2015, Policy Brief No. 5, pp1–2, at https://www.un.org/pga/70/wp-content/uploads/sites/10/2016/01/PolicyBrief2015_5_-Imlementing_the_HIPPO_Alexander-Ilitchev.pdf. For a general assessment of the wider implications of the HIPPO for the UN, see inter alia, Arthur Boutellis and Alexandra Novosseloff, *Road to a Better UN? Peace Operations and the Reform Agenda*, International Peace Institute, November 2017; William Durch, 'Implementing "Uniting Our Strengths for Peace": An approach to benchmarking 'HIPPO' recommendations in five key areas', *Background Paper: Challenges Forum 20th Anniversary*, May 2016, at https://www.challengesforum.org/wp-content/uploads/2019/06/Implementing-Uniting-Our-Strenghts-for-Peace.pdf.

Indeed, Brazil has since promoted the concept of 'tailored peace operations' to reflect the trend towards phased mandates and the need to anticipate and act in accordance with now well accepted supra-mission tasks such as protection of civilians and the promotion of enduring women, peace and security mandates.[155] Such an approach might also go some way to escaping the constraints imposed by the enslavement of planning, authorisation, and implementation of peace operations to a conceptual – and to some extent artificial – typological lexicon, rather than to the operational conditions on the ground and the express and implied requirements of the mission. The shadow of Rwanda is clearly evident in this conclusion, for as the *HIPPO* noted, 'the pronounced international failures to protect civilians during the 1990s, particularly in Rwanda and Srebrenica… still loom large over the United Nations and its peace operations today. The spectre of those experiences must continue to drive the Organization to spare no effort to protect those it is mandated to protect'.[156]

Nevertheless, the *HIPPO* has been criticised for some tacit sidestepping of RoE and use of force issues. The Netherlands Institute of International Relations ('Clingendael') has argued, for example, that:

> HIPPO ignored the fact that UN peace operations can be an easy target for terrorist acts, such as the bombing of UN headquarters in Bagdad, and are on occasion pulled into supporting military counterterrorism operations, albeit on the margins. Consequently, peace operations may require counter-terrorism capabilities for self-defence purposes and because, even if unintentionally, they may be drawn into military counter-terrorism.
>
> Moreover, HIPPO concluded that in case UN peace operations are deployed in operating environments with asymmetric threats, they should be provided with the necessary capabilities and training, and an appropriate concept of operations and rules of engagement. For this purpose, troop- and police-contributing countries should deploy with the required capability and political will, to enable missions to respond to threats, and to use force proactively in self-defence, to protect civilians and to dissuade spoilers. Yet, this is precisely one of the main reasons why

155 See, for example, Eduarda Hamann and Adriana Erthal Abdenur, *The Future of United Nations Peacekeeping Operations from a Brazilian Perspective (implementing the HIPPO report)*, Igarape Institute Strategic Note 25, March 2017, pp3–7.

156 HIPPO, para 83.

> HIPPO was set up: Peace operations are deployed in asymmetric threat environments, in the absence of the required capabilities and political will. So, what now?
>
> In the absence of satisfactory answers to these more strategic questions about the use of force and the future of peace operations, HIPPO dealt with some more concrete issues concerning the safety and security of peacekeepers.[157]

Whilst the Clingendael concerns are most certainly relevant and pressing, it should also be borne in mind that in attempting to chart a course for co-existence between the progressive and traditional approaches, engaging with these undoubtedly important justifications for progressively robust manifestations of UN peace operations RoE may simply have been a bridge to far for the *HIPPO*.

4.8 *A Really Useful Development: the 2017 Guidelines on Use of Force*

The DPKO / DFS 2017 *Guidelines: Use of Force by Military Components in United Nations Peacekeeping Operations* is 'intended to provide clarity in the appropriate use of force at the tactical and operational levels of United Nations peacekeeping missions.'[158] This has become necessary because:

> Numerous after action reviews and discussions with TCCs have identified a gap in the understanding of the use of force despite existing mission-specific rules of engagement. These guidelines are accordingly intended to address the hesitation or lack of willingness/readiness to use force, when appropriate, in order to carry out mandated activities as well as to address the use of excessive force. It provides guidance on the use of appropriate force.[159]

The *2017 Guidelines* then proceed through a series of tactical and operational considerations around RoE and use of force – evidence of a further refinement in RoE procedures from that evinced by the 2001 *UN RoE Guidelines and Master List* – and specifically state that it is 'Mission-specific ROE [that] provide

157 Jair van der Lijn et al, *Progress on UN peacekeeping reform: HIPPO and beyond*, The Netherlands Institute of International Relations 'Clingendael', October 2017, p29, at https://www.clingendael.org/sites/default/files/pdf/Progress_on_UN_peacekeeping_reform.pdf.

158 DPKO / DFS, *Guidelines: Use of Force by Military Components in United Nations Peacekeeping Operations*, 01 February 2017 (Ref: 2016.24), para 1.

159 Ibid, para 5.

the requisite authority for the use of force.'[160] This is a long march from the confusion that beset the UNAMIR RoE, although it has taken some time to get there. However, the lessons of Rwanda for RoE (in my view) are perhaps best evidenced in the long awaited and very welcome recognition of four different types of 'force' / 'self-defence' that may be addressed in RoE:

> 'Force' is defined as the use of, or threat to use, physical means to impose one's will. In peacekeeping operations, peacekeepers are authorized to use force in **self-defense** and to **execute their mandated tasks** in appropriate situations. Depending upon the mandate, this may include the authorization to use force for the **protection of civilians**. The objective of the use of force in peacekeeping operations is to influence and deter, not necessarily to defeat threats seeking to threaten or harm United Nations personnel or associated personnel or the civilian population. In some cases, the use of force may also be authorized to **respond to other threats, including those caused by armed spoilers** intending to distract peace processes.[161]

For the first time, it would seem, UN doctrine has gripped up, differentiated, and expressed the distinctions between sub-types within the amorphous UN conception of 'self-defence'. If this clarity had been available, and expressible in binding RoE for UNAMIR, perhaps some Rwandans and some peacekeepers might have been saved.

4.9 *But Lingering Concerns Remain…*

The progress outlined above is welcome and – in context – even admirable. Yet there are four sets of RoE concerns identified or presaged in (inter alia) the 1999 *Independent Inquiry Report*, which continue to animate UN peace operations doctrine and its approach to RoE. The first of these is ongoing confusion as to the UN concept of 'self-defence'.[162] As one analyst observed in 2008, 'the UN's efforts in Darfur are beginning to mirror its efforts in Rwanda…[and] without additional efforts, many lives are at risk.'[163] Similarly, *The*

160 Ibid, para 38.

161 Ibid, para 6 (my bolding).

162 Bruce Oswald, 'Soldier Self-Defense Symposium: The Evolution of the UN Doctrine of Self-Defence in UN Peacekeeping', *Opinio Juris*, 01 May 2019, at http://opiniojuris.org/2019/05/01/soldier-self-defense-symposium-the-evolution-of-the-un-doctrine-of-self-defence-in-un-peacekeeping/; Boss, *Law and Peace: A Legal Framework for United Nations Peacekeeping*, p300.

163 Faggart, 'UN Peacekeeping After Rwanda: Lessons Learned or Mistakes Forgotten?', p496.

Guardian could still ask, in 2015: 'What's the point of peacekeepers when they don't keep the peace? From Rwanda to Bosnia, Haiti to Congo, failures raise questions about future of United Nations blue helmets.'[164] And whilst the Secretary-General's *Independent Report on Improving the Security of United Nations Peacekeepers* in 2017 assessed that 'Each mission is unique, and even within each country, different situations require different actions given the threat that prevails in an area. But what never changes is that the interpretation of mandates, rules of engagements and other documents should support taking ACTION, and not be used to justify INACTION',[165] it nevertheless concluded that 'Simplistic interpretations of mandates, regulations, standard procedures, and rules of engagement continue to justify the military posture and approach to the use of force that allows attacks to occur.'[166] However, as noted above, the *HIPPO* and the 2017 *Use of Force Guidelines*, as well as the experience of the Force Intervention Brigade, have very usefully served to crystallise this debate, and progress in clarifying this key RoE issue is apparent and accelerating. These are welcome indicators of the UN's increasing momentum towards resolving doctrinal limitations around the concept of self-defence, and the use of RoE.

The second set of concerns is the fact that the existence of a doctrinal space beyond the traditional approach to use of force and RoE in UN peace operations – championed by (most recently) the Special Committee on Peacekeeping – which reflects the hesitancy of many states towards the progressive approach to robust RoE, and represents their wish to maintain the traditional caveats and principles, is still tenuous and contested. Any attempt to doctrinally generalize the progressive trend towards more robust and mission-tailored RoE – rather than doctrinally pure 'three pillars' RoE – will be resisted, at least in the immediate future. That is, for every *Brahimi Report*, there is a *Capstone Doctrine*; for every piece of Security Council or Secretariat advocacy for robust RoE, there is Special Committee advocacy of continuing caution and doctrinal orthodoxy. To some extent this impasse is resolving itself through the recognition of, effectively, separate doctrinal bailiwicks for peacekeeping and peace enforcement. But this will only carry co-existence so far, for the emergence of generally agreed supra-mission, and cross-doctrinal, thematic mandate

164 Chris McGreal, 'What's the point of peacekeepers when they don't keep the peace? From Rwanda to Bosnia, Haiti to Congo, failures raise questions about future of United Nations blue helmets', *The Guardian*, 17 September 2015, at https://www.theguardian.com/world/2015/sep/17/un-united-nations-peacekeepers-rwanda-bosnia.

165 *Improving Security of United Nations Peacekeepers: We need to change the way we are doing business*, 19 December 2017, Executive Summary.

166 Ibid, p16.

concerns identified in reports such as the 1999 *Independent Inquiry Report* – most particularly the protection of civilians – has reinvigorated the need to reflect more robust RoE even in the most traditional of peacekeeping missions.

The third lingering concern is that even within the Secretariat itself, whilst many centrally concerned UN organs – primarily DPKO, the UNSC, and the UNGA – have commissioned important and constructive reports and compiled intensely relevant lists of lessons learned, the degree to which practical implementation has followed remains patchy. In DPKO's 1996 *Multidisciplinary Peacekeeping: Lessons Learned from Recent Experience* report, it was noted under the section on 'Military' that 'Rules of Engagement should be sufficiently detailed to eliminate doubt as to individual and unit behaviours under various contingencies, and should include guidance concerning mutual support by personnel and units of the force as a whole'.[167] In a similar report for 1999, the lesson identified was that 'Rules of engagement should be sufficiently detailed to eliminate doubt as to individual and unit behaviour under various contingencies, and should include guidance concerning mutual support by personnel and units of the force as a whole.'[168] The question, however, is whether this indicated a lesson continuously re-identified, but unactioned, or a lesson the importance of which bore continuous reiteration. The winding history of UN doctrine on RoE, and the shadow of UNAMIR, leaves us at best uncertain.

The final concern is that even in its current, long term, 'draft' state of being, current *UN RoE Guidelines* are desperately in need of updating – they are functional and perhaps even occasionally adequate, but they are far from agile. Furthermore, as a recent Brazilian report reminds us – in language reminiscent of the 1999 *Independent Inquiry Report* – 'With or without RoE, peacekeepers have a moral duty to act, if he/she has the capacity to do so, when a crime happens during a mission (e.g. massacres, rape, illegal taxation, looting, etc.). This is a moral duty even if the mission does not have a mandate to protect civilians, that is, even if it a mission is under Chapter VI.'[169] The problem, of course, is that doctrine still does not adequately reflect this truism.

167 DPKO Lessons Learned Unit, *Multidisciplinary Peacekeeping: Lessons Learned from Recent Experience*, December 1996, p17, at https://reliefweb.int/sites/reliefweb.int/files/resources/C51B776A550FF1E8C1256D57004B1BE0-dpko-multi-dec96.pdf.

168 DPKO, *Multidisciplinary Peacekeeping: Lessons from Recent Experience*, April 1999, lesson 8 under the heading of 'military', at https://www.globalpolicy.org/component/content/article/199/40912.html#Military.

169 Hamann and Abdenur, *The Future of United Nations Peacekeeping Operations from a Brazilian Perspective (implementing the HIPPO report)*, p 7.

4.10 *Conclusion*

As Trevor Findlay concluded in 2002,

> Despite the force commander's bravery in staying in Kigali and pleading for more troops and the authorisation to use force, this had been denied by both the UN Secretariat and the Security Council. Clearly, UNAMIR could not have mounted a military campaign to stop the killing altogether once it had gathered momentum. With an extremely weak logistics base, it was rapidly running out of food, medical supplies and even sandbags for its own protection.[170]

Yet even if UNAMIR had been at authorised levels of troops (2600) and graced with sustainment, it still could not have 'contained the killings in April' unless it 'had been mandated to intervene for humanitarian protection purposes.'[171] As evidence of the difference a robust – and sufficiently robustly interpreted and implemented – RoE could make, Feil cites the fact that Operation Turquoise was 'a determined modern force that advertised its mission and its robust ROE had no difficulty in controlling the level of violence' in its area of operations.[172] This, above all else, is perhaps the most enduring doctrinal and operational legacy of the 1999 *Independent Inquiry Report* into UNAMIR and the genocide in Rwanda: RoE are the symptom but not the cause. If we fix and clarify doctrine, ensure a contextually relevant mandate, adequately resource the operation, and back it with political will, then the 'right' RoE will almost inevitably follow.

---

170 Findlay, *The Use of Force in UN Peace Operations*, p282.

171 Ibid, p283; see also Kuperman, 'Rwanda in Retrospect', pp94–95: 'Although some lives could have been saved by intervention of any size at any point during the genocide, the hard truth is that even a large force deployed immediately upon reports of attempted genocide would not have been able to save even half the ultimate victims.'

172 Feil, 'Preventing Genocide: How the early use of force might have succeeded in Rwanda', p13.

CHAPTER 16

Rwanda and the Rohingya

Learning the Wrong Lessons?

David J. Simon

1 Introduction

The 1994 genocide against the Tutsi in Rwanda elicited consternation about the hollowness of the post-Holocaust commitment to the mantra "Never Again." It also ushered in volumes of genocide studies scholarship and efforts at public policy reforms. Yet in the quarter century that has passed since the genocide in Rwanda, genocide and mass atrocity have continued. The genocidal persecution of the Rohingya in Burma/Myanmar[1] stands as a recent example, and one of the best to illustrate both the changes in the global atrocity prevention regime and, ultimately, the shortcomings of those changes in terms of leading to a better result.

The Rwandan crisis unfolded in the immediate wake of the cold war, with norms and institutions in flux, and with no precedent of hewing to the commitments seemingly required through the Genocide Convention. The United Nations (UN), its peacekeeping forces, and powerful states – both as members of the UN and its Security Council and as policy-making governments in their own right – all lacked the imagination to recognize genocide as a possibility even as it unfolded before their eyes; they also lacked the courage to commit troops and other resources protect threatened civilians.

In the wake of Rwanda, and in recognition of the failure of the system to respond accordingly to the crisis of genocide, the global atrocity prevention regime evolved. In 1994, at the dawn of the post-cold war era, the global atrocity prevention regime consisted of nothing more than the thought of a fifty-year old, seldom-invoked convention. The new regime, under the rubric of the Responsibility to Protect, embraced a more proactive approach involving an affirmative commitment to intercede when civilian populations face threats their own states cannot or will not abate on their own. The new dedication to atrocity prevention, buttressed by new global norms and institutions, inspired

1 I use both terms, generally consistent with whichever was contemporaneously acknowledged as official by the United Nations given the context at issue.

 | DOI:10.1163/9789004430129_018

the hope that there is a lower likelihood that an attempted atrocity campaign could succeed. Yet the failure of norms of protection-oriented intervention illustrates otherwise.

In this essay I examine the international response to the genocide against the Tutsi in Rwanda, the nature of the changes to the international atrocity prevention regime that ensued, and then the global response to the genocide against the Rohingya in Myanmar. I conclude with a discussion of why the current regime still falls short of what is necessary to prevent genocide.

2 The Global Response to Genocide in Rwanda

The global response to the crisis and genocide in Rwanda, which is covered extensively elsewhere in this volume, can be broken into three chronological segments that highlight its shortcomings. The first segment covers the eight months prior to the onset of genocide, beginning with the August 1993 signing of the internationally brokered Arusha Peace Accord between the Rwandan Patriotic Front (RPF – its army was known as the RPA) and the parties that comprised Rwanda's government – a group led by President Juvenal Habyarimana's Rwandan National Movement for Democracy and Development (MRND), but which also included several others that had been granted seats in the immediately preceding years. Those accords called for the presence of a UN peacekeeping force to provide security and prevent defections during the time required to pull together a coalition government featuring all the Accord's signatories. In October, the Security Council authorized the deployment of a 2500-troop force – about half the size that had initially been requested – which would come to be known by the acronym UNAMIR.[2] The force helped bring representatives of the various parties together for negotiations, but was unable to stem resistance to the deal. Such resistance was particularly acute from the wings of government parties (and a few not in government) known as "Hutu Power."

The second phase was the 100 days of genocide which began following the assassination of Habyarimana in April 1994. During this phase, the inability of the UNAMIR peacekeepers to protect the civilian population became the defining characteristic of the UN's mission to the country. The peacekeepers took some measures to protect Hutu and Tutsi politicians who supported the peace accord plan, as well as other civilians facing danger. However, in the face of overwhelming strength on the part of government and government-allied forces, and with little support from DPKO or the Security Council, they were unable to do so meaningfully or consistently. Two weeks after Habyarimana's assassination, with

2 The United Nations Assistance Mission In Rwanda.

attacks on Tutsis having taken thousands of lives already, the Security Council voted in Resolution 912 to evacuate all but 270 UNAMIR troops.[3]

The third phase of international involvement in Rwanda in 1994 consisted of confused re-engagement. The Security Council voted in May to authorize a re-imagined peacekeeping force, known as UNAMIR II, with more robust rules of engagement. However, disagreements of strategy, procurement snafus, and an inability to source troops from member states prevented UNAMIR II from putting boots on the ground until August. By that time, the RPA had seized Kigali, forced the genocidal interim government to flee into Zaire, and effectively ended the genocide against the Tutsis.

Meanwhile, under the authority of a Security Council Resolution[4] under Chapter VII of the UN Charter on 22 June 1994, France sent in its own troops in a venture known as Operation Turquoise. With an apparent inclination to support Hutu control of the government, Turquoise soldiers were cheered by Hutus and only acted to protect Tutsis after witnessing – to their surprise – attacks on Tutsi civilians.[5] Meanwhile, in controlling two provinces, the French operation prevented the RPA from chasing down the interim government, which had been orchestrating the genocide, and allowed the latter to make its escape.[6] Once in Zaire, the ousted government took military control over refugee camps and declared itself to be the Rwandan-government-in-exile – a source of instability for both Rwanda and Zaire that serves as the point of origin for the two-and-a-half decades of conflict in eastern Zaire/DRC that have ensued.

How did the international community get so much so wrong? Almost all of the action involved the UN, so one line of critique naturally focuses on the international organization's disfunctions. Indeed, the UN failed to appreciate the nature of the threat of violence before the genocide began and the nature of the violence itself once it did. Much of the blame lies with the DPKO, then headed by future UN Secretary-General Kofi Annan. It was the DPKO that denied the UNAMIR commander's request to act upon an informant's tip regarding genocidal preparations in January 1994, and DPKO that signed off on using UNAMIR troops and vehicles to assist in the evacuation of expatriates, abandoning large numbers of Tutsis they had been protecting, as the genocide was just getting underway.

3 In a passive rejection of Res. 912's guidance, approximately 400 UNAMIR troops actually remained. They actively engaged in civilian protection activities, which was also in defiance of the resolution.

4 S/RES/929 (1994) 22 June 1994.

5 Alison Liebhafsky Des Forges, Human Rights Watch, and International Federation of Human Rights. *"Leave none to tell the story": Genocide in Rwanda*. Vol. 3169. No. 189. (New York: Human Rights Watch, 1999) 516.

6 ibid 511–514.

Another problem involved the lack of engagement from the Secretary-General, Boutros Boutros-Ghali, who downplayed the urgency – or even the possibility – of intervening to protect civilians in Rwanda.[7] The Secretary-General's briefing to the Security Council in advance of its meeting that would lead to Resolution 912 "reflected the views of the interim government," focusing on civil war rather than genocide and blaming "unruly soldiers" for "anarchy and spontaneous slaughter".[8] Boutros-Ghali's special representative in Rwanda, Jacques-Roger Booh-Booh from Cameroon, failed to recognize the genocidal dynamics as they were unfolding. As a matter of policy, he favored a negotiation process that involved the genocidal interim regime, and presumably projected for it to maintain at least a partial hold on power. UNAMIR Commander Roméo Dallaire depicts Booh-Booh as "overwhelmed and uncertain about what to do" (265) at the outset of the genocide, and generally more concerned with trying to resurrect the peace deal than trying to protect civilians.

But the largest share of blame goes to the Security Council, which failed to authorize an adequately sized peacekeeping force in the first place. In debates about the possibility of extending UNAMIR's mandate, the Security Council portrayed UNAMIR as a privilege that Rwandans were at risk of losing – ignoring the fact that extremists were explicitly maneuvering to effect UNMIR's departure. And, of course, it was the Security Council that withdrew most of the force during the bloodiest days of the genocide.

There are three sets of reasons for the Security Council's Rwanda myopia. The first is *ignorance*, stemming from the gaps in the flow of information from the Secretariat to the Council. For example, the Security Council never discussed the situation on the ground in terms of a possible (indeed, actual) genocide as it debated Res. 912. A more thorough description would not have omitted the term. To the extent that those gaps reflected willful under-informing on the part of people like Booh-Booh and Boutros-Ghali, these are errors that originate with the Secretariat as noted above. But UNAMIR commander Dallaire has also suggested that the French, Belgian, and American embassies likely maintained their own intelligence operations, which they did not share with the UN.[9]

---

7 Boutros-Ghali, an Egyptian, has also been accused of favoring the Hutu regime in the Rwandan conflict, as Egypt sold arms to the Rwandan military after the initial RPA invasion in 1990 – when Boutros-Ghali was Egypt's Minister of Foreign Affairs. See Linda Melvern, *A People Betrayed: The Role of the West in Rwanda's Genocide* (2009) Zed Books Ltd., 2009) 38–9.

8 ibid 192.

9 Roméo Dallaire, *Shake Hands with the Devil: The Failure of Humanity in Rwanda* (Vintage Canada 2004) 148; Daniela Kroslak, *The French Betrayal of Rwanda* (Indiana University Press 2008) 184.

The second set of reasons involve *deception* within the Security Council. The primary culprit is the somewhat anomalous occurrence that Rwanda held a non-permanent seat on the Council in 1994. The Rwandan representative, Jean-Damscene Bizimana had been appointed by the Habyarimana regime and served at the behest of the genocidal interim government after Habyarimana was killed. He was treated with deference and allowed to present an account of the situation in Rwanda as a conflict initiated by the RPA from outside the country.[10] In fact, Bizimana called for the strengthening of UNAMIR, provided its focus would be on helping to protect the interim government from the RPA.[11] While the rest of the Security Council did not endorse the implications of this perspective – i.e., a call for support to the interim government and perhaps sanctions against states seen as assisting the RPA – there is little in the public record that indicates anyone on the Council directly rebuked or censured the Rwandan representative.[12] France may also have been somewhat deceptive, allegedly coaching Boutros-Ghali to avoid making a case for a more robust involvement,[13] and "doggedly (holding) the line that only a ceasefire" – and not intervention or action taken against the perpetrators of the unfolding genocide – "would end the conflict in Rwanda.[14]

The final, and most consequential set of explanations for the Security Council's behavior is *cowardice*. The Security Council kept UNAMIR weak and later ordered UNAMIR's retreat because it was scared: scared of taking casualties, scared of losing, scared of bad publicity. Barnett writes that "when the Secretariat proceeded to reject the possibility of intervention at the outset of the crisis, it cited not only pragmatics, but also principles and the need to use peacekeepers only when there was a workable ceasefire"[15] and that "[k]nowing the [Security] Council was in no mood to authorize reinforcements, the Secretariat might have concluded that the only way to protect the peacekeepers was to remove them from danger."[16] After ten Belgian peacekeepers were killed by Rwandan forces shortly Habyarimana's

10 Linda Melvern *Conspiracy to Murder: The Rwandan Genocide* (Verso Books 2004) 202.

11 Arthur Jay Klinghoffer, *The International Dimension of Genocide in Rwanda* (New York University Press 1998) 51–2.

12 Samantha Power, "Bystanders to genocide." *Atlantic Monthly* 288.2 (2001) 102. See also Dallaire (n 9) 195.

13 Michael Barnett, *Eyewitness to a Genocide: The United Nations and Rwanda* (Cornell University Press 2002) 121; Kroslak (n 9) 186–9.

14 Kroslak (n 9) 194.

15 Barnett (n 13) 116.

16 Ibid 122.

assassination, Belgium unilaterally withdrew the rest of its contingent within UNAMIR. Belgian officials lobbied Belgium's allies, included the United States, to follow suit with the rest of the force. The United States, still feeling the burn from the deaths of 19 American soldiers working with UN peacekeepers in Somalia the previous October, eagerly agreed. There was practically zero support among the P5 for more robust UN peacekeeping engagement. Russia and China were tepid, at best, towards the very concept of multilateral interventions, wary of allowing operations that seemingly allowed Western powers to challenge global norms of sovereignty. For their part, the U.S. and the U.K. had little tolerance for putting lives (or even resources) at risk, and France overly inclined to trust Hutu political power (if not Hutu Power more specifically).

3 The Global Response to the UN's Failure in Rwanda

In the wake of the genocide against the Tutsi in Rwanda, as well as the murder of approximately 8000 Bosnian men who had nominally been under UN protection in Srebrenica, the United Nations and several national governments reconsidered their approach to atrocity prevention. The most potentially consequential reforms took place at the multilateral level, within or centered on the United Nations. Now Secretary-General, Kofi Annan created the Office of the Special Adviser for the Prevention of Genocide, a body that would operate within the Secretariat with access to the Security Council, charged with making sure the possibility and risk of genocide are not overlooked in the course of UN policy-making. The point of the new office was to ensure that UN decision-makers could not claim ignorance of genocide risks in a given situation, as well as to identify (and ideally preempt situations that might have the potential to develop more acute genocide risks.

Annan also convened the International Commission on Intervention and State Sovereignty (ICISS), which developed the concept of "Responsibility to Protect" (R2P) to guide decision-making when a risk of genocide and other atrocities are present. Specifically, as articulated in the 2005 World Summit Outcome document and later elaborated upon in an annual series of Secretary-General's reports, the doctrine establishes 1) that states have a responsibility to protect all populations under their control from genocide, crimes against humanity, war crimes, and ethnic cleansing; but 2) that when states abjure that responsibility, the international community has a responsibility to do what it can – whether through intervention or otherwise – to protect populations that are at risk of facing atrocity.[17] To avoid a situation in which powerful countries twist the doctrine to attain for themselves a right to intervene, the elaboration of the doctrine specifies that the Security Council bears primary responsibility for identifying atrocity risk situations wherein the international community has a responsibility to become involved. The U.N. General Assembly is granted an underspecified measure of secondary responsibility should the Security Council become paralyzed.[18]

Regional organizations could serve as delegates for R2P actions so long as they are coordinated with the U.N. In the late 1990s and throughout the 2000s, regional organizations also made an effort to be more ready to confront and stop atrocities. Most notably, the Organization for African Unity, notoriously a "dictator's club" at which sovereignty concerns invariably rose above all others, was refashioned as the African Union. The new version's charter explicitly gave the organization the right to intervene in its own members' affairs when there might be a risk of genocide, war crimes, or crimes against humanity. The Association of Southeast Asian Nations (ASEAN) remains more outwardly focused on preserving and promoting the sovereignty of its members, but even its 2007 charter features the clause "ADHERING to the principles of democracy, the rule of law and good governance, respect for and protection of human rights and fundamental freedoms."[19] Finally, many national governments pursued reforms designed to make them responsive to mass atrocity risks abroad. Several established "R2P Focal Points" – essentially offices within national governments mirroring the role of the Office of the Special Advisor for the Prevention of Genocide within the UN. In 2011, the United States established the Atrocities Prevention Board, similarly designed to serve as an interagency watchdog that would ensure that national policy was undertaken with an awareness of the attendant consequences for atrocity risks.

In theory, these reforms should have led for a more robust response to mass atrocities in what was hoped would be a strictly hypothetical analogous situation to Rwanda. The international environment would appear to be have

17 These two points comprise the first and third "pillars," respectively, of what is known as the "three pillars" approach to the doctrine. The second pillar states that the international community must help states realize their own responsibility to protect through aid, intelligence, and other forms of assistance. See United Nations Secretary General, UN Document A/63/677 (2009).

18 United Nations Secretary General (n 17) 27.

19 Association of South-East Asian States [ASEAN]. "Charter of the Association of South-East Asian States." <https://www.asean.org/uploads/archive/21069.pdf> accessed July 15, 2019.

changed substantially between 1994 and 2017. The struggles of meeting that ideal became apparent repeatedly in the 2010s (by which the new regime was, at least on paper, in place). In case after case – most notably including Libya, Côte d'Ivoire, South Sudan, Burundi, Iraq, Syria – the application of the R2P doctrine proved to be anything but straightforward, and amid some relative successes, more frequently an outright failure. The persecution – and genocide – of Myanmar's Rohingya population illustrates most starkly the shortcomings of the post-Rwanda atrocity prevention regime.

4 The Responses of the United Nations to Genocide in Myanmar

As in Rwanda, the conflict that spiraled into genocide had been percolating for several years (even discounting the notional expulsion of the Tutsi and Rohingya, respectively, that had been ongoing for decades). In Rwanda, "percolation" took the form of the civil war between the RPA and the government, which began in 1990. In Myanmar, it was the periodic episodes of pogrom-like anti-Rohingya violence that erupted in June 2012 and October 2016 (following several more distant precedents, 1978–9 and 1991–2).[20] In 2017 in Myanmar, though, unlike Rwanda in 1994, there was no peacekeeping force on the ground when genocidal violence erupted in Rakhine state. As a result, the most obvious lesson from Rwanda – that peacekeepers on the ground should intercede and not retreat – had no application. Instead, the international community (primarily in the form of the UN) struggled to gain access to the arena of persecution and lacked leverage over the government of Myanmar. R2P, while invoked, thus faced a heavy lift in Myanmar. In the end, it can scarcely be said to have been acted upon, raising the issue of whether the post-Rwanda anti-atrocity regime has any heft at all.

To understand the international community's passivity at the point of the 2017 violence, it is helpful to note the UN's reaction to the 2012 episode. In 2012, attacks on civilians led to as many as 100,000 Rohingya to flee their home villages and take refuge in displacement camps.[21] At the time, several UN officials

---

20 Cheung S, "Migration Control and the Solutions Impasse in South and Southeast Asia: Implications from the Rohingya Experience" (2011) 25 Journal of Refugee Studies 50, 51–2.

21 Alina Lindblom, Elizabeth Marsh, Tasnim Motala, and Katherine Munyan, "Persecution of the Rohingya Muslims: Is Genocide Occurring in Myanmar's Rakhine State," October 2015, *Allard K. Lowenstein International Human Rights Clinic at Yale Law for Fortify Rights* <https://law.yale.edu/system/files/documents/pdf/Clinics/fortifyrights.pdf> accessed 16 July 2019, 19–20.

raised concerns about the violence, and especially the prospects that ethnic cleansing and torture might be occurring.[22] ReliefWeb documents 14 different occasions when the UN's special rapporteur on the human rights situation in Myanmar, Tomás Ojea Quintana, called out the Myanmar government on human rights concerns, and 15 occasions when New York-based UN statements (whether from the High Commissioner for Human Rights, the Special Advisor for the Prevention of Genocide, the General Assembly, or a report of the Secretary-General) questioned or condemned the violence against the Rohingya between June 2012 and January 2014.[23]

UN scrutiny led the government of Myanmar to develop a counter-offensive, of sorts, on the ground. It began to target international organizations, including the UN and non-governmental organizations. At least 5 UN employees and nine NGO workers were jailed in 2012 on charges of fomenting ethnic hatred.[24] Human Rights Watch reported that after the June 2012 flare-up had prompted an evacuation, the government refused to permit officials back into the region.[25] Meanwhile, local animus towards the UN hindered the delivery of badly needed humanitarian relief. A Human Rights Watch report observed

> …widespread animosity among the local Arakanese community towards UN agencies and international humanitarian organizations providing relief to displaced Muslim populations. Local Arakanese, in some cases led by Buddhist monks, have publicly protested against and physically obstructed aid to Rohingya, issued threats against aid workers, and distributed pamphlets calling on the Arakanese community to attack staff and supporters of specific organizations.[26]

The threats to the UN, initially made to the agencies and officials active in Rakhine state, soon had the effect that security forces and the government had presumably desired: a more pliant UN that seemed reluctant to raise concerns about violence against the Rohingya. By 2013, in-country UN officials were avoiding pressing the government on human rights issues related to the

22 Human Rights Watch, "All You Can Do Is Pray." April 2013 <https://www.hrw.org/report/2013/04/22/all-you-can-do-pray/crimes-against-humanity-and-ethnic-cleansing-rohingya-muslims> accessed 16 July 2019.

23 "Timeline of International Response to the Situation of the Rohingya and Anti-Muslim Violence in Burma/Myanmar," Undated <https://reliefweb.int/sites/reliefweb.int/files/resources/timeline-of-international-response-to-burma-9.pdf> accessed 15 July 2019.

24 Human Rights Watch (n 22).

25 ibid.

26 ibid.

persecution of the Rohingya. Aung San Suu Kyi had only recently risen to power, and her international backers feared that her hold on power was tenuous. Prominent diplomats inside and outside the UN feared that to challenge her on human rights would weaken her, leading the military to resume full control over the state.

Ultimately 'constructive engagement' meant 'willful ignorance.' Charles Petrie, author of the UN's highly critical self-examination of its inaction and accommodation of an atrocity-committing force in Sri Lanka, diplomatically expressed concern that similar dynamics were in play in Myanmar after 2012:

> I think the key lesson for Myanmar from Sri Lanka is the lack of a focal point. A senior level focal point addressing the situation in Myanmar in its totality – the political, the human rights, the humanitarian and the development. It remains diffuse. And that means over the last few years there have been almost competing agendas.[27]

An internal UN document reportedly concluded that "the UN team in Myanmar [was found to be] 'glaringly dysfunctional' with 'strong tensions' between different parts of the UN system."[28] Officials concerned with human rights issues effectively had to do battle with officials focused on democracy (who desired to coddle the new democratically elected regime) and development (who saw a good relationship with the state as essential for economic planning and results). The resident co-ordinator, Renata Lok-Dessallien was left to sort out the competing priorities, and seemed to have chosen the global story of democratic revival over what must have been deemed a relatively local one of ethnic cleansing. Per a BBC journalist, "UN officials who did try to insist on addressing human rights issues were "humiliated" and "isolated."[29] According to one staffer, "publicly talking about the Rohingya became almost taboo. Many UN press releases about Rakhine avoided using the word completely," which played directly into the government stance that it would be impossible to persecute the Rohingya since – in its eyes – the category does not meaningfully exist.[30]

By August 2017, when violence targeting the Rohingya population returned with a much greater intensity than at any previous point, the UN was more

27 Quoted in Fisher J, "UN Failures on Rohingya Revealed" (*BBC News*, September 28, 2017) <https://www.bbc.com/news/world-asia-41420973> accessed July 16, 2019.

28 Fisher J, "Myanmar: Top UN Official in Myanmar to Be Changed" (*BBC News*, June 13, 2017) <https://www.bbc.com/news/world-asia-40256083> accessed July 16, 2019.

29 Fisher ("UN Failures . . ." (fn 27)).

30 ibid.

prepared to challenge the Myanmar government directly. The government, however, was also more prepared, taking several steps to prevent the United Nations from bearing witness to the violence. Following the October 2016 spate of violence, the UN Human Rights Commission authorized a three-person fact-finding mission (FFM). The government denied entry visas to the FFM, forcing its member to conduct research primarily from refugee camps in neighboring countries. Yanghee Lee had replaced Quintana as the special rapporteur, but was denied access to crucial communities in July of 2017 and then to the country as a whole in January 2018. The government requested that she be replaced.[31]

Lee, following Quintana before her, unequivocally condemned the Myanmar government for its inability to prevent (and possible complicity in) the violence against Rohingya in Rakhine state. The FFM strongly condemned the military's role in the violence, suggested that the legal criteria for classification of the violence as genocide against the Rohingya had likely been met, and called for further Security Council action, including the recommendation of an International Criminal Court investigation.

Back in New York, UN officials also ratcheted up their condemnations of Myanmar's treatment of the Rohingya, perhaps reflecting some measure of internalization of the lessons of Rwanda. In October 2017, not long after the initial outbreak of violence against the Rohingya that year, the Special Advisors for Genocide and R2P declared that "the Government of Myanmar has failed to meet its obligations under international law and primary responsibility to protect the Rohingya population from atrocity crimes."[32] In March 2018, the Special Adviser for the Prevention of Genocide, Adama Dieng – who had also been denied access to Myanmar proper – declared that

> [i]nternational crimes were committed in Myanmar. Rohingya Muslims have been killed, tortured, raped, burnt alive and humiliated, solely because of who they are. All the information I have received indicates that the intent of the perpetrators was to cleanse northern Rakhine state of

31 Schlein L, "Investigator: UN, International Community Fail to Hold Myanmar Accountable for Crimes Against Rohingya" (*Voice of America*) <https://www.voanews.com/east-asia-pacific/investigator-un-international-community-fail-hold-myanmar-accountable-crimes> accessed July 17, 2019.

32 Adama Dieng and Ivan Simonovic, "Statement by Adama Dieng, United Nations Special Adviser on the Prevention of Genocide and Ivan Simonovic, United Nations Special Adviser on the Responsibility to Protect, on the situation in northern Rakhine state, Myanmar," October 19, 2017 <https://www.un.org/en/genocideprevention/documents/201710 19%20Statement_Myanmar_Final.pdf> accessed 15 July 2019.

> their existence, possibly even to destroy the Rohingya as such, which, if proven, would constitute the crime of genocide.[33]

Despite also having been denied access to Myanmar, the FFM completed its work, and came to a similar conclusion. Its September 2018 report called for the Security Council to refer the situation, and specifically the roles played by several military officials, to the International Criminal Court, arguing that the violence against the Rohingya met the criteria for the commission of genocide (as well as those for war crimes and crimes against humanity). One of the FFM commissioners added that as of May 2019, there remained "no evidence that the Myanmar government is acting in good faith to resolve the crisis."[34]

To an extent, the lessons of Rwanda had been applied: concerned parties authorized observers on the ground to assess the existence and extent of atrocities. Those observers did not shy away from labeling the violence as atrocities for which the predominant share of the responsibility lay with the military and its government and civilian allies. The Secretary-General himself was completely aware of the atrocity dimensions of the conflict. These reports and statements illustrate the changes in the global atrocity prevention regime since the genocides in Rwanda and Srebrenica. Designated actors within the UN system (and also outside, to take into account the atrocity monitoring NGOs like the Global Centre for the Responsibility to Protect that had also called for the application of R2P[35]) raised the possibility that atrocity crimes were taking place, and that appropriate measures ought to be pursued to suppress them.

However, beyond that point, the "new" atrocity prevention regime was unable to differentiate itself from the old one. While strong words were spoken, strong actions were not taken. Aside from supporting refugee camps in neighboring countries, the UN undertook no concrete action to protect the Rohingya

---

33 Adama Dieng "Statement by Adama Dieng, United Nations Special Adviser on the Prevention of Genocide, on his visit to Bangladesh to assess the situation of Rohingya refugees from Myanmar," March 13, 2018 <http://www.un.org/en/genocideprevention/documents/2018-03-13%20Statement_visit%20Rohingya%20Bangladesh_FINAL.pdf> accessed 15 July 2019.

34 "UN Independent International Fact-Finding Mission on Myanmar Urges Financial Isolation of Myanmar Military" (*OHCHR*) <https://www.ohchr.org/EN/NewsEvents/Pages/DisplayNews.aspx?NewsID=24608&LangID=E> accessed July 17, 2019.

35 See the list of organizations that signed on to the Global Center's letter of concern in December 2017 (Global Center for the Responsibility to Protect, "Joint Appeal to the UN Security Council to Act on Myanmar's Rohingya Crisis," 12 December 2017, <http://www.globalr2p.org/publications/620> accessed 15 July 2019.

from genocidal persecution – even as the failure of the Myanmar government to "protect" its population became manifest.

Blame for this lies at the level of the Security Council and with the member states who have prevented a more robust response. Following the outbreak of violence in August 2017, the Security Council has issued a sum total of one presidential statement and – despite the calls for action from other UN bodies – zero resolutions addressing the situation in Myanmar. The Presidential Statement, from November 2017, notes the Council's concern with the outbreak of violence, the blame for which it allocates to both ARSA and state security forces. The report takes pains to "[reaffirm] its strong commitment to the sovereignty, political independence, territorial integrity, and unity of Myanmar" and emphasizes (per the fundamental tenet of the R2P doctrine) that the state bears primary responsibility for protecting its own citizens. However, it makes no mention of any path towards intervening should the state continue (at that point) to fail to exercise its responsibilities.

The United States and the United Kingdom pressed for action to follow up on the Special Advisors' and FFM's conclusions. In December 2018, a resolution framed around stipulating a process for the return of Rohingya refugees included language that would advance the prospects of holding those responsible for atrocity crimes accountable – presumably via some process invoking international criminal justice. China and the Russian Federation expressed their opposition, however, and the resolution never came to a vote.[36]

Similarly, when the Security Council devoted its agenda to the Rohingya crisis for one day in February 2019 – a year-and-a-half after the breakout of genocidal violence – no resolution and no meaningful action came out of it. (Although the Council did agree to investigate whether UN offices had been too accommodating of the Myanmar regime from 2012 to 2017). While several Security Council members called for an international accountability mechanism, and at least one (Belgium) echoed the FFM's effective charge of genocide, no resolution came up for a vote. Instead, the focus on the UN's attention became pledging to assist Bangladesh in managing the burden of hosting

---

36 Nichols M, "U.N. Security Council Mulls Myanmar Action; Russia, China Boycott…" (*Reuters*, December 17, 2018) <https://www.reuters.com/article/us-myanmar-rohingya-un/u-n-security-council-mulls-myanmar-action-russia-china-boycott-talks-idUSKBN1OG2CJ> accessed July 17, 2019; See also Chin J, "Call for Rohingya Genocide Prosecution to Deepen China's Support of Myanmar" (*The Wall Street Journal,* August 29, 2018) <https://www.wsj.com/articles/call-for-rohingya-genocide-prosecution-lets-china-rush-to-myanmars-rescue-1535536804> accessed July 17, 2019.

almost 800,000 Rohingya refugees, with little attention paid to the role or responsibility of the government of Myanmar.[37]

The veto is clearly at the heart of the problem. In situations where a veto was not applicable – that is, procedural votes rather than actual resolutions – actions in the spirit of R2P have gone through. China and Russia tried unsuccessfully to block the FFM chair Mazuki Darusman from addressing the Security Council in October 2018, when the decision was made via an un-vetoable procedural vote.[38] Again, in December 2018, a majority vote preserved funding for the UN Human Rights Council's work on Myanmar. Yet on matters involving a direct (as opposed to merely rhetorical) challenge to Myanmar's sovereignty, no progress could be made. Yanghee Lee, the United Nations special rapporteur on human rights in Myanmar, expressed her frustration on the failure to pursue accountability for the perpetrators of atrocity crimes in an interview with Radio Free Asia:

> The roadblock is, of course, the U.N. Security Council. China is backing the Myanmar government [by] objecting to a Security Council resolution for referral to the ICC [International Criminal Court]. China and Russia often work together in this kind of situation, which I think is shameful, so that the Security Council cannot move beyond this. I really wish China and Russia would revisit their decision.[39]

Whether they are protecting sovereignty at a conceptual level or promoting economic interests at a national one, China and the Russian Federation have been able to keep the UN's critiques of the Myanmar state and security forces at the level of rhetoric, without consequences for the government or for the government's approach to resolving what it sees as its "'Bengali' problem."

In sum, then, the core lesson from the UN's failure in Rwanda was *not* learned: that the current structure of the Security Council, which remains unaltered since 1994 – indeed since the UN's inception in 1944 – is unlikely to

37 "Crisis in Rakhine State, Violence Could Derail Gains in Myanmar's Peace Process, Special Envoy Warns Security Council, Calling for Unimpeded Humanitarian Access | Meetings Coverage and Press Releases" (*United Nations*) <https://www.un.org/press/en/2019/sc13727.doc.htm> accessed July 16, 2019.

38 Simon Adams, "'If not now, when?': The Responsibility to Protect, the Fate of the Rohingya and the Future of Human Rights." January 2019 (*Global Centre for the Responsibility to Protect Occasional Paper Series No. 8*) 18.

39 Staff RFA, "Interview: 'I Really Think That Myanmar Is Going Down a Dark Path Now'" (*Radio Free Asia,* July 2, 2019) <https://www.rfa.org/english/news/myanmar/interview-myanmar-going-down-a-dark-path-06272019163917.html> accessed July 17, 2019.

authorize either a protection-driven intervention mission or a punitive procedure. So long as the country in question can claim a measure of friendship with one of the five veto-holding permanent members, it will neither be prevented from nor held accountable for the commission of atrocity crimes. As much as the R2P framework attempts to spell out criteria and procedures for intervention, it does nothing to address the issue of will. It fails to produce a case for a country to subsume even relatively minor national interests to a logic of joint collective action in the name of civilian protection.

What, at this point, can be done? Critics seem to be increasingly frustrated with the principle of R2P, noting how its establishment appears to have failed to have abated the pace of atrocities being perpetrated across the globe. This view is unduly skeptical: R2P has indeed been invoked widely, and may deserve some credit for establishing a basis for avoiding or punishing atrocity crimes in several cases. And some of the criticism of R2P may be offered disingenuously, by opponents of the idea of intervention for civilian protection seeking to tar the best instrument for justifying that idea as ineffectual.

In reality, there is no alternative to R2P as an idea, save for giving up upon the enterprise of protecting civilians from atrocities altogether. What is needed are refinements to the doctrine that enable it to become more effectively self-actualizing. A greater role for the General Assembly, or an iron-clad commitment to abjure the use of the veto in atrocity cases could serve as a start. Certainly, in the latter case, opponents could still try to prevent the declaration of a given case as one in which atrocity concerns are invoked. But even then, objection would mean going on record as such in the face of specific bodies of evidence establishing the risk or existence of atrocity. For a Security Council power to do so would entail a potentially higher political cost than it would face from undermining an anti-atrocity effort at a procedural level, or pre-empting a vote on an R2P action to be negotiated within Council deliberations.

Tweaking the costs and payoffs for different courses of action – or of inaction – is an imprecise and remote strategy for improving powerful countries' buy-in to the responsibility to protect. Roméo Dallaire, seeking to find a path to more responsiveness in the face of atrocity threats, told an audience at the United States Holocaust Memorial Museum in 2002 (paraphrasing Kofi Annan), "we have entered a millennium where in fact humanity, the human race, is to become the dominant factor, not the self-interest."[40] Yet close to two

40 (*United States Holocaust Memorial Museum*) <https://www.ushmm.org/confront-genocide/speakers-and-events/all-speakers-and-events/a-good-man-in-hell-general-romeo-dallaire-and-the-rwanda-genocide> accessed July 17, 2019.

decades of the Responsibility to Protect era tells us that neither the new millennium nor the new doctrine has been sufficient to realize such an idealistic vision. Since neither can be discarded, proponents of a more robust atrocity prevention regime must chip away, slowly but steadily, at the sovereignty's vice grip on collective decision-making in times of atrocity threats.

CHAPTER 17

Humanitarian Intervention and R2P

Stacey Henderson

1 Introduction

The Rwandan genocide, which saw the international community fail to prevent or halt the slaughter of 800,000 people over a 100 day period,[1] was a catalyst for significant international reform, both political and legal. Among those reforms was the development and adoption of the concept of the responsibility to protect ('R2P'), the genesis of which is found in the tragedy of inaction by the international community when faced with impending genocide.

In the lead up to the Rwandan genocide, some permanent members of the Security Council 'knew that officials connected to the then government were planning genocide; UN forces were present, though not in sufficient number at the outset; and credible strategies were available to prevent, or at least greatly mitigate, the slaughter which followed'.[2] The international community chose to stand idle, rather than respond. In the aftermath of the genocide, 'many African peoples concluded that, for all the rhetoric about the universality of human rights, some human lives end up mattering a great deal less to the international community than others'.[3]

2 Rallying Call

In 2000, at least 133 States issued individual or joint statements rejecting the legality of 'the so-called 'right' of humanitarian intervention, which has no legal basis in the United Nations Charter or in the general principles of international law'.[4] Despite this, constructions of Rwanda as a moral failure in public debate, mass media, and apologies, led to a re-examination of the

1 'Rwanda: How the Genocide Happened' BBC Online (17 May 2011) <https://www.bbc.com/news/world-africa-13431486> accessed 13 May 2019.

2 International Commission on Intervention and State Sovereignty ('ICISS'), *The Responsibility to Protect* (IDRC, 2001) 1.

3 ibid.

4 Group of 77, *Declaration of the South Summit* (2000) [54]; Non-Aligned Movement, *Final Document of the XIII Ministerial Conference* (2000) [263].

 | DOI:10.1163/9789004430129_019

conceptualisations of sovereignty and the principle of non-intervention, and ultimately to the development of R2P.[5]

Then UN Secretary-General Kofi Annan highlighted the failures of the international community to act in Rwanda and Kosovo, and challenged the international community to 'find common ground in upholding the principles of the Charter, and acting in defence of our common humanity'.[6] He asked:

> if humanitarian intervention is, indeed, an unacceptable assault on sovereignty, how should we respond to a Rwanda, to a Srebrenica – to gross and systematic violations of human rights that offend every precept of our common humanity?
>
> We confront a real dilemma. Few would disagree that both the defence of humanity and the defence of sovereignty are principles that must be supported. Alas, that does not tell us which principle should prevail when they are in conflict.[7]

By 2005, the international community had an answer – at the conceptual level – in the form of R2P.

3 The ICISS Formulation of R2P

The International Commission on Intervention and State Sovereignty ('ICISS'), sponsored by the Canadian government, was charged with

> exploring the whole range of legal, moral, operational and political questions rolled up in this debate, in order to consult with the widest possible range of opinion around the world, and to generate a report that would help the Secretary-General and other concerned parties find some new common ground.[8]

The ICISS report, entitled *The Responsibility to Protect* was released in December 2001 in the aftermath of the 9/11 terror attacks. Unsurprisingly, it

5 Wesley Widmaier & Luke Glanville, 'The benefits of norm ambiguity: constructing the responsibility to protect across Rwanda, Iraq and Libya' (2015) 21 *Contemporary Politics* 367, 368.

6 ICISS (n 2) 2.

7 Kofi Annan, *We the Peoples: The Role of theUNin the 21st Century* (*Millennium Report of the Secretary-General*) (UNDPI, 2000) 48.

8 ICISS (n 2) vii.

received little attention when it was released, given that the focus of the international community was then firmly on national security and protection from global terrorism. However, the ICISS report, which provided a framework of policy tools designed to prevent the recurrence of mass atrocities, found a champion in then UN Secretary-General Kofi Annan.

The ICISS report sought to change the focus of the debate surrounding humanitarian intervention from the rights of States to considerations of human security and human rights. The ICISS report noted, by reference to the Rwandan genocide, that too often the problem is a lack of 'analysis and translation [of data] into policy prescription, and the will to do something about it'.[9] The report drew upon the reconceptualization of sovereignty as responsibility, emphasising that

> [t]hinking of sovereignty as responsibility…has a threefold significance. First, it implies that the [S]tate authorities are responsible for the functions of protecting the safety and lives of citizens and promotion of their welfare. Secondly, it suggests that the national political authorities are responsible to the citizens internally and to the international community through the UN. And, thirdly, it means that the agents of the [S]tate are responsible for their actions; that is to say, they are accountable for their acts of commission and omission.[10]

The ICISS approach conceptualised sovereignty as incorporating legal responsibility, not simply political accountability to be enforced by voters in elections or the international community through diplomacy.[11]

Changing the language from a discussion about 'rights' to one about 'responsibility', as proposed by the ICISS report, had three main benefits.[12] First, the change in focus meant that issues are evaluated from the point of view of those in need of protection, rather than those considering intervention. Second, the primary responsibility to protect its population rests with the State concerned – only if that State is unable or unwilling to fulfil its responsibility to protect, or is itself the perpetrator, should the international community take the responsibility in its place. Third, R2P is an umbrella concept, not restricted to military intervention, encompassing the responsibility to react, the responsibility to prevent, and the responsibility to rebuild.

---

9 ibid 21.

10 ibid 13.

11 Anne Peters, 'Humanity as the A and Ω of Sovereignty' (2009) 20 *EJIL* 513, 526.

12 Gareth Evans & Mohamed Sahnoun, 'The Responsibility to Protect' (2002) 81 *Foreign Affairs* 6, 99.

3.1 *The Primary Duty*

R2P placed the primary duty on States to protect their own populations from atrocity crimes.[13] The ICISS report noted

> The defence of state sovereignty, by even its strongest supporters, does not include any claim of the unlimited power of a state to do what it wants to its own people….It is acknowledged that sovereignty implies a dual responsibility: externally – to respect the sovereignty of other states, and internally, to respect the dignity and basic rights of all the people within the state. In international human rights covenants, in UN practice, and in state practice itself, sovereignty is now understood as embracing this dual responsibility. Sovereignty as responsibility has become the minimum content of good international citizenship.[14]

The ICISS report was widely praised for 'preserving the integrity of the principle of state sovereignty'.[15]

3.2 *The Secondary Duty*

More controversially, the ICISS report provided that where a State is unable or unwilling, either through deliberate inaction or inability, to carry out its primary duty to protect its population, the international community has a secondary duty to step in and protect populations at risk. Indeed, it has been claimed that '[t]his foundational concept – that the State owes a duty its citizens, the neglect or flouting of which opens the door to international intervention – is the core'[16] of R2P.

The ICISS report suggested that intervention by the international community under R2P could only occur where six criteria were satisfied:

1 the 'just cause' threshold: civilians must be faced with the threat of serious and irreparable harm, either large scale loss of life or large scale ethnic cleansing, which is the product of deliberate State action, State neglect, inability to act or State failure;[17]

2 the four precautionary principles:

---

13 ICISS (n 2) xi.

14 ibid 8.

15 Max Matthews, 'Tracking the Emergence of a New International Norm: The Responsibility to Protect and the Crisis in Darfur' (2008) 31 *BCIntl&CompLRev* 137, 140.

16 Tessa Davis, 'Taking International Law At Its Word And Its Spirit: Re-Envisioning Responsibility To Protect As A Binding Principle Of International Law' (2010) 38 *Fla St UL Rev* 883, 893.

17 ICISS (n 2) xii & 32–35.

a. right intention – the primary purpose must be to halt or avert human suffering;[18]
b. last resort – every non-military option for the prevention or peaceful resolution of the crisis must have been explored with reasonable grounds for believing lesser measures would not have succeeded;[19]
c. proportional means – the scale, duration and intensity of the planned military intervention should be the minimum necessary to secure the defined objective of protecting civilians;[20] and
d. reasonable prospects – there must be a reasonable chance of success in halting or averting the suffering that has justified intervention; the consequences of action must be no worse than the consequences of inaction;[21]

3 the requirement of right authority: Security Council authorisation should, in all cases, be sought prior to any military intervention being carried out.[22] Only if the Security Council fails to act should the matter proceed either to an emergency special session of the General Assembly under the Uniting for Peace procedure or to action within an area of jurisdiction by regional or subregional organisations under Chapter VIII of the UN Charter subject to their seeking subsequent authorisation from the Security Council.[23] The ICISS report specifically noted that the Rwandan genocide might conceivably have been a case where the General Assembly could have achieved the required two-thirds majority of votes in favour of action under the Uniting for Peace procedure.[24]

Several commentators have argued that the ICISS formulation of R2P and the six criteria are nothing more than a modern restatement of Saint Augustine's Just War theory of the 400s.[25]

18 ibid xii & 35–36.
19 ibid xii & 36–37.
20 ibid xii & 37.
21 ibid.
22 ibid xii–xiii & 49–55.
23 ibid 53–55.
24 ibid 53.
25 Rebecca Hamilton, 'The Responsibility to Protect: From Document to Doctrine – But What of Implementation?' (2006) 19 *HarvHumRtsJ* 289, 292; Susan Breau, *The Responsibility to Protect in International Law: An emerging paradigm shift* (Routledge, 2016) 11–12; Ivan Shearer, 'A Revival of the Just War Theory?' in Michael Schmitt and Jelena Pejic (eds), *International Law and Armed Conflict: Exploring the Faultlines* (Koninkliike Brill BV, 2007) 3; Gareth Evans, 'From Humanitarian Intervention to the Responsibility to Protect' (2006) 24 *WisIntlLJ* 703, 710.

To the disappointment of many, these six criteria or indeed any set of guiding principles, were absent from the agreed version of R2P adopted at the 2005 UN World Summit (discussed below). Evans explains the absence of the six criteria from the 2005 *World Summit Outcome* document as follows:

> they fell at the last hurdle: caught, in effect, in a pincer movement between, on the one hand, the hostility of the United States, which very definitely did not want any guidelines adopted that could limit in any way the Security Council's – and by extension, its own – complete freedom to make judgments on a case-by-case basis, and on the other, the hostility of a number of developing countries who argued, with more passion than intelligibility, that to have a set of principles purporting to limit the use of force to exceptional, highly defensible cases was somehow to encourage it.[26]

Importantly, the secondary duty, even in its original formulation, has always been about more than military intervention. R2P is not a binary choice between the international community using force and doing nothing, as happened in Rwanda. The ICISS report confirmed the 'need for a range of escalating non-coercive and coercive measures to prevent or halt' atrocity crimes, with military intervention being reserved as a remedy of last resort.[27] The report expressly noted that

> we are also very much concerned with alternatives to military action, including all forms of preventive measures, and coercive intervention measures – sanctions and criminal prosecutions – falling short of military intervention. Such coercive measures are discussed in this report in two contexts: their threatened use as a preventive measure, designed to avoid the need for military intervention arising; and their actual use as a restrictive measure, but as an alternative to military force.[28]

Amongst other measures, the ICISS report specifically discussed the use of targeted sanctions, including asset freezes, arms embargoes and travel bans,[29] withdrawal of investment or aid,[30] suspension of membership or expulsion

26 Evans (n 25) 716–717.
27 ICISS (n 2) 29–31 & 36–37.
28 ibid 8.
29 ibid 29–30.
30 ibid 23.

from international or regional bodies,[31] and ending military cooperation and training programmes. The ICISS report made clear its view that while approval was required for military intervention, States did not need to seek approval from the Security Council when using measures less than force.[32] The ICISS report stated that '[t]he most compelling task now is to work to ensure that when the call goes out to the community of states for action, that call will be answered. There must never again be mass killing or ethnic cleansing. There must be no more Rwandas'.[33]

4 The Journey to Adoption of R2P at the 2005 UN World Summit

R2P as a concept was embraced and developed in two UN reports in 2004 and 2005. The 2004 report by the Secretary-General's High Level Panel on Threats, Challenges and Change endorsed the ideas and principles of R2P from the ICISS report.[34] The report stated that:

> We endorse the emerging norm that there is a collective international responsibility to protect, exercisable by the Security Council authorizing military intervention as a last resort, in the event of genocide and other large scale killing, ethnic cleansing, or serious violations of international humanitarian law which sovereign governments have proved powerless or unwilling to prevent.[35]

The report noted that the 'biggest failures of the United Nations in civil violence have been in halting ethnic cleansing and genocide'.[36] The report explicitly identified the failure of Secretariat officers to provide the Security Council with early warning of the impending Rwandan genocide,[37] the withdrawal of peacekeepers when the killings began,[38] and the slow response to the unfolding Rwandan genocide.[39] By affirming the status of R2P and the secondary

31 ibid 31.
32 ibid xii–xiii & 49–55.
33 ibid 70.
34 *A More Secure World: Our Shared Responsibility – Report of the Secretary-General's High Level Panel on Threats, Challenges and Change* (2004) UN Doc A/59/565.
35 ibid [203].
36 ibid [87].
37 ibid.
38 ibid.
39 ibid [41].

duty of the international community as an emerging norm, the report increased the international credibility of R2P as a concept. The report also firmly grounded R2P in existing obligations under the *Genocide Convention*,[40] which reinforced R2P as 'a valid development in international law, rather than a figment of its imagination'.[41]

Building on this groundwork, the Secretary-General's 2005 report expressly asked States not to simply recognise the principle of R2P but to recognise it 'as a doctrine that requires action, rather than merely an aspirational statement'.[42] It was against this backdrop, that the 2005 UN World Summit took place.

5 The 2005 UN World Summit

The 2005 UN World Summit was a significant moment in the evolution of R2P. It concluded 'with an agreement that the international community, acting through the United Nations, bears a responsibility to help to protect populations from genocide and other atrocities when their own government fails to do so'.[43] The agreed version of R2P adopted by consensus by the General Assembly was as follows:

> 138. Each individual State has the responsibility to protect its populations from genocide, war crimes, ethnic cleansing and crimes against humanity. This responsibility entails the prevention of such crimes, including their incitement, through appropriate and necessary means. We accept that responsibility and will act in accordance with it. The international community should, as appropriate, encourage and help States to exercise this responsibility and support the United Nations in establishing an early warning capability.
>
> 139. The international community, through the United Nations, also has the responsibility to use appropriate diplomatic, humanitarian and other peaceful means, in accordance with Chapters VI and VIII of the Charter, to help to protect populations from genocide,

40 ibid [200].

41 Davis (n 16) 897.

42 Kofi Annan, *In Larger Freedom: Towards Development, Security and Human Rights for All – Report of the Secretary-General* (2005) UN Doc A/59/2005 [7(a)]–[7(b)].

43 Alicia Bannon, 'The Responsibility to Protect: The UN World Summit and the Question of Unilateralism' (2006) 115 *YaleLJ* 1157, 1157.

> war crimes, ethnic cleansing and crimes against humanity. In this context, we are prepared to take collective action, in a timely and decisive manner, through the Security Council, in accordance with the Charter, including Chapter VII, on a case-by-case basis and in cooperation with relevant regional organisations as appropriate, should peaceful means be inadequate and national authorities are manifestly failing to protect their populations from genocide, war crimes, ethnic cleansing and crimes against humanity. We stress the need for the General Assembly to continue consideration of the responsibility to protect populations from genocide, war crimes, ethnic cleansing and crimes against humanity and its implications, bearing in mind the principles of the Charter and international law. We also intend to commit ourselves, as necessary and appropriate, to helping States build capacity to protect their populations from genocide, war crimes, ethnic cleansing and crimes against humanity and to assisting those which are under stress before crises and conflicts break out.[44]

For the first time, the international community had expressed a clear acceptance of the existence of a responsibility to protect populations from genocide, war crimes, ethnic cleansing, and crimes against humanity.[45] '[I]t is not unreasonable to say strongly that, in 2005, the world wanted to look at itself in a mirror and to begin a kind of introspection and, indeed, to examine its conscience so that it could acknowledge that there have been serious failures in recent decades'.[46] Inaction by the international community in Rwanda was clearly among those failures.

In April 2014, on the twentieth anniversary of the Rwandan genocide, the United Nations Security Council unanimously passed Resolution 2150, which reaffirmed paragraphs 138 and 139 of the 2005 World Summit Outcome Document.[47] Paragraph 1 of Resolution 2150 also called upon States to 'recommit to prevent and fight against genocide, and other serious crimes under international law',[48] and underscored 'the importance of taking into account lessons learned from the 1994 Genocide against the Tutsi in Rwanda, during which Hutu and others who opposed the genocide were also killed'.[49]

---

44 *2005 World Summit Outcome Document*, UN Doc A/RES/60/1 [138]–[139].
45 Matthews (n 15) 137.
46 *General Assembly Debates* (2009) UN Doc A/63/PV.98, 29.
47 *Security Council Resolution 2150* (16 April 2014) [1].
48 ibid.
49 ibid.

6 Significance of the 2005 UN World Summit Outcome Document

The first significant outcome from the 2005 UN World Summit is that it affirms the reconceptualization of sovereignty as entailing the responsibility of the State to protect their populations and those within their territory from atrocity crimes; 'the primary raison d'être and duty' of every State is to protect its population.[50] Further, the international community is willing to act (intervene) in the State should there be a manifest failure to provide such protection. The international community implicitly agreed that it will never again stand idle in the face of genocide.

A second significant result of the *2005 UN World Summit Outcome* document is the implicit acknowledgement by the international community that prevention of atrocity crimes is better than reaction after the crimes have already been committed. There are two parts to the secondary duty on the international community under R2P. The first part is the responsibility to 'use appropriate diplomatic, humanitarian and other peaceful means, in accordance with Chapters VI and VIII of the *Charter*, to help to protect populations from genocide, war crimes, ethnic cleansing and crimes against humanity'.[51] The second part of the secondary duty under R2P is the willingness to 'take collective action, in a timely and decisive manner, through the Security Council, in accordance with the Charter, including Chapter VII, on a case-by-case basis and in cooperation with relevant regional organisations as appropriate, should peaceful means be inadequate and national authorities are manifestly failing to protect their populations from genocide, war crimes, ethnic cleansing and crimes against humanity'.[52] This part of the secondary duty cements the privileged position of the Security Council in relation to the use of force.[53]

Neither part of the secondary duty imposes new legal obligations on the international community to act either unilaterally or collectively in response to atrocity crimes occurring in third States, in the sense of there being a legal compulsion to act or respond in some way to the commission of atrocity crimes. Crawford posits that the R2P triggering crimes 'are not matters of domestic jurisdiction in any event' and that R2P does not suggest the imposition of specific legal obligations 'over and above existing obligations under human

50 Annan (n 42) [135]; Roberta Cohen & Francis Deng, 'Sovereignty as Responsibility: Building Block for R2P' in Alex Bellamy & Tim Dunne (eds), *The Oxford Handbook of the Responsibility to Protect* (Oxford University Press, 2016).

51 *2005 World Summit Outcome Document* (n 44) [139].

52 ibid.

53 Anne Orford, *International Authority and the Responsibility to Protect* (Cambridge University Press, 2011).

rights, humanitarian law and international criminal law'.[54] The decision about whether to act remains a matter for the State and is not prescribed by the secondary duty under R2P. However, paragraph 139 is an express commitment by the international community to help 'States build capacity to protect their populations from genocide, war crimes, ethnic cleansing and crimes against humanity and to [assist] those which are under stress before crises and conflicts break out'.[55]

7 Criticism of the UN World Summit Outcome Document

Many scholars viewed R2P 'as the most comprehensive framework for approaching humanitarian intervention ever put forth'.[56] Evans argues that R2P is a 'brand new international norm of really quite fundamental importance and novelty…that is unquestionably a major breakthrough'.[57] Others claimed that it merely legitimised the status quo by relying on the Security Council as the authorising body for military intervention.[58] The secondary duty on the international community under R2P was heavily criticised as being an 'imperfect duty'.[59] As the secondary duty was allocated to the international community generally, it was argued that this 'diffuse responsibility can make it easier for [S]tates and international organisations to shirk their obligations'.[60] There was also criticism of the concept as raising unfulfilled expectations amongst populations at risk, and for the noticeable 'absence of mechanisms for holding the international community accountable retrospectively for its failure to play its remedial role'.[61]

---

54 James Crawford, 'Sovereignty as a legal value', in James Crawford & Martii Koskenniemi (eds), *The Cambridge Companion to International Law* (Cambridge University Press, 2012) 131.

55 *2005 World Summit Outcome Document* (n 44) [139].

56 Hamilton (n 25) 291; Matthews (n 15) 146.

57 Gareth Evans, 'The Responsibility to Protect: From an idea to an international norm' in R Cooper & J Kohler (eds), *Responsibility to Protect: The Global Moral Compact for the 21st Century* (Palgrave Macmillan, 2009) 16.

58 Jeremy Levitt, 'The Responsibility to Protect: A Beaver Without a Dam?' (2003) 25 *MichJIntlL* 153, 176.

59 Jennifer Welsh & Maria Banda, 'International Law and the Responsibility to Protect: Clarifying or Expanding States' Responsibilities?' (2010) 2 *Global Responsibility to Protect* 213, 219; Terry Nardin, 'From Right to Intervene to Duty to Protect: Michael Walzer on Humanitarian Intervention' (2013) 24 *EJIL* 67, 74.

60 Welsh & Banda (n 59) 219.

61 ibid.

Weiss argues that the secondary duty on the international community in the version of R2P adopted at the World Summit was so much narrower than the original ICISS proposal, that it is better described as 'R2P-lite'.[62] Chesterman pessimistically asserts that 'by the time RtoP was endorsed by the World Summit in 2005, its normative content had been emasculated to the point where it essentially provided that the Security Council could authorize, on a case-by-case basis, things that it had been authorizing for more than a decade'.[63] Mohamed argues that '[w]hen it comes to the international community, there is little responsibility remaining in the responsibility to protect'.[64] Miller argues that 'the anemic legal implementation of R2P belies the strength of the moral commitment that underpins the emerging consensus that states must not be permitted to rape, torture, and slaughter their citizens with impunity'.[65]

Much of the criticism levelled against R2P mirrored previous debates about humanitarian intervention. Some scholars argued that the simple change in language to R2P did not resolve the fundamental debates that have always existed regarding humanitarian intervention.[66] Still others argued that R2P was simply a 'cover for legitimating the neo-colonialist tendencies of major powers'.[67]

In addition to the criticism above, three key issues form the basis of the criticism of R2P as reflected in the *2005 World Summit Outcome* document. First, the original ICISS proposal defined the triggering crimes for R2P as 'large scale loss of life or large scale ethnic cleansing',[68] whereas the World Summit limits the triggering crimes to 'genocide, war crimes, ethnic cleansing or crimes against humanity'.[69] However, the triggering crimes are not as important as the

62 Thomas Weiss, 'R2P after 9/11 and the World Summit' (2006) 24 *WisIntlLJ* 741, 750.

63 Simon Chesterman, '"Leading from Behind": The Responsibility to Protect, the Obama Doctrine, and Humanitarian Intervention after Libya' (2011) *Ethics & International Affairs* 279, 280.

64 Saira Mohamed, 'Taking Stock of the Responsibility to Protect' (2012) 48 *StanJIntlL* 319, 330.

65 Nathan Miller, 'International Civil Disobedience: Unauthorised Intervention and the Conscience of the International Community' (2015) 74 *Maryland Law Review* 315, 332.

66 Jennifer Welsh, Carolin Thielking & Neil MacFarlane, 'The Responsibility to Protect: Assessing the Report of the International Commission on Intervention and State Sovereignty' (2002) 57 *International Journal* 489, 500; Matthews (n 15) 146; James Pattison, *Humanitarian Intervention and the Responsibility to Protect: Who Should Intervene?* (Oxford University Press, 2010).

67 Hamilton (n 25) 292; Mohamed Ayoob, 'Third World Perspectives on Humanitarian Intervention and International Administration' (2004) 10 *Global Governance* 99, 115.

68 ICISS (n 2) xii.

69 *2005 World Summit Outcome Document* (n 44) [138].

adoption of the principle of R2P itself, and, further, the threshold can change through State practice. Second, the threshold for action by the international community in the original ICISS proposal was that a State be 'unwilling or unable' to prevent the triggering crimes. The World Summit, however, increased this threshold requirement to 'manifestly failing to protect their populations' from the four triggering crimes,[70] although what would amount to a manifest failure was left undefined. In practice, however, there may not be much difference between a State which is 'unable or unwilling' or 'manifestly failing' to protect its population from atrocity crimes. Third, the original ICISS proposal had left open the possibility of forceful action through the General Assembly or regional or subregional organisations if the Security Council failed to act.[71] As discussed above, the ICISS report had identified the Rwandan genocide as a possible situation where the General Assembly could have taken action under the Uniting for Peace procedure. However, the World Summit version of R2P places the duty to exercise collective action solely in the hands of the Security Council.[72]

These changes reflect the compromise position that was necessary to construct a version of R2P 'that is sufficiently broad to be effective, but also narrow enough that nations will agree to be bound by the doctrine'.[73] Even if R2P as formulated in the *2005 World Summit Outcome* document is far from perfect or complete, 'it still represents a significant step away from the culture of indifference that has dominated the international state system for so long, and for which millions of people have paid the ultimate price'.[74]

8 After the 2005 UN World Summit

Since its acceptance and adoption at the 2005 World Summit, debate at the UN regarding R2P has moved from a discussion about R2P's legal status and boundaries, to a discussion about developing 'strategy, standards, processes, tools and practices for [implementing] the responsibility to protect'.[75]

70 ibid [139].

71 ICISS (n 2) xiii.

72 *2005 World Summit Outcome Document* (n 44) [139].

73 Davis (n 16) 898.

74 Eli Stamnes, 'Speaking R2P' and the Prevention of Mass Atrocities' (2009) 1 *Global Responsibility to Protect* 70, 70–71.

75 *Implementing the Responsibility to Protect – Report of the Secretary-General* (2009) UN Doc A/63/677.

8.1 *Three Pillars*

In his 2009 report, *Implementing the Responsibility to Protect*, then UN Secretary-General Ban Ki-moon put forward a three pillar strategy, with three equally weighted pillars, to advance the implementation of R2P.[76] The first pillar is the primary responsibility of a State to protect its citizens from the four atrocity crimes of genocide, war crimes, ethnic cleansing and crimes against humanity. The first pillar affirms the reconceptualization of sovereignty as responsibility, highlighting that States have the primary responsibility to protect their citizens from atrocity crimes. The second pillar is international assistance and capacity building to assist a State to fulfil its primary responsibility to its citizens. The third pillar is the international community's responsibility to take timely and decisive action in accordance with the UN Charter, where a State has manifestly failed in its responsibility to protect its citizens.

The report emphasised that the three pillar strategy 'stresses the value of prevention and, when it fails, of early and flexible response tailored to the specific circumstances of each case'.[77] It stated that

> [w]hile the scope [of R2P] should be kept narrow, the response ought to be deep, employing the wide array of prevention and protection instruments available to Member States, the United Nations system, regional and subregional organizations and their civil society partners.[78]

During the General Assembly debates on this report, many States expressed support for R2P and the three pillar approach to its implementation.[79]

While there was unanimity within the General Assembly on the first two pillars, many States expressed concern about the coercive aspect of the third pillar. Although States raised concerns in relation to the use of force, the use of measures less than force under the third pillar was accepted by States. Singapore noted that responses under the third pillar 'can and should take different forms, without necessarily resorting to the use of force'.[80] Chile stated that the third pillar 'is forceful, but also cautious. It refers to peaceful measures that could be taken'.[81] South Africa observed 'that there are a myriad of instruments at the disposal of the international community to utilize in response' to

76 ibid.
77 ibid 2.
78 ibid [10(c)].
79 UN Doc A/63/PV.98 (n 46); *General Assembly Debates* (2009) UN Doc A/63/PV.101.
80 UN Doc A/63/PV.98 (n 46) 8.
81 ibid 11.

atrocity crimes under the third pillar.[82] Japan stated that '[t]he international community should use, initially, diplomatic, humanitarian and other peaceful means. If those means are inadequate, collective action will be necessary to protect populations'.[83] China, too, noted that 'the third pillar...highlights the role of the international community within the framework of the United Nations: to favour diplomatic, humanitarian and other appropriate peaceful means to help protect populations from mass crimes and atrocities'.[84] Kenya stated that 'necessary measures should...not be equated with the threat of use of force'.[85] Lesotho stated that '[t]he invocation of pillar three would not necessarily translate into recourse to the use of force. This is because that pillar encompasses many measures that are non-coercive and non-violent in nature'.[86] The Holy See noted that 'this element has too often focussed solely on the use of violence in order to prevent or stop violence, rather than on the various ways in which intervention can be carried out in a non-violent manner'.[87]

8.2 *More than the Use of Force*

Subsequent reports of the Secretary-General on the implementation of R2P have confirmed the wide range of tools available to the international community in implementing the secondary duty under R2P. The 2012 report clearly identifies the importance of using all available tools, not just the use of force, to help to protect populations from atrocity crimes.[88] Amongst the tools discussed in the report are measures such as fact-finding missions and commissions of inquiry,[89] monitoring and observer missions deployed under Chapter VI,[90] threats of referrals to the ICC,[91] and naming and shaming.[92] More coercive measures, which still fall below the use of force, such as sanctions, travel bans, asset freezes, and embargoes, are also discussed.[93]

82 ibid 17.
83 ibid 22.
84 ibid 25.
85 UN Doc A/63/PV.101 (n 79) 3.
86 ibid 5.
87 ibid 17.
88 *Responsibility to protect: timely and decisive response – Report of the Secretary-General* (2012) UN Doc A/66/874-S/2012/578 [21].
89 ibid [27].
90 ibid [28].
91 ibid [29].
92 ibid [30].
93 ibid [31].

The 2015 report notes that the crises in Libya and Syria 'contributed to wider misperceptions that the responsibility to protect is primarily concerned with coercive measures'.[94]

> Notwithstanding this range of options, the third pillar of the responsibility to protect is still commonly perceived as being solely concerned with the use of force. This perception needs to be countered. First, the choice is not between inaction and the use of force. Non-military tools have made a tangible difference in responding to the commission of atrocity crimes and preventing their escalation. Second, even in intractable situations characterized by continuing violence, international actors have attempted to fulfil their responsibility to protect through political, diplomatic and humanitarian means. These efforts may at times have fallen short of delivering a long-term protective environment, but they have succeeded in saving lives. Finally, in some circumstances it may not be judged possible to employ force for protection purposes without potentially causing more harm than good.[95]

Highlighting the 'full range of tools at the disposal of the international community – non-military as well as military – to respond to the imminent risk or commission of genocide, war crimes, ethnic cleansing and crimes against humanity',[96] the report stresses the continued need for 'an early and flexible approach to acting on pillar III responsibilities that focuses on non-coercive means, but that takes into consideration from the outset all the mechanisms available under the Charter'.[97]

The Secretary-General's 2016 report on R2P notes that '[t]he views of Member States converge on many important elements, including ... that any international action should employ the full range of diplomatic, political and humanitarian measures and that military force should be considered as a measure of last resort'.[98] The report emphasises the 'ongoing responsibility to use peaceful means to protect populations',[99] and reiterates the 'broad range of peaceful tools available to protect populations affected by atrocity crimes'.[100]

94 *A vital and enduring commitment: implementing the responsibility to protect – Report of the Secretary-General* (2015) UN Doc A/69/981-S/2015/500 [9].
95 ibid [38].
96 ibid [37].
97 ibid [39].
98 *Mobilizing collective action: the next decade of the responsibility to protect – Report of the Secretary-General* (2016) UN Doc A/70/999-S/2016/620 [18].
99 ibid [45].
100 ibid [47].

8.3 *Restraint*

The Secretary-General's reports on implementation also demonstrate that R2P contains within it a set of restraints on potential action taken by the international community in response to the commission of atrocity crimes. While restraint as a part of R2P first appeared in the four precautionary principles contained with the ICISS version of R2P (discussed above), the reports on implementation confirm that restraint remains a part of R2P following the adoption of the modified version of R2P at the 2005 World Summit. Indeed, the element of restraint was noted to be a key component of R2P and the three pillar approach to implementation during the debates in the General Assembly. For example, Vietnam stated '[u]nder all circumstances, the impact of such acts on the population – particularly its most vulnerable sectors – should be the consideration of top priority'.[101]

The 2010 report confirms that peaceful and preventive measures 'are most likely to be effective if they are undertaken at an early point and are carefully targeted and calibrated' to the circumstances of the case.[102] The 2012 report notes that at 'every stage of the implementation process, from identification and assessment to policy formulation and action, international actors need to act responsibly'.[103] The 2014 report states

> Experience has shown that poorly designed international assistance can inadvertently create or exacerbate social cleavages, thereby contributing to the development of atrocity crimes. International support or technical advice that contributes to discrimination and disparities or causes groups to compete over sources of revenue is particularly damaging. International partners should therefore make all possible efforts to "do no harm" by incorporating atrocity crime prevention into the assessment, planning and monitoring processes that guide their assistance.[104]

This report specifically notes that one of the ways the international community can assist States under stress to protect their own populations is through denial of the means to commit atrocities. The *Arms Trade Treaty* is noted to be a 'significant step forward in this respect and reinforces the obligation of States not to knowingly provide arms that could be used for atrocity crimes'.[105]

---

101 UN Doc A/63/PV.98 (n 46) 28.

102 *Early warning, assessment and the responsibility to protect- Report of the Secretary-General* (2010) UN Doc A/64/864 [3].

103 UN Doc A/66/874-S/2012/578 (n 88) [51].

104 *Fulfilling our collective responsibility: international assistance and the responsibility to protect – Report of the Secretary-General* (2014) UN Doc A/68/947-S/2014/449 [17].

105 ibid [60].

Further, the 2015 report emphasises the 'responsibility to anticipate, as far as possible, any harmful effects of ... policy responses and to mitigate those potential consequences'.[106]

9 Conclusion

The inaction on the part of the international community when faced with atrocities in Rwanda, led to a re-examination of the fundamental international law principles of sovereignty and non-intervention, and ultimately to the adoption of R2P. At its heart, R2P is about duty: the primary duty of States to protect those within their borders from atrocity crimes and the secondary duty of the international community to help to protect populations from atrocity crimes. R2P is a powerful concept of statecraft, providing a conceptual solution to the failings of Westphalian sovereignty from a humanitarian perspective by articulating when and how States *may* respond to atrocity crimes in other States. While R2P may not impose an enforceable legal obligation on the international community to intervene in response to every situation of mass atrocity, it raises the possibility that a greater range of measures may be taken in response to the commission, or anticipation of, atrocity crimes in the future. The legacy of Rwanda is the hope, reflected in R2P, that silence and idleness will never again be the international community's response to genocide.

106 UN Doc A/69/981-S/2015/500 (n 94) [40].

Index

www.ingramcontent.com/pod-product-compliance
Ingram Content Group UK Ltd.
Pitfield, Milton Keynes, MK11 3LW, UK
UKHW022209051026
15624UKWH00001B/68